THE FLASH PRESS

HISTORICAL STUDIES OF URBAN AMERICA
Edited by Timothy J. Gilfoyle, James R. Grossman, and Becky M. Nicolaides

Also in the series:

THE FLASH PRESS
SPORTING MALE WEEKLIES IN 1840S NEW YORK

PATRICIA CLINE COHEN,

TIMOTHY J. GILFOYLE,

and HELEN LEFKOWITZ HOROWITZ

in association with the AMERICAN ANTIQUARIAN SOCIETY

THE UNIVERSITY OF CHICAGO PRESS • CHICAGO AND LONDON

PATRICIA CLINE COHEN is professor of history at the
University of California, Santa Barbara, and the author
of *The Murder of Helen Jewett: The Life and Death of a
Prostitute in Nineteenth-Century New York.*
TIMOTHY J. GILFOYLE is professor of history at Loyola
University Chicago and the author of *City of Eros: New
York City, Prostitution, and the Commercialization of Sex,
1790 –1920.*
HELEN LEFKOWITZ HOROWITZ is professor of American
studies and history at Smith College and the author of
*Rereading Sex: Battles over Sexual Knowledge and Sup-
pression in Nineteenth-Century America.*

The University of Chicago Press, Chicago 60637
The University of Chicago Press, Ltd., London
© 2008 by The University of Chicago
All rights reserved. Published 2008
Printed in the United States of America

17 16 15 14 13 12 11 10 09 08   1 2 3 4 5

ISBN-13: 978-0-226-11233-6 (cloth)
ISBN-13: 978-0-226-11234-3 (paper)
ISBN-10: 0-226-11233-0 (cloth)
ISBN-10: 0-226-11234-9 (paper)

Library of Congress Cataloging-in-Publication Data

Cohen, Patricia Cline.
 The flash press : sporting male weeklies in 1840s
New York / Patricia Cline Cohen, Timothy J. Gilfoyle,
and Helen Lefkowitz Horowitz ; in association with the
American Antiquarian Society.
   p. cm.—(Historical studies of urban America)
 Includes bibliographical references and index.
 ISBN-13: 978-0-226-11233-6 (cloth : alk. paper)
 ISBN-10: 0-226-11233-0 (cloth : alk. paper)
 ISBN-13: 978-0-226-11234-3 (pbk. : alk. paper)
 ISBN-10: 0-226-11234-9 (pbk. : alk. paper) 1. Men's
magazines—New York (State)—New York—History—
20th century. 2. Sensationalism in journalism—
New York (State)—New York—History—20th century.
I. Gilfoyle, Timothy J. II. Horowitz, Helen Lefkowitz.
III. American Antiquarian Society. IV. Title.
 PN4899 .N41C64 2008
 051.081—dc22
                                    2007039994

The paper used in this publication meets the minimum
requirements of the American National Standard for
Information Sciences—Permanence of Paper for
Printed Library Materials, ANSI Z39.48-1992.

To

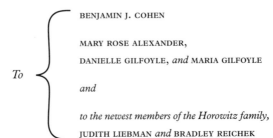

BENJAMIN J. COHEN

MARY ROSE ALEXANDER,
DANIELLE GILFOYLE, *and* MARIA GILFOYLE

and

to the newest members of the Horowitz family,
JUDITH LIEBMAN *and* BRADLEY REICHEK

CONTENTS

INTRODUCTION

From the fall of 1841 to the spring of 1843, an extensive sexual under-world of New York City came to sudden public notice through an eruption of small weekly newspapers with bold titles. The *Flash,* the *Whip,* the *Rake,* and the *Libertine* aimed to entertain and enlighten literate sporting men about leisure-time activities and erotic entertainments available in New York. Distinguished by a trenchant, mocking humor and a titillating brew of gossip about prostitutes, theatrical denizens, and sports contests, the papers offered guidance to men young and old intent on navigating the new world of unrestricted pleasure and commercialized leisure in the city. They frequently defended such behaviors in the vernacular of republicanism and democracy.

Customers could easily acquire the papers in saloons and oyster bars, on steamboats and in barbershops. Young newsboys pitched them to likely looking readers on the streets, outside hotels, and at the public promenade at Battery Park at the southern end of Manhattan. Papers graced parlor tables in the elegant brothels of the city's Fifth Ward and circulated in the third-tier balconies of the Park and Bowery Theatres, where prostitutes regularly congregated for evening amusement and to arrange business deals. Handbills advertising coming issues were posted openly and notoriously. The flurry of scandalizing papers reached a peak in the summer of 1842, at a time when all four titles squawked in competition; their presence proved difficult to ignore.

New York was no stranger to the cacophony of competing newspapers. In the 1830s and 1840s the city of more than 300,000 inhabitants supported somewhere between forty and fifty daily and weekly publications. Some featured commercial news, others political; some sheets took a religious or reform slant, while others were primarily literary or cultural. The major dailies had recently faced and absorbed a challenge from what were called the "penny papers," a cheap alternative press combining limited hard news, human-interest features, and more than a dollop of crime and sensationalism, along with a highly personalized editorial voice, all contrived to augment newspaper readership with the more plebian and street-smart crowd.[1] There were specialty weeklies devoted to labor or to sports and theater, along with a remarkable number of short-lived papers combining humor, gossip, crime stories, and social notes on elite balls. The reading public of New York City certainly had abundant choices, reflecting both a reading revolution and dramatic innovations in the technology, economics, and production of newspapers that started in the 1830s.[2]

But until the "flash" papers came along, no newspapers dared to trumpet the attractions of prostitutes, provide tour guides to the city's brothels, and give voice to an otherwise hidden community in the city. Reportage of theater, sports, balls, and politics in these papers took on "flash" attributes as well, emphasizing racy details and colorful characters, pitched to a "man-about-town" readership. The editors brandished satirical humor, often striking a pose of great shock—bogus shock, to be sure—at the scandalous activities they described for their appreciative readers.

The term "flash press" was just one of several descriptors applied to these short-lived papers. Producers and admirers used such adjectives as racy, satirical, spicy, or sporting to describe them, while their outraged adversaries called them obscene, libidinous, loathsome, lascivious, and disgusting. We have settled on *flash* for its in-the-moment, slangy connotations, and also because the genre-setting first paper was titled the *Sunday Flash*. First coined among the swindling underworld of eighteenth-century London, *flash* denoted an elaborate slang vocabulary used by thieves to communicate among themselves and mystify outsiders. It carried core meanings of smartness and deceit. A New York glossary of "flash terms" from 1847 defined *flash* as "the language of thieves," while an 1859 slang dictionary also from New York defined a *flash-man* as "a fellow that has no visible means of living, yet goes dressed in fine clothes, exhibiting a profusion of jewelry about his person," suggesting an income derived from pimping or thieving. A British slang dictionary of 1874 defined it as:

> *Flash,* showy, smart, knowing; a word with various meanings. A person is said to be dressed FLASH when his garb is showy, and after a fashion, but without taste. A person is said to be FLASH when he apes the appearance or manners of his betters, or when he is trying to be superior to his friends and relations. FLASH also means "fast," roguish, and sometimes infers counterfeit or deceptive—and this, perhaps, is its general signification.[3]

The New York flash papers actually did not have much obscure slang in them, but they described a world of deceit and counterfeit, where

FIGURE I. *SUNDAY FLASH*, OCT. 24, 1841. COURTESY AMERICAN ANTIQUARIAN SOCIETY.
THE FLASH PRESS THRIVED FROM 1841 TO 1843.

attractively innocent young women turn out to be sexually available, where respectable men young and old lead double lives and fear exposure, where swindlers and cheats abound among the lowlife and the elite—where things, in short, are seldom what they seem. This quality of "flash," of deceit and ambiguity, applied equally well to the editors themselves, who trumpeted their lofty mission as one of exposing vice and iniquity even as they fawned over particular brothels and prostitutes and engaged in blackmail. They attempted to walk a fine line, projecting moral outrage and winking humor simultaneously; certainly their dedicated and enthusiastic readers understood their main mode to be satirical.

As bold, noisy, and provocative as these papers were, in their time, for many years they were completely forgotten. Historians of journalism and even sensational journalism had no knowledge of them. A near-exhaustive book-length bibliography of New York antebellum newspapers published in 1928 by Louis H. Fox merely noted the titles *Rake, Whip,* and *Flash* with no extant copies.[4] Twentieth-century lawyers and judges arguing obscenity cases did not know to use them as legal precedents, and historians studying the history of sex, gender, and sports were ignorant of them.

Not until 1985 did a significant collection of nearly a hundred issues land in the world of scholarship, in a single purchase made by the American Antiquarian Society (AAS) in Worcester, Massachusetts, from a private party living in New Hampshire. The Antiquarian Society, the premier library in the United States for antebellum printed materials, was well suited for this acquisition. It already owned a small set of antebellum racy papers from the 1840s and 1850s, two of which were flash papers of early 1840s New York: the *Libertine* (June 15, 1842) and the *Weekly Rake* (July 9, 1842), the latter given to the AAS in 1946 by New York scholar and noted bibliophile Thomas O. Mabbott.[5]

FIGURE 2. *WEEKLY RAKE,* JULY 9, 1842. COURTESY AMERICAN ANTIQUARIAN SOCIETY.

Patricia Cline Cohen appears to have been the first historian to see the 1985 set, during a fellowship year she spent at the Society in 1987–88. She was assiduously tracking New York City newspapers for her research on the murder of a prostitute in 1836, using Fox's bibliography to ferret out unusual titles. On one memorable day, Dennis R. Laurie, reference specialist of newspapers and periodicals, asked her if she might like to see some uncatalogued New York titles of a somewhat disreputable character. (Their uncatalogued state should not be interpreted as reticence or suppression; in the pre-computer era, the AAS perpetually faced a large backlog of uncatalogued materials.) Laurie brought out the papers in successive batches; Cohen recalls that they were not yet filed in the large acid-free folders regularly used for old newsprint but seemed to be wrapped in a loose, gauzy paper.

About two years later Cohen met Timothy J. Gilfoyle and tipped him off to the flash papers. His book, *City of Eros: New York City, Prostitution, and the Commercialization of Sex, 1790–1920,* published in 1992, was the first to cite them in print. Cohen also made brief use of them in a 1992 article. Musicologist Dale Cockrell was the third to cite them, in articles in 1996 and then in his 1997 book, *Demons of Disorder: Early Blackface Minstrels and Their World,* which featured two figures from the flash press

FIGURE 3. *WHIP AND SATIRIST OF NEW-YORK AND BROOKLYN,* FEB. 12, 1842. COURTESY AMERICAN ANTIQUARIAN SOCIETY.

world who also had notable careers performing or managing minstrel acts. Cohen drew on the flash papers to expand on the customs of elegant brothels in New York's Fifth Ward for her 1998 book, *The Murder of Helen Jewett: The Life and Death of a Prostitute in Nineteenth-Century New York*. Helen Lefkowitz Horowitz, our third coauthor, learned of the Antiquarian Society's collection on her first visit to the AAS when research librarian Joanne D. Chaison showed her a sheet of "racy" primary sources at the AAS that included the papers' titles. A fellowship year allowed her to research them extensively for her 2002 study *Rereading Sex: Battles over Sexual Knowledge and Suppression in Nineteenth-Century America*.[6]

The idea for our collaboration was sparked in 1999, when Cohen, Gilfoyle, and Horowitz teamed up in a session at the American Studies Association meeting in Montreal, in a session titled "Three Takes on the New York Flash Press." By this time, Horowitz had discovered that a private collector, Professor Leo Hershkowitz of Queens College, held another ten issues originally gathered in evidence files by New York City's district attorney in the 1840s. After visiting Professor Hershkowitz's home, Horowitz returned with Cohen to examine these papers thoroughly. She then helped persuade him to donate his materials to the AAS in 2001.[7]

It is remarkable that so many of these disreputable flash papers have survived. The combined set of 104 issues constitutes 73 percent of the implied full set of the weeklies, calculated to be 142 issues. The district attorney's office had reason to preserve the ten issues, at least in the short run, as material evidence in potential libel and obscenity trials; these issues are marked by the district attorney's hand, with paragraphs highlighted and notes in the margins. Indeed, existing indictment files at the New York Municipal Archives for the cases that went to trial still contain a few single issues of the papers. But who initially preserved the large and privately held collection? One strong candidate is an editor or writer for the *Whip*. That newspaper's run is complete for its first six months and nearly complete for the rest. Moreover, the *Whip*'s editor was previously a reporter for the *Sunday Flash*, so he had motive and opportunity to save many of those issues. But this collection also included many issues of the rival papers the *Flash* and the *Weekly Rake*; we can conclude that the collector was clearly intent on saving the entire production. How and where the collection survived for its first sixty or eighty years remains unknown, but it seems probable that it continued to be held within the sphere of sports journalism, the later career of at least two of the flash press editors. Sometime between about 1910 and the 1930s, a well-known

New York sportswriter, George B. Underwood, acquired the collection. Underwood was an athlete himself, with a gold medal in track from the 1904 Olympics, and a man with a passion for boxing. Over the years he wrote a sports column for various New York newspapers—the *World*, the *Evening Telegram*, the *Press*, and the *Sun*—and in the 1920s he was also a regular writer for the *Ring*, a boxing magazine. For a time he managed publicity for Madison Square Garden, the New York sports arena. A descendant recalls that he was a popular figure with famous boxers, socializing with them at his home. He very likely shared train trips with athletes and sportswriters to cover sporting events, and camaraderie in saloons as well. At some point in this cozy community of men's men, the flash papers surfaced, and George B. Underwood came to be the steward of the set, whether by gift or by purchase. A trajectory through sports journalism channels to Underwood is far more likely than a transit via the other main readership of the papers, prostitutes and madams, with their shorter careers and their minimal involvement in publishing. A chain of sports journalists with a high appreciation for unique specimens of print culture offers the most plausible explanation of the collection's survival. Underwood died in 1943, and in 1985 his son sold them to the Antiquarian Society.[8]

The contemporary readers of the papers, men (and women) who bought them in theaters, saloons, and barbershops, had little reason to save their copies and perhaps much reason to dispose of them quickly. What hooked buyers—gossip about sex accompanied by names and initials of real people—would be exactly why they would be quickly discarded. These are not the kind of papers typically saved for posterity, especially if one's own identity were exposed to public view and ridicule.

What can we learn of the contemporary readers of the flash press? New York City and other urban centers in the 1830s were rapidly expanding in numbers of single white men and women aged 15 to 30. Some among the young men were native New Yorkers, from artisan and working-class families of the city's lower wards, well described by one scholar as an urban "bachelor subculture" of unattached men expressing male camaraderie around sporting events and saloon-hall drinking. But probably as many flash press readers were newcomers drawn to the city by the promise of entry-level jobs in a rapidly commercializing economy. By the thousands they left homes in the rural countryside of New England and the mid-Atlantic states, skilled in the reading, writing, and arithmetic essential for white-collar jobs as sales clerks, bookkeepers, and secretaries. Crowded together in largely unsupervised boarding houses in lower Manhattan, they took their meals in oyster bars and cheap saloons. Moralistic guidance literature aimed at such youths warned them to steer clear of the temptations of urban vice; the flash press offered contrary guidance, steering them straight to the locales and institutions of the sexual and sporting underworld.[9]

Some flash press readers were to be found among the young women who arrived in New York daily, seeking work as domestic servants or seamstresses. Some of these working women joined New York's rapidly growing ranks of prostitutes, said to number between five and ten thousand around 1840, at a time when the city's population was 312,000. The flash newspapers elevated a handful of these women to celebrity status and bantered about others in editorial columns. And one paper featured a regular column titled "Fair Sex" that covered balls and fashions for its female readership.[10]

Still, male readers predominated. Male clients far outnumbered prostitutes, and literate young men flocking to white-collar work far outnumbered literate girls of the servant/seamstress/sex-worker stratum. Factor in the newly arrived greenhorns, inexperienced in the protocol of commercial sex but wanting to learn, along with readers interested in vicarious thrills but not looking to cross a brothel threshold, and the reason for the strong male flavor of the flash press becomes clear. The real surprise is that there was any cultivation of female readership at all.

As that large number of prostitutes implies, commercial sex in antebellum New York City was not in short supply, and it seemed to many to be rapidly increasing. In response, a moral reform movement, led by evangelical ministers and mostly female congregants protesting sexual immorality, launched itself in 1833 in New York and spread to other cities. Soon the New York group began publishing its own bimonthly periodical, the *Advocate of Moral Reform*, filled with stern articles about a rising tide of "licentiousness," a judgmental and fear-mongering term that framed illicit sex as lascivious, lustful, and lewd. The moral reformers were criticized for their unladylike attention to sexual sin, but they were far from alone in their alarm. One striking way to demonstrate the moral panic over sex is to chart the printed usage of "licentious" and "licentiousness," as measured in computer-assisted searches in over a thousand periodical publications in the years 1800 to 1865. The dramatic peak of 1841–45 represents 3,179 repetitions of those two words and coincides perfectly with the years of the flash press.[11]

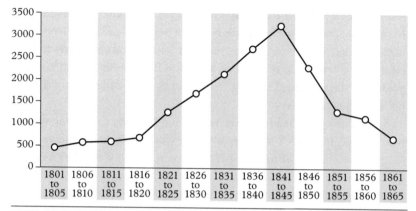

FIGURE 4: DATA ON THE FREQUENCY OF THE TERMS "LICENTIOUS" AND "LICENTIOUSNESS" IN FIVE-YEAR INTERVALS IN THE AMERICAN PERIODICAL SERIES ONLINE (APS), PROQUEST, ACCESSED AUG. 2, 2006. THE APS CONTAINS 900 SERIAL TITLES FROM 1800 TO 1860, AND ANOTHER 118 UP TO 1877, TOTALING MORE THAN SEVEN MILLION PAGES. NEITHER THE *ADVOCATE OF MORAL REFORM* NOR ANY OF THE FLASH PAPERS IS PART OF THE DATABASE. THE DATA REVEAL AN ESCALATION OF CONCERN ABOUT ILLICIT SEX AND A SATURATION OF THE WORD LICENTIOUSNESS PEAKING IN 1841–45, WITH OVER THREE THOUSAND REFERENCES TO THE TWO KEYWORDS. SOME PORTION OF THE UPSWING FROM 1800 TO 1840 REFLECTS THE INCREASED NUMBERS OF PRINTED PAGES OVER TIME, BUT THAT MAKES THE FALL-OFF AFTER THE EARLY 1840S PEAK ALL THE MORE REMARKABLE. ILLICIT SEX PROBABLY CONTINUED UNABATED INTO THE 1850S AND 1860S, BUT AFTER 1850 IT WAS EITHER DISCUSSED IN PRINT LESS OFTEN, OR THE TERMS OF THE DISCUSSION LITERALLY CHANGED. ACCORDING TO THE *OX-FORD ENGLISH DICTIONARY*, THE ORIGINAL MEANING OF "LICENTIOUSNESS" AS LICENSE FROM LEGAL RESTRAINT WAS SUPPLANTED BY THE SEXUAL MEANING, LEWDNESS, BY THE NINETEENTH CENTURY.

A surging concern over sexual licentiousness was at once both the precondition and consequence of the flash press. New York already had one periodical attending closely to sexual sin, published by the moral reform women, and it was not so great a leap to imagine the comic possibilities of satirizing it. In an era when the start-up costs of producing a weekly newspaper were surprisingly low, it probably did not take astute business sense to appreciate the potential sales of periodicals serving as trade journals for the high-end brothel business yet masquerading as moral-reform publications when they came under fire. And the large population involved in commercial sex meant the readership would be strong.

Prostitution was quite visible in the neighborhoods of the western lower wards of New York City, where high-priced brothels stood adjacent to the solid and spacious dwellings of the middle and upper classes, and in the densely crowded eastern wards, where down-on-their-luck girls sold sex in alleyways and dingy tenement rooms. Dressed in silks, streetwalkers openly cruised Broadway, the city's main north-south thoroughfare, and prostitutes had their exclusive seating section in all the city's theaters.

Prostitution and other forms of non-marital sex were not absent before the 1830s; New York had a version of the "pleasure culture" that a recent scholar has so well described in detail for Philadelphia in the years from 1760 to 1800.[12] That old, looser sexual regime treated moral lapses as regrettable rather than catastrophic; an out-of-wedlock pregnancy—not uncommon up to the 1790s—could be put right by marriage.

This tolerant attitude, however, was completely reshaped between 1800 and 1830 among members of the emerging middle classes. A newly emphasized ethic of sexual restraint took hold, ostensibly directed at both sexes. Women perhaps more readily than men adopted the strictures on sexual behavior and policed the boundaries of respectability of their sex, drawing clear lines between sexually pure versus unchaste women. What was particularly novel was the penalty attached to loss of female virginity: "fallen" women were ruined, in the language of the day, shunned by decent society, unfit for respectable married life, and doomed to swell the ranks of the "frail," i.e., prostitutes. Many men of the growing middle classes also honored the sharp distinction between pure and fallen women, but since it was male sexual privilege that created the category of unchaste women, it is clear that hypocrisy about moral standards for men flourished widely. A corresponding vocabulary described sexually experienced men—such epithets as "rake" and "libertine" were in everyday use—but a man so designated did not usually suffer exile from respectable society. As female moral reformers often complained, a man with a fast reputation for sexual experience was sometimes especially sought after for his allure and sophistication. In short, an especially acute double standard of sexual morality was in play.

The distinctive contribution of the flash press to this evolving sexual scene was to embrace words like "rake" and "libertine" and to build a sense of shared community around them. By publicizing the locales and participants engaged in non-marital sex, the papers familiarized and normalized those activities and thereby emboldened men to feel comfortable asserting male sexual prerogatives in opposition to the emerging canons of respectability. Male readers of these papers were no longer individual hypocrites, slinking guiltily through dark streets in search of illicit sex. They could recognize themselves as members of a subculture defined by shared values and activities, forging a male sociability through their nonconforming sexual behaviors that flaunted conventions. Readers also shared enthusiasms for sports, like pugilism, pedestrianism, and dog fighting, and for theatrical performances as well, with attentive coverage of skimpily clad female dancers and minstrel shows, acts that pushed the boundaries on body exposure and disguise. The flash press played a vital part in constituting this community of men, giving it a language and an identity popularly called *flash.*

This flash community soon took on regional and even national dimensions, thanks to a system of agents who contracted to sell the papers in far-flung places. Letters and articles submitted by correspondents to the *Flash,* the *Whip,* and the *Rake* reveal that tendrils extended out from the city, to other larger cities and small villages all over the Northeast and mid-Atlantic states and even to the South, where one communication line stretched deep into Georgia. Rather well along on research for this project, we discovered that a number of flash-like newspapers also dotted the landscape from the late 1830s to the early 1850s, some precursors to the New York City set and others clearly copycat enterprises. In Philadelphia there was the *Spy and Philadelphia Paul Pry* (1842), in Baltimore the *Viper's Sting and Paul Pry* (1849–50), and in Boston the *Satirist* (1842–43) and the *Boston Blade* (1848). The New York set was centered in a cluster of risqué humor papers: the *Polyanthos* (1838–41), the *Two-Penny Trumpet* (1841), the *Uncle Sam* (1841), the *Arena* (1842), the *Sportsman* (1843), the *Packet* (1845), *Ned Buntline's Own* (1849), the *Scorpion* (1849), and the *Pick* (1852). In the 1850s, the *Broadway Belle* (1858) and *Venus's Miscellany* (1857–58) moved the genre into the category of erotic fiction, quite different from the flash papers.[13]

Such a rich array of sex and humor papers helped us to isolate distinctive features in our original set of flash papers. As with a medical nosology, we elaborated eleven diagnostic symptoms: (1) coverage of sporting events and theater; (2) malicious gossip tidbits submitted by readers; (3) stories condemning immoral men; (4) reports from regular correspondents detailing sexual scandals; (5) anticlerical themes; (6) coverage of criminal underworld activity, such as gambling, abortion, or confidence games; (7) critical coverage of prostitution and other illicit sexual behaviors; (8) rough populism or republicanism critical of hierarchy and privilege; (9) cartoon lithographs with sexual and ribald themes; (10) a defense of active, male heterosexuality; and (11) favorable coverage of prostitution and other illicit sexual behaviors. A range of publications in the antebellum era, both serious and humorous, contained from one to five of these features, while our core flash papers had nine to eleven. The distinctive character of flash came principally with the last two on our list.

The fully flash papers of New York established and maintained their preeminence among satirical papers not only by their content but by their razor-sharp wit and style. They originated from the country's center and heart of journalism, and their talented set of editors and writers managed to make local stories and characters speak to the entire country—or at least a certain stratum of like-minded readers around the country, proving that New York's reputation as a cultural capital able to set styles was as true of this low echelon as it was of the high culture of art and literature. These papers innovated recurring features, such as profiles of notables written with artful cunning and clever "wants" on the model of gossip want-ads, that enticed readers to buy every issue and follow the foibles of characters. The *Flash,* the *Whip,* the *Rake,* and the *Libertine* were brash and brazen, boldly embracing the brothel scene and touting allegiances (when not picking feuds) with the women there. At times, they invoked republican language that introduced a new form of political commentary. The less cosmopolitan papers of the 1840s do not score as high in flashiness. The editors, of a nature more timid or less ribald, took their sexual content where it naturally occurred in public view, as in trials of seduction and adultery suits, or from police reports of brothel raids. In general they were not as willing to engage their readers with boundary-breaking topics or to thumb their noses at authorities.

At this writing, a small but growing number of other scholars have drawn on the flash press for a range of projects including popular dancing, sports, interracial entertainments, homosexuality, pornography, obscenity, women's underwear, and New York nightlife and nocturnal activities.[14] The American Antiquarian Society has now microfilmed the entire rich trove of satirical materials, including a number of the flash-like papers as well. We expect their greater accessibility will lend substantial aid to future studies of early American humor and satire, of adolescence and youth, of class and race mixing, of sports like pugilism and pedestrianism, as well as to further work on sexuality and gender.

The flash papers describe on their own terms and in their own flippant tone an underworld that formed a larger part of antebellum American culture than hitherto acknowledged, a world that drew in a surprising range of participants and offered a challenge to what has often been seen as a monolithic Victorian sexual regime emphasizing suppression if not outright denial of sexual urges. The papers illuminate an erotic universe with models of masculine and feminine behavior differing from those of the dominant culture. With humor and sarcasm, the editors challenged

FIGURE 5. "A STREET VIEW." WOMEN'S UNDERWEAR IN THE MID-NINETEENTH CENTURY FEATURED AN OPEN INSEAM BETWEEN THE LEGS, FOR EASE IN TOILETING FUNCTIONS. THE MAN BELOW THE GRATING HOPES TO CATCH A PRIVATE VIEW. *WEEKLY RAKE*, JULY 9, 1842. COURTESY AMERICAN ANTIQUARIAN SOCIETY.

the ethos of sexual purity that constituted the official story about respectable sexual morality. Perhaps such subcultures have always existed, on the margins and behind closed doors. Too often historians have learned about such alternative universes from crime reports or from the moralistic critiques of reformers. Guided by denizens of the subculture, the flash papers take readers, both then and today, behind those closed doors.

But we also need to be cautious: our amusing flash men are not always reliable reporters. They were, after all, satirical writers competing with one another, settling scores against each other as well as poking fun at hypocrisy in the larger world. Ambiguity and deceit are the hallmarks of flash; and so we find that even while presenting prostitution in a positive light, the editors might bizarrely insist that their goal was to promote morality by exposing sexual sin, and they freely lobbed charges and countercharges of immorality at each other. Cracking their own code, their flash-take on an inverted world of easy male sexuality that co-existed (for many of them) with simultaneous participation in respectable society, is our aim in this book, and to that end we provide substantial excerpts from the papers and illustrations to allow readers the challenge and fun of interpreting the satirical, sarcastic evidence for themselves.

PART I
THE FLASH PRESS

BEGINNINGS

Rivalry and Satire

In July 1842, two editors of a distinguished New York literary weekly called the *New World* sounded the alarm about four "licentious publications" which are "thrust in our faces at all the landings, ferries, and other places of resort." Comparing the onslaught of printed immorality to the worst libertine period of the French Revolution, the men chose their words carefully, to communicate the transgression without being tainted by it themselves. "Pictorial representations, calculated to excite the imaginations and passions of the young, and to gratify the morbid and beastly appetites of the worthless debauchee, are issued by the thousands." Why, they asked, are the press apathetic and the police silent? The papers were hard to miss: "The city has been covered with placards for the last six months, giving minute particulars of the revolting contents of every new publication in staring capitals."[1]

An out-of-town daily newspaper, the *Philadelphia Journal,* expressed amazement that such papers existed:

> There are now published in New York at least three papers, the chief end of which is not to disseminate general intelligence, nor intelligence of any kind which is usually the sustenance of the periodical press. Their aim is neither religious, literary, nor political. They have nothing to do with science or art, nothing with trade or finance, nothing with the agricultural, mechanical, or liberal professions, nothing with benevolent institutions or associations. "What, then, is their purpose?" asks the innocent reader. It is to promote vice and crime—to point out the facilities for immoral practices which are afforded in large cities—to propagate slanders—to blast character—to debase intelligence—corrupt the heart—and fill the paths to perdition![2]

Another New York paper, a new community weekly called the *Gazette Extraordinary,* sternly called for legal action against the notorious publications "weekly thrust into the face and eyes of the mayor, the District Attorney, the Grand Jury, and of every officer in the city—[yet] nothing is done to suppress them. The city is disgraced at home and abroad; the ribaldry and beastliness to which it gives utterance, through the medium of these obscene presses, calls forth the rebuke and the reproach of sister communities; and all because our police is too imbecile, or too cowardly, or too wanton, to do its duty and execute the laws." The *Gazette* demanded crackdowns on the editors and publishers, urging stronger laws if existing ones were inadequate, to get the "loathsome, horribly disgusting, and obscenely damnable publications" off the streets. "Let Mr. District Attorney Whiting look to it," or, the *Gazette* darkly hinted, an enraged mob would take up the job.[3]

The leading daily newspapers, on the other hand, gave little attention to the flash papers. Even the female-edited bimonthly periodical dedicated to rooting out licentiousness, the *Advocate of Moral Reform,* barely took note of the racy publications—which only shows that silence in no way implied approval or consent.[4] To write about the flash papers was tantamount to admission that one had seen them, handled them, perhaps even read them, and that was more than the moral reform women or the male editors of the mainstream daily papers were willing to do.

Clearly these innovative little weeklies touched a nerve. Thousands of New Yorkers loved their audacious charge and sent circulation soaring, while others became angry or fearful, nerve-wracked, perhaps, about the immorality the papers endorsed. District attorney James R. Whiting was not known as a particular friend to moral reform, but at several points from 1841 to 1843 he brought legal action against the aggressively marketed weeklies.[5] Only when the flash editors were on the court docket did they finally rate coverage in the major New York dailies, confined to the police office or court of sessions columns.

Enjoying high circulation and mostly stony silence from the authorities, the spirited editors gave free rein to bawdy humor as well as spleen and pioneered a new genre of American publication, drawing on British prototypes skillfully adapted to American forms of ribald humor and sexual sensibilities. This chapter introduces the editors and sketches out the day-to-day workings of the flash press. Five remarkably talented men, intimately familiar with urban male sporting culture, were responsible for transgressing the limits on what could be published in the antebellum United States: William J. Snelling, George Washington Dixon, George Wilkes, George B. Wooldridge, and Thaddeus W. Meighan. A sixth editor, Thomas L. Nichols, also deserves notice for his consistent role in promoting other flash papers and perhaps for publishing one himself, sufficient copies of which have not survived to make a definitive call.

FIGURE 6. "THE PEWTER MUG, ON A SATURDAY NIGHT." NOTED LITHOGRAPHER JOHN H. MANNING SHOWS HIGH-HATTED MALE PATRONS OF A NOTABLE PUB ON FRANKFORT STREET, READING THE *RAKE* AMIDST CLOUDS OF SMOKE. *WEEKLY RAKE,* OCT. 22, 1842. COURTESY AMERICAN ANTIQUARIAN SOCIETY.

Several more men also worked on the papers, in secondary or understudy roles: Charles G. Scott, John Vandewater, George Colburn, and Henry Renshaw.

Who were these men, and why did they get involved in what turned out to be a legally risky business? What did the papers print, and what was controversial about their contents? What was their distribution, and what clues do we have about the presumed and actual readership of the papers? How did the editors make money? What about blackmail? And finally, what can we learn about the urban sexual subculture to which they spoke, and indeed helped to create and enliven?

The *Flash,* the *Whip,* the *Rake,* and the *Libertine* burst forth in quick succession. A timeline mapping their dates of issue suggests the synergy among them, a combination of rivalry and mimicry. Their heavy presence in summer 1842 indicates an enthusiastic readership.

The flash papers differed one from another in particulars, but they shared a pattern and style. They were salacious and sex-oriented, hu-

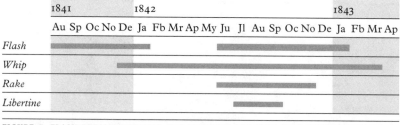

	1841	1842		1843
	Au Sp Oc No De	Ja Fb Mr Ap My Ju Jl	Au Sp Oc No De	Ja Fb Mr Ap
Flash				
Whip				
Rake				
Libertine				

FIGURE 7. FLASH PRESS TIMELINES. SEE APPENDIX FOR FULL PUBLICATION DETAILS.

morous and ribald, in league with the brothel world and also in varying degrees attuned to the saloon culture and competitive athletic sporting life of young "bloods"—the fast young men—of the city.[6] Seeking to expose the hypocrisy in high places, their editorial voices were often infused with a distinctive republican or democratic rhetoric. They were issued as four-page sheets, then the common length of many daily and weekly papers (though near the end of its run, the *Sporting Whip* expanded to eight pages). The front page typically carried an engraving depicting a character profiled in an adjoining story or else a picture of stock figures in a humorously compromising situation. Page-one articles often lifted up either a specific local person or a generic character (the serving girl, the milliner) to highlight a quarry's foibles and sexual quirks. The *Flash* titled this feature the "Gallery of Rascalities and Notorieties" and focused on locally well-known men connected to newspapers, theaters, brothels, or crime, whose exploits and weaknesses—for sex, for drink—were scathingly ridiculed. These were never admiring profiles. Other profiles under the rubric "Lives of the Nymphs" or "Nymphs by Daylight" featured individual "frail" young women giving sympathetic and compelling stories of their descent into prostitution. ("Frail" was not a flash word but a common code word used by the dominant culture to describe a woman of compromised sexual virtue, whose fall thus indicated moral weakness on her part.) Some papers might run on page one a scandalous "crim. con." article ("criminal conversation" in English law, meaning a charge of adulterous sex), regaling readers with some sexual entanglement, purportedly of real people; other front pages featured short fictional pieces involving seduction or adultery.

The second page always carried an editorial column on the left, where the editors castigated their opponents, puffed their favorites, or commented on events of the week. Then came short items of news relating the comings and goings of prostitutes, fancy men, pimps, and dandies,

GALLERY OF RASCALITIES AND NOTORIETIES.—No. 10.

THE COLONEL AFTER HAVING BEEN WAYLAID AND SHAVED BY OLD WOMEN ON BOSTON COMMON.

JAMES WATSON WEBB.

FIGURE 8. "GALLERY OF RASCALITIES AND NOTORIETIES.—NO. 10.: JAMES WATSON WEBB." A VILLAINOUS RENDERING OF COL. JAMES WATSON WEBB, EDITOR OF THE *COURIER AND ENQUIRER* NEWSPAPER, RAKED OVER THE COALS IN A RASCALITIES FEATURE. *FLASH*, NOV. 20, 1841. COURTESY AMERICAN ANTIQUARIAN SOCIETY.

interspersed with articles delivering insults to other newsmen and to certain madams described as old hags and harridans. Assorted feature columns appeared with regularity as well: weekly tours of some half dozen brothels, naming and appraising the charms of the young women in each; observations of pick-ups at the New York Battery park; theater and dancehall reviews; an "Ancient Pistols" column telling the life story of various colorful scoundrels of the local scene; accounts of seduction cases in the courts; social and fashion notes from various prostitutes' balls. The third page had spillover from page two and then theater and sporting news

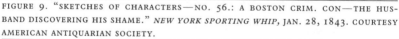

FIGURE 9. "SKETCHES OF CHARACTERS—NO. 56.: A BOSTON CRIM. CON—THE HUS-
BAND DISCOVERING HIS SHAME." *NEW YORK SPORTING WHIP,* JAN. 28, 1843. COURTESY
AMERICAN ANTIQUARIAN SOCIETY.

of various kinds. Over time, the sporting news increased, and included
pugilistic fights, both impromptu quarrels and formal challenges between
trained fighters; dog and horse racing; foot races and walking competitions ("pedestrianism"); and instances of news on boating races, cock-
fights, and firehouse competitions. The theater reviews often included
entertainments in the balconies as well as on stage.

Much of the fourth page of the papers carried advertisements, as was
true for regular newspapers. Some were quite ordinary ads, for hats or corsets, for stoves and pianos, some placed by women milliners or merchants;
most improbably, a young ladies' boarding school sought pupils among
the flash readership.[7] A great number of the advertisements marketed doctor's services or medical remedies such as Hunter's Red Drops for sexually
transmitted diseases. Similar sex-targeted advertisements also appeared

FIGURE 10. "WANTS TO KNOW." HEADER ILLUSTRATION FOR A REGULAR COLUMN. *NEW YORK SPORTING WHIP*, MARCH 4, 1843. COURTESY AMERICAN ANTIQUARIAN SOCIETY.

in the mainstream press, although not in such abundance. Multiple ads for saloons and oyster houses spoke to the flash audience as well.

The papers always assumed a heterosexual stance and addressed the readership accordingly. But there was recognition of the existence of alternative practices. One paper, the *Whip*, ran a blistering six-part series on "Sodomites," strongly condemning the "fiends" and their "monstrous and wicked acts" (with specific details of names and location of the action provided), and a few scattered items in the *Rake* also outed and condemned sodomites.[8]

The papers exhibit a lively, interactive quality, still somewhat unusual for more mainstream newspapers of this era. Flash gossip columns called "wants" carried many paid insertions contributed by readers that commented on or directed inquiries at people usually identified by initials or first names only. These were not businesslike "want ads" but "wants to know" columns, which one paper routinely illustrated by a sketch of a man peeping through a keyhole at a couple beyond. "What old lecher from Bond street went with a little girl to a house of assignation in Elm street, on Tuesday evening. Look out, old sinner. . . . What C. J. was at in the dark box at Vauxhall, with the girl in the blue bonnet. Her draperies seemed to hang rather odd. Be more careful, next time, Charley." Some of the "wants" were fairly risqué: "Why J–S—carried his 'rope' over the upper part of his pants in Sand street the other day. We do not think it right to *stand* so much."[9] Such clever, taunting insertions not only created a cash flow for each paper, they raised the potential for libel suits or, indeed, blackmail threats.

Regular correspondents from distant locales also contributed letters that could fill a page or more of print, providing updates on the reception of the flash press and juicy gossip about the local sexual action of the correspondent's village or town. Whether completely genuine or not—a question that needs to be kept in mind about every insertion in the flash papers—these letters map out an impressively wide community of readers, up the Hudson River (Fishkill, Poughkeepsie, Kingston, and Albany), into Connecticut and Massachusetts (New Haven, and up the old turnpike to Middletown, Worcester, and Boston), south through Newark and New Brunswick, to Philadelphia, Baltimore, and even Augusta, Georgia, and west to Cleveland and Cincinnati. The *Whip*'s editor once disparaged the *Flash* by claiming its compositor caught the drunken editor penning fake letters; but that story itself was of a piece with the bogus insults these men often traded.[10] When read over many issues, the letters from regular correspondents reflect consistent voices and consistent pictures of, say, the sexual doings of Poughkeepsie as distinct from New Brunswick, with a fairly steady cast of characters described. Possibly some of the tattled tales were fabricated or embroidered; but the authors were persuasively locals from those places, forging links between their small towns and the sinful city of New York.

Once a town was anchored with a regular correspondent, a special "wants" column for that town usually appeared, revealing the synergy between gossipy disclosure and eager readership. The *Whip*'s correspondent from Poughkeepsie once reported that he staked out the front porch of the main hotel in that Hudson River town to observe the rush of readers buying copies of the flash paper fresh off the steamboat from New York City. The purchasers immediately turned to the "wants" column, he claimed, to check out "their own exposure; some squatting on stoops, others on the packing boxes in front of their stores; here a few lawyers, there a dry goods merchant with his clerks looking over his shoulder; further on several collected about a grocery store—some with consternation visible on their countenances, others with compressed lips and lowering brow; others again with smiles on their faces but terror in their hearts." Their sins? Lying, slander, and fornication, "which is carried on to a great extent in this community," according to the correspondent.[11]

In one instance, confirmation exists that real characters and correspondents in a small town were entangled in New York City's flash subculture. In June 1842 the *Flash* ran several "wants" items about Middletown, New York, a small village in Orange County some fifteen miles west of Newburgh. One was: "Who was that young milliner reading the Whip at her bedroom window one Sunday lately. Do you take, Miss Newcome." A week later a letter to the editor in the upright *Middletown*

Courier charged that "an outrage [has] lately been committed upon the character of some of our most respectable citizens, through the agency of a scurrilous print published in the city of New York, and bearing the title of 'The Flash.'" Leaving Miss Newcome unnamed, the village defender suggested that the local who fed the story to the *Flash* should be tarred and feathered and run out of town on a rail. Indeed, the anonymous letter outdid the *Flash* in its heated speech, calling the New York paper "the organ of blacklegs, debauchees and loafers, who take this method to disgorge upon the community the slime and putrefaction of their corrupt and polluted minds." The *Flash* responded a week later with smooth restraint, even as it seized the opportunity to wound the young woman again: "Miss Newcome is a pretty milliner in the place, and by what we can glean from our correspondent there, is a member of the church. The fact of her reading the Whip being made public, grieved her sorely; why, we cannot imagine, for ladies of New York, with as spotless a reputation as she or any other lady of Middletown, read not only the Whip, but all papers of that caliber, which they have access to." Whether or not young ladies in Middletown actually read flash papers cannot be determined from this evidence, although one was so charged and named. What is clear is that readers in the village of Middletown, New York, knew about the *Flash* and understood that a local correspondent retailed their sexual gossip in the big city.[12]

Sometimes local authorities moved to squash distribution of flash papers, as happened in Norwich, Connecticut, where a court fined two men $10 for selling "horribly obscene papers" from New York City in December 1842. The Albany newspaper reporting this story thought a fine ten times greater for the vendors more appropriate: "The man who will consent to pander to the vicious appetites of the low minded and vulgar by disseminating the blistering obscenity and filth which these papers teem with, and which poison the minds of hundreds of the young and virtuous, is far more guilty than the midnight thief or the highway robber." Albany too was subjected to a barrage of immoral weeklies out of New York, the editor complained. "It is almost impossible to turn a corner without having them thrust in your face."[13]

II The flash papers brought a new form of sexual speech to the print world of New York, but they were not without immediate precedents, both indirect (moral reform periodicals) and direct (several London papers). In the 1830s, New York's burgeoning commercial sex trade prompted the emergence of several moral reform publications daringly blunt about the evils of licentiousness. How to name and describe a taboo subject without reproducing its harm was a delicate task for the reformers, one their critics felt they did not always accomplish. Exposés meant to warn readers might titillate instead, depending on who was reading them. The flash papers took some cues from the moral reform press and shrewdly exploited that ambiguity.

McDowall's Journal pioneered the moral reform genre in 1833. John R. McDowall, a maverick young Presbyterian clergyman, described his near-nightly missions of mercy to Manhattan brothels. He generated shocking "Magdalene Facts" (numbers of prostitutes and of clients) and told affecting stories of girls gone wrong. Suspicious minds in the district attorney's office worried that his publication in effect served as a tour-guide to dens of iniquity, and a grand jury investigated him in 1834 but did not indict. Two years later a church trial by Presbyterian superiors suspended him for "unministerial conduct."[14] By then his journal was taken over by a set of evangelical women equally determined to make an issue of sexual sin.

Renaming it the *Advocate of Moral Reform,* the lady editors expanded their focus beyond prostitution to hazardous courtship customs, the dangers of unescorted girls on public transport, and their drive to criminalize seduction. By steering clear of specific descriptions of brothels and prostitutes, they avoided McDowall's resemblance to a brothel tour guide. They endured criticism for injecting sexual content into print but, significantly, never came under a legal cloud. As wives and daughters of prominent religious leaders, they were apparently beyond reproach. Not so lucky was a twenty-five-year-old male crusader, Joseph A. Whitmarsh, who heavily featured New York sexual sin in his 1835 periodical, *Light; or, the Two-Edged Sword.* Just one issue of the thirteen published survives, and it shouts in heavy boldface type about whoremongers, adulterers, and masturbators. Reviving brothel tours, Whitmarsh relished entering the parlors of prostitutes under false pretenses and springing missionary sermons on the revelers. The district attorney brought the *Light* before the grand jury, and soon after, Whitmarsh relocated to Boston, where he started another periodical equally strident in its attacks on lust.[15]

The moral reformers drew inspiration for their breach of the polite silence around sex from what they regarded as an avalanche of licentiousness engulfing cities and towns in the 1830s. The flash editors also drew inspiration from that avalanche but equally from the moral reform press, which provided an inviting target of satire. Time and again, when under challenge for indecency, the flash editors wrapped themselves in the mantle of the moral reform school. When a grand jury called the *Whip* a "scandalous" and "scurrilous" paper, its editor drew himself up in a feigned huff at the very idea: "We, who never wrote or printed an immodest line; we, who never thought an immoral thought."[16]

In honing that satire, the editors had benefit of at least three satirical weeklies all inaugurated in London by 1838: the *Town*, the *Satirist*, and the *Crim. Con. Gazette*. The *Town* was a large-format, four-page paper featuring woodcuts of comely young serving women, profiles of well-known courtesans, and articles puffing pubs and saloons. New York's *Whip* regularly pirated woodcuts and text from the *Town* without credit. When the London editor of the *Town* was indicted for "corrupting public morals," his incensed response was exactly what the flash editors in New York would soon say: "Was there ever such impudent hypocrisy! We, who have always unflinchingly exposed and attacked every breach of public morals that presented itself to our notice, and made ourselves enemies among the few for the benefit of the many, to be charged, not only with encouraging but affording an incitement to vice!" In 1840 the *Town* started to run a "Questions and Answers" column, precursor to the New York "wants" columns, but different in that not just questions but answers were supplied. The added material greatly heightened the risk of libel suits: "Who is the lady fair and frail who receives the visits of the Earl of Munster?—Mrs. Bedford, of York-street." The *Town* did not include letters from correspondents, however, or provide weekly ratings of brothels and their inmates. It projected the single voice of its editor, Renton Nicholson, a self-described *swell*, a "man of importance" with a "showy jaunty exterior," a man about town. Nicholson's goal was to provide guidance to the leisure establishments of pubs, theaters, and literary lectures, amusing notes on the doings of the upper classes along with news of noted courtesans.[17]

Newcomers to the London metropolis relied on the *Town* as a guide to the swells' style of urban living, but, perhaps because the British capital was so much larger than New York, the *Town* never captured a sense of a community with individuated readers. New York's flash papers, by contrast, were not elegant and mannered. They offered a cynical and sarcastic view of real people with real names (or fake, as the case may be), pursuing activities the broader culture defined as vice. London's *Town* depicted the venues of suave *swells;* New York's flash press tapped into the world of American humbug.

III At least a dozen men were centrally involved in publishing the flash papers, but only three of them forthrightly put their true names on mastheads. Others used fake names, like the Dickensian trio of "Scorpion, Startle, & Sly" on the *Sunday Flash,* while some employed more ordinary but still invented names, noted as aliases in the court records. The core group of editors consisted of city-born youth in their early twenties, and no doubt a significant generational component contributed to their brashness. The true originators of the genre were two somewhat older men, William J. Snelling and George Washington Dixon, both in their thirties and neither native-born New Yorkers.[18]

William J. Snelling, born in Boston, stands at their head. In 1842 a rival flash editor dubbed him "the father of the smutty papers. . . . What would any of us have been without him?"[19] Snelling was the main writer and editor for the *Sunday Flash,* the first known fully flash paper, launched in August 1841. For three years previous he supplied the main copy for the *Polyanthos,* inaugurated by George Washington Dixon in 1838, a New York paper that by summer of 1841 attended closely to the doings of prostitutes and abortionists, under the non-credible but oft-asserted guise of being a moral reform paper. The assemblage of a multitude of small pieces of Snelling's history reveals a lonesome boyhood marked by promise but also loss, and a defiant young adulthood of a bright but oddball character, one either strong enough, or uncaring enough about his own reputation, to flaunt conventions and become the progenitor of "the smutty papers."

Before he was twenty-five, Snelling experienced a life packed with both serious learning and adventure. Born into a middling Boston family in late 1804, he lost his mother when he was six. His father, Josiah Snelling, left his son first with relatives and then at a boarding school in Medford, Massachusetts. Reportedly the small boy once threw a treasured coin collection into the Charles River in anger over his many displacements during this time. Colonel Snelling left him to pursue a rapidly rising military career, including an important post at Detroit during the War of 1812 and resolute action in the Battle of Tippecanoe in Indiana; he next was rewarded with the command of a fort in the Dakota Indian territory (soon called Fort Snelling, now a historic site along the upper Mississippi River near present-day Minneapolis). Meanwhile young William Joseph prospered in classical training at Medford Academy and then was honored with an appointment to West Point Military Academy in 1818.[20] Just thirteen, he fell below the stated minimum entry age of fourteen; but evidently William was very bright. He had to pass a demanding entrance exam and then dive into a challenging curriculum of advanced mathematics including "fluxions" (calculus), engineering, and French, a necessary language skill since France at the time produced the top engineering and technology treatises. Perhaps not surprisingly, young William struggled in his studies, competing for grades with much older boys. He had to repeat coursework, a common experience among the cadets, and to his credit he stuck it out for three years, besting more than half the class that had entered with him.[21]

But 1822 William resigned from West Point, "on account of a difficulty which he had with one of the instructors," a later observer reported. The seventeen-year-old traveled to the high Midwest plains to join his indulgent father, with whom he had not lived for over a dozen years. The family included a disapproving stepmother and several half siblings. A family servant at the fort later recalled that "Mrs. Snelling did not seem to have any great fondness or respect for him, and perhaps with good reasons; the colonel was greatly attached to him, and would do anything for him."[22]

In Minnesota, William Joseph did a complete about-face from his military training and spent the next six years as a woodsman and a licensed fur trapper working for a trading company headquartered in St. Louis, Missouri. For a winter he lived with the Dakota Indians, learning their language, "sharing their food and blankets," and, by one report, their women.[23] Apparently Snelling bragged about his exploits: "He freely fraternized with the Indian hunters and trappers, partaking of their wild fare and wilder pursuits," wrote an impressed younger man who met Snelling a few years later. By age eighteen he was a proficient guide and interpreter for a U.S.-sponsored geological expedition of scientists and artists which explored northern Minnesota for two months in 1823. When not in the woods in pursuit of fur trades with Indians, he stayed at Fort Snelling, where daily life offered abundant elements of a masculine world of drinking, card playing, and even dueling; young Snelling was injured in one duel, losing part of his left hand. Women also inhabited the fort, and the officers' wives valiantly fashioned a "select and aristocratic" circle of female gentility, marked by pianos, jewelry, and occasional full-dress receptions.[24]

In the fall of 1826 William met and married an eighteen-year-old immigrant Swiss girl passing by the fort on a multi-family migration heading south from Canada; the couple lived together at Prairie du Chien with her people over a bitterly cold winter, but the young woman died six months later. Later in life, Snelling demonstrated fluency in French, learned first at West Point and cemented in this short marriage. Snelling's last major exploit in the West came at age twenty-three, when he joined his father's troops in quelling a two-month revolt of Winnebago Indians. All of this was adventure aplenty for the West Point dropout.[25]

In 1828, William's world changed radically. His father's heretofore valiant military career was called into question: subordinates at the fort were uneasy about Josiah Snelling's increasingly heavy drinking and questionable handling of money and supplies; his superiors did not like the reports of dueling. The colonel traveled to Washington, D.C., to defend his station but there suddenly dropped dead, at age forty-six.[26] William, just twenty-four, was now without his protector and champion. Estranged from his stepmother and half siblings, he returned to his natal city, Boston.

There he took up literary pursuits, writing ready essays and poems for a wide variety of periodicals. He had stored up enough material on Minnesota Indians to write *Tales of the Northwest*, a set of appealing stories portraying Dakota and Mandan Indians as sympathetic, intelligent protagonists. *Tales* won favorable review, and Snelling was pronounced a budding and gifted literary talent in 1830 by what was arguably the leading review journal of the country, the *North American Review*, which then commissioned him to contribute reviews, a real mark of distinction.[27]

Snelling's decade in Boston was surely more physically sedate than his life on the Minnesota frontier, but still he courted danger, often betraying a disturbingly belligerent personality and a "wiry and active" physicality. He published a short, anonymous, and disparaging biography of President Andrew Jackson, and then plunged forward with his most famous literary production, a fifty-page cruelly satirical poem titled "Truth; A New Year's Gift for Scribblers" published as a stand-alone pamphlet in 1831. In it he named and castigated nearly every literary figure in the country, comparing the writers to vermin and complaining of the puffery that passed for literary criticism. A negative, dismissive review of the satire dryly commented on Snelling's rich "vocabulary of vituperation" as demonstrated in his overeager deployment of words like *booby, dunce,* and *blackguard.* One literary lion did not take to the joke: Snelling and the author and journalist Nathaniel P. Willis traded dueling challenges in 1836.[28]

Snelling's antagonistic poetic dig at the literary establishment makes his next career move hard to fathom: he was hired on as an editor at the *New England Galaxy*, a distinguished literary periodical. Snelling immediately used the *Galaxy* to mount an aggressive campaign against gamblers in Boston, publicizing their illegal hangouts and taunting the police to make arrests. It boosted subscriptions by 500, he claimed. In a theatrical stunt, he decorated his editorial office with all "the paraphernalia of an extensive gambling establishment. All sorts of threats we made against him by the gamblers. It was the sensation of that day," reported a contemporary. His friends feared for his physical safety, said another. His campaign indeed had serious legal consequences—for Snelling. Several accused gamblers sued him for libel, and Snelling developed a deep distrust of the judge in the case. The truculent journalist blasted the judge in print for "disgracing his office" and "perverting law," at which provocation the judge sued Snelling for libel and won. An appeal to the state supreme court lost, and Snelling was sentenced to sixty days in jail and a $50 fine. His very short career editing the *New England Galaxy* was over. In his remaining years in Boston, between 1834 and 1837, he contributed piecework writing and short-term editorial work to an assortment of publications.[29]

Snelling's experience in the Boston city jail was not his last. By the mid 1830s if not earlier, he suffered from a serious drinking problem. While he had managed to marry—a Yankee woman this time named Mary Adelaide—this relationship was evidently rocky, and he deliberately sought arrest by violating laws on public drunkenness and announcing to the judge that "I deserve all the punishment the court can put upon me," plainly requesting a long sentence to conquer his "insidious demon." The judge obliged with a four-month incarceration. Never one to miss a telling a good tale, he produced a hundred-page pamphlet titled *Rat-Trap; or, Cogitations of a Convict in the House of Correction* (1837) which included a moving passage on his view that alcohol abuse was akin to a mental illness whose first cause should be sought in "unpleasant homes and sorrow." Years later an acquaintance recalled encountering a determinedly sober Snelling after his June release from jail, but at a subsequent meeting "his presence disgusted me with the odor of liquor." And suddenly the thirty-year-old Mrs. Snelling died in September. She was also "guilty of too freely indulging in the use of liquor," the acquaintance wrote. Many retrospective assessments of Snelling's career offered variations on a theme: "a very bright and talented man . . . and as dissipated as he was talented."[30]

As this brief sketch of his life indicates, Snelling was an adventurous, talented and energetic writer with a caustic wit, a chip on his shoulder, and a debilitating problem with alcohol. His literary stock rose in the late twentieth century among scholars who found his early writings on Native Americans to be sensitive and surprisingly free of racism. Snelling could see past other cultural blinders as well: he was one of just a dozen men, along with William Lloyd Garrison, who founded the New England Antislavery Society in Boston in 1832, and he published poems in Garrison's *Liberator* starting in 1831. In a one-time-only lecturing stint in 1832, Snelling stirred a public audience with a powerful antislavery speech in which he "spoke from his own personal knowledge of the evils of slavery, as well as from conviction, having visited the plantations, and witnessed the sufferings of the oppressed." (If true, this witnessing could only have occurred in the 1820s on trips to Missouri where his fur trading company headquarters was located.) Snelling's ready sympathy for Indians and enslaved blacks stood in marked contrast to his posture of aggressive insult easily turned on judges, famous writers, and journalists.[31]

All accounts of Snelling's life leave out the years from 1838 to 1844, when he lived in New York and pioneered the flash papers. Possibly the Boston literary types who wrote his obituaries after his early death in 1848 did not really know what he was up to in New York; maybe they assumed he was ill or incapacitated. (One obituary writer waved a hand over a decade of newspaper work "which we have not space to describe here.") He apparently dropped out of his third marriage in those years, having taken a new wife in 1838 fast on the demise of the second Mrs. Snelling. The new bride, Lucy Jordan, aged twenty-four, daughter of a Boston baker, bore three children: one in June 1839, the next in 1848, and the last in 1849, when the mother was a new widow, all in Massachusetts. The unusual nine-year break in childbearing may indicate that Lucy Snelling returned to Boston soon after William moved to New York in March 1838.[32]

However, Snelling was far from inactive in New York. Within two weeks of his arrival he had a new paper on the streets. He ambitiously inaugurated a daily and called it the *Censor*, a name announcing a censorious stance on things, an appropriate fit with his abusive personality. Only five copies of the paper remain extant, April 11–15, 1838; they may constitute the entire run. The *Censor* resembled many other such papers that arrived and disappeared quickly: a man-about-town drifts though the cityscape, offering wry observational humor about political rallies, the theatre, religious or medical quacks, and so forth. There were unique and telltale Snelling touches to it: articles on the Seneca Indians and the Mohawk leader Joseph Brant, and more caustic verbal dueling with the author Nathaniel P. Willis, called by Snelling a "mean-spirited hound" and an "emasculate," a term calculated to wound a lady's man like Willis. In general it appears that the paper offered little to New Yorkers that they could not get in several other breezy papers. The *Censor* quickly folded.[33]

In June, all that changed. A scandal involving the mysterious death of a beautiful young actress charged up Snelling's vindictive character and set him on a course towards the sex-scandal-mongering journalism of the flash press. It also put him in partnership with the ostentatious, eccentric George Washington Dixon, a man keen to bring his unique style of theatrical pretense into the world of journalism.

Louisa Missouri Miller was the girl in question, an eighteen-year-old who made her lead-role debut in 1838 at the National Theatre in New York. Miss Missouri (her stage name) was by all reports lovely, guileless, and charming. She had attended the most prestigious girls' school in the United States, Emma Willard's Troy Academy, just across the Hudson River from Albany, New York. Willard's 300 students hailed from states stretching from Maine to South Carolina and west to Kentucky, with a sprinkling from Quebec, Paris, and Scotland. Elizabeth Cady Stanton, later a famous pioneer for woman's rights, attended the Troy Academy, and her sister Margaret Cady was a classmate of Missouri's. The high tuition and strict entry requirements ensured its exclusivity.[34]

Louisa Missouri did not come from a family of the professional or upper class, as did most of her fellow students. Her father was unknown to her, and indeed possibly unknown to her mother: Adeline Miller was an established madam who presided over a series of elegant brothels for at least three decades in New York. When Miss Missouri's familial identity became public, in the summer of 1838, the redoubtable principal Emma Willard rushed to protect her school's reputation by disclaiming all knowledge of the girl's origins. She was represented to be an orphan, Willard explained, when she arrived at age twelve with an aunt and older brother. Her initial deportment struck Willard as "somewhat wild and thoughtless," but three years at the Academy had matured her into "not only an accomplished lady, but a good woman." All at the school felt great regret over her subsequent fate, insisted Willard.[35]

By fate, Willard meant something worse than Missouri's choice to be a stage actress, although that alone was a very large step away from the sort of respectability Willard's pupils were trained to embrace. Missouri followed in the footsteps of her older half sister, Josephine Clifton, by seeking theatrical training under the tutelage of Thomas S. Hamblin, an English actor and director who ran the famous Bowery Theatre in New York City. Hamblin had transformed Clifton into a star, as he had also done for Naomi Vincent, another well-known New York madam's daughter. Hamblin took Vincent into his bed as well, and she died in his house while giving birth.[36] All of this was a fate Emma Willard would not approve for her girls; indeed, it was a fate at which Adeline Miller, Missouri's mother and doyen of brothel madams, also drew the line. If being an actress represented a threat to one's character, being an actress under the mentorship of Hamblin was many times worse.

Hamblin encouraged the teenaged ingénue, putting her in a lead role in a play opposite himself. Louisa Missouri's mother objected, and Louisa in an anti-maternal gesture moved from her mother's house to lodge in a respectable boarding house. A tug of war ensued, her mother and brother pulling her one way and Hamblin seeking—and finding, with the help of a shady reporter for the *New York Herald* named William H. Attree— legal means to acquire her. Attree maneuvered the girl to choose a police court justice named John M. Bloodgood as her legal guardian, allegedly to save her from her disreputable mother. And then he transferred her to Hamblin's own quite irregular household in early June 1838. In addition to Naomi Vincent's two illegitimate children, Hamblin lived with a lover, Louise Medina, a twenty-five-year-old Spanish playwright. Medina had moved in five years earlier to be a governess to Hamblin's children by his legally wedded English wife. The wife returned to England, and Medina took her place, even as Hamblin also romanced Clifton and Vincent.[37] On the face of it, Missouri Miller's family was right to be alarmed.

How Snelling got involved in this story is unknown; either his prior championing of Josephine Clifton, his writings as a theater critic, or a link as yet undiscovered with Adeline Miller and her brothel, are possibilities. (Another flash paper later profiled Snelling in a hostile article in December 1841 and alleged that he was the "protégé of the notorious woman Miller" as soon as he arrived in New York, serving her "in every capacity," a clear sexual insinuation. This was exactly the sort of contemptuous potshot rival flash editors often fired off.)[38] With the *Censor* now folded, Snelling's response to Missouri's dire situation of early June was to start

FIGURE 11. "GALLERY OF RASCALITIES AND NOTORIETIES.—NO. 8.: IL JATTATORE; OR THE EVIL EYE." THOMAS S. HAMBLIN ON THE STAGE; THE ITALIAN WORD APPROXIMATES BOASTER, BRAGGART, OR ENCHANTER. *SUNDAY FLASH,* OCT. 31, 1841. COURTESY AMERICAN ANTIQUARIAN SOCIETY.

yet another paper, called the *Polyanthos,* as an organ for criticizing Hamblin and agitating the public about the potential dangers to Missouri.

Snelling's senior partner in the *Polyanthos,* George Washington Dixon, already had a national reputation as a blackface singer and stage performer. The two men, both in their thirties, would in the course of three years transform the *Polyanthos* into the direct progenitor of the flash press, paving the way for the satirical weeklies. After that, the two became sworn enemies, working on rival flash papers. But in 1838, they joined forces to gang up on Hamblin and defend Missouri Miller.

The *Polyanthos* was far more censorious than the *Censor*. It accused Thomas Hamblin and other intermediaries of immorally enticing and removing the girl from her mother. Snelling derided Hamblin as a wretch, a criminal, and a villain; Hamblin was, in Snelling's words, "a hoary leper," a "Scoundrel whom even Texas vomited from her afflicted bowels." The journalist who initiated Missouri's removal (Attree) was described in classic Snelling-speak as a "bloated letcher . . . who has not drawn a sober breath since he picked his mother's pocket of her gin bottle while she was listening to his father's last words and dying speech at the foot of the gallows." [39] Snelling's verbal pyrotechnics slammed Hamblin and caught the attention of other New York newspapers. Their concern over Missouri's fate was not misplaced: in two weeks' time she suddenly took sick and died, tended to the end by Louise Medina in Hamblin's house.

Her death propelled the story of the tug-of-war over a sixteen-year-old actress into the national distribution circuits, but with a quite surprising twist in the plotline: the national reportage blamed the *Polyanthos* for killing her! The cause of death, according to autopsy, was inflammation of the brain, which many newspapers attributed to the shock Missouri suffered upon reading Snelling's articles about the dastardly Hamblin and his evil intentions to ruin the girl. She was driven mad "by the violent conduct of her mother, and the publication of an abusive article in the *Polyanthos*" according to one well-circulated report. [40]

No grand jury investigated Missouri's death; Hamblin seemed untouchable by the law. His protected position grew even more curious when, just six months after Missouri's dramatic demise, his playwright and young lover Louise Medina also unaccountably died at the Hamblin residence. In the immediate wake of these tragedies, Hamblin's golden touch in the theater business faltered, and he bowed out of the Bowery and left town for a while. When he returned in the summer of 1841 and resumed management of the theater, the Miller family had had enough.

Missouri's unforgiving family—mother Adeline, brother Nelson— determined to seek revenge on Hamblin by generously financing a scathing publication willing to blast the Bowery Theatre and its manager. Snelling rose to the challenge and started publishing the *Sunday Flash* in August 1841, with vicious and smarmy "rascality" features blasting Hamblin and Attree, the *Herald* reporter who abetted the girl's removal from her mother's house. [41]

GEORGE WASHINGTON DIXON,
The American Melodist.

FIGURE 12. IN 1836, GEORGE WASHINGTON DIXON GAVE HIMSELF CELEBRITY TREAT-
MENT BY HAVING MULTIPLE COPIES OF HIS PORTRAIT PRINTED BY PENDLETON'S LITH-
OGRAPHY IN BOSTON. COURTESY AMERICAN ANTIQUARIAN SOCIETY.

George Washington Dixon was far from a silent partner in this tirade in defense of Louisa Missouri Miller. He was unquestionably delighted to have a sizzling story to launch his paper, and equally glad for the financial assistance that almost certainly flowed his way from the wealthy Mrs. Miller. Dixon and Snelling had run in the same journalism circles in Boston, and probably the same bars and theaters too. While they shared a satirical sense of humor and no doubt bouts of excessive drinking, in other ways they were strikingly different. Snelling, the New England Whig and West Point cadet who once lived with Indians and championed slaves, was a sharp contrast to the southern-born Dixon, a native of Virginia and reputedly the son of a barber. Dixon had genuine talent as a popular singer, songwriter, and ventriloquist, and he gained national celebrity on the performance circuit in the 1820s as *the* "buffo" singer, with his act of songs, slapstick, and impersonations. ("Buffo" from the Italian for *clownish* lives on in modern English in *buffoonery*.) Stories clung to

FIGURE 13. "GALLERY OF RASCALITIES AND NOTERIETIES [sic].: SOME PASSAGES IN THE LIFE OF G. W. DIXON, THE AMERICAN COCO LA COUR." SNELLING CHOSE THIS ILLUSTRATION OF A COMIC BLACKFACE DANCER TO ILLUSTRATE THE HOSTILE PROFILE OF HIS ONE-TIME COLLABORATOR GEORGE WASHINGTON DIXON. *FLASH*, DEC. 18, 1841. COURTESY AMERICAN ANTIQUARIAN SOCIETY.

Dixon throughout his life that he had African ancestry, a charge he cagily but apparently never flatly denied. (A paper in Portland, Maine, in plugging his local appearance, said "George is a rare bird," to which a Boston paper retorted, "A black swan?") Dixon penned several hit tunes, most famously "Ole' Zip Coon," published sheet-music books, and performed in blackface—"he jumps Jim Crow with startling energy," reported an early critic, who also characterized him as a "stupendous" humbug, a standout among all the many charlatans of the era. In the early 1830s, Dixon the "American Melodist" was a nationally-known entertainment sensation.[42]

Dixon sought greater fame beyond his comic singing career. He had a gift of gab, showcased in many out-of-doors performances to crowds of hundreds. Several times in courts of law he chose to play his own lawyer—and succeeded. His writing talent was less notable, yet still he had turned his considerable energy to the enterprise of newspaper editing and publishing, first in Stonington, Connecticut, and then Lowell, Massachusetts, and finally in Boston in 1836 where he first met Snelling. None of these papers lasted more than a few months, and Dixon typically left a string of creditors in his wake. At least three times he found himself in court for swindling, forgery, or theft; in all cases he was found innocent. A Boston newspaper covering one of Dixon's forgery trials characterized the singer-editor as "an inoffensive young man, of very considerable musical talent, but a great lack of discretion" in business, a view confirmed by the court trial where the defense strategy of *non compos mentis* succeeded; all of which demonstrated how skillfully Dixon perfected his buffo, humbugging persona.[43] When Dixon arrived in New York in April 1838, Snelling trumpeted the arrival of his friend in the *Censor*, and the two teamed up to champion Missouri Miller and bash Hamblin. Alone, each man had a history of trouble keeping a paper going, but the *Polyanthos*, their joint project, remained off and on in circulation for nearly four years.

Once the *Polyanthos* moved past the Missouri Miller story, Dixon became the sole named editor on the masthead; but Snelling later claimed that he did nearly all the writing and merely let Dixon take the potential legal heat in case anyone sued. Clearly he anticipated that occasional articles in the *Polyanthos* verged on the actionable. Typically the paper featured theater reviews, gossipy tales, poetry, and satire, but at two salient moments, the writers crossed the line into sex scandals involving respectable citizens, a highly-placed Episcopalian minister and a merchant who committed suicide after being exposed in print. Dixon quickly found himself in court and then in jail for libel. He implausibly insisted his paper was really a moral beacon, helpfully repeating scandalous gossip about the minister so that the man learned of the rumors and could take corrective action. His article on the merchant, he said, could not be offensive because it was lifted right from the church women's *Advocate of Moral Reform*![44]

The court had none of it: Dixon's bail in *each* case was set at $9,000, amounts far exceeding typical bail sums of the day. Amazingly, Adeline Miller stepped forward and pledged security for this enormous sum, but a month later she too had second thoughts about her one-time champion and withdrew her financial support. As a consequence, Dixon was jailed pre-trial from January to April 1839, when the first libel (brought by the surviving family members of the merchant-suicide) was heard in court. Dixon dazzled his audience with his hours-long opening statement, but let a lawyer handle the rest of the three-day trial, which garnered many inches of sensational newsprint and concluded with a hung jury. The second case involving the Episcopal clergyman, Francis L. Hawks, was tried a month later, at which point Dixon surprised all by pleading guilty to the set of libels. (He later claimed the minister had paid him $1,000 for his guilty plea, hoping to avoid the exposure of intimate details at trial.) A six-month term in Blackwell's Island ensued, during which the *Polyanthos* suspended publication.[45]

The revived *Polyanthos* of 1840 and 1841 shifted gears into flagrant moral reform mode, so seriously that some scholars have taken the paper at its word—always a mistake with a character like Dixon. A shrill and insistent campaign against the well-known New York abortionist Madame Restell led the way, making the woman medical practitioner out to be an absolute monster causing the death of young women. Other articles listed the names of "blackguards and seducers" and published the addresses of houses of prostitution to help readers avoid the debauchery they offered. The *Polyanthos* thundered about its sacred mission: "Ours is a high and sublime one—to uphold virtue and chastise vice and wickedness in every form, but chiefly the vice of the social and domestic state; to defend the sacredness of the marriage institution, to scourge as with a whip of scorpion, the lewd adulterer, and cover with shame and disgrace the heartless seducer." Yet the more the paper ranted about a "fearless determination" to uphold virtue and condemn vice, and the more it featured moralistic (but juicy) stories about the evils of abortion and seduction, the more modern readers are inclined to doubt its stated motives. By early 1841 the paper was cleverly salting righteous moral reform pronouncements with increasing sprinkles of lighthearted coverage about women on the town, prostitutes' balls, and seduction stories; the wolf was slowly shedding its sheep's clothing. The last extant issue of the paper, November 6, 1841, promised that the next edition would be "the most beautiful, racy and spicy sheet ever issued" with a description of a recent ball hosted by "Princess" Julia Brown, a prominent brothel madam. Dixon had finally revealed himself, and on November 20 the district attorney's office brought a charge of "publishing an obscene paper." Twice his case came to trial, and twice he skipped and forfeited his bail.[46]

Meanwhile, the cheeky spirit of the *Polyanthos* found a kindred spirit in the first full-blown flash paper, the *Sunday Flash,* launched in August 1841 by Dixon's one-time partner, William Snelling. During Dixon's legal troubles, Snelling abandoned the *Polyanthos* and had started in mid-1841 a frothy weekly with literary pretensions called the *Sunday Times,* a paper he continued to edit for the next two years. But Snelling's wicked wit yearned for an outlet; as he wrote in a private letter, he found writing poetry a bore ("weary, stale, and unprofitable") and claimed "I can only write in the excitement of strong feeling, which is not enkindled every day." The *Sunday Flash* answered his need for excitement, allowing him to vent his spleen and flash his satirical humor under the cognomen Scorpion, in partnership with coeditors George B. Wooldridge (Sly) and George Wilkes (Startle).[47] Wooldridge seemed an unlikely prospect for a career in journalism. The twenty-four-year-old youth came out of a food provider background; his recently deceased father owned an eating establishment and bathhouse near City Hall in lower Manhattan, and his widowed mother Lydia continued to run a refectory at least through the 1840s. In 1841, young Wooldridge managed an oyster bar on lower Broadway called the Elssler Saloon (honoring the celebrated Viennese ballet dancer Fanny Elssler who toured the U.S. in 1840–42 and was famous both for her grace and her daringly revealed legs). Oyster bars were down a step from refectories or restaurants (figuratively as well as literally, most often being in basements), and they catered to a mainly male clientele with alcoholic drinks and snacks of small raw mollusks and apple cobbler (or so the Elssler Saloon advertised). Wooldridge's bar was a hangout for young unmarried men and evidently an assignation spot for illicit couples and street prostitutes seeking space for sexual encounters; ads discreetly emphasized that "private rooms can be had, where visiters [sic] can sit without observation." What Wooldridge brought to flash journalism was his ready access to unseemly gossip.[48]

Wooldridge had a more intimate connection to prostitution as well: at the tender age of eighteen, back in 1836, he actually courted and married a girl named Julia Warren living at a bawdy house on Centre Street. A Methodist minister, no doubt unaware of the status of the bride, officiated. Wooldridge's incensed father sued the brothel keeper, charging she enticed his son and encouraged the marriage. The senior Wooldridge dropped the suit, however, upon learning that Julia Warren was already married to a man who had abandoned her, making her marriage to George null.[49]

George Wilkes, aka Startle, the twenty-four-year-old son of a New York cabinet maker and a German-born mother, was street-smart and well read, making his first move into what would be a life-long career in journalistic publications. He became the key player in the *Sunday Flash*, despite his youthful age. Snelling provided the newspaper experience, the connection to Adeline Miller's financial backing, and the witty pen that

FIGURE 14. GEORGE WILKES, FRONTISPIECE FROM HIS 1852 TRAVELOGUE, *EUROPE IN A HURRY.*

produced the caustic "rascalities" essays; but his battle with alcohol periodically sidelined him. Wilkes could get a paper out on deadline, and he knew the shadowy depths of New York intimately. "No one knew life in the metropolis more thoroughly than Wilkes," reminisced a veteran New York newsman; no doubt Wilkes acquired his city knowledge early.[50]

As a youth, Wilkes garnered his first arrest record in 1836 when he and some other rowdy lads burst into a brothel and made mischief. In the late 1830s, he chummed with laboring men who soon formed the leadership of the Spartans, a political gang that delivered a pugnacious Five-Points-style challenge to the political backside of the Democrats of Tammany Hall. Wilkes grew up with Mike Walsh and David Broderick: Walsh was a Spartan leader and editor of the 1840s *Subterranean,* a rancorous workingman's newspaper; Broderick, a stonecutter's son and owner of the

Subterranean saloon, who, once tutored by Wilkes, rose to prominence as a colorful United States senator from California in the 1850s.[51] When Wilkes's friendship with Walsh shattered in 1845, Walsh pounded him in print specifically for his flash-press days:

> He was formerly brothel chronicler for a beastly, fraudulent and disgusting obscene paper which was suppressed by the authorities as a "public nuisance," called the Sunday Flash—has been a common loafer in groggeries and brothels, and actually spit in the face of a decent hard-working woman in the public street, who was defrauded out of some money either by him or the person who fed him. I have administered several kickings to the white-livered wretch for his conduct towards others, and I understand that he is now trying to commence blackmail again.[52]

The occasion of Walsh's diatribe was a libel suit in 1845. Wilkes had recently worked on the *Subterreanean* but Walsh fired him in a blistering volley of abusive language, calling him in print "a miserable, white livered thief, who formerly swept out my office" and a "stool-pigeon and false witness." Wilkes sued over this character-damaging description, but a jury failed to convict. Walsh did know how to love as well as hate, as shown in these extravagant words about Snelling, also from 1845: "I have loved Snelling from the first hour I ever saw him, and never expect to have cause to change my good opinion of him. I love him for his lofty and vigorous intellect—for his frankness and sincerity—for his devotion to friends and his hatred of cowardly and malignant enemies—for his good humor when roughly handled by fortune, and in short I love him as a whole."[53] Walsh and Snelling were kindred—and not gentle—spirits, plainly.

Walsh's allegation of new blackmail activity by Wilkes in 1845 referred to the recently founded publication, the *National Police Gazette*, which, despite Walsh's aspersions, was Wilkes' first wholly legitimate and successful enterprise. Under later editors the *Police Gazette* indeed became openly prurient over sex and violence, but its original formulation in the hands of Wilkes and his coeditor Enoch E. Camp was actually—considering its focus on crime—admirably restrained about sensationalizing sex crimes. The *Gazette* made good on the claim that such a publication would help police by identifying career criminals, their haunts, and their patterns of malfeasance. Coeditor Camp was six years older than Wilkes and already well established as a professional (lawyer, journalist, politician) and a family man; the *National Police Gazette* was not to be a flash-press derivative. But Camp was not in the dark about his partner's ongoing brothel-world connections. The two met when Camp took Wilkes into his law office as a clerk in 1842, during the heyday of the flash press. And while they shared editorial duties on the *Police Gazette*, between 1845 and 1848, Wilkes continued his close ties with prostitution, reportedly living for a time at Kate Ridgely's brothel. Wilkes drew on his brothel contacts to write a serialized history for the *Police Gazette* about the murder of Helen Jewett, a prostitute murdered in a highly sensationalized case from 1836. Despite being a boon to policework, the *Police Gazette* also offered opportunities for blackmail, as Walsh charged, inherent in its choices about which blackguard to expose and which to ignore. It certainly angled for readership by lively reporting and by romanticizing stories such as the one on Helen Jewett; and it featured a "Lives of the Felons" series, with some resemblance to the flash "Gallery of Rascalities." But, it was not remotely a flash paper.[54]

Wilkes was described by friend and foe alike as a dapper, tall, slender man of fastidious taste in clothes and "gifted with a rare nervous energy" that gave him a great capacity for work. In the late summer and fall of 1841, when he signed on with Snelling to help edit the *Sunday Flash*, he pressed his talents as a wordsmith into turning Wooldridge's sordid saloon gossip into snappy articles. There were profiles of scoundrels and prostitutes, unmaskings of various humbugs, accounts of prize fights and balls, and, as the weeks progressed, letters to the editor and reports from out-of-town correspondents. Snelling did all or most of the editorials and also the page-one "rascalities" profiles, where his cutting wit shone through.[55]

When "Scorpion, Startle, & Sly" fell out over a lawsuit brought against them by a Wall Street broker named Myer Levy (discussed in chapter 3), Wooldridge quit the *Flash* and mocked it by issuing two issues of the *True Flash*. Wooldridge was aided by George Washington Dixon, once good friend and *Polyanthos* partner with Snelling but now a turncoat (in Snelling's eyes). Snelling took revenge by maligning Dixon in a vicious two-part rascalities feature, the first illustrated with a cartoon of a "traitor" hanging from a gallows. The embittered Snelling, facing a court trial and eventually jail over an obscene libel charge linked to the Levy lawsuit, battered Dixon for cheating writers out of pay on the *Polyanthos*, sponging off the earnings of prostitutes, and—most ghastly of all— secretly rejoicing over the death of Miss Missouri back in 1838, because "it would make his paper sell!" Snelling christened Dixon the "negro swindler" and recounted in detail various deceptions that he had perpetuated that repeatedly landed the comic singer in court in Massachusetts.[56]

Snelling's anger at Dixon's abandonment was understandable, and much of his narrative was actually true. However, the heated rant was par for the course in this and subsequent titles of the flash papers. Arguably the most distinctive feature of the flash genre (beyond the attention to illicit sex) was the well-honed insult, hurled against men (and sometimes women) all known to each other as members of a community. To a degree, this explains the pose of the moral reform mission, in addition to its efficacy in throwing the district attorney off balance: each author could lash out at other sleazy lowlife types, pretending to be on a pedestal themselves while they issued correction to the others. "We are the police," claimed the *Sunday Flash* (as had the *Polyanthos* before it, and the *Whip* and *Rake* to come): "We follow vice and folly where a police officer dare not show his head, as the small, but intrepid weasle [sic] pursues vermin in paths which the licensed cat or dog cannot enter. We detect and redress and punish crimes beyond the reach of police or law."[57] Weasels and vermin were fitting characterizations of these worthy opponents.

Naturally, Wooldridge earned strong condemnation from both Snelling and Wilkes for betraying them in court. They portrayed young George as a contemptible puppy who simply could not write. (Nineteenth-century derogatory slang made rich use of canine synonyms, *cur, bitch, hound,* and *puppy* being frequent epithets.) Wooldridge proved them wrong by regularizing his rival paper under a new name, the *Whip and Satirist.* As the *Flash* petered out in January 1842, the *Whip* claimed the field alone, covering the brothel beat ("Diary of a Rake," later called "The Brothel Exposé," to maintain the fiction of exposing what they termed vice) and inaugurating the "wants to know" feature that all later flash papers copied. Wooldridge gave more coverage to the theater and dared to raise the subject of "sodomites." He aimed some barbs at "Scorpion," and claimed his *Whip* was a lash for punishing libertines and exposing "Palaces of Lust." But with just a few exceptions—Mrs. Adeline Miller being the key one—Wooldridge sang the praises of individual prostitutes, described their ball gowns and hairstyles as breathlessly as would a fashion magazine today, and in general exonerated women in the trade. (It is clear that Wooldridge aimed at a female readership for these fashion columns; indeed, it is entirely possible the fashion notes were written by a woman, since it would take a rare type of brothel-going man to be as well versed in the cut of fabric and style of feminine outfits as this columnist

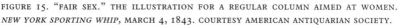

FIGURE 15. "FAIR SEX." THE ILLUSTRATION FOR A REGULAR COLUMN AIMED AT WOMEN. *NEW YORK SPORTING WHIP*, MARCH 4, 1843. COURTESY AMERICAN ANTIQUARIAN SOCIETY.

proved to be.) Most surprisingly, William J. Snelling himself became a writer for the *Whip* in March and April 1842![58] Satire indeed, when sworn enemies conveniently overlooked their rivalry.

The *Whip* proved to be the most durable of the flash papers, running for nearly fifteen months into early 1843. As the paper matured, it expanded its coverage of the sports and fashion scene; of all the various editors, Wooldridge had more direct connections with the burgeoning world of pugilism in New York, and sports in general received more attention, especially when the paper doubled in size in 1843 and changed its name to the *New York Sporting Whip*. From an early point, editor Wooldridge had the assistance of two men, George Colburn and Henry Renshaw, names identified as aliases in the police office records; under any name, they remain elusive and unknown.[59]

With solid editorial help and apparent financial success, Wooldridge launched a second paper in June 1842, a sixteen-page bimonthly titled the *Libertine,* positioned differently in the market for flash papers. The new eight-page paper had more racy fiction with titles like "Confessions of a Wanton" and "The Neglected Daughter." It carried longer profiles of four or five well-known prostitutes, and it attended to crim. com. cases and the "errors of the English Nobility." Its prospectus announced it was "a chronicler of libertinism" but not itself libertine, a fine distinction asserted but not explained; it would (somehow) send errant wives and husbands back to their spouses, Woodridge claimed. He promised that

FIGURE 16. MASTHEAD OF THE *LIBERTINE*, JUNE 15, 1842. COURTESY AMERICAN ANTI-QUARIAN SOCIETY.

its contents would be "entirely original, or have never been published in this country." Given the crim. con. and English nobility references, it is probable that most of the *Libertine* was plagiarized from one of the London satirical papers. Like the *Town* of London, the single issue of the *Libertine* that remains seems more than a step removed from the New York streets.[60]

June 1842 was the high point for the flash papers: the *Whip* and the *Libertine* were in full swing, and two new entries joined them, a revitalized *Flash* and a newcomer the *Rake*. Charles G. Scott's name now graced the *Flash*'s masthead, assisted by John Vandewater as agent. Almost nothing can be learned about them in the 1840s, until they both left for the California Gold Rush and quit the newspaper world for good. Scott was very possibly the same Charles Scott who stood as best man to George Wooldridge in his ill-fated Methodist marriage to a prostitute, a hunch further strengthened by finding Charles G. Scott also marrying in a Methodist ceremony in 1844. Scott was twenty-three and Vandewater just eighteen in 1842, but they benefited from experienced help on the paper: the biting wit of William J. Snelling shows up as early as their second issue, in a particularly nasty profile of Thomas L. Nichols. (Nichols was the editor of a small daily paper called the *Arena* that was beginning to turn rather flash itself, publishing justifications for prostitution and male sexual needs, unclouded by any smirking attempts to hide behind the skirts of moral reform.) Snelling tumbled from the first *Flash* in late January, worked for the *Whip* in March and April, went to jail for a month in May over libel charges from the first *Flash*, and in June agreed to write for the new *Flash*, an opportunity to skewer old foes again. He was probably of little help on the business side of producing a paper, and credit for keeping the *Flash* to its regular schedule from June to January should go to Charles G. Scott.[61]

The *Weekly Rake*, the fourth distinct New York flash paper, also started up in June and lasted at least until November 1842. Thaddeus W. Meighan was a lad not quite twenty, born in Westchester County but raised in New York City. Meighan coedited another weekly paper called the *Star*, so he was juggling two publications at once; he was "an industrious writer," a friend later recalled. His "rake" appeared in cartoons as a farm implement, not a womanizing dandy, and he poked gentle fun at the *Whip* and the *Flash*. Despite his youthful age, Meighan was not a newcomer to the sporting world. Back in February, four months before the start of the *Rake*, the *Whip* had attacked Meighan, lampooning him as a "male prostitute" who lived with a baud who was "fat, fair, and forty." In his opening issues, Meighan ribbed the other editors who derided him and politely asked for a truce, but soon his *Rake* was as lurid and mock-insulting as the others. He slammed Wooldridge for betraying Snelling and Wilkes in the first suit against the *Sunday Flash*, portraying Wooldridge's *Whip* as a paper "devoted to lies, slander and virulent personal abuse." He offered the now-familiar defense that he condemned libertinism— "we loathe, detest, abhor, condemn, abjure licentiousness, in every form and shape" and merely hold the mirror to society. His overinsistence was the tip-off: the day-to-day contents of the paper clearly endorsed what "is in the nature of man itself," his sexual appetite. While the other flash papers expressed shock—feigned or not—over New York abortionists, Meighan's *Rake* was on record as matter-of-factly pro-abortion. He told of a Boston girl in trouble who came to New York and was "relieved" with no danger or pain. "From a personal knowledge of this and many other similar cases, we can recommend Madam Restell, who is a beautiful, intelligent and kind-hearted woman, to our readers to perform any little jobs in her line. Her address may be learned from her advertisements in the *Sun* and *Herald*."[62]

IV How did the flash papers make money, and how could such young men enter the business? In general, start-up costs for any new four-page weekly produced on speculation were low if an editor subcontracted production to print jobbing firms, an option increasingly available in the 1830s and 1840s in New York City. Or, if an editor already worked on another paper (as did Thaddeus Meighan), he might have access, either ready or after-hours, to a printing press.

Because of a legal dispute over a promissory note that stretched out for a year, we have an unusually clear picture of how the *Sunday Flash* was produced. Snelling and Wilkes testified in a trial in November 1842 that they wrote their fall 1841 articles in Brooklyn and in West Broadway, probably in their living quarters. The type was set at various jobbers' shops, after which the locked-up forms of the type for each page were conveyed to William Applegate, a major print jobber. Applegate ran frequent ads soliciting business for his shop at 17 Ann Street, on the corner of Theatre Alley, where he had thirteen presses including a "mammoth" press for printing large wall signage.[63]

When Myer Levy sued the *Sunday Flash* for libel, Applegate worried about his own liability. He had printed the paper for four months, on a cash-and-carry basis, but now he wanted to stop. He offered to sell a press to the men for $750 so they could print the *Sunday Flash* themselves. Lacking cash reserves, Snelling approached Adeline Miller, and the wealthy female entrepreneur endorsed a note for the full amount to Applegate, who made it abundantly clear that he preferred Miller's credit rather than Snelling's. The press was removed to a rented site in Jersey City, and one of Applegate's pressmen was hired to run it. Wilkes and Snelling intended to pay Miller back out of the future earnings of the paper, but in fact the paper had only a short future. The Jersey City site was unheated and the cold weather chilled the ink, producing marred copies. Three issues were printed in December, followed by a long break until late January when the final two issues were struck. The trial of the two editors for libel against Myer Levy and for obscenity intervened, and though the obscenity count ended in a hung jury, Wilkes quit the paper. By the end of January Snelling, unable to carry it alone, shut down the *Sunday Flash*. Applegate demanded either full payment on the note, or partial payment of $500 plus return of the press; Mrs. Miller refused, and their legal battle dragged on for ten more months, at which point a court rendered a judgment of $433 in favor of Applegate.[64]

Wooldridge's spin-off paper, the *Whip*, followed a similar course. For its first month of publication, from late December 1841 to mid-January 1842, the editorial office was George Wooldridge's home address on Duane Street. Once on its feet, the *Whip* (and soon the revived *Flash* and then the *Rake*) paid production costs out of revenue for rented office space, compositors' wages, reams of paper, and printers' charges. Despite Applegate's concerns about printing the *Sunday Flash*, before long he was producing the *Whip*, along with Thomas Nichols's near-flash paper, the *Arena*. Possibly he concluded that Snelling's style of verbal attack was trouble, whereas the sexual innuendos of Wooldridge and the frank appreciation of sex by Nichols were less likely to attract lawsuits. As with the *Sunday Flash* (and indeed all the cheap penny papers of New York), the distribution of the *Whip* was handled in public by city newsboys or

FIGURE 17. FLASH PAPERS FOUND WILLING STREET VENDORS. NICOLINO CALYO, *THE NEWS-PAPER STAND*, 1840–44. WATERCOLOR ON PAPER, 12 X 9.5 INCHES. MUSEUM OF THE CITY OF NEW YORK. GIFT IN MEMORY OF FRANCIS P. GARVAN 55.6.3.

by agents outside of New York, who earned a set fraction of a paper's unit price. Once a revenue stream was established, each editor contracted with reporters or correspondents who were paid for their submissions, in the penny-a-liner tradition. After the *Sunday Flash* lost Wooldridge, Snelling assured readers that he was training five young Scorpions, three Slys, and two Startles; Wooldridge also claimed to have helpers-in-training, nicknamed Snap, Snarl, and Slick.[65]

On the income side were advertisements and sales. All the flash papers carried advertisements, proffering legitimate goods and respectable services. Apparently the moral reform disguise of the papers was sufficient to make the advertising page safe for real merchants. Revenue from readers could be a tidy sum. The flash papers sold for six cents, the standard price of the major newspapers then; they were not competing with the penny dailies for market share. Usually one to two cents was retained by the newsboys who sold copies in the streets. Self-reported—and no doubt exaggerated—figures for circulation range from 4,000 to 12,000, the larger number the claim of the *Whip* at its height, in summer 1842, when it also announced a readership of 100,000, a figure that assumed ten readers shared each copy. Comparative daily and weekly figures exist for 1842 for other urban papers: the *Courier and Enquirer,* 5,000 dailies and 3,000 weeklies; the *Sun,* 19,000 and 3,000; and the *Herald,* 13,000 and 14,000. So sales—if we can accept their claims—rivaled those of the legitimate press. Those figures included out-of-town sales, of course.[66]

The flash papers also relied on three other significant and nearly unique sources of income. Readers typically paid twenty-five cents to insert items in the "wants to know" gossip columns, which ran thirty to fifty or more items each week. A second less visible income stream came from bribe money, solicited from brothels to earn favorable notice in a paper's columns. The *Rake* revealed the mechanics of this process when it charged that the prostitute Julia Brown kept sending the editor $5 to puff her house on Leonard Street, but the editor refused to cooperate.[67] Of course, this could well have been a bogus claim, perfectly in keeping with the way scores were settled in the flash world.

Blackmail was a third and highly lucrative path. It might work through private extortion, as in this letter purportedly from an editor to a lady: "I've received $10 to expose you in print—if you wish to hide—pay $10." Notices in the "wants" column functioned as blackmail threats, and no doubt many a citizen whose initials appeared there hurried down to a paper's office to hush a story. One editor testified in court that an initial motivation in starting the *Sunday Flash* was "for the purpose of levying blackmail" and that $50 of hush money had been collected from one of their first targets. Fairly direct blackmail in print looked like this: To "Mr. J.R.L. We think this gentleman will feel rather sore when we acquaint him with the fact that we are preparing a list of the houses he lets to frail women for the purpose of carrying on the sinful trade of prostitution." The *Whip* promised that their list was shortly to be sent to the city marshal. Their target here was probably the very wealthy and very old John R. Livingston, brother of the famous Livingston politicians (Robert, Edward) and chief brothel owner of all New York. No list appeared in subsequent papers, so it appears that J.R.L. found a way to stifle the exposure.[68]

Of course, blackmail is effective only when the threat involves exposing a true or plausible scandal; if a flash paper went over-the-top with sly winks and wild accusations, it risked losing all credibility. Early on, an editor of another city weekly remarked that the *Sunday Flash* with its "utter contempt of truth and decency" and its "bold and villainous levies of black mail" had indeed "overshot its mark." "Those who are now foolish enough to accede to its demands of black mail, which hitherto it has freely levied, have only their folly to reproach, for the stamp of false-hood is so indelible upon the sheet, that money paid to buy its silence is thrown away." [69]

Quite so: the *Flash*'s Snelling preferred heaping abuse on individuals and daring them to sue. By contrast, Wooldridge, Meighan, and Scott perfected the subtle art of announcing untold scandal about to break in next week's paper—which then never appeared, once the payoff material-ized. The editor who so breezily denounced the blackmail racket as fool-ish was Thomas L. Nichols, whose name appeared in compromising news items repeatedly in all the flash papers over their duration. Running jokes about Ego Nichols, Handsome Tom, or, all in lower case, t. l. nichols portrayed him as an arrogant fool who romanced prostitutes. Perhaps if Nichols had taken threats of blackmail seriously and paid up, he could have avoided the continuous ridicule of the flash papers. Evidently his ego was so strong that he did not fear the ridicule; or else he enjoyed the publicity.

High readership, low production costs, "wants," puffs, and blackmail: the flash papers had the potential to be quite profitable. Wooldridge bragged that he cleared $5,000 in the *Whip*'s first four months, a believ-able figure in view of the *Whip*'s evident robust circulation outside of New York City and its "wants" column going into the many hundreds of insertions.[70] Very young men could enter this business if they had tal-ent as writers, connections to the brothel world (a major and necessary source of stories, gossip, and capital), and a willingness to risk libel and obscenity suits.

The concatenation of four flash papers cluttering the streets in June and July 1842 finally caused respectable newspapers to com-plain. It worked; the district attorney brought charges before the grand jury, which handed down indictments against Wooldridge, Colburn, Renshaw, Meighan, Scott, and Vandewater. (Snelling also appeared in a separate trial in mid-September, still fighting obscenity charges from the fall of 1841.) After trials in September, at least four were sentenced to sixty days in the city jail on Blackwell's Island.[71] On the day they arrived there, the prominent New England author Lydia Maria Child happened to tour the jail for her series called "Letters from New York" she was penning for the *National Antislavery Standard*. She cast a surprisingly sympathetic eye on the young flash editors: "While I was there, they brought in the editors of the Flash, the Libertine, and the Weekly Rake. My very soul loathes such polluted publications; yet a sense of justice made me refractory. These men were perhaps trained to such service by all the social influences they had ever known. They dared to *publish* what nine-tenths of all around them *lived* unreproved . . . Why should the Weekly Rake be shut up, when daily rakes walk Broadway in fine broadcloth and silk velvet?"[72] Child's observation echoed a theme common in the flash papers: why should writing about illicit sex be worse that the actual commission of it?

Even with the lead editors incarcerated, all but one of the flash papers continued to publish. The *Rake* listed a new editor, P. Henry, and the *Whip* had a Peter Dobbs; nothing is known about either of these men, and they may well have been false names. The *Flash* also continued, but by January 1843 it claimed a new editor, A. D. Munson, and then it immediately folded. The *Libertine* ceased to publish at the time of Wooldridge's arrest. When the jailed editors were released, two of them, Wooldridge and Meighan, resumed flash work, but the *Rake* only lasted another month, at which point Meighan went to work on the *Whip* with Wooldridge. The following March, the *Whip* too ended its long run, brought down by yet another indictment for obscenity.[73]

After 1843, this particular set of editors moved on to other outlets for their professional energies and entrepreneurial ambitions. Their papers concluded, but new titles published by new editors continued some of the themes and subjects pioneered by the flash press. In the later 1840s and 1850s, these new men were emboldened to try their luck in a market that had shown itself to be enthusiastic, lucrative, and not prohibitively dangerous. Our concluding chapter will lift the curtain on the future careers of the original flash editors and also survey the derivative papers, some in New York but also significantly a number from other cities, papers that consciously borrowed flash elements but also pioneered new developments in the unfolding story of printed sexual speech in the United States.

New York remained distinctive as the source of this new genre of publication. By the 1840s, the city had consolidated its position as the center of the country's publishing industry. And with the country's largest urban population, New York supplied the most visible and concentrated subculture of commercial sex, providing fertile ground for the flash papers to take firm root there, early and noisily, with four of them going strong at once in the summer of 1842. The *Flash*, the *Whip*, the *Rake*, and perhaps to a lesser extent the *Libertine* achieved an extensive distribution, spurring imitators and shocking critics well beyond the island of Manhattan. They and their emulators from Baltimore to Boston, from Manchester to Philadelphia, and perhaps many other places beyond, flourished in the 1840s as they could not have a decade before, and indeed did not a decade later, or at least not in the same satirical form. Flash papers were purposely paradoxical, and that was part of the joke. They gave voice to both bawdy satire and moral indignation; they combined trenchant critiques of class privilege with endorsements of heterosexual indulgence; and they supported male sexual prerogative while defending and admiring individuals of the "frail" sisterhood of prostitutes. Their complex sexual politics makes them slippery subjects indeed.

SEXUAL POLITICS

The editors, publishers, and writers affiliated with the flash press of the 1840s were a confusing bunch. They included men who at various points in their lives were brothel bullies and water-cure vegetarians, abolitionists and blackface minstrels, spiritualists and sporting men, Whigs and Democrats. To say the least, the flash press made for strange bedfellows. Their weekly papers were quickly composed, slipshod, and blatantly emulative of one another. They existed in a world of highly emotional rivalries, personal invective and competitive journalism among sporting and penny press publications. Papers like the *Whip*, the *Flash*, and the *Rake* employed gossip, revelatory threats, and satirical descriptions of competitors.[1] A combination of money and honor seemed to define their purposes.

The multiple conflicts and political views of the flash press editors, however, camouflaged what they had in common. Admittedly, the flash writers never shared a distinct or explicit set of beliefs in a programmatic sense; their views were ill-defined, personal, fluid, and paradoxical. Yet despite their problematic (and at times inconsistent) political beliefs, public rivalries, and entrepreneurial motives, the flash papers represented a unique and distinct antebellum genre. A close inspection shows they shared a certain (albeit imprecise) ideology, reflecting a variety of values originating in their daily experiences and validated in their social life.[2]

Specifically, the flash weeklies of the 1840s espoused an ideology best labeled "libertine republicanism." This was never as sophisticated or as complex as the "religion of libertinism" described by historian Randolph Trumbach that emerged in eighteenth-century Europe, nor did it replicate the republicanism associated with the American Revolution.[3] Indeed many nineteenth-century Americans would have considered the concept of libertine republicanism an oxymoron. Republicanism was critical of patriarchy, privilege, luxury, and corruption. Originally these characteristics were associated with European aristocracies, but by the nineteenth century numerous critics complained that certain American elites and social groups were guilty of the same. In particular, corruption and luxury were frequently equated with licentiousness, "vice," and other forms of libertine sexuality. One literary weekly described the libertine as the antithesis of the virtuous republican, "a monster whose breath is poison, and whose grasp is death."[4]

Contemporaries, however, ignored the unique combination of libertine and republican beliefs found within the flash press. Four broad themes repeatedly infused the reportage of writers and editors alike. First, the flash press consistently promoted male heterosexual indulgence. Sex was a natural, positive, and central part of human life.[5] Second, the flash press devoted considerable attention to prostitution, paradoxically defending and attacking it at the same time. Some critics even referred to the weeklies as the "licentious press" and the "profligate press," their editors as "brothel chroniclers." Third, the libertine republicanism of the press espoused a radical, democratic critique of privilege and hierarchy. Finally, editors and writers affiliated with the flash press displayed a skeptical rationalism and a vehement, anticlerical hostility to organized religion and social groups defined by their religious beliefs. In contrast to European anticlericalism which was profoundly and primarily anti-Catholic, this American version combined anti-Catholic, anti-evangelical, and anti-Semitic sentiments. The flash press's combination of republicanism and libertinism was never consistently displayed; indeed, at times some of these views were contradictorily expressed. Significantly, critics like *New York Tribune* editor and future U.S. presidential nominee Horace Greeley referred to the flash papers as "the ribald and infidel press, owned and conducted by notorious libertines."[6]

Libertine republicanism was a conception of freedom quickly repressed by mid-nineteenth-century contemporaries and largely forgotten by later historians. In their comprehensive studies on the changing definitions and perceptions of "freedom," for example, historians Eric Foner and David Hackett Fischer ignore libertine ideas. Libertine behaviors associated with a "pleasure culture" in Revolutionary-era cities were seemingly undermined and suppressed by evangelical and moral-reform forces early in the nineteenth century.[7] Furthermore, libertine republicanism presented a dramatic contrast to the more common portrayals of masculinity defined by either the responsible, self-restrained, pious, pure, intelligent Christian gentlemen or the rugged, romantic man of the frontier.[8] By contrast, the libertine republican mixed an emotional critique of privilege and hierarchy with language more often associated with an expressive, promiscuous, male-centered sexuality.

The flash press and its associated subculture was a strange mixture of Tom Paine's revolutionary politics infused with aspects of the sexual ideology of the Marquis de Sade.[9]

The editors of the flash press, however, never explicitly invoked Paine or Sade. Rather, Paine's republican ideals were evidenced by the flash press's promotion of individualism, their satirical commentaries on institutional and evangelical religion, their sometimes scathing attacks on wealth and the economically advantaged, and their cosmopolitan urbanism and entrepreneurship. The discussions of sexuality in the flash press at times reflected the influence of freethinking contemporaries such as the utopian reformer Robert Dale Owen, editor Abner Kneeland, and physician and birth-control advocate Charles Knowlton.[10]

Similarly, sympathetic critics believed the flash press promulgated a "polite libertinism" and, in truth, certain Sadean beliefs permeated the flash weeklies. What the New York plebian writers borrowed from the French aristocrat were not the violent perversions, cruel tortures, and reprobate pleasures commonly associated with Sade, but the side of his writing that defined freedom as the right to satisfy one's own individual pleasure. One can see this in the key Sadean libertine ideas underlying flash articles that advertised—and sometimes valorized—the openly erotic behaviors of so-called rakes, roués, and sporting men who engaged in a promiscuous heterosexuality. Sexual passion was natural, its elimination impossible, and its repression injurious. All natural desires were useful and worthy of satisfaction. Forbidden pleasures were good, sexual pleasures supreme. By exchanging money for sex, prostitution offered a liberating form of sexual pleasure. Smearing with sexual slander was a means to assail the powerful. Attacks on religion, priests, convents, civil officials, and influential citizens reflected an unsystematic but nonetheless fervent anticlericalism and anti-statism.[11]

Equally significant was the distinctive way libertinism in the flash press departed from European counterparts: discussions of libertinism were often clothed in moralistic language which at times criticized libertinism itself. Most of this moralism was tongue in cheek, written with a literary wink and a nod. Yet the result was a libertinism that mixed the moral with the licentious. For instance, George Wooldridge defended the *Libertine* as "a moral paper." When one Richard B. Jones was attacked and criticized, he was pejoratively identified as "a libertine at worst." Similarly, when an adulterous physician was threatened with exposure, he was described as "the libertine Dr. B." In an article on dress and style, the

Flash was critical of libertine trends in fashion and culture. In drawing sympathetic portraits of prostitutes, women were frequently portrayed as victims of male libertines. When the *Whip* wrote in defense of the *Libertine*, Wooldridge used irony: "The *Libertine* is not itself a libertine but a chronicler of libertinism."[12]

Therein lay the paradox: in chronicling libertinism, the flash press advertised that very philosophy, exemplified by their endorsement of unrestrained male heterosexual indulgence. The *Libertine*, for example, identified its audience as "the epicures" of America's leading cities. The *New York Sporting Whip* defended sexual profligacy, arguing that "Man is endowed by nature with passions that must be gratified, and no blame can be attached to him, who for that purpose occasionally seeks the woman of pleasure." Municipal suppression of commercial sex was futile, argued the *Whip*, because fornication was a universal pleasure, present since the creation of humankind; it would so remain "till time is no more." The editors of the *Rake* proclaimed that the "seeds of [man's] intemperance" were "broadly scattered" and being "pregnant with soft desires, they covet a genial growth." The male sex drive, insisted Thomas Nichols in the *New York Arena*, had to be gratified, and that it was "madness to expect them to refrain from intercourse with the other sex."[13] Not surprisingly, such views mirrored those found in brothel guidebooks.[14]

This pleasure principle sometimes extended to female sexuality. The *Weekly Rake* challenged opinions that women who departed from "virtuous propriety" and engaged in "illicit intercourse with one or two men" were thus stigmatized by "the abyss of shame." This was, simply put, "a mistaken idea." Kept mistresses and "*higher* grade" courtesans were hardly in the same category as the impoverished prostitutes in Corlears Hook and Five Points. Rather, the elegant concubine epitomized by the murdered prostitute Helen Jewett represented sophistication and erudition. Such women were "full of noble sentiment and indicative of a cultivated and reflecting mind."[15]

Proponents of this libertine, heterosexual ideal enlisted antiquity as a defense. The *Weekly Rake*, for example, reminded readers that ancient Greek women like Sappho, Erinna, Lais, Aspasia, Pythonice, and Phrayne were really common harlots or kept mistresses in their time. Greek mythology, for example, was riddled with blatant sexual display:

> Even the halls of heaven itself were not free from the pollution; and criminal conspiracies, adulteries, lewdness, drunkenness, and other

debaucheries, were as rife in the courts of Jove, as in our sinful world at this time. Themes like these have engaged the loftiest intellects, and have been sung in strains the most melodious and divine, that ever enraptured or soothed the ear; or ministered to the prurient impulses of our nature.

In sum, the "great occupation" of both Greek and Roman divinities, pointed out the *Rake*, was "the gratification of their immortal lust." [16]

Other times, the flash papers summoned Greek or Roman mythology to promote their indulgent heterosexuality. The *Flash*, for example, included a front page lithograph of Hero and Leander, subjects of a romantic Greek tragedy. In discussing sexual seduction in another issue, the *Flash* employed an illustration of the mythological Greek nymph Arethusa being sexually pursued by the river god Alpheus. Prostitutes attending Julia Brown's ball were noted for their "Juno-like form," comparable to "a second Venus de Medicis" [*sic*].[17]

References to antiquity revealed a certain level of sophistication by the presumed audience. Young men with some classical education were familiar with such characters. While little evidence supports the claim that the poetesses Sappho or Erinna were prostitutes or mistresses (indeed many thought them to be lesbians), the flash press writers assumed that readers knew Aspasia, the influential mistress of Pericles who appears in the texts of Aristophanes, Plato, Aristotle, Xenophon, and Plutarch. A similar familiarity was associated with Lais, a courtesan from Corinth who lived with the philosopher Aristippus, and Pythonice, the mistress of Harpalus in Plutarch's *Phocion*. Some brothels, like the Alcibiades Club House, even adopted classical appellations.[18]

Even youths and young men with less formal educations were most likely familiar with certain classical subjects. John Vanderlyn's painting *Ariadne Asleep on the Island of Naxos* (1814), for example, portrayed a mythical Greek figure in a sexually provocative pose. Not only was *Ariadne* among the earliest large-scale nudes by an American-born artist, but the painting was frequently and publicly displayed during the 1820s and 1830s. In various theaters, "model artist" shows, or tableaux vivants, were popular. Actresses on stage, replicating classical narratives such as "Venus Rising from the Sea" or "the Greek Slave," assumed stationary poses dressed in tights, transparent clothing, or nothing at all. As the historian Lawrence Levine has shown, plebian audiences in antebellum New York were far more familiar with classical, Shakespearean,

GALLERY OF COMICALITIES.

THE LOVES OF HERO AND LEANDER.

FIGURE 18. "GALLERY OF COMICALITIES.: THE LOVES OF HERO AND LEANDER." THE FLASH PRESS EMPLOYED GREEK TRAGEDY IN PROMOTING HETEROSEXUAL INDULGENCE. *FLASH*, SEPT. 18, 1842. COURTESY AMERICAN ANTIQUARIAN SOCIETY.

and other texts later defined as "high culture" than their counterparts a century or more later.[19]

The endorsement of heterosexual indulgence within the flash press was magnified by its homophobia. The *Whip*, in what historian Jonathan Ned Katz describes as the earliest-known crusade against homosexuals, was the most strident. Young men with "genteel" backgrounds and

GALLERY OF COMICALITIES.

PIETY IN A NEW GARB.

" ON BOARD OF THE ARETHUSA." ' lighten the ship by the head,"—nor could he conceive

FIGURE 19. "GALLERY OF COMICALITIES.: PIETY IN A NEW GARB." IN GREEK MYTHOLOGY, THE RIVER GOD ALPHEUS PURSUED THE NYMPH ARETHUSA. *FLASH*, SEPT. 4, 1842. COURTESY AMERICAN ANTIQUARIAN SOCIETY.

"feminine . . . manners" congregated nightly in the vicinity of City Hall Park, complained the *Whip,* thus turning that public space into "a second Palais Royale," a reference to the Parisian locale noted for various kinds of illicit and homosexual behaviors. Throughout 1842, the *Whip* blasted gay men with a cacophony of insults: "brutal sodomites," "abominable sinners," "a set of *fiends* bearing the form of men," "a beastly crew," "old and lecherous villains," "polluted persons," all of whom were "in the habit of disgusting nature with their monstrous and wicked acts." The homosexual was, simply put, "a man-monster."[20]

But the *Whip* was hardly alone in such homophobic condemnation. The *Weekly Rake*, for example, complained of "a vile wretch" who reportedly enticed boys and young men to his hotel and office for the purposes of sodomy and masturbation. Such homosexual behaviors represented "terrible enormities now winked at." The *Flash* similarly complained "that the worst and most unnatural of vices of ancient Athens is extensively practiced in modern Gotham." They estimated that "a score of habitual sodomites" resided in the city.[21]

The *Whip*, in particular, attributed such behavior to immigrants and actors. Theaters like Palmo's had "these monsters among [their] performers." Johnny L'Epine was identified as a French "sodomite" who portrayed "feminine parts" for a theatrical troupe identified with St. John's Hall on Frankfort Street. Elsewhere they charged that only Frenchmen and English were "*beasts* who follow that unhallowed practice." Yet, a month later they singled out the Portuguese Jewish immigrant John Emmanuel for his "unnatural intercourse" with a journeyman printer.[22]

Libertine republicanism promulgated the right of heterosexual males to indulge in commercial sex, yet the prostitute was a paradoxical icon. At times, the flash press assumed a tolerant, Augustinian view, again echoing themes frequently found in brothel guidebooks. The *Weekly Rake* argued that brothels were necessary "as bread or water," but required orderly regulation. "The cause of morality is not served by the suppression of open brothels," added the *Rake*, "they are as essential to the well-being of society as churches."[23] The *Whip* insisted that human passion "must have a vent," and one way was the licensing of brothels as in France. Regulated prostitution would result in more social order: less streetwalking, fewer pickpockets, and the elimination of "the whole tribe of brothel bullies." Prostitutes were categorized as victims, "oppressed and unfortunate." "All prostitutes are not alike," stated the *Rake*. "Some have tender feeling, intellectual gifts, are charitable, no more to be despised than the male libertine."[24]

More significantly, flash papers joined brothel guidebooks as among the first American publications to consciously celebrate prostitution. "Away with the false notion that a woman who once sins is irrecoverably lost," the *Whip* recommended. While penny papers like the *Herald* and the *Transcript* included occasional stories about "women on the town," none offered the detailed reportage on the lives of prostitutes found in the flash press. Leading madams like Rebecca Weyman and Sophia Austin, respectively identified as "Lady Weyman" and "La Belle Austin," were acknowledged as "fashionable ladies" based on their dress and frequent visits to Stewart's department store.[25] Regular column's such as the *Weekly Rake*'s "From Our Office Window," the *Flash*'s "Lives of the Nymphs," and the *Whip*'s "Diary of a Rake" and "Nymphs By Daylight" glorified leading madams and prostitutes. Each chronicled the origins, qualities, and personalities of streetwalkers.[26] In "Lives of the Nymphs," an engraved image usually accompanied a biographical sketch of the subject. Amanda B. Thompson was one such example:

> Among the gay sisters of our city, this is without doubt the most remarkable and if respectability belongs to such a peculiar profession as that which she follows, she may be called respectable. Amanda is extremely beautiful with tresses black as get [*sic*], which she wears in the highest style of fashion, and eyes that might challenge comparison with the brightest things of earth. A figure magnificent beyond description, a bust that defies the imitation of the sculptor, and a smile sweet beyond expression, are but a few among the mighty charms she possesses.

Thompson reportedly grew up in a respectable family and was well educated. After her seduction by a local minister, she became the mistress to "young Buonaparte" [*sic*] during his visit to the United States. Thompson allegedly joined her aristocratic suitor on his travels throughout the country. Under his tutelage, she was repeatedly introduced to local elites, "her beauty" being "the theme of boundless admiration" wherever they went. After he abandoned her, Thompson opened an expensive Broome Street brothel. "Scarcely any of the palaces of beauty set out in magnificence as the temples of licentiousness can bear a comparison with hers," claimed the *True Flash*.[27]

Julia Brown, however, was the queen of all madams for the flash press. The *Whip* regularly extolled praise upon Brown, describing her elaborate brothel ball and referring to her as "the head of her profession" and "Princess Julia."[28] "All the ladies looked charming, and were the true representatives of angels themselves," reported the *Flash* after a visit to Brown's establishment. The women "seemed as if they had come down from heaven to charm man from this worldly state of misery to that of eternal happiness and pleasure." Brown was not only elegant, pretty, and intelligent, preached the *New York Arena*, but she possessed "a rosy

A GRAND BALL GIVEN BY JULIA BROWN, AT HER MANSION, 55 LEONARD ST.

FIGURE 20. "A GRAND BALL GIVEN BY JULIA BROWN, AT HER MANSION, 55 LEONARD ST."
FLASH, JAN. 14, 1843. COURTESY AMERICAN ANTIQUARIAN SOCIETY.

cheek, a bright eye, sweet smile, and a hand whose softness is absolutely bewildering." The *Weekly Rake* claimed that Charles Dickens visited Brown's establishment during his 1842 tour of the United States. "He says not a word about his visit to Julia Brown," the editors complained, "and we cannot forgive him."[29]

Not all prostitutes, however, merited celebrity status. At times, the flash press resorted to satire, attacking vice while sensationalizing and glorifying sexual profligacy. Most likely, criticism of commercial and other forms of public sexuality was designed to assuage grand juries and prosecutorial authorities. The *New York Sporting Whip* claimed to be "devoted to the eradication of abuses," particularly the suppression of fornication, adultery, and seduction; it then commenced publishing the names and addresses of Gotham's most prominent madams.[30] The *Whip* announced its intentions to describe "city life, and take a bird's eye view of that wickedness which is lurking in the security of its hiding places." The newspaper's goal was to expose crime and "put in every honest hand a whip" to root it out. Yet, the same journal devoted front-page coverage to the memoirs of Mary Robinson, the mistress of King George IV. The editors of the *Rake* similarly insisted they were not apologists for libertinism. "We loathe, detest, abhor, condemn, abjure licentiousness in every form and shape," they proclaimed. Rather, their intent was to "show vice in its own image."[31] Meanwhile, excerpts from *Decameron* and other erotic narratives were featured on the front page.[32]

Some prostitutes were used to insult. Phoebe Doty, for example, was portrayed as fat, ugly, and too old for men to enjoy her sexual services.[33] When her name appeared in the flash press, she was a frequent vehicle for ridicule. The *Sunday Flash*, in their attack on Myer Levy, described him as her "fancy man." To mock George Washington Dixon, he was identified as Doty's paramour, soon to bring her "to the hymenial altar." The *Whip and Satirist of New-York and Brooklyn* stated that Doty was writing her memoirs and would implicate "many *great* names" like penny press editors Moses Beach and James Gordon Bennett.[34]

Descriptions of Harriet "Hal" Grandy were similarly employed by certain flash press editors to vilify their enemies. Numerous columns derided her behavior and looks, describing her as degraded, dirty, and disgusting. But mockery of Grandy departed from insults levied against other prostitutes in a significant way: her masculine deportment was singled out for attack. The *Whip*, for instance, depicted her as an intimidating woman with considerable physical strength, "a *she*-male" by one account. Grandy was criticized for openly promenading along Broadway in men's clothing and jostling "respectable" women off the sidewalk. Another time she "cow-hided" a former lover in broad daylight for allegedly sharing "her affections with a host of lawless fellows." One article entitled "Grand Pitch Battle between Harriet Grandy and the Gingerbread Man at 100 Church Street" described how Grandy insulted her lover with the nickname "Gingerballs." When he returned the insult, she challenged him to a fight in the back yard of a well-known brothel. Grandy won in the seventh round.[35]

FIGURE 21. "SKETCHES OF CHARACTERS—NO. 41.: THE GREAT CHARITY SUPPER, GIVEN TO MRS. PHOEBE DOTY." A COMIC DEPICTION OF PROMINENT NEW YORK MADAMS AND PROSTITUTES, INCLUDING HAL GRANDY (FAR RIGHT). *WHIP,* OCT. 22, 1842. COURTESY AMERICAN ANTIQUARIAN SOCIETY.

Some of this was most likely hyperbole. Yet, criticism and negative portrayals of individual prostitutes represented more than personal invective or sensational titillation. They served a third ideological purpose: prostitution was equated with the antithesis of republicanism—aristocracy, privilege, and luxury. While individual prostitutes (particularly madams) were singled out for criticism, clients, landlords, and "protectors" were equally the subject of attack. Prominent church members and social elites—"the front rank of society"—were guilty of nothing less than "prostituting themselves to the lowest species of crime," charged the *Whip.* "Reader," queried the anonymous editor, "what think you of a professing Christian who lives on wealth earned by prostitution?" The *Whip* envisioned itself as an advocate for the oppressed and the unfortunate, and thereby opposed "the vicious," irrespective of wealth or status. The *Flash* objected not to the prostitution in the Alcibiades Club House, but "its aristocratic character," that "none but the rich and powerful" were admitted. When the same brothel was closed, the *Weekly Rake* rejoiced, claiming that the madam kept the brothel too exclusive. "Select things don't do here," charged the paper, "our Republican stomachs rebel against and sicken at any thing *recherche*."[36] The profiteers of commercial sex were metaphors invoked to express class resentments associated with patrician privilege and anti-republican politics.

Pimps epitomized the symbiotic and symbolic association of prostitution and privilege. Elites and "aristocrats" were vilified as "dandies" and "fancy men," the consorts of "fancy women, or favorite prostitutes." The *True Flash* defined fancy men as little more than pimps, that "class of the community who strut about the town well dressed" and were "supported by the small change and extras of the frail sisterhood." One critic described pimps as "things in the shape of young men, who mingle with the best society" and "live by the prostitution of lewd women." Their aristocratic pretensions and fine dress were purchased not with their labors, but "by the harlots whom they mingle with."[37] One issue of the *Whip* equated the fancy man with the "brothel bully," "a debased delinquent" known for violent assaults on houses of prostitution.[38]

Sexual seduction and marital infidelity were likewise translated into metaphors of aristocratic privilege and elite hypocrisy. When Myer Levy sued Snelling, Wooldridge, and Wilkes for libel, Snelling accused Levy of acting as a surrogate for other wealthy adulterers, specifically the "upper crust soaplocks and highbinders." The *Flash* editors further implied that the court system was stacked against them because the grand jury was composed of sinners and fornicators, all of whom feared "the *Flash* more than the summons of the last trump to appear before the judgement seat." Snelling later charged he was treated differently than editors like the *Herald*'s James Gordon Bennett because "Bennett is rich and Snelling is poor." The *Flash* bluntly insisted that their purpose was to expose the "vice and immorality in the SALONS of the rich."[39]

George Wooldridge most emphatically linked upper-class privilege with sexual duplicity. On one occasion, he complained that a wealthy merchant, after seducing the wife of his closest friend, successfully covered up the scandal. No newspaper exposed the deed, charged

Wooldridge, "because they are wealthy, and are styled respectable." Wooldridge found this not just appalling, but representative of larger forms of social corruption.

> We ask, who destroy and bring disgrace upon most families? We answer, the rich! Who are the cause of harlotry? We repeat, the rich! Who rob the poor by means of banking? The rich! Who rob the banks? Again we say, the rich, the aristocracy of New York! Let this be ended.[40]

Elsewhere, libertine republican attacks on privilege were wrapped in unabashed racism. Although William Snelling was an early leader in the abolitionist movement in the 1830s, his sympathy for enslaved Americans was not shared by other flash press editors. African Americans were regularly referred to as "darkies," "niggers," or "amusing vagabonds," a reflection of the anti-abolitionist views of Snelling's fellow editors. George Wooldridge, for instance, described pickpocket Charley Quinn as "a coal-black, thick-lipped, crooked shinned [sic] brother of Arthur Tappan," thereby associating African American crime with abolition. Another time he attacked the merchant and broker Myer Levy as a "practical amalgamationist," someone who "sees Paradise in the arms of thick-lipped, wooly-headed wench." If Levy preferred "negresses to white women, let him marry them and we shall hear less about amalgamation," Wooldridge charged. "That is the true way to suppress the abolitionists."[41]

The attack on Levy was part of a larger pattern of invoking interracial sex as a metaphor of insult against enemies of the flash press. Interracial coupling was evidence of a "morbid appetite," concluded the *Whip*. The *Sunday Flash* derided the low-status occupations of men who attended the "Grand Nigger Ball" in Brooklyn. When the *Weekly Rake* criticized the madam Julia Brown, they charged that she liked to "kiss negroes." The *New York Sporting Whip* mocked a group of "amorous whites" who frequented a brothel filled with African American women and "fell desperately in love with the fascinating Dinahs," thus violating racial etiquette. Upon learning that a white cartman had a child with an African American woman, the *Weekly Rake* vilified him as a wretch, skunk, and polecat, rhetorically asking "why not gratify his dirty, beastly desires with women of his own color—not penetrate to the cellars of blacks and wallow with strapping half-humans?"[42]

Other times, the *Whip* eroticized racial differences. One letter to the editor from "Hornet" in Baltimore depicted interracial intercourse in prurient and sexually arousing language:

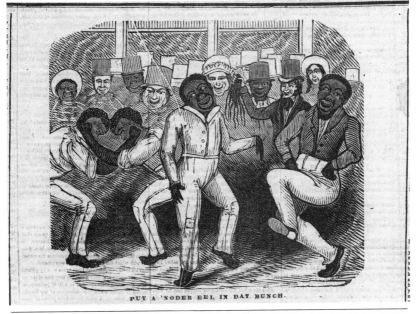

FIGURE 22. "PUT A 'NODER EEL IN DAT BUNCH." AN ILLUSTRATION FOR A STORY ABOUT
COMPETITIVE DANCING BY AFRICAN AMERICANS AT AN OUTDOOR FISH MARKET SUNDAY
MORNINGS. THE APPRECIATIVE AUDIENCE INCLUDES MEN AND WOMEN OF BOTH RACES.
FLASH, NOV. 12, 1842. COURTESY AMERICAN ANTIQUARIAN SOCIETY.

Here you will find houses that surpass the 'Five Points' in the richness of
filth and putrid matter; enter some and view the Circassian and sable race
beautifully blended together, and their arms intermingled so as to form
a lovely contrast between the alabaster whiteness of the one, and the polished blackness of the other; what a charming sight to thus see two lowly
and loving couple entwined in Cupid's Silken Knots. What abolitionist
is there but who could admire this? How I admire it, and a Southerner,
too. Yes, I love amalgamation as the devil does holy water.[43]

More often, the *Whip* was vociferously critical, describing amalgamation
in Five Points as "worse, by far, than sodomy."[44]

The combination of attacks on elite privilege with a defense of male heterosexual indulgence generated a fourth characteristic of the flash press:
a mixture of anticlerical, anti-Catholic, and anti-evangelical views. By
1800, a vast body of anti-monastic and anti-Catholic erotica had spread
throughout England, much of it translated from French. American Prot-
estants easily assimilated this literature into their own critiques of Roman
Catholicism. Such seamy novels as George Bourne's *Lorette* (1833), the

anonymously written *Female Convents* (1834), Rebecca Reed's *Six Months in a Convent* (1835), and Maria Monk's *Awful Disclosures* (1836) depicted convents as places of alcoholism, flagellation, prostitution, and infanticide. The latter proved so popular it sold over 300,000 copies.[45]

The flash press borrowed this salacious convent imagery. The *Sunday Flash* and the *Rake* reprinted portions of Boccaccio's *Decameron,* including parts depicting various forms of sexual seduction. The alleged mute Masetto da Lamporecchio, for example, is hired as a gardener in a convent. Two nuns conspire "to gratify a certain [sexual] curiosity with this fellow; for he is the fittest in the world for our purpose, being such an idiot, that he cannot expose us if he would." In time, all the nuns partake, including the abbess. When he finally talks, he claims it is a miracle.[46]

Catholicism was not the sole object of this anticlerical attack. Indeed, the very name of the *Sunday Flash,* published by Snelling, Wilkes, and Wooldridge on the Christian Sabbath, may have been an open repudiation of the Sabbatarian movement. Snelling later charged that Sabbatarians walked through Five Points, ignoring the poverty and prostitution around them while quarreling with the Sunday newsboys. Such men, he complained, "would rather sit contentedly and inhale the odor of dunghill than command it to be removed by its proper name." Evangelical Protestantism was similarly ridiculed. The *New York Sporting Whip* mocked millennial predictions of apocalypse. "We believe that, on the 32nd of April next all sinful and unholy acts will be stopped, and that (as in the case of Niblo's Saloon) theatres will be turned into churches, drinking shops to Croton Reservoirs, and newspapers to tracts, except the *Whip* and *Herald.*" The weekly also added that a good library should include *Fanny Hill, The Cabinet of Venus Unlocked,* and all of Paul DeKock's novels.[47]

Anticlericism frequently assumed the guise of linking church members with commercial sex. One Hudson Street brothel, for example, was charged with attracting male clients from the nearby Broadway Tabernacle. The landlord (Mr. B———) was identified as a deacon at St. Paul's Church. When confronted with the nature of his tenants, he replied they paid the rent and their affairs were none of his business. "So much for the morals of this church member," mocked the *Flash.*[48]

The flash press editors believed their anticlerical views and criticisms of organized religion enjoyed public support. The editors insisted they offered a necessary and alternative press, that they were representative of popular will, and that religious-oriented publications ignored the daily interests of many readers. "We wish to be considered the advocate of the people and their pastimes, so long as they are of an innocent nature," proclaimed the *Whip*. Such pastimes included traditional male sports—horse racing, boxing, pedestrian races—as well the theater and other forms male leisure, particularly saloons. While these subjects appeared in other sporting papers like *Spirit of the Times,* as well as certain penny papers like the *Herald*, none defined their purpose in opposition to organized religion. The "rigidly righteous may condemn the public taste," acknowledged the *Sunday Flash,* but sporting male activities deserved coverage and discussion. "The pulpit or a professedly religious paper is not the proper place to disseminate such information."[49]

Other times, the flash press's antagonism toward religion appeared as anti-Semitism. When Snelling, Wilkes, and Wooldridge of the *Sunday Flash* were sued for libel by Myer Levy, they mocked his genitalia by referring to him as "the circumcised Israelite" and "the circumscised [sic] Philistine." After Snelling and Wilkes were incarcerated in the Tombs, they described Levy as little more than "a broken down, scoundrel debauchee, [someone] who would be honored by cleaning my shoes." To expect forgiveness or sympathy was beyond the man because, "this fellow is a Jew." In another issue, the *Flash* attacked Moses Mallan on the front page. Described as a Manchester Jew and "quack dentist of the very vilest description," Mallan allegedly hired "scores of young Hebrews" who assumed his name, passed for his offspring, and engaged in dental practices where they literally stole teeth from the jaws of patients. "One rogue makes many—they multiply as fast as rabbits," wrote the *Flash*. Mallan "is the progenitar [sic] of these noxious vermin."[50]

Anti-Semitism even overlapped with homophobia. When the *Whip* attacked Andrew Isaacs as a "sodomite," George Wooldridge attributed such behavior to his religious and racial origins. Sodomites were "mostly of the Hebrew race," charged the *Whip*, "at least, we find no laws, save in Leviticus, to punish them." Linking anti-Semitism and homophobia served to simultaneously denigrate two groups considered perpetual outsiders.[51]

II The combination of male heterosexual indulgence, the defense of prostitution, hostility to privilege, and anticlericalism combined with blatant discussions of sexuality raises a perplexing question: Were the publications espousing libertine republicanism pornographic? More precisely, by popularizing certain forms of commercialized heterosexual promiscuity, were the flash press editors among

America's earliest pornographers? Did the libertine republicanism espoused by the editors of the flash press truly embody a Sadean view of prostitution, that the grafting of sex onto money was liberating, and represented the ideal form of sexual exchange?[52]

The answer depends on how one defines pornography. The meaning of terms like "obscenity" and "pornography" have changed over time. Historians disagree over the precise definition of pornography, in part because nineteenth-century Americans rarely employed the term. Historian Randolph Trumbach, for example, argues that most eighteenth-century sexual writing was erotic, not pornographic. Sexual courtship leading to consummation was more often verbally described than portrayed with visual images of erect penises and sexual acts. The sexual content of poems and ballads was convivial and humorous, never approaching the seriousness of twentieth-century "pornotopia."[53] By this definition, eighteenth-century publications such as *Fanny Hill* were erotic, but not pornographic.

Other historians adopt a broader definition. Montgomery Hyde, Walter Kendrick, and most recently Lisa Sigel acknowledge that "pornography" originally had a narrow application. But that limited meaning was important: pornography was derived from the Greek words *porne* which meant "harlot," and *graphos*, or "writing." *Pornographos* thus pertained to writing about prostitutes. The initial application of the term applied to works which discussed the lives, customs, and habits of prostitutes and their patrons. Over time, pornography assumed a broader meaning, including a wide array of sexual images. Significantly, visual images were supplementary to the printed word; most pornography prior to 1850 came in the form of novels, plays, and poetry.[54] Relying upon this definition, the flash press was pornographic.

Furthermore, in nineteenth- and twentieth-century Anglo-American courts, the term "obscene" or "obscenity" was applied to images and subjects considered "offensive to modesty," "indecent," or "filthy." Contemporaries applied the term to visual and *verbal* images of sexuality employed for purposes of shock or male titillation. Using this more umbrella-like definition, historians like David Reynolds equate erotica and pornography, arguing that the subversive fiction of radical democrats like George Lippard and George Thompson undermined stylistic and political modes of writing by employing erotic or pornographic themes in their political protests and critiques of antebellum America. Karen Halttunen insists that reform literature assumed pornographic dimensions because it eroticized pain. "Spectacles of suffering" were commonplace conventions of sexual pornography in the early nineteenth century. Peter Wagner defines pornography as any realistic written or visual depiction of sexual behavior intended to deliberately violate widely accepted social taboos. In general, a writing, image, or sculpture is obscene or pornographic if it induces sexual arousal.[55]

The broader, less precise, but more encompassing definition of pornography provides a vehicle to historicize the very concept of "the obscene" or "the pornographic."[56] If those terms meant visual and verbal sexual images and subjects considered "offensive to modesty" and employed for purposes of shock or male sexual arousal, then the flash press editors were among America's earliest pornographers. Contemporaries saw them so. William Snelling, for example, was labeled "the father of the smutty papers," by the *Weekly Rake*. Furthermore, social and religious conservatives considered most penny papers obscene, even though their content was far less sexually inflammatory. New York's former mayor and successful merchant Philip Hone, for example, complained that the penny press was "scurrilous," filled with "impious ribaldry," "licentiousness," and "the most profligate and disorganizing sentiments."[57] Opponents referred to the *Herald*'s James Gordon Bennett (hardly a flash press editor) as "licentious," an "obscene vagabond," a "polluted wretch," a "profligate adventurer," "a reptile," while accusing the *Herald* of "obscenity," "blasphemy," and "moral leprosy."[58] Tellingly, flash press editors indicted for obscenity were charged in boilerplate language for attempting "to debauch, injure, debase and corrupt and to raise and create in their minds inordinate and lustful desires."[59]

The flash press revealed the emergence of a trans-Atlantic, pornographic dialogue. The topics and themes repeatedly found in the flash press between 1840 and 1844 echoed those in European pornographic literature. Alluring portraits of prostitutes, anticlerical depictions of parsons as "reverend rakes," and seductive portrayals of orgies in Roman Catholic nunneries were routine in eighteenth- and early nineteenth-century English and French pornography. Pornographic reprints of Boccaccio's *Decameron* were commonplace. The flash press's references to madams as royalty—"Princess Julia," "Queen Sweet," and the "Countess de Roberts of Mott Street"—played upon stereotypes of a sexually decadent and polymorphously perverse European aristocracy. The assumed names of certain prostitutes reflected the influence European pornographic novels; the New York madam Mary Berry was identified as the "Duchess de Berri," a pseudonym probably borrowed from *The Authentic Memoirs of the Countess de Barre*, first printed in English in 1771. In general, libertine ideas—attacks on privilege, an emphasis on erotic pleasure, sexuality as intrinsic and natural—infused European pornography between 1750 and 1850.[60] The same was true for the flash press.

Herein was the great paradox of the flash press: it indulged in verbal pornographic image-making while simultaneously employing the language and rhetoric of moral reformers. The editors of the *Sunday Flash* defended the prominent madam Adeline Miller on one page, and attacked Thomas Hamblin and Myer Levy for their infidelity on another. They not only quoted Scripture—"thou shalt not commit adultery"—but urged the state legislature to criminalize adultery and fornication as statutory offenses.[61] Elsewhere, they vilified the *Herald* for publishing advertisements by abortionist Madam Restell, while doing the same for Madam Costello. The *Whip* regularly referred to Julia Brown as "Princess Julia," yet expressed outrage when Thomas Nichols's *Arena* sang her praises and the "beauty of her prostitutes." The *New York Sporting Whip* described the Bowery Theater as little more than "a semi-bawdy house," while offering detailed accounts of the outrageous sexual behavior of prostitutes sitting in the third tier.[62] The press castigated homosexual behavior while identifying numerous locales in which to find it.

At times, the editors defended themselves as moral guardians. When charged with libel, the *Sunday Flash* pontificated: "Our purpose is to effect a moral regeneration of New York."[63] While public authorities were "dozing on their seats," they "acted as the only true police."

> When we first commenced our course, this city presented a picture of moral depravity that has never before been equalled [*sic*] in any age or country. Vice went openly abroad. Lust walked about stark naked and crime of every form and degree, was committed with impunity. The city presented in short, a spectacle of a modern Sodom.[64]

The editors of the *Sunday Flash* proclaimed they occupied high moral ground, that they sacrificed their self-interest for the greater good. "It is sheer nonsense to say that there is no police," they blustered. "We are the police."[65]

Flash editors claimed they were one with the moral reformers. George Wooldridge, for example, insisted that the "morals of the *Whip*" were not indecent, but rather his goals mirrored that of the *Advocate of Moral Reform*—to suppress illicit sex and force brothels to close or move. "Why do you indict us alone?" he queried the district attorney. "Why don't you present Bennett's *Herald* and the *Advocate of Moral Reform*?" On another occasion, the *Whip* described the Moral Reform Society as "one of the greatest charities." While some argued that publications like the *Advocate* did more harm than good because "they create the evil they would remedy," pronounced the *Whip*, "we are not one of these." [66]

But what the flash press editors wrote and what they genuinely believed were difficult to discern precisely. Money was probably a motive. Editors like Snelling and Wooldridge were well aware of the considerable quantities of erotica circulating on the streets of New York by the late 1830s. The Whig printer and political cartoonist Henry R. Robinson, for example, published the earliest seminude lithographs of the murdered prostitute Helen Jewett for a mass market in 1836. [67] Then in 1842, city officials raided Robinson's Cortlandt Street warehouse. Inside were engravings, etchings, paintings, lithographs, pamphlets, books "with every possible characteristic of obscenity and lewdness," according to penny press reports. Robinson's inventory not only included popular European imports like *Memoirs of a Woman of Pleasure* and eroticized Biblical images, but some of the earliest American-produced pornography. One entitled "A Standing Member of the Abolition Society, Giving an Example of Practical Amalgamation" depicted a Quaker abolitionist in sexual congress with an African American woman. Other prints entitled "Do you Like this Sort of Thing?" and "The Wedding Night" illustrated men and women in various states of undress and copulation. Like Robinson, the flash press editors appealed to the expanding male audience in search of sexual adventure. [68]

By invoking the language of moral reform, the editors were simultaneously ironic, satirical, and opportunistic. This linguistic duplicity made the flash press confusing to contemporaries and confounding to later historians. The moral reformer John McDowall and flash editor George Wooldridge mixed the moral with the erotic. [69] Each identified prostitutes and clients in their publications; each defended themselves as moral policemen out to expose sexual hypocrisy. Yet Wooldridge and his associates departed from moral reformers with their celebratory exposés of prostitutes, their tongue-in-cheek critiques of bachelors, dandies, and libertines, and their titillating accounts of Gotham's sexual commerce. The flash press broached topics previously considered unbroachable. What was once deemed a hidden sexual underworld became a part of public culture. And as popular literature, the flash press writers taught working- and middle-class male readers how to think about sexuality, how to define their masculinity. Most significantly, they endeavored to more than simply educate their audience; they wanted to arouse readers. Sometimes they did so—in more ways than one.

In the flash press, liberty and libertinism were flip sides of the republican coin. For a brief time, Whigs like George Washington Dixon and Democrats like George Wilkes enlisted obscene images and pornographic language to convey political ideology, sexual beliefs, and personal vilification. Editors offered an intriguing mix of erotic celebration and personal vituperation, sexual idealism and monetary motive. By invoking a language of licentiousness, the flash press employed obscenity and prostitution to illuminate the hypocrisy of the privileged, challenge religious duplicity, and promote a promiscuous heterosexuality. Flash reportage contested multiple nineteenth-century conventions: the limits on public discussions of sexuality, the maltreatment of sexual and public women, the exploitative behaviors of the socially and economically privileged. This liminal underworld of the 1830s and 1840s not only linked different elements of American politics, the penny press, and the flash weeklies, but offered social and political commentary lost in later sporting and pornographic publications.

Libertine republicanism represented a new male heterosexuality centered in America's rapidly growing urban centers, a transgressive, erotic ideal that celebrated unfettered male (and sometimes female) sexual expression. Sexual images found in the flash press embodied a pleasure principle validated and valorized by the marketplace. The prostitute epitomized this distinctive, imagined sexuality, available to anyone willing and able to pay. In their descriptions of New York, the flash press transformed the city into a symbolic seraglio. In naming names and identifying the most alluring and seductive in Gotham's commercial sexual universe, the flash press removed restraints and challenged traditions. Male freedom meant unbridled heterosexual fulfillment. Forbidden pleasures were no longer forbidden. Male heterosexual gratification was democratized, available to anyone with the means. Political liberation or republicanism was meaningless without sexual freedom. Sex in the flash press not only represented liberty; it made one a better republican.

But the liberty promulgated by this new journalism proved short-lived. The flash press editors, beneficiaries of a legal system and print culture which protected and defended dissident forms of speech, were finally challenged by that very system. They were sued.

3 TRIALS AND TRIBULATIONS

illiam Joseph Snelling of the *Sunday Flash* recounted that on October 26, 1841, as he sat "quietly smoking his cegar at 6 Center Street," a police officer arrested him on two bench warrants issued from the Court of Sessions. The arrest was hardly unusual. Newspaper editors in the antebellum years were frequently incarcerated for libel, and indeed that was the case here. Snelling was hauled into court for publishing "the amorous adventures of a very great rascal designated as Big Levy." [1]

"That's a dem fine gal!" read the caption underneath the woodcut of a corpulent, hatted man, labeled "Big Levy" in the *Sunday Flash* of October 17, 1841. The image quite likely bore little resemblance to its ostensible subject, Myer Levy. Such pictures normally originated from the second-hand stock of suppliers. Levy was described as a fashionable "dandy" and impugned as a "walking scarlet sin." The article accused him of flirting and skirt chasing. It linked him to many women, some of them prostitutes. Most notably, it insulted him by identifying him as the "fancy man" of Phoebe Doty, a well-known older prostitute frequently denounced in the publication. The *Sunday Flash* evoked racist imagery, charging that Levy was a "practical amalgamationist." A poem captured the violation of race mixing:

> Black, white or yellow, nothing came amiss;
> "Give me," lewd Levy cried, "a melting kiss." [2]

Some or all of these insults may well have been falsehoods, like the image, stock invective pulled out of nowhere, or they may have been accurate. The charge that Levy cared for the son of the sister of Eliza Boardman, a deceased mistress, in his house on Sullivan Street has the specificity of truth. The Sullivan Street address, at least, was verified by a city directory. [3]

The article on Levy appeared in the paper's "Gallery of Rascalities and Notorieties," a first-page feature that normally presented illustrated stories of celebrities and felons. Criminals were in no position to complain, and

GALLERY OF RASCALITIES AND NOTORIETIES.—No. 6.

"THAT'S A DEM FINE GAL!"

BIG LEVY.   dressed in the extreme of the fashion, peering under

FIGURE 23. "GALLERY OF RASCALITIES AND NOTORIETIES.—NO. 6.: 'THAT'S A DEM FINE GAL!'" ILLUSTRATION FOR THE STORY HEADLINED "BIG LEVY," PRODUCING THE FIRST FLASH LIBEL SUIT. *SUNDAY FLASH,* OCT. 17, 1841. COURTESY AMERICAN ANTIQUARIAN SOCIETY.

most of its other subjects—newspapermen and actors—were frequent targets of such ill treatment by the press. But Levy was different; he was a businessman. Born in 1898 in Kingston, Jamaica, Levy immigrated with his family to New York City as a child. His father, Jacob, was a practicing member of Shearith Israel, the city's oldest Jewish congregation founded by Spanish and Portuguese Jews. Myer was the only son and apparently a lifelong bachelor, but his sisters married into three of the most prominent Jewish families in the city. Myer Levy took an active part in the religious and philanthropic life of Shearith Israel, and in the late 1830s served with his brother-in-law Moses B. Seixas as an occasional cantor. In this same period he was a founding member and contributor to the New York Hebrew Assistance Society to aid new Jewish immigrants to the city. City directories list him as a merchant, initially on Cedar Street. His business shifted to Wall Street in 1835, where it remained through 1839.[4]

According to a later report, Emanuel Hart provided some of the embarrassing details on Levy. Hart was closely associated with Levy as a broker, congregant of Shearith Israel, and family member, but had a bitter grievance against him. Hart's father was the secretary of the New York Stock Exchange; his mother was daughter of Benjamin Mendez Seixas, a pillar of the Jewish community. Yet Hart traveled with the rough sporting crowd around the Elssler Saloon that included Wooldridge. When he entered ward politics as a Tammany Democrat in the mid-1840s, another Democrat privately disparaged him as a man with a "very bad" reputation who was "well known here as the associate of Gamblers, and still more notorious as the *Companion* of a brothel keeper." Whether true or not, the charges against Levy in the *Sunday Flash* article—accusations of sexual misconduct, business fraud, counterfeiting—originated with a man closely familiar with Levy and intimately familiar with gambling and commercial sex. The article tipped its hand in exposing Hart's bitter grievance, in this final charge meant to insult Levy: "Having called in question the character of Mr. E—H—, a young gentleman who has been unfortunate in business and was unable to pay him a balance due in stock speculations, the latter [Hart] publicly horse whipped him in Wall Street, and he [Levy] had recourse to the law for protection as usual."[5]

Even if Emanuel Hart supplied specific details to bash Levy, he was likely surprised by the strong streak of anti-Semitism the *Sunday Flash* editors worked into their roast of his co-religionist. "The Hebrews are strict in the manner of genealogies, and thus it appears that Levy is a lineal descendent of him who sold his lord for thirty pieces of silver. The younger Judas would sell him for half as many pieces of copper; so true it is that, with that unfortunate race, the sins of the father descend to the children." Among the accusations against Levy, repeated several times, was that he did not fight in the street. For example, the *Sunday Flash* stated, "He may be a Jew in other matters; but, when it comes to fighting, he is a Quaker meeker than Moses." Rather than return a blow in a manly fashion, Levy was lampooned for relying on the law for redress. Thus it should not have been a surprise to Emanuel Hart or the editors of the *Sunday Flash* that Levy quickly instigated legal action.

Myer Levy went to district attorney James R. Whiting charging libel. Whiting then demanded the grand jury of the Court of General Sessions indict the editors—Snelling, George Wilkes, and George B. Wooldridge—on a criminal charge of libel. This was a well-established

legal path. Both aspects of the case—written assault on a person's character and the charge of libel—were standard fare in the newspaper world
in New York in the 1840s.

But this case contained a striking new element. Snelling and his coeditors were arrested on a second warrant for "publishing the Flash in general." The district attorney not only secured an indictment for criminal
libel, he obtained one for publishing an obscene paper.[6]

As a result Snelling, Wooldridge, and Wilkes were brought before the
Court of General Sessions of New York. At an initial trial on January 14,
1842, Snelling and Wilkes stood before the judges, accused of criminal
libel and obscene libel. Wooldridge, their former confederate, now testified against them. Both Snelling and Wilkes pleaded guilty to criminal
libel against Levy but not guilty to the obscenity charge. After hearing
evidence, the jury failed to convict both men on the second offense. The
matter did not end, however, for in April both returned to court to be
retried for obscenity. This time Wilkes pled guilty and was given a suspended sentence. Snelling, however, maintained his innocence, and the
jury found him guilty. He was sent to the Tombs to serve out his sentence, most likely a month in prison.[7]

Wooldridge, now publisher of the *Whip and Satirist of New-York
and Brooklyn,* relished Snelling's conviction. Within months, however,
he was indicted in a manner similar to the initial case involving Myer
Levy. Wooldridge had instigated a vendetta against another private citizen, which led to a criminal charge of libel. Once again suspicion of libel
against an editor led to close scrutiny of his paper, and he was charged
with obscenity. Wooldridge was again indicted for "publishing an obscene sheet," the July 9, 1842 edition of the *Whip.*[8]

Then on July 14, a wholesale set of indictments was served against the
proprietors of the flash press, covering not only the owner of the *Whip,*
but also those of the *Rake,* the *Flash,* and the *Libertine.* The indictment
of Wooldridge in the district attorney's records stated that the accused,
"being a scandalous and evil disposed person and devising, contriving
and intending the morals as well of youth as of divers other citizens of
the state of New York to debauch injure debase and corrupt and to raise
and create in their minds inordinate and lustful desires . . . unlawfully,
wickedly, maliciously and scandalously did print publish and circulate in
the said city of New York and utter a certain lewd wicked and scandalous paper." The indictment listed the specific articles deemed obscene,
published "to the manifest corruption of the morals of youth as of divers
other citizens . . . in contempt of the people of the state of New York

and their laws, to the evil example of all others in the like case offending and against the peace of the People of the State of New York and their dignity." [9]

I Why was Snelling arrested on October 26, 1841, on a second warrant for "publishing the Flash in general"? Why were Wooldridge and other flash paper editors indicted in July 1842? New York, like most states in the union, had no laws in the 1840s against obscenity. How could charges of obscenity lead to indictments, arrests, trials, guilty verdicts, and jail time?

The answer is common law. Antebellum New York had no need for a statute to prosecute cases for obscenity. Instead, the state relied on the English common law tradition as adopted and adapted in the United States.

Scholars have long thought that, with a few notable exceptions, obscenity cases in the United States began in 1873 with the prosecutions by Anthony Comstock. These well-known later trials were based on a federal statute and accompanying state laws that criminalized pornography, contraception, abortion, and related advertising. But the flash press indictments in the early 1840s reveal that before 1873, common law tradition was maintained by the courts, supported by legal treatises. In New York in 1841 and 1842, the outcropping of racy weekly papers designed for sporting men caught the eye of local authorities. They resorted to common law practices to shut the publications down. Although generally unknown to legal investigators, the trials of the flash press editors were of great consequence. They profoundly influenced the well-known legal proceedings after 1873 that were supported by anti-obscenity statutes.[10]

What makes the early cases more significant is that the common law of obscene libel, as applied by the courts in the flash press trials, is inimical to First Amendment protections, as understood by later generations. At the time, however, as defendants gained important and sobering experience in courts and jails, they realized some of the harms of common law practice and initiated a critical tradition of dissent. Thus the New York trials of 1841 and 1842 of the flash press play a key, but largely forgotten, role in the national struggle between censorship and the right of free expression.

II Why did the English common law tradition enjoy such a profound influence in the new American nation, presumably committed to the principles of freedom articulated in the Bill of Rights, and especially those protected by the First Amendment? The answer requires an examination of the law and the First Amendment.

In legal history, it is a mistake to see the United States as new. Colonial authorities relied on the legal tradition and practices that originated in England. During and after the Revolution, states confirmed their legal systems based on common law, British statutes not in opposition to their constitutions, and acts of colonial legislatures. As a result, common law undergirded decisions of state courts in civil and criminal cases in the new republic. The traffic in domestic "obscene" materials, that is, those not coming from Europe, was understood before the Civil War as a matter for states (and through them, local communities) to regulate, falling within the domain of their police powers.

Common law differs from statutory law in several key respects. A law based on statute is one passed by the legislature of a colony, state, or federal government. By contrast, common law governing civil and criminal matters consists of judicial decisions. Statutory laws cannot be applied retroactively, but in the eighteenth and early nineteenth century, common-law rulings could. Using the argument that the law "always existed, and a breach of it was criminal," judges ruled that it was unnecessary for a court to determine violations in advance. This made sense at the time because common law was equated with natural law. Legal experts understood judges to discover, not create, law. Common law tradition derived from study of previous judicial decisions and treatises that grounded them in principles.[11]

Furthermore, twentieth-century interpretations confuse and obscure the meaning of the American Bill of Rights in the nineteenth century. Then the First Amendment held no sway in the area of obscenity, at least in the mainstream legal tradition. In that era the First Amendment was primarily seen as protecting the rights of the states of the union against the federal government, not of citizens against government intrusion. Only in the dissenting legal tradition that emerged after the Civil War in the wake of obscenity rulings did defendants' lawyers finally argue for First Amendment freedoms as countering common law and protecting the right of free speech.[12]

In Britain, the common law of obscene libel began in 1727 when Edmund Curl was prosecuted for publishing *Venus in the Cloister; or, The Nun in her Smock*. The British Attorney General argued that the book, in tending "to corrupt the morals of the King's subjects," was "against the peace of the King." In ruling for the prosecution, the court extended the notion of criminal libel to include obscenity. The court stated that even without "an actual force," a book had the power to destroy the basis of public order—morality.[13]

Eighteenth-century British digests and treatises tamed the common law, systematizing it and grounding it in principles. The most weighty effort was the comprehensive *Commentaries on the Laws of England* by William Blackstone. Although Blackstone never addressed obscenity nor identified it as a crime or misdemeanor, he laid the necessary groundwork. In two sections of his fourth volume *On Public Wrongs* (1765–69), he distinguished between a private vice and a public wrong. If one was drunk alone in one's home, one was beyond the reach of the law. If one was drunk, however, "publicly, in the face of the world," the evil example this set made the act "liable to temporal censures." Some public wrongs were high crimes, striking "at our national religion." But a lower class of crimes of "gross impieties and general immoralities" included lewdness, swearing and cursing, and blasphemy. Blackstone defined lewdness as "some grossly scandalous and public indecency" and linked it with obscenity.[14]

Obscene images and words were not located in this category of offense but belonged among libels. This meaning of "libel" changed dramatically over time. Blackstone invoked the word to "signify any writings, pictures, or the like, of an *immoral or illegal tendency.*" The critical test of "bad tendency" was that words served to "harm the public welfare." This standard was taken directly from British law into American courts and applied to published words that a prosecutor considered seditious, blasphemous, or obscene. While a critical line of defense in the eighteenth century was the issue of "truth," Blackstone insisted that this had no weight. In a criminal prosecution for libel, it mattered not to Blackstone whether the words be true or false. The only issue was the tendency "to create animosities, and to disturb the public peace"; and the only facts to be considered were "the making or publishing of the book or writing" and whether the matter within was "criminal."[15]

Punishment of these criminal libels, Blackstone argued, did not violate "the liberty of the press." This important liberty came from freedom from prior restraint, not from "freedom from censure for criminal matter when published." Blackstone's distinction was between, on the one hand, suppression of a publication and punishment of its maker after it was determined to be libelous and, on the other, censorship that occurred prior to publication. Blackstone and his legal successors defended this distinction as compatible with liberty of the press, contending that the common law suppressed libelous speech that had already occurred. By contrast, common law did not censor such language in advance. In effect, suppression was reactive, in contrast to censorship, which was proactive. This enabled

Blackstone to insist that in the punishment of the criminal libels "the *liberty of the press,* properly understood, is by no means infringed or violated."

Although a person had the right to express his thoughts, Blackstone theorized, one had to accept the consequences if one published something that was "improper, mischievous, or illegal." This seemingly benign statement posed what became perhaps the most serious obstacle to free speech in America: "To punish . . . any dangerous or offensive writings, which, when published, shall on a fair and impartial trial be adjudged of a pernicious tendency, is necessary for the preservation of peace and good order." [16]

Blackstone was the bedrock upon which American courts defined obscenity, but *The Law of Libel* by Francis Ludlow Holt, published in many editions in England and the United States in the early nineteenth century, served as the fundamental treatise for obscenity. It dealt directly with obscene libels. In the 1816 edition, Holt defined them as "libels against morality and the law of nature," and he set out the logic. Morality or "the law of nature . . . is necessary to society, and society, therefore, must maintain it. This is the reason of the English law in prohibiting and punishing all open and public immoralities, obscene writings, speaking, and exhibitions, the tendency of which is evidently to poison the springs and principles of manners, and disturb the peace and economy of the realm." Like Blackstone, Holt distinguished between public example, which was prosecutable by the state, and private vice and sin, punishable only by the Almighty. When he considered the public and prosecutable libel of obscenity, Holt emphasized the legal responsibility of booksellers and publishers for any wrongful dissemination of obscene printed matter on their part. [17]

But what constituted obscenity? This was (and remains) a fluid term in the law, encompassing different aspects in succeeding generations. Two important cases in the early decades of the nineteenth century illustrate what obscenity meant in the antebellum years.

Commonwealth v. Sharpless, the 1815 ruling by the Supreme Court of Pennsylvania, is well known. Jesse Sharpless, a tavern-keeper in Philadelphia, charged patrons a fee in his place of business to view a picture that the mayor's court of Philadelphia found obscene. The image was never identified, but was described as "representing a man in an obscene, impudent, and indecent posture with a woman." On appeal, when the chief justice found against Sharpless, he connected obscenity to "lascivious pictures" capable of "inflaming" the "passions" of the "youth of the city." He upheld the conviction of obscene libel because he perceived an imaginative representation offered to the public for a fee potentially incited lust in the young.[18]

The 1834 blasphemy trial of Abner Kneeland in Massachusetts added another important element: the nature of the dissemination. Here obscenity was cited only secondarily within a charge of blasphemy. Convicted in a lower court, Kneeland's case ultimately came before the Supreme Court of the Commonwealth of Massachusetts, presided over by Chief Justice Lemuel Shaw, a man of great learning and prestige. After exhausting his legal options, Kneeland became the only American to serve a sentence for blasphemy, ultimately spending sixty days in jail.

Kneeland was a former pastor who came to Boston as a freethinker in the early 1830s. He earned his living as a writer, speaker, and publisher of the weekly *Boston Investigator*. In his writings, he employed intentionally shocking words. The particular obscene element cited by the courts was a secondhand quote from Voltaire in an 1833 issue of the *Investigator:* "The Frenchman will ask *why* the Hottentot allow their boys but one testicle,—but that same Frenchman, though he be too stupid to understand the laws of evidence, or too illiterate to apply them to history, firmly believes that Jesus Christ was begotten without any testicles at all." In making its case, the prosecution contrasted writings in the books by authors such as Voltaire, "read only by men of literary habits—necessarily a few," and presumably not indictable, with the publication of their words in a newspaper "so widely circulated, so easily read—so coarsely expressed—so industriously spread abroad." Thus an important element of Kneeland's offense was that he made certain words of sexual anatomy available through cheap publication. Together these two cases provide an 1840 definition of an "obscene paper": a cheap publication, widely available, whose erotic content might inflame lustful passions in young people.[19]

To prosecute obscenity cases in New York, courts found the work of British jurist Thomas Starkie, writing in the early nineteenth century, the most useful. In his *Treatise on the Law of Slander and Libel* (1830), Starkie provided both a rationale for obscene libel and a blueprint for trials. Resting on the firm foundation of Blackstone and Holt, Starkie argued that the logic behind civil libel suits and criminal libel cases differed. In bringing a criminal case, the state had a clear interest in protecting its citizens against any libel that might weaken social bonds or threaten its security. These dangers included obscene libel, labeled by him as "Publications tending to subvert Morality." Starkie wrote, "It is now fully established, that any immodest and immoral publication, tending to corrupt the mind, and to destroy the love of decency, morality, and good order, is punishable in the temporal courts."

Criminal libel was concerned not with the creation of an expression. A person might write exactly what he wanted—as long as he kept it to himself. Rather, criminal libel concerned publication, defined most comprehensively as putting words or images into the hands of another. Following Blackstone, Starkie argued that the truth or accuracy of a statement was unimportant; what mattered was whether the words had a "tendency to provoke and injure." Starkie elaborated on the perplexing consequences of a truth test. He asked rhetorically, "Would proof that indecent transactions have actually occurred, supply any excuse for the public exhibition of them in a print or a pamphlet?" Blackstone's distinction between a private and a public wrong lay behind the element of obscene libel that the acts depicted or described were not necessarily crimes under the law. Starkie replied, "Although many vicious and immoral acts are not indictable, yet if they tend to the destruction of morality in general, if they do or may affect the mass of society, they become offices of a public nature." Published material had the capacity of being a public wrong, however truthful it might be.[20]

This feature of obscenity jurisprudence was often questioned by the American editors who ran afoul of it. To those who imagined themselves as truth-tellers, exposing the hypocrisy of the mighty, this aspect of common law not only flew in the face of common sense, it stood against genuine morality.

When Starkie dealt with the question—Did a publisher "intend" to do harm?—he laid out the element of English common law that plagued American defendants charged with obscene libel. Essential determinants for conviction in Britain were "malice" and "intention." What went against common sense were the definitions that Starkie gave those words. "Malice," Starkie stated, was "the absence of legal excuse" when an act was "injurious and unlawful." When there failed to be "circumstances which justify, excuse, or at least modify the act, a rational being *must*, in law as well as morals, *be taken to contemplate and intend the immediate and natural consequences of his act.*" Neither a madman nor a servant delivering a sealed letter without knowing its contents can be held responsible for his acts. "But where the act is knowingly and intentionally done, it is plain that the mere absence of an actual intention to injure cannot absolve from criminal responsibility." Simply put, this meant that any sane person who acted in his or her own behalf and did wrong therefore *intended* to do wrong.[21]

There was no escape from this logic in Starkie, even for those with the best and purest of purposes. Starkie argued that it went against legal principles to excuse a freely chosen illegal and injurious act because a man insisted that he had good motives. "The law allows no man to defend himself by saying, 'I did an act, in itself injurious, mischievous, and illegal, but I did it with an excellent intention.'" Although counterintuitive in ordinary language, these words of the law were echoed in American obscenity trials.[22]

In Britain, the tasks of the jury in criminal libel cases were straightforward. The jury was only to decide the facts of the libel and whether the defendant pursued it with legal malice, i.e., "the entire absence of legal excuse." The judge decided the quality of the libel and directed the jury, as to "the criminal quality of the acts which the evidence tends to prove." American law modified this by the turn of the nineteenth century, allowing the jury the right to determine the law as well as the facts of cases of seditious libel and individual criminal libel.[23] In the case of obscene libel, however, the role of the jury remained fluid, at times reflecting the limitations that Starkie imposed.

The first American edition of Starkie's work, published in 1826, gave some evidence that he or his publisher feared a potential conflict between English common law and American protections of freedom of expression. This work was an adaptation of the previous one-volume English edition. It gave references to American cases and reconciled Starkie's treatise with the First Amendment and with state constitutions guaranteeing freedom of the press. A detailed footnote established protections provided in each state, including the all-important defense of truth as justification. By contrast, in the trials of the flash press, the New York Court of General Sessions relied on the two-volume 1830 English edition with its more extensive practical guidance. As a work directed toward the British legal system, this edition included no mention of constitutional protections.[24]

Starkie was particularly useful in the practical guidance it gave to American courts. For example, the 1830 edition offered a standard indictment for obscene libel:

That A.B., late of, &c. being a scandalous and evil disposed person, and not having the fear of God in his heart, but devising, contriving, and intending the morals as well of youth as of divers other liege subjects of our said Lord the King, to debauch and corrupt, and to raise and create in their minds inordinate and lustful desires, on, &c. with force and arms, at, &c. in a certain open and public shop of him the said A.B. there situate, unlawfully, wickedly, maliciously, and scandalously, did publish, sell, and utter to one C.D., a liege subject of our Lord the King, a certain lewd, wicked, scandalous, infamous, and obscene print, on paper, entitled _____, representing, &c. (*as in the print,*) and which said lewd, wicked, scandalous, infamous, and obscene print, on paper, was contained in a certain printed pamphlet, then and there uttered and sold by him the said A.B. to the said C.D. entitled _____, to the manifest corruption and subversion of youth, and other liege subjects of our said Lord the King, in their manners and conversation, in contempt of our said Lord the King and his laws, and against the peace, &c.[25]

The Court of General Sessions of New York knew its Starkie. In 1842, when Wooldridge and the other editors of the flash press were indicted for obscenity, Starkie was the model, specifically the 1830 edition. The only changes the American court made were to exchange the British king and his subjects for New York equivalents. More generally, in its logic, legal definitions of words such as "malice" and "intention," and specific practices, Starkie's *Law of Slander and Libel* (1830) served as a working manual for American courts.[26]

III The New York courts had the means to prosecute the flash papers under common law, including a definition of obscenity and the tools offered by Holt and Starkie. Why did they use them? Why did legal authorities choose to move against the editors and thereby shut the papers down? What led to the indictments and trials of the flash press?

These questions have several parts. The first concerns the legal system's relation to other elements of society, especially as the law engaged issues of sexuality and obscenity. Some argue that nineteenth-century Americans were "Victorian," and therefore sought to repress sexual drives and suppress sexual speech. Quite the contrary. In New York and elsewhere in the 1840s, sexual matters were high on the list of contentious issues about which Americans disagreed.

Many discussions about sexual matters appeared in print. Debates over sexuality were, in fact, part of a vast conversation in which contending voices held different and sometimes conflicting frameworks for understanding sex. Three basic formulations were in play in the 1840s—folk or vernacular wisdom, evangelical religion, and popular science. Vernacular understandings held an earthy acceptance of sex and desire as vital parts of life for men and women. Sexual desire was imagined to spring from hot blood. Lying at the base of conscious awareness and corresponding to strong bodily urges, vernacular sexuality retained power throughout the nineteenth century. As the source of bawdy humor in America, many popular terms, and numerous sexually arousing texts, folk beliefs shaped much of the copy of the flash papers. By contrast, evangelical Christianity, spurred by the revivals of the Second Great Awakening, held a deep distrust of the flesh. Sunday schools and societies to promote missions and the Bible spread. Revivals unleashed campaigns against alcohol, prostitution, slavery, stimulating food and drink, desecration of the Sabbath, and obscene images and words.

Beginning in the late 1820s, a new and important popular science of the body emerged. This third perspective brought together scientific notions of the body, nerves, health, and the relation of mind and body. Divided from the outset, some voices sought sexual expression less constrained by traditional morality, while others urged restraint and inhibition. The new popular physiology saw sexual desire as located in the mind, originating in messages sent from the brain through the nerves, rather than the heated blood of folk understandings. Masturbation became a special, even obsessive fear. Beginning in the early 1830s, a time when more and more teenage youths left home for school or work, anti-masturbation tracts proliferated, counseling parents to guard their offspring against the practice. Locating sex in the mind at a time when poems and fiction centered on heightened emotion emphasized the potential power of imaginative literature and thus its danger.[27]

Into this cacophony of voices, the law intervened. Unlike others, the legal voice had authority to repress materials of an erotic nature. Although at one level, legal arguments represented one discourse among others, it was a discourse with unique power. Antebellum judges had opportunities to impose their will on others clearly and directly. They gave public expression in court to what they understood as the standards of the community. They enjoyed the power to make others obey their will. They kept order in the court, judged points of the law, and held authority in criminal trials to decide punishment if a jury determined guilt. When they imposed a sentence, the convicted person was shackled and led to prison by armed officers of the law. As legal scholar Robert Cover states, "Legal interpretation takes place in a field of pain and death." When a judge utters an understanding of a text, "somebody loses his freedom, his property, his children, even his life." [28]

However abstractly Blackstone, Holt, or Starkie discussed the law, it was invoked in practice by real people with real issues at stake. The critical actors who managed the apparatus of the legal system in 1840s New York—the police, judges, juries, legislators, and lawyers—were men. Not only were women denied the vote and the right to hold public office, they were ineligible to serve on juries, work as lawyers, or be appointed judges. The legal apparatus was an all-male domain. Moreover, the most powerful men in the court, the judges, represented only a small segment of the population. Whether elected or appointed, most were affluent and well connected. If, as was likely, the judges originated from the ranks of lawyers, they were educated in the traditions of the law and sworn to uphold it. As a result, judges generally represented a deeply conservative element of society. In court a judge's words took place within an institutional structure derived from Britain, where precedents had great power. [29]

So the question then shifts from the abstraction of common law and the staffing of New York courts to a more specific one: What pushed the conservative men of New York courts to suppress the flash press through the courts in 1841 and 1842, using the common law?

First, concern about erotic materials was in the air. This was hardly surprising because plenty of examples abounded and generated concern at the federal level. The U.S. Congress wrote a measure in section 28 of the Tariff Act in 1842 prohibiting the importation of all "indecent and obscene prints, paintings, lithographs, engravings, and transparencies." Any such matter could be "proceeded against, seized, and forfeited, by due course of law, and the said articles shall be forthwith destroyed." Although the public record contains no evidence that the bill elicited discussion or debate, something moved the federal government to exert one of the few means it had to control pornographic materials—the regulation of foreign trade. Immediately the provision was put into force, and a New York district court trial for imported snuffboxes with obscene paintings ensued. Because of the importance of the city's port, citizens of New York were perhaps more aware of this effort than those elsewhere. [30]

Moreover, antebellum New Yorkers lived in an era of unprecedented change and urbanization, some of which gave them grave concern. The rise of a distinct sporting culture, with its institutions and attractions available to a widening group of men on the town, posed a particular threat to traditional understandings of civic order.

Against this perceived threat, the courts flexed their muscles in the early 1840s. Agents of the law arrested, tried, and convicted the abortionist Madame Restell. They went after booksellers and their suppliers for selling and publishing pornographic prints and texts. And, beginning in July 1842, they waged a full-scale campaign against the flash papers.[31]

Hawked on the streets, the *Flash, the Whip,* the *Libertine,* and the *Rake* offered a vivid and public emblem of sporting culture and the dangers it posed to youth. These public prints presented a range of harms in critics' eyes. The flash papers, whatever their nods to reform, encouraged young fellows to seek the company of prostitutes and provided the necessary information to find them. Despite the papers' own condemnation of the "solitary vice," perusing the papers, both text and images, could excite young men to masturbate. Finally, the libertine republicanism of these weeklies challenged the established order and turned many of its values upside down. Not only did the flash press include titillating words and images, portray the games and pastimes of men on the town, and encourage heterosexual indulgence outside of marriage, it challenged many of the presumptions of power. Playing on sexual scandal, the flash press ridiculed respected citizens and exposed hypocrisy in high places. In the minds of socially conservative men of the legal profession, these weeklies clearly imperiled public order.

An important purpose of the flash papers was to sell a sheet that entertained and guided its buyers. The *Sunday Flash* and its successors gave male readers paths to navigate the city without being conned or embarrassed as a greenhorn. Moreover, some of the pleasure was vicarious. Even a shy fellow who stayed in his boardinghouse could imagine himself as a blade making a sophisticated entry into a brothel parlor. The printed pages allowed him to partake of, even create, a fantasized identity as a sporting man. The courts focused on this aspect of the flash papers, but perceived in a somewhat different manner. They saw the sexual narratives and the argot of men on the town in these cheap publications as having the power to incite lust in the young. The common law, with its provision for obscene libel, gave them the hook they needed to rout out both this danger to youth and the larger one the flash press posed to the city.[32]

IV In the trials against the flash press that ensued, the judge and prosecutor relied on common law derived from England. In the absence of statutory law to guide them, they echoed Blackstone and Holt and, most importantly, invoked Starkie. In doing so, they brought to the United States precedents and procedures from England that allowed for the prosecution and punishment of editors guilty of "obscene libel." In effect, the men of the New York City courts created new procedures on American soil and a new legal tradition to prosecute obscenity. These wore a deep groove in the law, with influence beyond the antebellum period. When the New York state legislature wrote new statutes against obscenity, beginning in the 1860s, the impact of the 1840s trials was felt. In the 1870s, a key decision by an important New York appellate judge confirmed existing court practices dealing with obscene libel and important elements of the common law tradition. This confirmation reached the national level when the judge was elevated to the federal Supreme Court in the 1880s.

After indictment by the grand jury, Snelling, Wooldridge, and Wilkes of the *Sunday Flash* appeared before the Court of General Sessions of New York. This was the court which heard important felony trials, such as those for larceny and counterfeit. Its judges were appointed by the state governor. Three judges and two aldermen sat as a panel, headed by the chief judge, called the recorder, one of the highest-paid officers in the city. At the start of each monthly session, the judges impaneled both a grand jury to hear indictments brought by the district attorney and a petit jury to try the cases brought before them.

Frederick A. Tallmadge, the recorder in the trials of the flash press, was a conservative in life and law. Devoted to public service and Christianity, he lived in the shadow of his father, a Revolutionary War hero and a Connecticut representative to the U.S. Congress. Tallmadge served as recorder for a decade beginning in 1841, except for two years in the U.S. House of Representatives. In 1849, he assumed command over civil authorities after the Astor Place riot. When the Metropolitan Police was organized in 1857, he became its first superintendent.[33]

The associate judges under Tallmadge were James Lynch and Mordecai Noah. About the former, little is known, although he was criticized in his day for being an incompetent benchwarmer. Noah was, however, well known, and from a background unusual for a judge. He was a newspaper editor, a playwright, and active in the Democratic Party. But during the 1840s, he turned briefly to the Whig Party. In 1841 he was rewarded with a judgeship. A maverick and iconoclast, Noah was an unpredictable actor in this real-life courtroom drama. He did have, however, two known predispositions important to the outcome of the trial of the flash press. Probably the first Jew named as a criminal court judge in America, he was sensitive to anti-Semitic slurs, such as those the *Sunday Flash* leveled against Myer Levy. Noah was also a partisan in the New York theater wars on the side of Thomas S. Hamblin, the tempestuous actor and theatrical impresario of the Bowery Theater. Noah's pro-Hamblin bias posed a particular danger to the editors of the *Sunday Flash*, given that the paper began in defense of ingénue Louisa Missouri's family, who accused Hamblin of spiriting the young actress away from them and causing her death.[34]

Quite likely district attorney James R. Whiting knew that Tallmadge and Noah would support him from the bench if he moved against the editors of the *Sunday Flash*. When selected by the county court as chief prosecutor in 1838, Whiting, a member of the Whig Party, was an odd choice. He came not from criminal law but from the world of civil law and banking. The atmosphere around him in fall 1841 was highly charged, for earlier in the year he oversaw the indictment and conviction of Madame Restell and during the initial trials of the flash press was awaiting her appeal.[35]

Snelling, Wilkes, and Wooldridge were indicted by a grand jury. In October 1841, this body consisted of a collection of solid citizens that included newspaperman William G. Boggs, a carter, a hosier, a brush maker, at least one grocer, a bank teller, a gilder, a distiller, a bookseller, two butchers, and a hardware dealer. When he swore in the October 1841 grand jury, recorder Tallmadge conveyed his sense of the importance of their work. He told the jurors that they were part of an "institution . . . of ancient origin . . . kept up in all countries professing any regard for civil liberty." The judge emphasized their responsible role and then prepared them for what was to come—cases of criminal libel—by attempting to clarify the rationale for libel as a felony. By criminalizing such behavior, the court prevented violent acts of revenge. At the same time the grand jury "extended the shield of its protective powers to every man" by keeping him from indictment without the consent of twelve jurors.[36]

Grand juries customarily offered general reflections after issuing indictments at the end of their term. Juror Boggs read these for the foreman at the close of the October term. He spoke against the Sunday papers, of which the *Sunday Flash* was only one, and the need for laws to regulate their sale: "The shrill cry of the newsboys pierced to the fireside and the altars of the citizen, and disturbed the quiet, and profaned the sanctity of the Sabbath. It was also a system which destroyed all regard for the Sabbath in the minds of the boys themselves, and was preparing them for a life of vice and crime."[37]

Snelling saw Boggs, the publisher of William Cullen Bryant's Democratic *Evening Post,* as an interested party to the case and believed that he was influenced by recent ministerial denunciations against the flash press. In the *Flash,* his renamed weekly, Snelling called the grand jury a "Star Chamber" and compared it to the Inquisition. He wrote, "Is it not a horrible thing that three innocent men should be accused and judged in private, on the information of such land sharks as this Levy, arrested without know[ing] what they are charged with and sent to prison without a copy of the indictment and without a moment allowed to procure bail or engage counsel." He intoned, "Mr. Boggs, Mr. Boggs, you and your fellows have brayed a little too loudly and too early this time. Scorpion, Startle & Sly are not news boys and are not to be silenced so easily." Snelling also broadcast anti-Semitic slurs against Levy and accused the grand jury of sexual scandal. They were hardly impartial jurors, but consisted of "several sinners and one fornicator" who wanted to shut down the *Flash* because they were threatened with exposure. Snelling insinuated that he would make real that threat, but his words were a smokescreen for his own powerlessness. He was at the time in jail awaiting trial, the sole editor unable to find money for bail.[38]

On January 14, 1842, the editors of the *Sunday Flash* went on trial in the courtroom at the Halls of Justice on Centre Street, known as the Tombs, a building that combined courtrooms and prison. Judge Noah opened the January 1842 session of the court with an unusual speech to the grand jurors in which he considered the press and libel in the manner of Blackstone. He stated that liberty of the press did not permit the invasion of others' rights. Governments establish laws, he said, to prevent the "rights of reputation" from being "recklessly infringed, or cruelly trampled upon." Although the federal Constitution "allows a citizen to speak, write and print whatever he may think proper," that citizen is responsible and accountable if he abuses this right. In reflecting on the way that the penny press maligned bankers and banking practices, Noah emphasized, "I have never witnessed so great an abuse of the liberty of the press as I have of late in this city." The jurors themselves held the cure, believed Noah; he promised them that as judge he would support their efforts. "Gentlemen," he intoned, the remedy is "in your hands."[39]

On January 14, William J. Snelling and George Wilkes stood before the judges, accused of two charges: one of criminal libel and the other of obscene libel. George B. Wooldridge turned state's evidence, agreeing to testify against Snelling and Wilkes in return for being cleared of charges. On the matter of the criminal libel against Levy, both Snelling and Wilkes pleaded guilty. Snelling published a letter of apology to Levy in the *Flash* and the *Herald*. On the obscenity charge, however, the two maintained their innocence, and the jury heard the evidence and arguments of the defendants' lawyers.

This particular indictment for obscene libel is missing from the files of the district attorney indictment papers, but according to the *New York Herald* account, "The prosecution stated that they should prove that the sheet contained obscene matter, such as should not be allowed to appear in a public print, and therefore they presumed that it was only necessary to prove who were the actual publishers of the paper." This was textbook Starkie: judges alone determined what was obscene; the jury dealt only with the facts of the case. The specific matter isolated as obscene for the court was the article in the *Sunday Flash* of October 17, 1841, on the life of Amanda Green, an eroticized "seduced-and-abandoned" narrative. Wooldridge testified that Amanda Green, a known prostitute, was the source of the information contained in the article.[40]

The *Herald* stated that Wooldridge testified that "he was solicited by George Wilks [*sic*] to take a share in the paper, and that if he would go in with him they would make a good thing of it." He explained that his role for the *Sunday Flash* was "as the collector of items, from which certain articles were written." Amanda Green's life was one such example. He explained that he "turned states evidence to prevent others from getting ahead of him," suggesting that if he had not testified against his confederates, then Wilkes or Snelling would have turned on him, and he would be in their place. The *New-York Spectator* added several significant details. Wooldridge stated to the court in reference to the *Sunday Flash* that "Snelling was a good writer, and that both Snelling and Wilkes would write for it." Wooldridge also admitted that he had provided notes for "attacking Myer Levy, which he gave to Mr. Snelling to write," including those provided by Emanuel Hart, a member of Levy's extended family. Without giving details, the paper stated, "It was proved that the character of Wooldridge for truth was very bad."[41]

On this final point the *Herald* offered the necessary background. The defense called several witnesses to counter Wooldridge's testimony, including one who "stated he would not believe him [Wooldridge] under oath." This was none other than Nelson H. Miller, the son of brothel madam Adeline Miller. His presence in the court recalled the critical story of the short life and death of his sister, the actress Louisa Missouri, which contributed to the very origins of the New York flash press. A week after the trial, Snelling printed in the *Flash*—and challenged—Wooldridge's testimony by giving full attention to Miller's statement in court. According to Snelling, Miller admitted that he knew Wooldridge for some time and that he was a "bad character." Miller insisted that Wooldridge's actions were motivated by the desire for vengeance against Levy. Had Miller known in advance that Wilkes and Snelling were forming an alliance with Wooldridge, he would "have warned them against such infamy." [42]

The jury deliberated for several hours, but failed to agree. Although eleven of the men voted for conviction, one supported acquittal. No record exists of this one man's "reasonable doubt," but it is significant that there was one person who did not find the harm of the flash paper so egregious that he was willing to suppress the paper by sending its editors to prison. His refusal offers evidence, partial and fragmentary to be sure, that the judges' perspectives on racy reading matter were not universally shared by New Yorkers. [43]

Trouble did not end for Wilkes and Snelling, however. In April 1842, both men returned to Recorder Tallmadge's court for publishing an obscene paper. This time Wilkes pled guilty. He originally sought a dismissal, plea of *nolle prosequi,* on the grounds that the paper had ceased publication and he was engaged in different pursuits, but his lawyer persuaded him otherwise. When, a year and a half later, Wilkes again testified in court, further details of his guilty plea emerged. According to the *Herald,* Wilkes stated that his counsel in 1842 met with the district attorney, who advised Wilkes to go to court, plead guilty, separate himself from the paper, and thereby end the proceedings, since "the only object of the prosecution appeared to be to suppress the publication of the sheet." In return, Wilkes received a thirty-day suspended sentence: he could keep out of jail so long as he never again wrote for an obscene publication. [44]

Snelling met a different fate. Despite his declared innocence, the jury convicted him. As the proceeding ended, "the recognizances of W. J. Snelling were declared forfeited." Nelson Miller, who had put up his bond money now "surrendered him [Snelling], and he was committed to prison." [45]

In the meantime, beginning December 25, 1841, Wooldridge established the *Whip and Satirist of New-York and Brooklyn,* and served as editor and publisher. In this new publication, Wooldridge reveled in vanquishing his opponents. He must have enjoyed the moment when

Snelling, after serving his prison time, joined the *Whip*, not as proprietor and equal but simply as a writer in Wooldridge's employ. The latter was not satisfied, however, for he had not crushed Adeline Miller. Wooldridge deliberately set out to ruin her business. In so doing, he helped to bring down his own.

In his weekly, Wooldridge repeatedly accused Miller of operating a disorderly house and threatened in each issue to station a watch at her brothel and publish the names of her clients. Several times he gave a list of names. In one article, he treated roughly Willis G. Thompson, a business associate and friend of Nelson Miller. Wooldridge stated that Miller, who was staying with Thompson, removed some steaks from his mother's brothel pantry to Thompson's house. In "The Whip Wants to Know" appeared the question: "How often a notorious liar sleeps at the house of Mr. Thompson, and if Mrs. Thompson knows that her husband visits his house in return." Thompson, like Levy, was a private citizen. Faced with an insult to his wife and himself, Thompson initiated the criminal charge of libel. Once again libel against an editor led the district attorney to scrutinize his paper closely and then to indict him for obscene libel.

One can see this process on the pages of the flash papers once held in the district attorney's office. Beginning in fall 1841, when Myer Levy first complained, Whiting collected copies of the flash papers, marking them in ways that reveal what he saw as potential violations of common law. An important example is the way he marked the *True Flash,* the paper created by Wooldridge after he first broke with his associates to turn state's evidence. Wooldridge blasted Snelling visually and verbally. The woodcut "Mary M'Ka's Fancy Man" portrays a man in tatters in the foreground and a gallows with a rum bottle in the background. "Spirit-gas Scorpion" mocked Snelling's attachment to Miller's brothel and his drunkenness: Snelling "served her [Miller] in every capacity, and revelled in his situation as pander to a wanton, nay a common procuress. Obeying the behests of this foul stain on her sex, he attacked the character of Hamblin—the more rum she gave him, the more reckless became his articles." It asserted that one day after Miller locked him in his room to both keep him from drink and to encourage him to write a play, Snelling consumed his lamp alcohol to drunkenness. When Snelling approached Whiting in an attempt to prosecute Wooldridge for criminal libel, Whiting must have refused. In the margin of the December 5, 1841, *True Flash* Whiting wrote, "Libellous[.] The aff[idavi]t. of W. Snelling must shew what words or name denotes that he is this person alluded to, & an

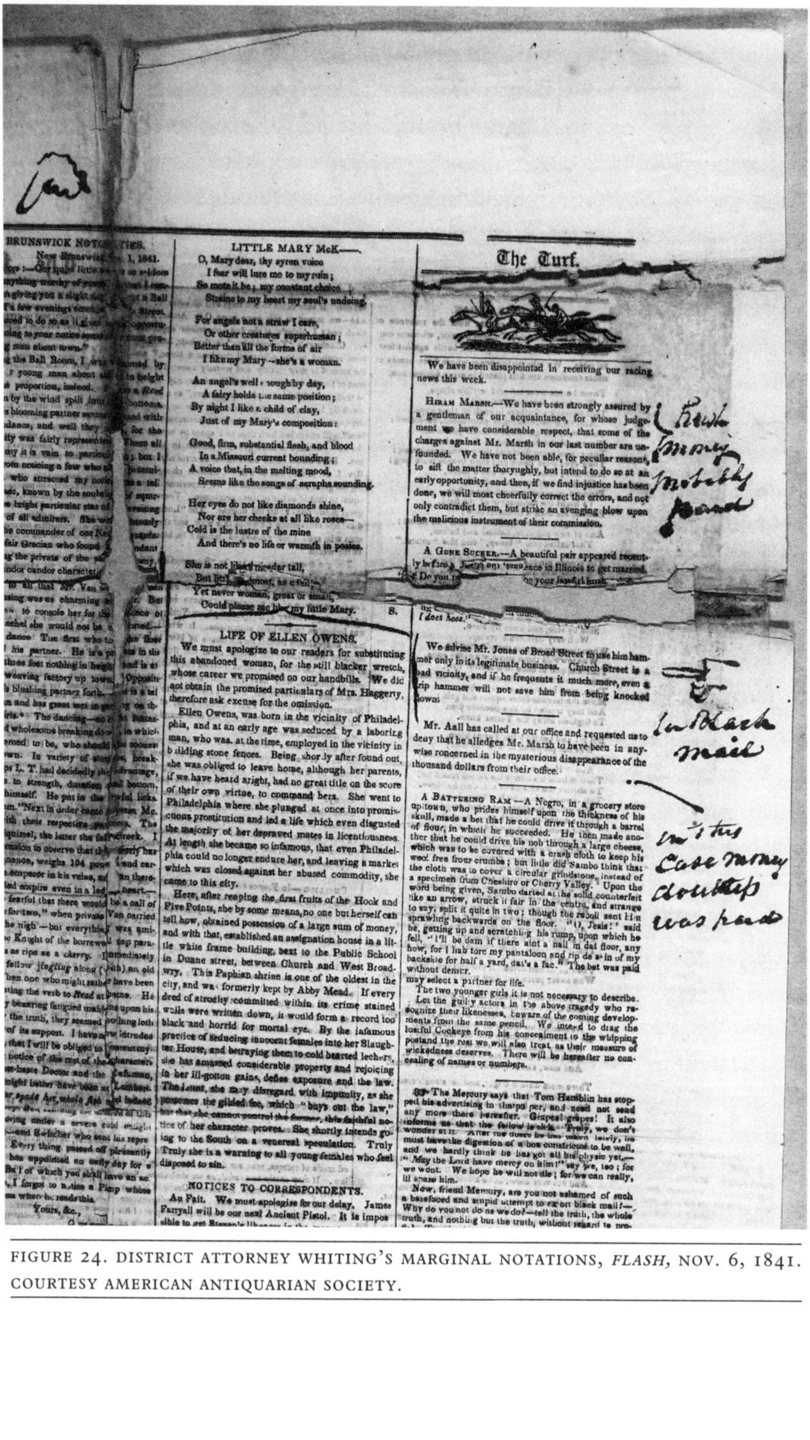

GALLARY OF OFRASCALITIES AND NOTORIETIES

MARY M'KA'S FANCY MAN

FIGURE 25. "GALLARY OF RASCALITIES AND NOTORIETIES: MARY M'KA'S FANCY MAN."
WOOLDRIDGE CHOSE THIS IMAGE TO ILLUSTRATE THE HOSTILE PROFILE OF HIS ONE-TIME
COLLABORATOR SNELLING. *TRUE FLASH,* DEC. 5, 1841. COURTESY AMERICAN ANTIQUARIAN
SOCIETY.

aff[idavi]t. of some witness to prove he is the man referred—J.R.W." Essentially, Whiting refused Snelling's request for an indictment for libel.[46]

In this case Whiting signed the note with his initials. That same hand appears in unsigned penned markings on other copies of sporting papers. Whiting was clearly searching for different violations. For example, on the *Whip and Satirist* of April 2, 1842, he placed boxes around articles, drew lines along the side of paragraphs, and underlined and marked with symbols significant sentences and phrases. The content of the marked passages reveals that Whiting was determined to find potentially libelous or obscene statements.[47]

As a result, Wooldridge was again indicted several months later for "publishing an obscene sheet," the July 9, 1842 edition of the *Whip*. The articles named in the second indictment were "The Battery Spy," "The Libertine Dr. B," "Pictures from Fancy No 2," "Poughkeepsee Rakes," and "Seduction—Conviction of the Libertine." This time, July 14, Wooldridge was part of a larger sweep of the flash press. In July and August 1842 indictments were levied against not only the owner of the *Whip* and the *Libertine* but also those of the *Flash* and the *Rake*. Those who were not indicted were as important as those who were. George Wilkes was now applying his talents elsewhere. William Snelling was merely a writer for the *Whip*, not an owner. He was not named because obscenity prosecutions involved the publishers of words and images, not their creators.[48]

In an editorial in the *Whip*, Wooldridge insisted that his indictment was a continuation of his old quarrel with Adeline Miller, and he was partially correct. Oddly, Wooldridge also suggested that what probably was the most offending was the following: "A chambermaid is lighting an old gentleman to bed, who, no doubt, becomes heated with love and endeavors to kiss her; in the struggle to obtain it, he manages to straddle the handle of a warming pan which she holds in her hand, and in type is made to say, 'Take care of the warming pan, sir!'" The engraving supplied by Robert H. Elton and copied from the London weekly the *Town* displayed an older man attempting to seduce a pretty young chambermaid carrying a warming pan. The stick of the pan was provocatively placed so that it looked like an erect penis. Her grasp of the stick implies that she was masturbating him.[49]

Wooldridge offered a weak defense of the illustration. He claimed he took it from "an English newspaper" and failed to fully note its content before publishing it in his own. Wooldridge did not mention the openly erotic articles listed in the indictment. For example, the "The Battery Spy" describes the prostitutes seen on a visit to the Battery on a Thursday afternoon by "all roués, libertines and sportsmen present . . . [and] suckers, sharps, diners-out, pimps, and drummers with white hats." The author compliments the costume of Mary Smith for being "rich with simplicity, elegant with neatness," in contrast to that of Harriet Grandy, which is "dirty, slovenly and disgusting as usual."[50]

SKETCHES OF CHARACTERS---NO. 16.

ELTON

THE CHAMBERMAID.

"*Take care of the Warming-pan, Sir.*"

FIGURE 26. "SKETCHES OF CHARACTERS—NO. 16.: THE CHAMBERMAID." AN IMAGE COP-
IED PERFECTLY FROM THE LONDON *TOWN* OF JAN. 20, 1838. *WHIP AND SATIRIST OF NEW-
YORK AND BROOKLYN,* APRIL 9, 1842. COURTESY AMERICAN ANTIQUARIAN SOCIETY.

The July 14 indictment is in the records. An adaptation of Starkie, it
declared that Wooldridge "being a scandalous and evil disposed person
and devising, contriving and intending the morals as well of youth as of
divers other citizens of the state of New York to debauch injure debase and
corrupt and to raise and create in their minds inordinate and lustful desires . . . unlawfully, wickedly, maliciously and scandalously did print
publish and circulate in the said city of New York and utter a certain
lewd wicked and scandalous paper." The indictment listed the specific

articles deemed obscene, published "to the manifest corruption of the morals of youth as of divers other citizens . . . in contempt of the people of the state of New York and their laws, to the evil example of all others in the like case offending and against the peace of the People of the State of New York and their dignity." Although the language was strong, it does not provide evidence of any deep fear of obscenity on the part of New York authorities, but only of the power of the common law tradition and of Starkie's utility to the social conservatives in the court who wished to shut the flash press down.[51]

On September 14, 1842, the cases went to trial. The following day, the *Herald* dealt briefly with the trial of John Vandewater of the *Flash*, who pleaded guilty along with Charles G. Scott. Attorneys Richard Voorhees, who formerly represented Vandewater, and C. W. Terhune Jr., who currently represented Scott, both appeared. The two defendants sought a lesser sentence. The advocate for Vandewater, while admitting that the paper was obscene, sought to mitigate the lad's punishment by introducing his father, who stated that his son had ceased to be connected to the publication.[52]

The proceedings against Wooldridge, charged as publisher of the *Libertine,* were of more interest to the *Herald,* and the paper gave an unusually full report. District Attorney Whiting insisted that no witnesses could testify as to whether or not the paper was obscene. One witness might refuse to answer. Others might be untrustworthy. "Those who bought the paper and gloated over its contents, would be very likely not to consider it obscene, while the decent man would lay it down after reading the first two lines." Whiting also declined to read the offending articles to the court. He did not want indecent language to become part of the public record, for, as he stated, to do so would allow newspaper reporters to republish the material. In effect, he argued that he would not be a party to any promulgation of the republican libertinism he was trying to staunch. What he did say was that the very name of the *Libertine* and titles of its articles revealed their content. In this Whiting was supported by Starkie's *Law of Slander and Libel* (1830).

Wooldridge was represented by James M. Smith Jr., a young novice lawyer. The attorney gave a long reply, stated reasons why the articles should be read to the jury, and demanded that witnesses be called. Smith insisted that the articles themselves might serve the cause of virtue by pointing out the results of vice. If a title alone or an isolated passage from the text were the sole guide, he argued, then important works of literature could be found obscene. "If a book or publication was to be judged by its title, or the selection of isolated passages, there is scarcely a publisher but would be liable to prosecution for obscene publications, and many of the works of Moore and Byron could not be defended with as much propriety as the articles named by the District Attorney." [53]

The court refused to allow witnesses but required the district attorney to read the articles in their entirety to the jury. Whiting, who earlier threatened to resign rather than read the offending works, obeyed, giving the court the full content of "Matilda Rollins, alias Daniels, alias Dutch Till" and "Catharine Alley, alias Kate Horn." This departure from Starkie was not to be repeated. In trials dealing with obscenity in the years following, subsequent district attorneys were never compelled to read aloud whole works in the courtroom.

Smith called no witnesses on behalf of Wooldridge, but according to the *Herald* made an "able and judicious defence of his client, in a speech abounding with eloquence, in the course of which he read several articles and extracts from the paper." The district attorney followed with his own "powerful speech, in which he forcibly depicted the consequences that must ensue if these licentious papers were countenanced and allowed to exist." Recorder Tallmadge then charged the jury. He spoke to them of "the blessings of a properly conducted press, and of the evils of an abandoned and profligate press." With these words, both Whiting and Tallmadge were forthright in their opposition to the libertine republicanism of the flash papers. The jury retired for five minutes and returned a guilty verdict against Wooldridge.

In addition, Henry Renshaw (under the name Henry McVey) and George Colburn faced indictments as publishers of the *Whip*. At the trial the following day, both entered guilty pleas. Counselor Smith requested a delay in sentencing until the beginning of the court's next term in order to prepare affidavits for a lesser punishment for his three clients. It was granted, but to no avail. Ultimately Wooldridge, Renshaw, and Colburn, as well as the other publishers of the flash papers, served prison sentences of sixty days. [54]

The indictments and trials stemming from the summer 1842 sweep attempted to be comprehensive. Although Wooldridge of the *Whip* and the *Libertine* garnered the lion's share of attention from the penny press, his legal fate was shared by Scott of the *Flash* and Thaddeus W. Meighan of the *Rake*. In addition, in August 1842, eight booksellers were arrested selling pornographic prints and books in New York City, and a hunt followed for the printer who supplied them with material. [55]

Initially the flash papers survived efforts to suppress them, for some editors were flexible and wily. In February 1843, for example, the *Whip* announced that its former rival was now to be its star. The weekly crowed: "T. W. Meighan: The ex-editor of the 'Rake,' 'Flash,' 'Messenger,' 'Sunday Star,' &c., is hard at work with a series of Tales, to be published in one of our principal periodicals. We have his life at our pen's end, and Elton his engraved portrait." But New York authorities were unrelenting in their campaign against the flash papers. In March 1843, Meighan came before General Sessions, pleaded guilty to being an editor of the *Whip,* and was remanded for sentence. This ended his career in the flash press, but he resurfaced in later years as a writer.[56]

In the month following Meighan's trial, it became clear that the actions of the courts in New York City from 1841 to 1843 were really about censorship, not simply suppression, an important legal distinction when considering liberty of the press. In April 1843, the publishers of the *Whip* were allowed to walk out of court "on their own recognizance, on condition of promising not to engage in the publication of any sheet of similar kind in future under pain of being rearrested and tried." Blackstone insisted that liberty of the press consisted of freedom from prior restraint, not "freedom from censure for criminal matter when published." Starkie dealt with the logic and practice of obscene libel, again for materials already published. However, the Court of General Sessions in 1843 was involved in administering censorship, which involved prior restraint, not in merely suppressing libelous material after its publication.[57]

This distinction was explicit in the retrial of George Wilkes in November 1843. When the first case of the *Flash* was settled in January 1842, Wilkes received a thirty-day suspended sentence under condition that he never again write for an obscene publication. A year later he was a reporter for Mike Walsh's *Subterranean* and returned to the courtroom to observe the radical politician-editor's trial for libel. As Walsh stood before him, recorder Tallmadge spoke in a manner that echoed his handling of the trials of the editors of the flash press and his opposition to the libertine republicanism of the papers. Tallmadge said, "the licentiousness that had recently presented itself among many of the public journals of this city was more of a curse to the community than a benefit." What Tallmadge emphasized in this case, perhaps because Wilkes was now associated with the *Subterranean,* was not the obscenity but the libel against persons and the violations of privacy. The journals had "entered the private sanctuary of families, which they have assailed in a manner that calls loudly upon the public authorities to suppress." The press must be condemned when it "attacks individuals and assails private character and relations without justification."[58]

In Tallmadge's eyes, because he was in the courtroom as a reporter for the *Subterranean* and an employee of Walsh, George Wilkes violated the terms of his suspended April 1842 sentence. The judge brought Wilkes before the court. Although he now spoke on his own behalf, Wilkes failed to change Tallmadge's decision to put him behind bars.

When Tallmadge administered the sentence, he spoke to the court. In a kind of backhanded compliment, the judge said that he was previously moved by "the youth of the accused, his talents." But now it was the dangers of libelous publications that were forefront. Tallmadge told the court that there was "a certain portion of the public press—particularly the penny press" that harmed the public. They made "personal attacks, harrowing up the feelings of families, and innocent and unoffending persons." In his court, "parties so offending should be visited with the most severe punishment." With that, he sentenced Wilkes to imprisonment in the Tombs for one month. Tallmadge hoped that this was "not only as a warning to him, but to all others who were concerned in publishing sheets of an infamous and libellous character." By Tallmadge's use of a suspended sentence in Wilkes' case, his statement at his retrial, and his sentencing of the reporter, Tallmadge clarified that he was using the law not just to suppress sheets printed in the past, but also to censor the press, preventing publications "of an infamous and libellous character" in the future.[59]

V Following the trials of the flash press, the *Herald* published an intriguing editorial. James Gordon Bennett, the paper's editor, a defendant himself in many libel cases, did not defend the editors of the sporting papers. Rather, he used them to slam his principal rivals, the established subscription papers. But in doing so, he gave them an odd kind of legitimization. In "The Tweedle-dum and Tweedle-dee in Morals—The Ann Street Licentious Press, and the Wall Street Licentious Press," he compared the flash papers, typically published on grubby Ann Street, and the subscription papers, printed in the respectable area around Wall Street. Why was one prosecuted in the courts and the other allowed to go free? In asking this question, Bennett revealed both his opposition to the bankers of Wall Street and his view of the Ann Street publishers. Each belonged to a class of "demoralized newspapers" published in New York—one, the business press centered on Wall Street, the other, "licentious" competitors on Ann Street. While the business press "patronizes theft, plunder, and wholesale robberies, through the agencies of banks, loan companies, and all species of incorporated bodies," Bennett editorialized, the flash press "patronizes the same species of plunder by means of faro banks, pool, roulette, hazard, betting, picking pockets, and every other species of robbery." Writing immediately after a prominent pugilist died in an illegal match, Bennett wrote that while the sporting papers sanctioned death through fights in the ring, the business papers upheld dueling as an honorable way to resolve a conflict. If the licentious press of Ann Street was jailed, why was that of Wall Street allowed to remain free? Cold comfort, perhaps, to the imprisoned editors of the flash papers, but at least a bit of recognition.[60]

The *Herald*'s coverage of the trial described efforts of flash press editors to defend themselves, but in editorials in their own papers they presented a more detailed defense. Usually Snelling and Wooldridge alleged that the original libel charges were the result of personal vendettas against them. They hurled invectives at their enemies, calling them names such as "dirty vagabonds" and "prostitute pimps." They insisted that they were innocent of all wrongdoing, that their sheets were put forward for moral reformation. They were the advocates of the underdog, people who had the right to enjoyment of innocent pastimes. In the matter of melodrama, Snelling declaimed in the *Flash*, "You have chosen your libel ill. . . . At present we bid defiance alike to Jews and negroes, Hell and Hamblin, Farce, Comedy and Tragedy."[61]

In the autumn of 1841, as Snelling fulminated about the wrong of the legal proceedings against him as editor of the *Flash*, he developed the arguments that Wooldridge's lawyer employed a year later. Snelling sought to put his treatment of prostitutes in a moral light, posing as a reformer: he only exposed the evil that existed, he did not create it. Was his language coarse? Only to his accusers: "Gentlemen; most righteous, virtuous and delicate gentlemen, the dirt of the Flash is all in your own imaginations. You have been looking for naughty words, and it is no wonder that you have found them." To call his writings into question was to threaten the publication of literary works. Invoking the great names of satire and libertinism, respectively, Snelling exclaimed: "Let them punish the publishers of Dean Swift. Let them suppress Byron." Snelling may have been rather nervy, given what he published, but he was a man who knew the world of letters. Prior to his New York interlude, he was a recognized poet in Boston.[62]

Wooldridge made the usual ritualistic promise to reform after his second trial, but his paper did not change. The *Whip*'s new editor, now anonymous, promised an even more licentious weekly: "When we happen to see an elegant female promenading Broadway or any other way, we shall, if she pleases our fancy, endeavor to describe her figure and gay dress with all the power of love itself—not caring whether she is frail or fair, for that is not our business. . . . We intend visiting all the first-rate seraglios, and with the pen of truth speak of *things* as we find them—draw out the lovely from their lurking places, and tell the world what flowers are 'wasting their fragrance on the desert air.'" In an article entitled, "Our First Walk About Town," the reader was taken on a lighthearted tour of brothels in New York City.[63]

It was George Wilkes who initiated an argument with legal strength. Wilkes challenged key assumptions in Blackstone, Starkie, and the common law. After his retrial in November 1843, Wilkes served time in prison. He kept a journal in jail, later published as *The Mysteries of the Tombs*. In it, he pondered broader issues. What bedeviled publishers and advocates for freedom of the press was not simply a judge or a court but a system of law that accepted elements of British common law. Wilkes understood this, at least in part. In *The Mysteries of the Tombs*, he stated his opposition to the common law of obscene libel and took on some of the premises behind Blackstone, Holt, and Starkie.

Wilkes focused on the contrast between the sanctions for words and deeds. Words that might provoke violence, in the case of libel, or licentiousness, in the case of obscenity, received harsh penalties. At the same time, deeds might be treated lightly or not at all: assault and battery merited mild punishment, and it was no crime at all to engage in sexual relations outside marriage. Wilkes regarded the common law governing obscenity as particularly illogical, if not hypocritical. As he put it, obscene materials for purchase "are subject to the same penalties as libel, because they tend to promote licentiousness; while adultery and fornication, the very evils which their prosecution is intended to prevent, go scot free of the law. Is not this supremely absurd?" Wilkes issued a challenge: "can the proposition stand, that it is criminal to incite to an act, the actual commission of which is innocent by law?" For Wilkes, no distinction existed between a public and a private wrong.

Furthermore, Wilkes rejected a jurisprudence originating in tradition rather than written statutes. He contrasted the common law governing obscene libel with the illegal sale of lottery tickets. Here, Wilkes argued, the courts act because such sale is "a direct violation of an imperative statute." Linked with his rejection was the vagueness of obscenity rulings in the common law tradition. As Wilkes put it, "the sale of obscene papers is merely an offence against taste, according to the common law, or in other words, common opinion." [64]

Snelling's editorials and Wilkes' *Mysteries of the Tomb* may have been forgotten, but their substance enjoyed a long life. Later in the century, as advocates of free speech mounted legal defenses for those accused of obscenity, they, too, challenged where lines should be drawn. They, too, argued that to reject works because of "naughty words" threatened a great deal of the world's literature. Once definite statutes against obscenity were written, free speech defenders protested against their vague language and their subjection to the vagaries of taste. By then, these advocates also perceived the First Amendment as applicable in their struggle to free speech. [65]

In the era of Snelling, Wooldridge, and Wilkes, the prevailing force in the war over sexual words was that of recorder Tallmadge. A conservative judge, he saw danger in the libertine republicanism of the flash papers. They were, as he put it, "an abandoned and profligate press," one of the "evils" of the city in need of censorship. He enjoyed the power to persuade juries of artisans and merchants. Whatever their personal behavior, these men shared Tallmadge's view that the press should not report the affairs of prostitutes, threaten to expose those guilty of misdeeds, or tell stories of seduction and betrayal. These men assumed that when they convicted editors of the flash papers, their judgments represented acts done in the public interest. Supported by the court, this socially conservative position had great power. And long life: Tallmadge's position and many of the practices of his court held sway over the law of obscenity until early in the twentieth century. Echoes of his voice remain today in those who seek to censor sexual words and images.

LEGACIES

The trials of 1843 shut down the flash papers. Few shed tears or gnashed their teeth over the fate of the fined and imprisoned editors, and in the ensuing decades, few even remembered that the papers had ever existed. Several of the editors themselves clearly tried to expunge their association with the flash press from their public records; the obituary of only one of them made reference to a shady youthful indiscretion of involvement with "sensational periodicals."[1] Yet important legacies emerged from these innovative weeklies. Although the flash papers evoked vehement condemnation, they also inspired pale copycat publications in several cities among the young urban male population that found them valuable and entertaining, if not titillating. The flash editors' use of sex to attack privilege and hypocrisy had an extended life in yet other periodicals of the late 1840s and 1850s, and their embrace of a lusty sexuality gave courage to a distinctly different and small set of editors in the 1850s who moved forward with frankly erotic periodicals, stripped of any politics. And though forgotten in the major legal conflicts over obscenity law in the twentieth century, the convictions of flash editors had an invisible but critical role in both shaping and implementing the Comstock Act of 1873, long seen as the landmark and sole originator of U.S. obscenity law.

The shutdown in 1843 came by legal means, at the hands of New York's deeply conservative judiciary motivated by its opposition to libertine republicanism. At least three additional identifiable groups beyond the legal establishment had a strong stake in eradicating the weeklies on other grounds. Evangelical Christians—the moral reformers and all for whom they spoke, both female and male—certainly interpreted the sporting weeklies' discussions of prostitutes and their clients as sinful; their religious moralism condemned all public sexual expression, whether cloaked in political ideology or not. Other less fervently religious segments of the novel-reading public embraced the romanticized sexuality of popular fiction but drew the line at the flash papers' depiction of commercialized sex, stripped of love. Love, not lust, properly motivated sexual expression, and on those grounds the flash papers were reprehensible. A third set of readers avidly sought new ideas about the physiology of sex as set forth in a burgeoning popular medical literature gaining significant audience in the 1840s. This new science of sex increasingly emphasized the connection of sexual desire to a complex nervous system rather than to heated blood. From this perspective, the racy language of the flash press probably appeared crude and uninformed, more archaic than satanic. From these multiple points of view, the demise of the New York flash press was welcome news.

It is possible that even the editors of the flash press were themselves glad the papers came to an end. They were resourceful young men with other opportunities to grab. If they made good money on these papers, they also suffered the serious headaches of periodic libel suits, arrests, and jail time. And they all jumped to new venues without much difficulty.

The trio of the *Sunday Flash* who started it all—Scorpion, Startle, & Sly—went their separate ways. William J. Snelling, the eldest at thirty-eight and with serious enough medical problems (likely alcoholism) to delay his sentencing in the October 1842 trial, continued to edit his more respectable weekly, the *Sunday Times,* with a young editorial partner named Walter Whitman. In mid-1843 the two men merged their paper with another, Mordecai Noah's *Weekly Messenger,* and soon thereafter Snelling returned to Boston and resumed his marriage to Lucy Snelling. The union was sufficiently stable such that the couple had two more children. Snelling's health also apparently recovered, enabling him to secure the editorship of the mainstream daily paper, the *Boston Herald,* a position he held for two years. He brought his bluster and bite into his new position, publishing many clever satirical pieces that delivered the old Snelling punch, but without any reference to sex. For example, a hapless writer of a letter to the editor was denied space for his missive, called a "craven and contemptible scoundrel," a "blockhead," and a "booby." Snelling expressed disbelief that any *Herald* subscriber could be so stupid. An adjoining squib took aim at Elizur Wright, a well-known Boston reformer, abolitionist, and newspaper editor, who had evidently complimented Snelling on his "genius." Writing in the editorial third person, Snelling sneered back and described Wright as "the driveling and despicable wretch who thus like a true spaniel, seeks to kiss the foot which has so often kicked him." Snelling wrote a cruel satire on Michigan senator Lewis Cass over several issues, mocked Isaac Pray, a Boston journalist of the 1830s, and delivered a chilling and graphic exposé on illegal flogging in the army, claiming to have witnessed over a thousand such beatings in his youth. When a sudden surge of apoplexy (cerebral hemorrhage) ended his life on Christmas day, 1848, his colleagues at the *Herald* praised him extravagantly as "a distinguished advocate for the oppressed" and blessed with a "wonderful knowledge of men and things." He was, they wrote, "a man whose faults whatever they might have been, were overcome in his excessive affection for his family—his devotion to truth—his stern and unflinching integrity." A month later, a well-attended benefit performance at the Boston Museum raised over $400 for his widow and small children, with actors, speechmakers, and uniformed fire companies providing the pomp and entertainment.[2]

George Wilkes was a young man at the founding of the *Sunday Flash,* and his long life and considerable success made him the best known of the group. His was a life full of dramatic twists and turns. After his month-long jail sentence and the resulting publication of *Mysteries of the Tombs,* his exposé of the city prison, Wilkes next used his able pen to support "manifest destiny" in Oregon, promoting an early argument for a national transcontinental railroad in a pamphlet that was cited by legislators in Washington. Then in 1845 he founded the *National Police Gazette* with lawyer-journalist Enoch Camp. This long-lived paper, with a professed focus on exposing the professional criminal class and aiding in police work, was in Wilkes's control only until 1853. In his eight years at the helm, he provoked a host of small libel suits and one major lawsuit that caused him to flee the state and then the country in 1851. He spent time in Europe and made two trips to California in the early 1850s, where his brother Henry and good childhood friend David Broderick had settled.

In 1856 Wilkes purchased an established and successful New York paper, the *Spirit of the Times,* which he owned the rest of his life. The *Spirit of the Times* was a sporting paper in a different sense, read by those interested in horse racing, boxing, and athletic events. The publication also provided theatrical news and gossip about celebrities. When Broderick, then senator from California, was shot dead in a duel in 1859, Wilkes inherited a substantial part of his fortune of $300,000, enabling him to spend his remaining decades living in some style and traveling extensively. In the 1870s he often appeared in the news for lawsuits and threatened assaults, all of which he took in stride. He let others handle the daily chores of the *Spirit of the Times,* but he filed impressive accounts of Civil War battles, wrote a book on the authenticity and identity of Shakespeare, and covered European revolutions of the 1870s. He married two, and possibly three, times, but his wives almost never entered the public record. His final relationship, lasting just four years, was with a married American woman he met in Europe. He adopted her two children when she died in 1884; the younger was probably his own natural offspring. He died the following year, leaving a tangle of litigation over his estate.[3]

George B. Wooldridge, about the same age as Wilkes, followed his escapades as a flash press editor with a colorful and varied career, surfacing several times in the historical record. His life demonstrates the close relation of the flash papers to theater and popular culture. After ceding the *Whip* to Thaddeus Meighan in February 1843, he signed on as the booking agent for the Virginia Minstrels, a singing group of four white men in blackface, and accompanied them on six-month tour in England, Scotland, and Ireland. Back in New York in 1844, Wooldridge pledged his skills with the pen to the newly founded Empire Club, becoming the recording secretary of the rowdy Democratic club headed by Captain Isaiah Rynders that backed James K. Polk's election with rallies, torchlight parades, and high spirits and fists. Wooldridge was acquainted with the Empire leaders via the boxing world; Rynders and the others were fight promoters when Wooldridge edited the *Whip*, and all were implicated in the fatal fight of Thomas McCoy, a 120-round illegal fight covered extensively in the flash press. In a scathing exposé of the Empire Club, an unfriendly newspaper of 1844 singled out Wooldridge for condemnation: He was "a criminal who is known as a notorious bigamist, and who has kept himself out of prison by a base betrayal of his associates in other crimes as a 'states evidence.' He was the collector of the brothel news published in the 'Flash' and 'Whip'—the two infamous publications which were suppressed by the authorities, and whose responsible editors were sentenced to the Penitentiary. He has once been sentenced to the State's Prison, and has served out his time as keeper of the Hog Pen in that institution."[4]

Wooldridge was actually not a bigamist. His early marriage to a prostitute, predating his involvement with the flash press, was probably never legal, since the girl was already married before taking up the brothel life. His next marital union was with a young woman whose father ran a hotel in Brooklyn; she died in 1848. In the 1850 census, the thirty-three-year-old Wooldridge, now running an ale house, the old family business, lived in New York City with four children, aged one to eight, and a twenty-year-old woman; probably the one-year-old was hers. In 1860, he was still with the same woman, with three more children, living near the Catskill Mountains north of New York City.[5]

During the 1850s, Wooldridge moved to Albany due to his close association with Dan Sickles, another brash lad who rose from the gangs of New York to be an elected Democrat in New York's assembly and, later, an ill-famed member of the House of Representatives. Wooldridge followed Sickles to Albany and secured work as the sergeant-at-arms for that body; when Sickles moved to the District of Columbia, Wooldridge went along and garnered the job as sergeant-at-arms for the House, despite being crippled in a serious train accident in 1856. Wooldridge was Sickles's personal secretary in 1859, when Sickles murdered in broad daylight his wife's lover, the son of Francis Scott Key, and got away with it. Wooldridge was with Sickles at the time of the murder and testified in a court case that electrified the nation for weeks. In the 1850s and 1860s, Wooldridge ultimately returned to the newspaper world as the columnist Tom Quick in the *New York Leader,* whose "Old Sports of New York" reminisced about the masculine culture of the 1840s. In his final years in the late 1860s, he owned and operated a resort hotel in Bethel, New York.[6]

The exploits of George Washington Dixon continued to entertain newspaper readers around the nation. After his flash press work, Dixon took up "pedestrianism" as a competitive sport. In Baltimore he paced on a board for sixty hours, fortified by only water, raw oysters, and a single glass of wine. In another stunt covered nationally, he power-walked sixty miles between Philadelphia and Trenton in twelve hours. He continued performing songs of political satire on stage and at Whig rallies.[7]

In 1845 Dixon resumed journalism with a slyly satirical weekly, the *New York Packet.* Early issues criticized moral reformers for foisting seamy stories of illicit sex into chaste families, but two months later he reversed course and pretended the *Packet* was cooperatively published with the good ladies of the *Advocate of Moral Reform,* he handling their secular reportage of seduction and adultery while they confined themselves to religious matters. He addressed the lady editors confidingly and by name, gave them advice, and stole from their paper to demonstrate he was in league with them. The good ladies were not amused. The *Packet* disappeared after late November 1845, either out of steam or in legal trouble.[8]

Dixon, besotted with fantasies of empire, appeared at rallies promoting the invasion of Mexico and then abruptly left New York City in 1846, skipping bail on a libel charge. Newspapers around the country followed the zany travels of "General Dixon" and his four dozen followers on their way to New Orleans, in preparation for invading the Yucatan. The *New Orleans Picayune* ridiculed Dixon's over-decorated uniform and advised

FIGURE 27. DIXON'S *POLYANTHOS*, SEPT. 18, 1841, PROCLAIMED ITSELF THE DEFENDER OF FREE SPEECH WITH THE SLOGANS "LIBERTY OF SPEECH" AND "FREEDOM OF THE PRESS" ON ITS MASTHEAD. COURTESY AMERICAN ANTIQUARIAN SOCIETY.

the locals to "button their pockets" whenever this "dark complexioned man, with a heavy black moustache" was near. Before a week had passed, Dixon was in the Calaboose, New Orleans's notorious jail, not the Halls of Montezuma. "Served him right! A more consummate loafer, or a more degraded, yet pitiful specimen of humanity, New York, when it luckily got rid of him, could not well boast," wrote a New York correspondent to a North Carolina paper.[9]

Dixon's life in New Orleans cemented his reputation as an oddball, a dunce, and a knave; when not in jail he was running for Congress. He planned to start a paper, a *Southwestern Police Gazette*, which never materialized. The Prince of Humbugs, the Duke of Yucatan, the Earl of Poydras Market in New Orleans: that Dixon got others to confer such titles on him says something about his either campy or deluded state of mind. He died at the Charity Hospital in 1861.[10]

John Vandewater and Charles G. Scott, the youthful pair running the *Flash* in the summer and fall of 1842, when the former was eighteen and the latter twenty-three, disappear from view for a time but reappear in Gold Rush California in the late 1840s. Scott arrived first, in March 1847, having left his wife and year-old daughter with her family in New York. Vandewater arrived in June 1849 and traveled to Tuolumne County in the gold country, where he appears as a miner in the 1850 census along with another young man, Garry Vandewater. In 1851, both John Vandewater and Scott lived on Powell Street in San Francisco and inscribed as members of the 700-man San Francisco Vigilance Committee. Vandewater left his tracks in several small newspaper items: a marriage notice, an involvement with an executed felon, and as a shooting victim. The 1852 special census of the city shows that Scott's wife Jane and daughter Indiana had joined him, along with a new baby boy born that year; Scott's occupation was "builder." Scott had died by 1860, but his widow landed on her feet. In 1870 she ran a boarding house and claimed property worth $17,000.[11]

Almost nothing is known of George Colburn and Henry Renshaw, who worked with Wooldridge on the various versions of the *Whip*. A new team called "Colburn and Madison" launched the *Sportsman* in July 1843, with flash-like cartoons, multiple humorous quips about Mike Walsh, a general plea to legalize prostitution, and a truly funny observation about the insult of small plaster statues of George Washington in tight pants that failed to put manly bulk in the genital region. Only one issue survives, leaving few clues as to who Colburn was. When indicted in April and again in July 1842, Colburn and Renshaw were entered in the court docket book with aliases (Henry McVey and George Serle), and none of these four names proves traceable; possibly in later life they took yet other names. At his sentencing in September 1842, Renshaw failed to show up and forfeited his bail; his codefendants received sixty-day sentences. Possibly he fled and never returned to New York.[12]

Thaddeus W. Meighan was also a young man in his flash press years and, like the *Sunday Flash* trio, spent much of his career in the newspaper world. Meighan's editorial stints in New York papers included the *Sunday Times* (coedited with Mordecai Noah), the *Express* (the paper quoted above that was so hostile to Wooldridge in 1844), and the *Evening Press*. A prolific man, he published in many genres, including several gold-rush songs and a humorous book on the mania associated with Jenny Lind, an immensely popular Swedish singer who toured the United States in 1850–51. Like Wooldridge, Meighan was connected both with the world of print and popular entertainments. For a time in the 1850s he was the manager of the Old Bowery Theatre, and he wrote several plays: the *Fairy Circle*, the *Waifs of New York*, and the *Mystic Bride*. He served in the Union army during the Civil War, rising to the rank of captain. When he died in 1873, he left a wife and eight children; friends in New York City organized a benefit concert at a major theater to raise money for the widow and orphans.[13]

II As these men went on with their lives after the trials, they left the world of obscene writing and images. That world changed with their departure. The conviction of Snelling, Wilkes, Wooldridge, Meighan, and their associates transformed obscenity. Future publishers of sporting newspapers were discouraged from celebrating prostitution and employing blatantly sexual images in their political and social critiques. Conversely, obscene or pornographic texts grew increasingly detached over time from their early political contexts. By mid-century, missing from the scene were periodicals that linked obscene libel or pornographic sensationalism with political ideologies in the manner of the libertine republicanism of the flash press of the early 1840s. Pornography, cut off from the original political associations in the flash press, evolved into a more singularly erotic literature.

Initially, one paper continued to invoke the language of the brothel and metaphor of the prostitute in its attacks on aristocracy and privilege. This was the *Subterranean* (1843–45), edited by the radical Democrat Mike Walsh, with reportorial assistance from George Wilkes in its first year of issue. Walsh consistently assailed opponents with sensational allusions to prostitution. He vilified the New York police for extorting "hush" money from madams, for gratifying "their goatish lusts" in brothels, for raping innocent servant girls arrested on false charges of streetwalking.[14] Walsh referred to political opponents as "pandering pimps" and "panel thieves." After Wilkes left the *Subterranean*, Walsh castigated him as little more than a "brothel chronicler." Walsh even linked an unnamed Custom House official with madam Adeline Furman, an alias for Adeline Miller, in one gossip column.

Walsh's most vehement insults were directed at New York City police chief George Matsell, once a bookseller and later to be *National Police Gazette* editor. Walsh smeared him as an "ex-vendor of . . . obscene prints," "a noisy whig brawler," a "walking mass of moral and physical putrefaction [*sic*]," a "degraded and pitiful lump of blubber and meanness," a man "infamous" for his "degraded passions" and "notorious for excessive and disgusting indulgence in the most beastly desires." Employing racist imagery, Walsh charged Matsell with frequent visits "to the lowest courtezans" in Five Points.[15] Yet while Walsh employed the cant and argot associated with prostitution, he never resorted to the laudatory and touristic coverage of Gotham's commercial sexual universe found in the flash weeklies.

By midcentury, the *National Police Gazette* exemplified the new style and content of the sporting weekly. Under the editorship of George Wilkes and later George Matsell and Richard Kyle Fox, the *National Police Gazette* abandoned the egalitarian agenda of the flash press. Undoubtedly certain themes and methods persisted: advertisements for venereal disease, male impotence, and concert saloons; gossip columns entitled "Murder and Suicide," "This Wicked World," "Glimpses of Gotham," and "Vice's Varieties." In an issue of 1847, Wilkes took pains to distinguish the *Police Gazette*'s coverage of sex and prostitution from inappropriate appeals to "sensualists" who crave "racy, unchaste, ribald disclosures." Was this a tacit acknowledgement that the flash papers like

FIGURE 28. THE *NATIONAL POLICE GAZETTE*, NOV. 24, 1849, REFLECTED THE NEW STYLE AND CONTENT OF SPORTING NEWSPAPERS AFTER 1845. COURTESY AMERICAN ANTIQUARIAN SOCIETY.

his own, earlier in the decade, truly aimed to feed the cravings of "sensualists"? Wilkes contrasted that low motive with the *Gazette*'s righteous-sounding goal, which was to expose vice and depravity in order to cure it—a near-exact replication of the recent claims staked by Dixon, Snelling, Wooldridge, and Scott. The sexual indiscretions of the wealthy and infidelities of the devout were covered, for the stated purpose of allegedly upholding "female virtue," but not incidentally for male titillation. The pleasure ethic remained prominent in *Police Gazette* stories, but absent any systematic critique of wealth or privilege. Leisure-time adventure replaced workplace equality.[16]

Several papers in the 1840s continued with the taunting humor and sexual innuendo of the flash papers, but without their full immersion in the brothel subculture and without the radical critique characterized by libertine republicanism. Spin-offs of this milder sort include three in New York whose editorial offices were graced by men with close associations to the original flash papers. Thomas L. Nichols, the butt of much insult in the *Whip* and the *Flash*, started his own daily paper, the *Arena*, in 1842, which adhered to acceptable social norms for about two months before veering into coverage of sexual doings about town. While Nichols championed prostitution in the abstract, he did not focus on individual prostitutes. The women he lauded in print were coy, flirty, and made out to be respectable young women with a keen appetite for romance, presenting his readers with a somewhat different picture of the sexual possibilities of Gotham.[17] George Colburn, as mentioned above, teamed with a new partner to create the *Sportsman* in 1843, a paper that (based on one extant issue) seems to have kept to the lighter side of humor. And George Washington Dixon kept up the *New York Packet* for part of a year in 1845, much in the spirit of early editions of his *Polyanthos* in the 1830s, gleefully claiming alliance with the moral reformers and goading them to notice and condemn him.

Near the end of the decade, *Ned Buntline's Own*, published by Edward Z. C. Judson under his pen name, aped elements of the flash papers. The publication expressed moral outrage over prostitution and gambling, published addresses of brothels and gambling dens, criticized editors such as Horace Greeley and James Gordon Bennett for advertising abortionists, and threatened blackmail. But *Ned Buntline's Own* promoted anti-immigrant nativism, not libertine republicanism. Much of the publication was devoted to championing Buntline's publications, if not Buntline himself. Absent was any of the satire or tongue-in- cheek style of the flash papers.[18]

Outside of New York, more spin-offs materialized. One extant issue of an 1842 paper titled the *Spy and Philadelphia Paul Pry* carried a subtitle indicating its mission as "wit, fun, and flash." Two of its four pages were packed with a local trial report on a seduction/adultery case, and the rest contained restrained humor about town gossip. Another "Paul Pry" paper was the *Viper's Sting and Paul Pry* of Baltimore, 1849–50, which danced around sexual jokes but mainly offered stings in its "wonder if" column, as in this pitch for either moral reformation—or blackmail: "Wonder who that widower is, that has been too fond of woman, especially a certain one who has presented him with a very striking likeness in the *Babee* line. How about it Mr. C.—? Pauls about these diggin's so be cautious hereafter, or your name will come next time." A number of other papers used the "Paul Pry" phrase, which originated in a popular British play of 1823 in which a busybody character named Paul Pry snooped, spied, and offered admonishments and gossip to everyone.[19]

More surprising is evidence that much smaller towns than Philadelphia and Baltimore supported scandal papers too. Manchester, New Hampshire, grew quickly from a tiny village to a factory town of some 7,000 by the early 1840s. Such rapid growth perhaps made for an unsteady sense of community among the newcomers, both young mill workers from the countryside and entrepreneurial adults arriving to build up the town's commercial services. Sometime before 1842, a scurrilous paper called the *Owl* appeared, irregularly, to tattle on immoralities observed; and its spirit was regularized in fall 1842 by the *Manchester Gleaner*, which teetered between outraged, sincere-sounding moral reform and clear sexual titillation—it is nearly impossible to tell which theme intentionally predominates. Fornicators were lashed, sexual harassers were outed by mill girls, and the "wants" column was rich with sinful behaviors. The *Gleaner* lasted into 1845; its offices were trashed, its editors jailed, but through all it maintained a fierce upright stance on exposing the licentious.[20]

And finally Boston gained its own racy paper, the *Satirist*, launched in the fall of 1842, and variously titled the *Satirist & Punch*, the *Satirist and Blade*, and finally just the *Blade* in 1848. This set comes closest to

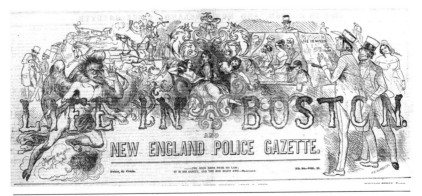

FIGURE 29. MASTHEAD OF THE *LIFE IN BOSTON AND NEW ENGLAND POLICE GAZETTE,* APRIL 6, 1850, FEATURING ASMODEUS, A FICTIONAL DEVIL WITH ORIGINS IN THE APOC-RYPHA, REFASHIONED IN NINETEENTH-CENTURY FICTION AND DRAMA AS A DEVIL/DANDY WHO COULD REVEAL URBAN SECRETS. COURTESY AMERICAN ANTIQUARIAN SOCIETY.

the New York flash papers: visits to brothels under the guise of exposing vice, a "wants" column of rich reportage. But missing is the competition with rival papers, and the boundary-pushing edge that such competition brought, which in New York contributed to the sense that the papers defined a fully rounded community. Boston's entry was a pale imitation of the New York originals.[21]

Another genre of midcentury publications displayed muted erotic elements, without the outrageous, sensational tone of the flash press. Publications like *Life in Boston* (1849–57), the *New York Scorpion* (1849), the *Weekly Whip* (1855), and the *Broadway Belle* (1855–58) included the sexualized writings of George Thompson; indeed, Thompson edited the latter two. *Life in Boston* offered a striking element, its masthead by the Boston delineator John H. Manning. He lived in New York in the early 1840s, drawing for a commercial firm that supplied images to the flash papers, especially the *Whip* and the *Rake*. In his Boston masthead, Manning offered dramatic scenes of male sporting life, with fast horses and buxom women, drunks in an open carriage, a policeman, a pickpocket, a warrant officer, and scenes in an opera box and a parlor where a gentleman read a titillating book to two reclining women. Looking at all of this was the devil-figure, Asmodeus, known in the nineteenth century as one who could take the roofs off houses to reveal the vices of city dwellers, a striking image for the sporting weekly itself and the complex enterprise of exposure, pleasure, and the pleasure of exposure.

These midcentury periodicals were filled with letters to the editor from various towns in the United States. Some included regular col-

FIGURE 30. GEORGE THOMPSON EDITED THE *WEEKLY WHIP* AND THE *BROADWAY BELLE* IN THE LATE 1850S. FROM *BROADWAY BELLE*, JAN. 22, 1855. COURTESY AMERICAN ANTIQUARIAN SOCIETY.

umns such as the *Broadway Belle*'s "Editor's Chit-Chat." Others, like the *Monthly Cosmopolite* (1849–50), the *Broadway Dandy* (1855), and the *Broadway Omnibus* (1858), covered topics which increasingly defined the sporting press and emerging "true crime" genres: gambling, theater, billiards, phrenology, suicide, adultery, indecent exposure, horse racing, "free and easies," prize fights, tales of seduction, domestic squabbles, Tombs incarcerations, firemen, balls, blackmailing, fraud, and even poetry. Advertisements offered cures for venereal disease, as well as marriage guides and "female medicines."[22]

The depiction of sex was different, however, for these later publications lacked the personalized, eroticized attacks of the flash press in the 1840s. Prostitution was a recurring topic, but, with the exception of certain George Thompson publications, it was usually portrayed as a perilous criminal activity. Commercial sex, for example, was to be avoided, "for disease, danger and death lurks upon every threshold, and you cannot cross them and escape contamination," charged the *Broadway Omnibus.* In 1850, the *Monthly Cosmopolite* complained:

> What is to be done with the thousands of unchaste females in our city, or with those promoters of vice and laughter to scorn who give them shelter and protection in palaces of pollution? . . . They are encircling us in our dwellings, drawing a cordon around us, and wherever we move we have the living picture of vice and immorality before us.

Similar articles feared the geographic spread of prostitution throughout the city, using language of loathing that defined the "woman of pleasure" as little more than "the abomination of her own sex." [23]

While sporting and crime publications eliminated or toned down their erotic content, more sexually oriented competitors did the same with political and social commentary. *Venus' Miscellany* (1856–57) illustrated this shift in obscene journalism. [24] Edited and published by George Ackerman (sometimes Akarman), *Venus' Miscellany* displayed a singular hedonist philosophy sans the republican and glamorized prostitution themes of the earlier flash press. [25] Bawdy jokes, short stories, vignettes, and letters promoted the "*pleasuriste*" or libertine lifestyle and subculture. The nonfictional coverage of brothel life and political critiques found in the flash press were replaced with fictional narratives depicting visits to elite houses of prostitution and grand balls resulting in the seduction of wealthy young teenage daughters. Women were recognized for their "perfect symmetry," "matchless form," and "bosoms boldly exposed," men for possessing genitalia "that would have done no dishonor to Priapus himself." Advertisements for sexual aides, abortionists, contraceptives, erotic publications, and other "rich, rare, and racy reading" were prominent in each issue. [26]

Venus' Miscellany and like publications reflected a dramatic shift in the printing subculture centered on sexuality: politically laced, literary forms of obscenity (or pornography) were supplanted by more visual and erotic ones. By no means was political commentary entirely eliminated. Mike Walsh's *Subterranean* and George Thompson's fiction, for example, employed erotic themes as vehicles for militant radical democrats to expose the perversity and corruption of American ruling class. And in some cases, Thompson's political critiques assumed more pornographic form after 1850. [27] Yet, when Thompson's novels were serialized in *Venus' Miscellany, Broadway Belle, Life in Boston* and the *Weekly Whip,* they were devoid of his republicanism. The serialized versions of *The Mysteries of*

DONNA INEZ—THE WANTON BATHER.

FIGURE 31. IMAGES LIKE "DONNA INEZ—THE WANTON BATHER" ON THE FRONT PAGE OF *VENUS'S MISCELLANY*, MAY 9, 1857, REFLECTED THE SHIFT TO MORE VISUAL FORMS OF OBSCENITY DEVOID OF POLITICAL COMMENTARY FOUND IN THE FLASH PRESS. COURTESY PRINCETON UNIVERSITY LIBRARY.

Bond Street and *The Amourous Adventures of Lola Montez* emphasized erotic male adventure without the political criticism found in the book versions.[28] Gone were the vivid, sensational, and often graphically realistic details of America's sexualized commercial landscape. Front-page correspondence describing the sexual adventures of flash newspaper readers from around the country was replaced by excerpts of romantic and sexual fiction. Simple titillation supplanted political outrage and radical critiques of privilege. Obscenity in the flash press served, at least in part, as a means to an end, a vehicle to express republican sympathies in the rhetoric and argot of the libertine. By contrast, obscenity for publishers like Ackerman was the end.[29]

III Although the trials of the flash press transformed the content of obscenity, they established legal precedents with great staying power. This became clear in the years after the Civil War when new laws and greater efforts at surveillance went into effect.

The flash press obscenity cases were part of an important tradition of court supervision of sexually explicit words and images in America. They established critical and important precedents, specifically criminalizing representations presumed to be sexually stimulating to the unattached, literate, urban young men partaking of New York City's sporting culture.

The New York courts' application of Starkie's text on the common law of obscenity cut an unusually deep groove in American legal practice. The jurisprudence that developed in the 1840s proved important when postwar legislation at the state and federal levels redefined obscenity, strengthened policing methods, and generated increasing numbers of indictments and convictions. The legislation itself is important, signaling an enhanced understanding that written statutes needed to govern criminal proceedings, something that George Wilkes emphasized in the 1840s.

In New York and some other states, laws were written that more systematically suppressed words about sex and applied obscenity to a greater range of materials. This was followed by the 1873 federal act for the "suppression of Trade in, and Circulation of, Obscene Literature and Articles of Immoral Use" best known as the Comstock Law. The 1873 federal statute gave the U.S. Postal Service broad and vague powers. It criminalized and established punishments of fines and imprisonment for sending through the mail six kinds of material: erotica; contraceptive medications or devices; contraceptive information; abortifacients; sexual implements (such as those used in masturbation); and advertisements for contraception, abortion, or sexual implements. A federal agent was charged with the power of arrest and the right of search and seizure. As the law was enforced, prosecutions and convictions included sellers of pamphlets and books on sex education, reform physiology, and sexual reform. Although contraceptive devices continued to be marketed and sold and abortions performed, words were carefully scrutinized and policed. Specifically targeted were radicals and free love exponents, such as D. M. Bennett, a post–Civil War maverick reformer and publisher of the free-thought weekly, the *Truth Seeker*. The Comstock Law fundamentally transformed the nature of the American sexual conversation for decades.

The precedents established in New York courts and the application of Starkie etched deeply into the rights of free speech and expression. In a key ruling on *U.S. v. Bennett* (1879), the New York appellate judge Samuel Blatchford wrote a landmark decision, upholding the actions of the lower court. Blatchford's ruling effectively established the constitutionality of the Comstock Law as it was applied in the federal courts in New York. In doing so, he confirmed existing court practices in New York state dealing with obscene libel and relying upon the common law tradition that reached back to the flash press trials of the early 1840s. Obscenity prosecution now rested upon three key common law assumptions and practices: the commission of an act was proof of intention; the denial of expert witnesses' testimony as to whether or not the matter was obscene; and the admission of excerpts as evidence, separated from the larger context of the work. Blatchford was later elevated to the federal Supreme Court in 1882. His judgment in *U.S. v. Bennett* governed obscenity for fifty years.[30]

From the beginning, however, the court's position was challenged. Early advocates for the defense returned to the concerns articulated by George Wilkes about the application of English common law in America. As time went on, opponents of censorship shifted the argument in ways that held great significance for American law. They added First Amendment rights of free expression, which, following the Civil War, were newly understood as protecting the rights of citizens against the state.

In the twentieth century, the U.S. Supreme Court revisited obscenity again and again. Over time, drawing on reinterpretation of the First Amendment, judges overturned many of the premises that determined obscenity rulings since the 1840s trials of the flash press. The new standards required a work to be judged in its entirety, not by an excerpt. Publishers were allowed to call expert witnesses for the defense. In ways that Wilkes valued, prosecution for sexual crimes increasingly focused on deeds rather than words. Finally, in line with Snelling's evocation of Swift and Byron, judges established that the potential cultural value of a work needed to be recognized; their understanding grew to protect material deemed to have any social importance. Although undertones of common law continue to haunt obscenity law, especially regarding images, Blackstone's and Starkie's interpretations of obscene libel were revised and rejected over time.[31]

Paths of history have many surprises and unexpected twists. In the years after 1843, as pale imitations of the flash papers appeared in towns and cities across the nation, the original New York publishers and editors went on to varied, interesting, and, in some cases, important lives. After their departures and the end of the *Flash, Whip,* and *Rake,* the republican libertinism that spurred them disappeared. Some periodicals occasionally used sexual scandal to oppose hypocrisy and privilege, but the virulent, caustic language found in the flash press waned with the 1840s.

By the 1850s, new highly eroticized publications emerged, shorn of politics. The legal struggles of the flash press publishers had a powerful, but hidden, impact. Initially they shaped the adjudication of the 1873 Comstock Law in New York courts and influenced the U.S. Supreme Court. Ultimately the arguments of the flash editors fed legal arguments opposing censorship. The protests of George Wilkes and William

Joseph Snelling in defense of the flash press were rejected in nineteenth-century jurisprudence, but by the late twentieth century, those same arguments were upheld in American courtrooms, and publishers today are free to print and sell almost all words. Seen from the perspective of the early twenty-first century, the editors of the flash press certainly have the last laugh.

PART II
FLASH PRESS EXCERPTS

These excerpts are reproduced here as they were printed in the flash papers. Typographical and spelling mistakes remain uncorrected, without the distracting use of [*sic*], so readers can achieve a fuller sense of the experience of reading the papers. Sections in italic indicate commentary by the authors of this book. Obscure terms and names are footnoted, insofar as possible. A rather large set of words designated prostitutes, so below is a glossary of euphemistic terms for such, many of which occur in these documents.

bawd.

courtesan (or often courtezan), derived from the class of women at a royal court used for the monarch's pleasure and not for reproduction.

Cyprian, derived from the island of Cyprus in the Mediterranean Sea, thought to be the location of the Temple of Aphrodite (also known as Venus), the goddess of love.

fair creatures.

frail, fair frail, or the frail sisterhood, marking prostitutes as morally weak women, unable to resist sexual temptation.

girl of the pavé, from the French and widely adopted in English to mean a girl of the street, a street walker.

harlot.

inmates.

lady of beauty.

lewd women.

lovers.

misguided girls.

nymphs.

procuress.

strumpet, a word from Chaucerian and Shakespearean English for an unchaste woman.

theatre-women.

trull.

unfortunate creatures.

wantons.

wretched girls.

|||||||||||||||||||||||||||||||||||||||||||||||||||||||||||||||||||||||||||||||||||||||||||||||||||||||||||||||

1 PURPOSES

|||||||||||||||||||||||||||||||||||||||||||||||||||||||||||||||||||||||||||||||||||||||||||||||||||||||||||||||

THE PURPOSE OF THE FLASH PRESS

From the *Whip*, October 15, 1842.

After George Wooldridge was convicted of obscene libel, his paper defended not only the convicted editor, but the right of journalists to cover and describe the world of commercial sex in New York, to "publish things as we find them."

REVIVAL OF THE WHIP.

Yes, kind and indulgent reader, revival is the word. The former editor of this paper has been indicted, tried, convicted, and imprisoned for conducting it in a truly moral and sedate course; we, too, shall endeavor to steer it in a moral path, and at the same time, having no fear before our eyes, speak boldly of men and matters as they shall present themselves. When we happen to see an elegant female promenading Broadway or any other way, we shall, if she pleases our fancy, endeavor to describe her figure and gay dress with all the power of love itself—not caring whether she is frail or fair, for that is not our business. At the balls, the season for which is nigh at hand, we shall notice all the beauties who grace the floor; not satisfied with this, we intend visiting all the first rate seraglios,[1] and with the pen of truth speak of things as we find them—draw out the lovely from their lurking places, and tell the world what flowers are "wasting their fragrance on the desert air." In fact, all shall find that we of the Whip publish things as we find them, not garbled, on account of the terrors of the law. Who and what I am you shall not know until I am ready to tell you, when you will find me a h-ll of a fellow; and what's the use of being a fellow unless you are a h-ll of a one? In a word, I hold in my hand the WHIP; the world is my plantation— mankind my slaves, and if they do not toll their hides shall feel my lash.

|||||||||||||||||||||||||||||||||||||||||||||||||||||||||||||||||||||||||||||||||||||||||||||||||||||||||||||||

2 LIBERTINISM

|||||||||||||||||||||||||||||||||||||||||||||||||||||||||||||||||||||||||||||||||||||||||||||||||||||||||||||||

IN DEFENSE OF THE FLASH PRESS

From the *Rake*, September 3, 1842.

The flash press editors vilified their more respectable competitors for failing to stand up for the public good. The excerpt below criticizes Brother Jonathan *and the* Sun *(specifically editor Moses Beach) for engaging in hypocrisy. The article also exemplifies the libertine philosophy and references to antiquity found in numerous flash press articles.*

THE CONSPIRACY AGAINST THE RAKE.

The savage and merciless attacks upon the conduct and principles of our paper, with which a portion of the press has teemed daily of late, are fast defeating the very object of their authors. To us they are utterly harmless provoking rather our pity and compassion, for the weakness and folly that characterize such manifestations of alarm, than resentment at the malice that prompted the hostility. Once or twice we have been put on the defensive, but enough has been said to place us in a proper attitude before the public. Already is its sympathy awakened in our behalf if we may judge from the communications which daily pour in upon us from every portion of the country, full of the most encouraging and cheering sentiments. Every additional invective that is hurled against us, every sentence pointed, as the writer no doubt fondly imagines, with a poison that must defeat our existence, but animates us with a new energy and wafts us more nearly to the haven of public approbation, to which our course is bent, while the voice of denunciation, hoarse with vituperation and abuse, is gradually and surely deafened by the plaudits that meet our ears on every side, form a right thinking and intelligent community. The unprecedented increase of our circulation is the rock upon which we lean, and firm in the position we have taken, we shall proceed on our way regardless of the senseless and stupid clamor that a few worthless and interested prints would raise against us. —Persecution ever fails to accomplish the purpose for which it is set on foot. Our faith is in the public; its judgment and decisions are never wrong. If our system is a false one—if the moral sense of mankind is shocked by its developements, either in principle or practice, it must fall—if, on the contrary, it finds favor in their eyes, it will be sustained. It is thus with all systems and with all religions. One is for a time in the ascendant; another springs up and finds its proselytes and has for a time its season; then another and another.

We are charged with misleading the minds of the youth. The fault is not with us; it is in the nature of man itself. The seeds of his intemperance are broadly scattered over its surface; pregnant with soft desires, they covet a genial growth and force themselves upward. Go to the mythology of the ancients, the religion that held possession of the world for so many ages. What is it but a tissue of intrigues and jealousies. The great occupation of their divinities seems to have been the gratification of their immortal lust. The saw the daughters of earth, that they were fair, and the great Thunderer himself did not hesitate to stoop from his high Olympus,[2] and throwing aside the dreadful bolt, cheat our terrestrial beauties into an embrace. Even the halls of heaven itself were not free from the pollution; and crim. cons.,[3] adulteries, lewdness, drunkenness, and other debaucheries, were as rife in the courts of Jove, as in our sinful world at this time. Themes like these have engaged the loftiest intellects, and have been sung in strains the most melodious and divine, that ever enraptured or soothed the ear; or ministered to the prurient impulses of our nature. And these are the productions which are put into our almost infant hands—with good cause—for what intellectual and accomplished or virtuous and pious parent would forbid to his child an acquaintance with those literary treasures with which their authors have enriched the store house of human learning.

We are told that we unlock the secret places of vice, and display to the fascinated and eager eye of passion the gorgeous embellishments and fatal temptations that are within. Reader, have you yet read the Tempter and the Tempted, just issued by the very respectable publisher of the Jonathan?[4] If not, we pray you to purchase it. Before you will have finished these pages you will find the heroine, a wedded wife, deep in the meshes of an adulterous web: and what it leads to God knows—no doubt to the usual results. Yet such are the papers that would oppose our advancement. Most worthy Editors!

We could retaliate if we pleased. Observe the course of the most violent of the crew that daily pours forth its tirade of abuse and calumny against our humble sheet—the Sun. From its commencement it has pursued a systematic course of assault on private character, and wherever the discerning eye of its Editor has perceived a momentary deviation in the morals of the otherwise innocent and virtuous, he has made his relentless sheet the instrument, whereby to compel the unfortunate offender to purchase immunity. Thus and by such means has it reached its present position. And Beach, boasts that he is rich. Yes, he is rich in the curses of his maddened victims in his recollections of the homes he has made desolate by his assassin hints rich in the catalogue of his violations of all honor and truth. Even yet his filthy sheet is daily deformed with the most licentious publications & finds its support in the largess of the empiric and the wages of the abortionist. His own movements are not hid from us. Our eye follows him into the luxurious haunts which his ingenuity has enabled him to purchase and reel in. We bid him beware.

DEFENDING PROSTITUTION

From the *Whip and Satirist of New-York and Brooklyn*, April 9, 1842.

The flash press spoke in multiple voices regarding commercial sex. Most controversial was their defense of prostitution. Flash press editors departed from contemporaries by openly defending prostitution as a necessary evil. To bolster such a defense, editors invoked Paris's century old system of regulation and downplayed the impact of venereal and other sexually transmitted diseases. Note their defense and description of heterosexuality as not only "natural," but pleasurable.

WHOREDOM IN NEW YORK.

There is an article on this subject in last Sunday's Times[5] which, though well intended and right in its general views, is incorrect in some of its details. These errors it is our present purpose to rectify. Imprimis,[6] it is headed "courtezanism." There is no such word in the English tongue; but we are not disposed to dwell upon inaccuracies of language. A newspaper editor has no time to pick his words.

"The courtezans of this city," says the Times, "are increasing at a fearful rate." Very true—so are thieves and burglars and the whole population. The supply always keeps pace with the demand. Where there is a market there will be goods. Witness the slave trade; which is brisker than ever, despite all efforts to suppress it. If there are more whores than formerly, it is only because there are more whoremasters. Geld these, and the evil will be radically cured. The course we have thus far pursued shews demonstratively that we are no friend to lewdness; but we do not think the cause of virtue can be promoted by falsehood or exaggeration. "Thousands," says our writer, "are laboring under diseases too disgusting to describe." "Vell, vot of it!" It is their own fault. The disease is perfectly understood and there are thousands of physicians to cure it. There is small reason for a Jeremiad[7] on this score. Those who suffer deserve no pity. If they will dance let them pay the fiddler. The Times reminds us of those who cry "Poor fellow!" when an attrocious malefactor is hanged.

"Every year the ranks of vice become more disgusting, forms are inoculated into our youth, and awful are the consequences. Parents mourn over the loss of their offspring, and grim death exults in his charnal halls over the headlong recklessness of our race."

Ochone! O wira sthrue![8] The world is coming to an end, sure enough. Why, Johnny Moore, what ails you? Do you think there shall be no more ginger and cayenne pepper? What's the use of crying for spilled milk?

What cannot be cured, must be endured. Fornication has been a pleasure ever since man and woman were created and will be till time is no more. You mistake the matter entirely. The disease it engenders are not at all dangerous; thanks to the improvement of medical science! Not ten percent of persons die of them in New York in a year. Ask doctor Vashay, to whose charge all the desperate cases are committed. Since Hunter's Red Drop[9] came into vogue the manufacture of noses has visibly declined—indeed, it is quite extinct. Yet you say that two thousand females and a thousand males die of venereal disease yearly! How the world is given to lying.

The Times estimates the number of prostitutes in New York at ten thousand. More power to your elbow, neighbor! Extend your experience, and you will find that there are treble that number. He says that the annual increase of their number is forty five percent. It is not so. The increase is in the exact ratio of the increase of the whole population. You say that "the imprudence of the parent is invariably visited on the offspring." Such is very seldom the case—in all our experience, and it has been pretty extensive, we have known but one instance.

The Times agrees with us that prostitution is a necessary evil, which cannot be repressed and therefore should be regulated. He proposes to license stews and, in a word, to introduce the police system of Paris; but he gives us no credit for having been the first paper to suggest the idea. We first proposed the measure, and before his article appeared we had procured the whole statistics and details of the French Sanitary Police, which we shall publish as soon as we have time to translate them.

The Times thinks that this system would "make courtezanism offensive to those who are sensually disposed." Not so—it would make it more respectable and, consequently more respected. There would be as many harlots as ever; but they would not be as much detested as they are; nor would they deserve to be so. The morals of the class would be raised. They would be an intermediate grade between the upper and lower classes of women; like the quadroon girls at New Orleans. There would be less street walking, less picking of pockets, less grossness and a great deal more safety. The whole tribe of brothel bullies would become extinct.

"We have given this ball the first kick." No; you have not. That honor belongs to us; but we forgive your presumption, because you know not what you say. Nay; more we thank you for your assistance and hope for its continuance; which, as you are a good man and entertain correct principles, we doubt not we shall have.

THE DANGERS OF LOVE

From the *Weekly Rake*, July 30, 1842.

*This short article celebrates the raptures of lovemaking, illustrated by an erotic litho-
graph of an ardent young couple with dress in disarray. Yet, young men are strongly
warned about the dangers of giving their hearts and affections to prostitutes. The article concludes with a puzzling sentence, perhaps disingenuous, about "putting down"
shameful sexual behaviors.*

AN AVOWAL OF LOVE.

" DON'T, LOVE—YOU'LL TAKE MY BREATH AWAY !"

FIGURE 32. "AN AVOWAL OF LOVE. 'DON'T, LOVE—YOU'LL TAKE MY BREATH AWAY.'"
THE "THRILLING SALUTE" OF "A KISS OF RAPTURE." *WEEKLY RAKE,* JULY 30, 1842.
COURTESY AMERICAN ANTIQUARIAN SOCIETY.

Our engraving should have represented a young couple just after they had
avowed their ardent affection for each other; but as he has given us something like a shingle with the picture engraved upon it with a jack-knife, we
trust you will imagine it and pardon us for presenting that as it was too late
to prepare another.

They are kissing, and it is a kiss of rapture which none but lovers know.
The prolonged thrilling salute which sends a feeling of joyous madness to
the brain and wraps the soul in an elysium of bliss.[10] Ah! what a moment is

that in which takes place an avowal of love, be it pure or illicit! The very life of the lover seems concentrated and ready to dissolve with joy or, leave the clay with disappointment and despair, according to the answer.

It must be rather amusing, though, to hear and witness the "first confession" of a bachelor of forty or its reception by a snuffy old maid, who has turned fifty; The prolonged kiss in this case must smack of barrenness and impotency. But when you come to behold the "first love" scene between a smooth chinned youth, and wily painted courtezan, then you will laugh and cry alternately at his folly a[nd] her treachery.

Yet, such things occur daily, and many a youth is drawn into a vortex of vice and dissipation which he can never again get rid of. To see a man place his heart in the keeping of a harlot is indeed a sorrowful sight. It must [be] terrible for a man to think that the only woman whom he loves on earth sells her body—hires it out for the use of any man who pays her her price—perhaps disposes of her charms to his bitterest enemy.

There are twenty thousand wantons in this city, each of whom boasts a man devoted entirely to her service, and who is termed a lover. These young men are generally good-hearted generous fellows, who by some uncontrollable circumstance have taken to this means of living, from which they are unable to escape.

God knows there is vice enough in this city, and if we take rather rough measure to put down the shameless proceedings hourly enacted does not the ends justify the means.

||||||||||||||||||||||||||||||||||||||||||||||||||||||||||||||||||||||||||||||||||||||||||||||||||||||||||||||||||||||||||||||||

3 BROTHEL LIFE

||||||||||||||||||||||||||||||||||||||||||||||||||||||||||||||||||||||||||||||||||||||||||||||||||||||||||||||||||||||||||||||||

THE PROSTITUTE AS A CELEBRITY

From *Dixon's Polyanthos*, June 6, 1841.

Julia Brown was among the most prosperous and well known madams in Gotham. Her Leonard Street brothel (no. 55) was adjacent to the National Theater, a reflection of the close connection between commercial sex and commercial entertainment in the antebellum era. Theaters frequently reserved the third tier for prostitutes and their potential clients. References to Brown as "Princess Julia" associate her with aristocratic decadence while her establishment is characterized as an elegant, refined, and magnificent "palace of love." The vivid description of Brown, combined with

FIGURE 33. THE NATIONAL THEATER, ON THE CORNER OF CHURCH AND LEONARD STREETS, BACKED UP TO JULIA BROWN'S BROTHEL. A MAJOR THEATER FIRE IN 1841 SPREAD TO HER PREMISES, KILLING AN INMATE AND GIVING DIXON AN EXCUSE TO FEATURE THE BROTHEL AS NEWSWORTHY. FROM *VALENTINE'S MANUAL* (1917).

a catalogue of her resident prostitutes, offers male readers a vicarious erotic adventure. Absent is the moral condemnation that typified most journalistic accounts.

DESTRUCTION OF THE NATIONAL THEATRE

Conflagration of Miss Julia Brown's House
AND DEATH OF A YOUNG WOMAN
With a full description of
PRINCESS JULIA'S PALACE OF LOVE.

Among the many buildings which delight the eye of the stranger, and make the New Yorker proud of his native city, is the elegant edifice, recently erected, next to the National Theatre in Leonard-street, and occupied by the Princess Julia, a lady of renown, whom we have several times had the honor to mention. This building is four stories high, made of brick and of the most fashionable structure. The house is built after the pattern of the Queen's mother, the Duchess of Kent. You enter the building by a magnificent entrance, an iron portico with seven steps; and the splendour of the interior does not disappoint the expectations which have been raised by a view of the outside.

On the first floor, the two parlours, seventy feet long, are finished in a style of Oriental magnificence—the elegant ottomans—the large and splendid mirrors,—the turkish carpets, imported from Europe—the drapery—the rich curtains—the ornaments of the mantel piece—every thing, in short, presents a scene which shows the most rich and exquisite taste in the fair lady of the domain, and the possession of a fortune to correspond with her desires. At the end of the parlour is the boudoir of the Princess. This apartment is furnished in a style of luxuriant elegance not surpassed by any establishment in the country. Feminine tastefulness, and exquisite delicacy, the tact and refinement of the sex are here impersonated in the most attractive form. The boudoir is mirrored all round and resembles one of those splendid grottos of nature in which all the glittering gems of the earth seem to be cemented together, and the inmate is constantly dazzled with a flood of glory. Yet, amid all this beauty stands the Princess of the mansion, more lovely than all, and, dazzling in the splendour of her charms, the rarest specimen of art and nature combined. As nearly as it could be done in this country the Princess' appartment is made to resemble that of Queen Victoria. The Princess, herself, is one of the most rare specimens of female grace and exquisite loveliness—the raven curls—the full orbed eyes, in which love seems to have stationed all his archers, who never draw bows in vain—the elastic step—the glorious bust—all proclaim her to be a woman born to tread on hearts and to reign over the vanquished and sighing victims of irrepressible tenderness. We know of no one to whom the princess could be more appropriately compared than to Flora Me Ivon, in spirit and feeling, and to the fair Jewess—the heroine in Ivanhoe—in feature complexion and form. Julia was one of the *cher ami* of ...., and after he parted from her it was like Napoleon parting from Josephine, his lowering fortunes followed hard upon—as the flames of Moscow lighted the defeated emperor to the isle of Elba. When Rathbone[11] commenced his fortunes he had the counsels of this fair one, when his fortune deserted him she had been sometime absent.

After she left ...., she came to New York, and here she became the "observed of all observers," the rare jewel, the pearl of price, the much sought and more valued, when found. Such was the Princess. Nor should we stop here—her charity is well known, as, indeed, how can it be otherwise than that those who dwell in love must be charitable? When the divine Fanny presented the manager of the B. H. monument with $500,[12] Julia was not behind her fair prototype, but presented the munificent sum of $200, with the very shrewd suggestion that now she and Fanny had taken hold of the stones the monument must rise. 'Twas nobly done and nobly said—like the maidens of Rome or Sparta—aye there were women in those pristine days who could cover monuments, and other elevated works with the aegis of their protection. It is estimated that the income of Julia's establishment, this pride of our city, is no less than $200 per night, for [vi]ands and other delicious luxuries. The Princess Julia is already accused of being worth from 80,000 to 100,000 dollars, nor is she parsimonious of her money; for she rents no less than three pews in different churches of this city—holds season tickets to at least two theatres, and gives yearly liberal annuities to the Bible and Tract Societies; and is what we may call, in every sense of the word, a glorious woman.

On ascending the second story, up the splendid steps, you fall in, with appartment, No. 1. This room is occupied by Lady Ellen, and a glorious lady she is, with the dark flashing orbs, and full of feeling—so full of intellect that one might stand and gaze, and gaze, and feast the eye, brain, and heart, for ever upon such a banquet of exquisite loveliness. Her beauty and her intellect captivated one of the greatest wits of the age. This fair form of nature's best and most classic chisseling, much reminds us of the Lady of the Lake, the wild and splendid daughter of the Douglas, and well we warn that if this modern Ellen could with oar and skiff become the presiding nymph of some romantic lake, she would touch even sterner hearts than that of the wandering knight of Snowden!

The splendid bed upon which she reposes is more like the nuptial couch of our first parents in Eden than like the beds of ordinary plodders of this world. A fine picture of Ovid hangs at the head of the bed, and Byron's at the foot; while a beautiful picture of Doctor Hawkes[13] decorates the right side of it, and on the left hangs the beautiful Cleopatra. On the mantle are neat ornaments, as coral shells, jewels, and fancy boxes. The book case composed of beautifully carved rose wood, contains the choicest volumes, among which are to found the works of Lord Byron, elegantly bound, and all the classic romances of the day, with the annual report of the Visiting Committee of the Female Moral Reform Society.[14]

No. 2 is occupied by the lovely Mary_who has been very aptly compared to the renowned Mary Queen of Scots. This room is splendidly furnished, yet in the most chaste and beautiful manner. Everything about it is in keeping with Eve's fairest daughter. Her complexion is of the finest and purest, her hair is of the most approved auburn, and her eyes are of the clearest and brightest hue. She has been a traveller and seen much of the world, having visited Europe in company with a gentleman who was anxious to take up his quarters with Hon. Sam. Swarthout.[15] The walls of this fair nymph are adorned with the queen of dance. Ellssler hanging on the head of the bed and Taglioni at the foot, while Count Reichstad is on the right and the Marquis of Waterford on the left, over the mantle is a splendid full length portrait of Charles Kemble, and one of Arbaces.[16] It would be no flattery to say that a prince might be proud to exhibit so fair a specimen of beauty in the Courts of Europe and call her his own.

No. 3 is decorated in a splendid manner as a tea and card room, where they hold their public soirees.

No. 4 is occupied by the Princess Lady of Honor, one of those fine Grecian forms that prepossesses one in her favor, in the moment that he sees her. Free and fragrant as an open rose, she bewitches the heart.

No. 5 is occupied by Alice_, a *facsimile* of Alice Grey, with her dark brown hair braided over a neck of spotless white; while her eyes beam with intelligence and flash with delight.

No. 6 is a maiden, shrewd and artful, who will never be monopolized by any one individual, but looks upon the whole sex with eyes of affection her mighty heart hath place for them all.

When you ascend the third flight, you fall in with some ten or twelve elegantly adorned rooms, filled with sylphs, Hebes and every description of beauties, like the third heaven of Mahomet. There is the place for epicures, to repose after the arduous toils and duties of Church and State, and lay their weary heads upon a downy bosom which deeply feel for all the sorrows to which our poor, unfortunate sex are doomed.

This is truly an establishment of the most refined pleasure, where the path of human life is strewed with roses, and the evil that flesh is held to is so well embellished that is seems as if virtue shook hands with vice, and compromised matters lest so splendid and glorious an establishment should fall through and be lost to the fashionable world.

THE PROSTITUTE AS MUSE

From the *Whip*, August 6, 1842.

Prostitutes (coded "frail") were the occasional subject of poetry in the flash press. The article below not only provides a titillating poem and lithograph, but offers a vivid, detailed description of the subculture of prostitution. The Whip *editors argue that "little is known" about the social structure of commercial sex. They point out that prostitution is riddled with class differences ("degrees") among the women, including*

SKETCHES OF CHARACTERS---NO 33.

THE FRAIL FAIR.

" This Cream is rich—Pray, sir, will you have a taste?"

FIGURE 34. "SKETCHES OF CHARACTERS—NO. 33.: THE FRAIL FAIR. 'THIS CREAM IS
RICH—PRAY, SIR, WILL YOU HAVE A TASTE?'" *WHIP*, AUG. 6, 1842. COURTESY
AMERICAN ANTIQUARIAN SOCIETY.

*those who solicit in theaters. Moral reform groups supporting Magdalen asylums and
the Society for the Suppression of Juvenile Prostitution are satirized.*

THE FRAIL FAIR:

Lady of beauty, frail yet fair,
Devoted to the shrine of folly,
Though decked in jewels rich and rare,
Thy life will close in melancholy.

"Good Mr. WHIP, pray hold your tongue,
And never mind my latter end;

I'm now both beautiful and young,
And just the girl to get a friend."

Man of the phiz[17] so dissipated,
'Tis such as you who are to blame;
That woman, when by wine elated,
Will on her sex bring scorn and shame.

"Hold, WHIP, your mortal bantering cease,
And turn your eagle eye so knowing,
To other "Breeches" of the "piece" [18]
Committed by the acting BLOWEN."

It has been said that there are degrees in all things; why not then in female prostitution? Indeed there are more degrees in that peculiar description of profligacy than in any other; but the public are not acquainted with the subject—little is known, even by the best informed persons of the day, of the degrees or quantity of misery under the weight of which their fellow-creatures are suffering. Some moral philosophers look upon the pallid though once lovely face of a street prostitute, and sigh, groan, or exclaim, "Poor thing! she *has been* pretty—what a pity to see a nice girl like her about the streets!" All this they imagine evinces their amiability, and extols their value in the eyes of their friends. Moreover, they, by this maudlin description of unaiding sympathy, obtain the credit of being kind hearted and charitable persons. But depend upon it these indirect self trumpeters are of all others the most useless set of beings to society. They infect others with their cant, and lead people to follow their example by administering for every ill a strong dose of pity without a single grain of relief.

But there are others who, possessing without professing the true spirit of Christian charity, are always up and stirring in the cause of philanthropy. Amongst the premiers of this class of well disposed persons we may notice those who have devoted their money and exertions to the support of institutions upon the Magdalen[19] principle, for the purpose of affording an asylum to the wretched and misguided girls who, in the very flower of their youth, have been led into a life of profligacy by the specious and seductive arts of man. It is matter of regret, that while America is, as a country, rich in charitable institutions, such as free-schools, hospitals, almshouses, &c. &c., its number of asylums for penitent prostitutes is comparatively few— and this too in an age when that destructive description of vice is daily, nay hourly, on the increase. The Society for the Suppression of Juvenile

Prostitution, so often made honorable mention of in our pages, has done much to abrogate that particular description of vice, by instituting prosecutions against those wretches who live upon its wages, but as we have some most interesting information to lay before our readers in connection with the late prosecution at the instance of that society, in our next, we shall defer further observation upon its merits till then.

We will now proceed to offer some remarks upon the subject illustrated, viz., the courtezan of fashion. Our readers will perceive that she is seated in the saloon of one of our theatres, apparently listening to the conversation, or, rather, small-talk of the downey-looking *roué* before her. The women who usually frequent the theatres may be said to be of the second class of courtezan, inasmuch as they are looked down upon by the first rate women who ride about in the carriage of rich protectors. Then the theatre-women think themselves degraded by comparison with those who do the excessively swellish on the *pavé*.[20] The dashing Cyprian who treads the pavement of Broadway by day, scorns an alliance, in thought or name, with those who do the same thing at night: and the well dressed evening street-harlot looks even with pitiable contempt upon the ragged, low-life creatures who wander the street for the same purpose as herself, but who, as their seedy attire proclaims, favored by the blind goddess. Thus, who shall say there are not degrees in public prostitution?

The leading characteristics of the theatre courtezan may be said to be black satin and rouge; they are very expensive dressers, and wear a profusion of jewellery when in luck—when out of luck the trinkets leave them one by one, until finally they all disappear. When however, fortune smiles again, out they come from my uncle's, sparkling in all their former glory.

We do not study to wound the feelings of these truly unfortunate creatures, nor would we countenance any act of oppression towards them while they conduct themselves with propriety, and dress according to the dictates of the dictates of decency. We conceive that, in this country as well as all others, they must, to some extent, be tolerated; yet we protest against the many indecent displays often witnessed in our patent[21] and minor theatres. Such places were never intended or designed as a rendezvous for half-naked women, nor as a rendezvous for half-naked men, nor as a regular promenade for unblushing prostitutes. The courtezans who nightly frequent the theaters should have the common decency to attire themselves decorously; it is the least they can do when permitted to mingle with respectable society.

PROSTITUTES AND HIGH SOCIETY

From the *Whip*, January 14, 1843.

Julia Brown and other prominent madams sponsored balls to entertain and attract clients. The flash press coverage of these events emphasized the economic exclusivity and visible wealth of patrons and prostitutes alike. The female residents in Brown's brothel not only possess beautiful bodies ("exquisite forms") but also considerable amounts of disposable income as reflected in their highly fashionable wardrobes.

THE PRINCESS JULIA'S BALL.

This magnificent affair, which for weeks has been the talk of the town, and which has been a rich harvest for mantue-makers,[22] tailors and costumers, came off as announced, on Tuesday evening last; and if it was expected to have been the most splendid affair that for years has been witnessed, there was no disappointment, for it was so.

The arrangements far surpassed anything our eyes ever beheld. The splendid Saloons lighted up by two superb chandileers reminded us of the Enchanted Halls told of in the Arabian Nights,[23] and they lost no charm from the crowd of lovely females who thronged them. We are inadequate to the task of describing the rich and massive furniture with which the rooms were lined. But to give our readers a faint idea we will attempt a description.

THE FRONT SALOON,

The furniture of which is gild, and composition instead of walnut or mahogany, and richly covered and lined with royal purple velvet. The principal chair is one of the pair used at the late National Theatre while under the management of Wallack and which was purchased by the Princess at the sale of his effects.[24] It is now styled the forfeit chair on account of the gent who occupies it is responsible for a bottle of champaigne which is handed to him while seated in it, and in return he kisses the pretty nymphs who are seated on his right and left.

THE BACK, OR MAIN SALOON

Is of still larger dimensions, and furnished after the manner of the principal parlours of our aristocracy. A piano of rosewood is also in this room which is ever discoursing most exquisite music from the hands of some one of her lady boarders, all of whom are proficient on that instrument.—This room

SKETCHES OF CHARACTERS---NO 52.

GRAND BALL AT MRS. SWEET'S IN CHURCH STREET.

FIGURE 35. "SKETCHES OF CHARACTERS—NO. 52.: GRAND BALL AT MRS. SWEET'S IN CHURCH STREET." A PROSTITUTES' BALL IN A BROTHEL PARLOR. *WHIP*, DEC. 31, 1842. COURTESY AMERICAN ANTIQUARIAN SOCIETY.

opens into the other through folding doors, which, when thrown open, are amply large enough to dance four quadrilles.[25]

"Hark what music strikes mine ear?"

'Tis the splendid band lightly touching their instruments previous to sending forth those delightful strains which enchanted all with their melody.

The roll of carriages are now heard—the bell sounds, and servants in the Princess's livery are bowing some fair creatures in—they pass to the ladies dressing room. We perched ourself in the chandelier where we could recognise all that entered. All is now ready and the ball goes on.

If there are moments when men feel as though beings of a happier sphere—as though the stars, that have caused them to wonder where space ends or where begins, have, like Apollyon[26] fallen from their high estate, among them, it is when among a throng of beautiful, though alas! frail, outcast females. God! God! The lustre of the eyes—is heightened to a glassy stare by the *rouge* on the otherwise pallid, care worn cheeks—the laugh, forced while grief springing from minds diseased is gnawing at the heart, sounds horrid and unnatural; but all! all! this—short sighted mortal that we are—was forgotten while the females whom we mention below were whirling with their gallants in the voluptuous waltz, the fascinating cotillion, the simple pleasing Cheat, and graceful Spanish dance. Amid all this, with choice snatches of the Bayadere, Diavelo, Massaniello, Semiramide, Tancredi,[27] Sich a gittin upstairs, and (in theatrical parlance) other "well known favorites," floating through the air, we noted down the following facts with our remarks attached:

The Princess Julia was habited in a red satin robe, trimmed neatly with silver flowers. Her brilliant complexion was admirably set off with a superb and *uniqe* Victoria hed-dress above and about which her dark hair appeared in charming profusion.

Ellen Thompson, thanks to the heavy purse of some profligate fool, changed her dress during the night. She first astonished us with an embroidered pink silk gown, handsomely trimmed, and arranged magnificently about her majestic Juno-like form. The second entree was as tasty, and as fanciful—a white watered silk, trimmed with down as soft and white as the splendid skin of the wearer.—Pass on, Empress of Harry's affections, till we note down

Rosina Jennings.—This female blazed away in a rich white satin gown, with blonde trimmings. A portion was looped up with a large rose, forming a rich and classic drapery.

Mary Walker was introduced in crimson, embroidered silk. Praxitiles never chiselled a more exquisite form, and Canova would have died in the vain endeavour to mould a bust like her own.[28]

Elizabeth Perry looked superb in a brown figured satin dress. Let us get out of the range of the beams of her elegant eyes—"those lovely eyes," as Mrs. Timm sings in the "Loves of the Angels."

Elvira Mills was attired in plain brown satin.—Her wit kept a host at her apron strings the whole evening.

Elizabeth Paulding robed herself in a gown of pale red satin. Something must have happened to this fair creature. Melancholy and sorrowful was she!

Sarah Adams, brown satin trim with down. The contrast was delightful.

Amanda Sparks dazzled us with her sparkling appearance. Her dress was magnificently embroidered, and her fairy-like feet were in a pair of spotty white satin slippers. When we pick a partner we invariably look at her feet!

Eliza Davenport.—This lady looked like a second Venus de Medicis,[29] in a loose flowing robe of velvet. Her conversational powers were put forth to please, and she succeeded.

Frances Lewis.—Her dress was of a hue facetiously termed by a gentleman present, quaker color. She is a woman of the Siddons style—tall, noble looking, commanding.[30]

Emma Place.—Her graceful figure of genuine classic mould was displayed to advantage in yellow sattin trimmed with deep costly blonde lace. Her voice is as musical as the song of a cherub, and her movements are particularly pleasing.

Mrs. Tucker of indicted notoriety won little admiration, though she had powerful *aides* in her blue satins, lace trimmings, and frizzled locks.—Take our advice old lady *a la* Hamlet—

"Go to a nunnery. Go!"

Henrietta Lancaster was also attired in a blue satin gown. Emblematic of her heart—*true blue.*

Louisa Roberts' dress was rather of the *fancy* cast; viz:—a black spencer, (we believe that is correct, though we might have called it a bodice,)[31] and cherry-colored skirt, (guess we seen the same "a long time ago" at a ball in Baltimore,) horribly defaced by black lace trimmings. Her head put us in mind of the snake-locks of Medusa.[32]

Sarah Wright of Thomas street was robed in virgin (?) white. Tom L. Nichols *was not* with her.[33] But we must "hold up," and conclude with one or two

REMARKS.—The Belvidere wore a set of diamonds presented to her by a southern gentleman, which cost him the nice little sum of $1500. She cannot receive aid from artificirls! her beauty is of a style that needs no decoration. The supper was *recherché*,[34] glarious! unparalled! and this is all the space we can devote to this elegant, important, exciting affair.

THE LIFE OF A PROSTITUTE

From the *Sunday Flash*, October 17, 1841.

A frequent feature in the flash press was the prostitute profile. Such narratives followed predictable and repeated tropes—a youthful innocent victimized by male lust and seduction, ultimately resulting in social exile and physical removal to a brothel. Titillation heavily salted the exposé; the profiles provided thrilling accounts of New York's brothel subculture. This particular example of a known prostitute formed part of the obscenity charge against the Sunday Flash *that sent its editors into court and* William Snelling *to jail. George Wooldridge testified in court that Amanda Green herself provided the information.*

LIVES OF THE NYMPHS, NO. 11.

AMANDA GREEN

This celebrated nymph was born in this city, though what particular street lane, or alley, or what house in such street, lane or alley, had the honor of producing her, we cannot pretend to say. She was born somewhere in the North side of town, her mother was a mantua maker,[35] and through industry and a good run of custom, pretty well to do is the world. At the age of six, Amanda was sent to school and achieved that invaluable accomplishment possessed by so few cyprians in this city, of being able to read. In due time, she also learned to write and cypher, and having now gained the *ne plus ultra* of her literary hopes, she left school and assisted her mother in her business. By and by, she grew up, and right pretty did she grow too and many a grocer's clerk and amorous shop boy, would find his mouth water and his heart beat as she went about the neighborhood on errands, and many a liquorish old goat and salacious young one, would wear out his ineffectual leather in following her about when business drew her far from home. But Amanda had not yet felt the throb of passion in a high degree, or if she had, had the discretion to master it, for the only answers which she returned to these unlawful solicitations were "Git along you sassy good for nothin feller, I can find my way home by myself," and so she battled off the annoyance.

One evening, a dress had been finished for a lady in Hudson Street and Amanda was to take it home. It was snowing at the time, and the distance was great, yet the dress must be carried. Unwillingly our heroine set out, performed her errand and on her return home, was about crossing Hudson Street when the jingle of a fast approaching sleigh warned her to stand back. The person driving, seeing a pretty female on the road, stopped the sleigh and apologizing for endangering her safety begged her to allow him to drive her home as a recompense. This Amanda refused and was about shipping to the other side, when the gentleman sprang out, clasped her in his arms, lifted her in, whistled to his horse and the next moment was flying along like mad; her complaints drowned by the clatter of the bells, and pursuit rendered fruitless by the speed at which they dashed over the ground. Giving his horse its head, the kidnapper took no notice of his course and only appeared anxious to convince Amanda of his kind intentions toward her; and to that end clasped her again and again in his arms and pressed upon her unwilling (so says Amanda) lips, a thousand kisses. After the proper quantum of struggling and crying, she became subdued and reposed unresistingly in his arms—perhaps she found a comfort in his bear's skin coat, for to say the truth the night was very cold.

At length, the horse, who appeared to understand his part as well as his master dashed up a long avenue and stopped at the gate of a very neat chateau, which from a ruddy light that shone through the windows, promised comfortable refuge from the storm. Lifting her in his arms like a child, though Amanda was by no means a chicken, the stalwart stranger bore her into a handsomely furnished room, where a most cheerful hickory fire was blazing high up in the chimney. Setting her down near it in a luxurious chair, he relieved her of her snow burdened bonnett and shawl, and leaving the room a moment, returned with his outer garments also cast off. Finding herself housed in a strange place, with no prospect of getting home, another fit of crying came on, but this the assiduous stranger, whom we shall now call Chambers, silenced and persuaded her to drink a glass of hot negus,[36] which was just then brought in the room by a stunted black waiter of about three feet high, who was at the same time one of the ugliest specimens of dingy humanity that Amanda had ever befeld. A hot and sumptuous supger followed this, and exhilerated by the share of a bottle of champaigne, she submitted without further opposition to his advances and toward the last returned them with interest. The sequel can be easily seen. At the crowing of the cock she was no more a maid. The next morning Amanda felt no inclination to return home and in accordance with her own and her lover's feelings, she resolved to abide with him for a time.

Far and near, and high and low, was she sought after, but no tidings heard, and at the end of a month, she was accounted by her friends as dead, and no further search made for her. Amanda remained at the Chateau some three months, when she discovered by a letter that Chambers was unfaithful to her, and sick at heart at the depravity of the man who owed her constancy, if nothing else, she left his establishment, returned to her mother, told her story and asked forgiveness. The softhearted parent, who looked upon her child as one arisen from the grave, forgave her at once and with a warning to stead her for the future, took her to her bosom.

For six months did Amanda lead a most exemplary life; but alas, who can control their fate! at the end of that time she fell in with a young German, whose profession it was to tune piano fortes, and soon fell a victim to his seductive arts. The affair was at length discovered by the mother herself, who caught the parties one evening, in *flagrante delicto*[37] in an attic, but enough, the contemplation of their sin, is too dreadful to dwell upon. Mrs. Green certainly thought it too vile for toleration and Amanda and her paramour, were *vi et armis*,[38] turned out of doors.

No resource was left her but open prostitution, and she accordingly took to that degraded calling, has followed it two years and now remains in it, another unhappy victim sacrificed at the altar of man's brutal passions. May those who have not yet sinned, take warning by her example. In person, Amanda Green is tall, very tall; her form is full, her complexion clear, and altogether she is very handsome. She resides at Mrs. Shannon's, No. 74 West Broadway.

By dint of long and patient investigation, we have at length gathered all the necessary particulars in the course of a harlot who assumes the title of the Countess de Valcour, and shall very shortly give them to our readers. We intend to cut down these strumpet noblesse. Next in order will follow Sophy Austin, Julia Brown, Mrs. Lewis, C_r's woman, &c. &c.

THE ATTRACTIONS OF PROSTITUTION

From the *True Flash*, December 4, 1841.

In October, 1841, William Snelling, George Wilkes, and George Wooldridge ended their shared editorship of their initial flash paper. Wooldridge not only testified against his former colleagues, but went off on his own and published his own weeklies, first the True Flash, *then the* Whip *and the* Libertine. *The profiles of prostitutes found in his new publications presented positive and erotic portrayals of commercial sex and the brothel world. Amanda Thompson, for example, is singled out for her respectability, fashionable wardrobe, and physical beauty.*

LIVES OF THE NYMPHS.

AMANDA B. THOMPSON AND HER ATTACHE

Our artist has engraved a most beautiful and exact likeness of this lady. Among the gay sisters of our city, this is without doubt the most remarkable and if respectability belongs to such a peculiar profession as that which she follows, she may be called respectable. Amanda is extremely beautiful with tresses black as get [jet], which she wears in the highest style of fashion, and eyes that might challenge comparison with the brightest things of earth.

LIVES OF THE NYMPHS.

AMANDA. B. THOMPSON AND HER ATTACHE.

FIGURE 36. "LIVES OF THE NYMPHS.: AMANDA B. THOMPSON AND HER ATTACHE." THE
PROSTITUTE THOMPSON IS DEPICTED WITH A MALE ATTENDANT, EITHER A CLIENT OR HER
LATEST "FANCY MAN." *TRUE FLASH,* DEC. 4 AND 5, 1841. COURTESY AMERICAN
ANTIQUARIAN SOCIETY.

A figure magnificent beyond description, a bust that defies the imitation
of the sculptor, and a smile sweet beyond expression, are but a few among
the many charms she possesses. She was born a_of parents in respectable circumstances and received the rudiments of a most excellent education. She was the belle of her native town and when at length the buds of
youthful promise burst into womanhood, she did not want admirers who
did her homage as their queen of beauty. But religion reigned supreme for
a young clergyman walked over the course and imprinted his image on
her too susceptible heart. At first a purely platonic affection, and then the
warmer feeling of love, until at length on a beautiful moonlight night after
mutual confessions of constancy till death, they fled together. Hours and
days, nay, months passed off, until one unlucky moment when a quarrel
ensued

> Alas how light a cause may move
> Dissension between hearts that love
> Hearts that the world in vain has tried
> And sorrow but more closely tried

That stood the storm when waves were rough
Yet in a sunny hour fall off
Like ships that have gone down at sea
When Heaven was all tranquility

When young Buonapart[39] visited this country, he became accidentally acquainted with Amanda and a second and severe affection sprang up which was not altogether of the Platonic order. Under his protection, and travelling with him, she was introduced to some of the first society in the country and wherever she went her beauty was the theme of boundless admiration. But, "hours will come to part," and once more she was left on her own resources. Other lovers followed scarcely less favored. Amanda now keeps a house in 474 Broome st where her arrangements are upon a gorgeous scale.—Scarcely any of the palaces of beauty set out in magnificence as the temples of licentiousness can bear a comparison with hers. She still retains all the beauty of her earlier years, and that fascination which once made her so distinguished.

SEXUAL GEOGRAPHY

From the *Whip*, October 15, 1842.

Flash press articles presented frequent and favorable tours of New York's sexual geography. Here the writer, who has just replaced the jailed George Wooldridge as editor of the Whip, *describes the comings and goings of a sporting man as he peruses the city's licentious offerings. He moves from saloons to streets to brothels, identifying well-known figures and institutions throughout. The article also continues the* Whip's *campaign against the prominent brothel madam Adeline Miller.*

OUR FIRST WALK ABOUT TOWN.

For the first time since we put on out new cap of editorialship we made up our minds to look into one or two *crack* shops[40] situated below Canal street. We smacked our lips over a brandy toddy at Thurston's, a Cockney, and withal a very clever fellow to all appearances, and who is blessed with a very pretty wife, who may always be found waiting upon her customers, with a sweet smile of welcome. We cast our eyes around the bar room and espied an acquaintance in the person of G. Lansing, who was enjoying himself smoking a segar and sipping beer with all the *sang froid* of a man about town. In a corner we saw W. Lewis, who is a "lover" to a black looking wanton, well known about town as Buffalo Jule. How this man lives we do not know, and how he intends to live is more than we can suppose, for it's well known that he does not even know himself. Who is that in yonder corner? a lawyer; well, as we dont like the profession he belongs to we shall leave him, and take up the boss baker, a pretty nice sort of a chap. We asked for a light and he handed us a segar. We bid the charming hostess good night, with a promise to call again and take another glance at her customers. In the street we saw a young man who works in our office in deep conversation with a frail one; we think he had better go and have his locks trimmed. Crossed to a confectioner's shop kept by a fine, black whiskered fellow, called French Henry: purchased an apple, and while in the act of paying for it, saw a devilish fine eye and set of teeth pass us and enter a back room; followed suit of course, expecting by so doing to pick up a few items, which the sequel will prove to be the case. On entering the room we found the lady and ourselves to be the only occupants; claimed an acquaintance, and was in the act of pressing her lips when a big blustering looking chap entered but again retired. She said she knew him well; had been bilked by him. From what she said of him we were led to believe that he was considerable of a *roué*; called him Riley. But mind, said she not *Peter* but the 'tatoe man of Fulton market. We liked his looks and the first good chance we have will drink a punch with him at Palmo's,[41] but at his expense. The lady, whose name for the present we shall keep dark, on account of future intentions, now called for a gin lemonade, for which we pointed, and would no doubt have called for and finished a few bumpers more had not limping George Gale and a black muzzled fellow entered. Their presence made the time pass dull and heavy, for not a single word escaped their lips save oaths and imprecations. We could not stand it so stepped out, bid our fair one good night, and sloped.[42] We next directed our steps to the house of the Duchess de Berri.[43] How or where she procured that high sounding title is to us a mystery. Found the house—rang the bell—and immediately heard a voice issuing from an iron blind asking the usual question of who's there?

"A friend."

"Indeed; why that's nothing. Who are you?"

"Well, in fact, madam, a stranger, entirely alone."

This seemed to be sufficient, for she immediately unbolted the door, and I for the first time walked into the palace of the Duchess de Berri alias Moll Cisco of Anthony street. We took a hurried glance at the smiling houris[44] that were seated around, partook of a glass of champaigne from another gent's bottle, bade all good evening with a polite invitation to call again. Wishing to take a few notes of what I had just seen, and requiring a light for that purpose, I went across the street into a bar room, kept, as I discovered, by a sporting cove[45] called Charley Locke, completed our purpose; happened to meet Johnson, the keeper of a livery stable, whom we had bilked out of many a ride. Crossed the street again to a three story brick house, directly in front of the Public School; without much difficulty we were admitted by a very pretty girl, and by her ushered into the back parlor where sat an old woman in deep but silent conversation with a small, slim fellow, dressed in black, and of a very pale countenance. He soon rose to depart, and we looked all sorts of colors when we heard him say, "Good night, Mrs. Miller," and in an instant we became conscious of being in the presence of that she devil who had been so severely castigated in the columns of the saucy paper which I was now to carry through. In a few seconds, however, we regained our confidence, and determined on cross examining the harridan[46] as to how she felt in regard to unjust incarceration of George Wooldridge:

"Well, madam, I perceive by the public papers that the editor of the [W]hip has received his just reward."

"He has, thank heaven," said she, "and I am very glad of it; indeed it was principally through my means he was indicted; it cost me considerable but I was determined. He came and offered me a thousand dollars to stop, but I told him that any sum would not bribe me."

"Well, I see he's at you again in last week's publication."

"Yes, I understand he had it done; but I can easily buy it off now; at one time I would have given him five hundred dollars to cease his attacks on me, but the villain said he would not for five thousand; he is poor now, and no doubt would take less."

"No, he is not poor, for I know one man he made pay $500 black mail; on the contrary I rather think he's rich, for he offered to pay a fine of a thousand dollars to the court, but they would not take it."

"Indeed; why then he is rich."

"Does he ever come here?"

"*Here?*" exclaimed she, "I wish he would or any of his gang: I would scald them."

As she uttered the last sentence she lifted the old black handkerchief from her head, her old gums chattered—and froth gushed from her mouth. She called her companion in iniquity, Cad Oakly, told her to fetch her best friend—the gin bottle. As she fell upon a chair we rushed from the house, and thus ended our "First walk about Town."

HARRIET GRANDY

From the *Whip*, July 30, 1842.

The prostitute Harriet "Hal" Grandy was subjected to frequent and vilifying invective by the flash press. Numerous columns described her as degraded, dirty, and disgusting. Her assumed aggressive, masculine behavior, in particular, was singled out for attack. Here she is portrayed as "a she-male" who physically assaults former male lovers, promenades along Broadway in male attire, and pushes "respectable" women off the sidewalk.

SCANDALOUS.

That infamous strumpet Hal Grandy has again been disgracing our city with her conduct. We think it is high time the police noticed this woman. She thinks nothing of Promenading Broadway in open day in men's apparel, or of jostling respectable females from the side walks. It was only the other day that she boldly walked into a hair dressers shop in Park Row, and grossly insulted a gentleman who was unfortunate enough to be acquainted with her, and who, if he had acted wisely, would have on the instant sent her to the or quietly lampblacked and floured the strumpet.[47] She is the same prostitute who cow hided in open day a young man, who at the same time shared her affections with a host of lawless fellows, but who chastised her severely for it on the spot, the marks of which she will carry to her grave. We would give the world to meet her in the street in any other appearance than that of a *she*-male.

PROSTITUTES AND PROMENADES

From the *Whip*, July 9, 1842.

New York's Battery, a public park and pleasure garden at the southern tip of Manhattan, was a prominent locale for promenading in the antebellum years. Castle Garden, a popular resort, beer garden, and later immigrant depot, was located in the Battery. This touristic account offers provocative glimpses of various men and women, sometimes giving names and evaluations of various prostitutes.

THE BATTERY SPY.

On Thursday afternoon we visited this delightful spot, and during our promenade noticed the following ladies, whose bearing elicited the admiration of all roués, libertines and sportsmen present, not neglecting the higher classes who wear goat beards and moustache, and are self styled gentlemen, but by us more rightly called suckers, sharps, diners out, pimps, and drummers with white hats.[48]

The elegant Mary Smith was there—dressed in the most splendid costume we ever saw—it was rich with simplicity, elegant with neatness.

Two splendid Belles from New Orleans, whom we have not the pleasure of knowing.

The superb Mary Capito, far more blooming than ever, dressed in the heighth of fashion.

The Misses Thompson and Clifton, and the lovely Misses Howes and Burke, The magnificent Mary Turner and Rose Berri both received much attention from the promenaders, who in an instant discovered them to be strangers, and many a wish was sighed for their quick return, as they glided from the battery.

Miss Emma Place made a splendid appearance on horseback; her costume we thought beautiful.

Harriet Grandy, dirty, slovenly and disgusting as usual.

WHERE TO FIND PROSTITUTES

From the *Flash*, July 3, 1842.

The short notices below typified how the flash press covered certain prostitutes. Such reportage not only provided specific details about the lives of and where to find women directly involved in commercial sex; it elevated a select few to celebrity status. In some cases, these squibs (also called puffs, inflated praise) constituted business notices and were very likely paid insertions.

The beautiful and divine Elizabeth Perkins we understand is about to leave the city for the east, where she intends to quit the paths of vice and immorality, and become the wife of a respectable merchant, of Boston. We hope it is true, as we always had a great regard for the charming Elizabeth.

From the *Whip* , February 11, 1843.

A STAR,— Bright, brilliant, beautiful—has fallen among us. It is called Miss Sarah Green (a queer name for a planet) and is in the harem of Julia Brown at present.

PROSTITUTION CRITICIZED

From the *Whip*, July 30, 1842.

The flash press treated prostitution in contradictory ways. At times, the editors assumed a highly moralistic stance. When criticizing commercial sex, they directed their ire and condemnation at older prostitutes and madams, perhaps as a way of encouraging monetary payoffs or settling old scores. This essay ends with a threat to publish the names of men who frequent a particular brothel, probably an effective way to deter business. The Whip *had already published names of clients at Mrs. Miller's brothel on Reade street (January 29, 1842), so this threat held some power.*

THE BROTHEL EXPOSE, —NO. 6.

MRS. BOWEN, OF CHURCH STREET.

"Reptile, despised one, horror of thy sex
Thy name, like dismal funeral knell,
Falls on the ear like potent terrific.
A scourge thou'st sent to warn the caring world:
Depicting vice in all its dread array."

Our exertions to stem the current of pollution that runs through every district of this large city have crowned with extraordinary success. The filthy creature whose character and pursuits we shall have occasion to exhibit to our readers in our present number is one mother Bowen, who resides in Church street. This abominable creature has for more than ten years devoted herself to every species of disgusting vice. This hag is of a most repulsive aspect, being fat and filthy. She has a face like a furnace, and covered with carbuncles,[49] and those eruptions which evidence a life of degraded debauchery. Moreover, this devil incarnate is a perfect tyrant to those unfortunate creatures who are under her control; acts of the most diabolical cruelty are perpetrated in her filthy den.

The principle traffic of this wretch is young girls from New Jersey as well as from Poughkeepsie, and rumor says that some sort of a connection exists between her and that filthy hag, Rachael Hendrickson, who resides near the latter place. Among those who reside with her at present, we shall mention her door keeper, Amelia Jones, a filthy, drunken wanton, whose whole life has been one ff degradation. Woe to the man who would enter this sink—disease and pollution is rank in every chamber.

To further prove the infamy attached to this den, we may as well state that she is connected with a man, who has the word fiend depicted on his very countenance, and who has left his wife, and even so far debased himself as to take away her own children, and place them under the protection of this foul prostitute. For this act he came near being "tarred and feathered," and 'tis indeed a pity that such was not the case, for he is deserving of nothing less.

Such is the den kept by old Bowen. Then who so base as to be a visitor at this den? Suresy not he who has a single feeling of self-respect. Do it not, for if nother remedy is left us, we must resort to that we ever wish to avoid—the publication of names.

4 HETEROSEXUALITY

PORNOGRAPHY

From the *New York Sporting Whip*, February 11, 1843.

The flash press was among the earliest to discuss the increasing availability of pornographic publications in New York. Like prostitution, the editors condemned the proliferation of such literature, while at the same time describing where to find it.

OBSCENE PICTURES.

Now that we have a Preventive Police, we hope and trust the numerous print shops about Gotham will receive, each a visit from the indefatigables.

These terrible engines of the destruction of youthful morals—those exciters of impure passions—those horrible evidences of the prurient state of French Society—richly colored and beautifully engraved prints, representing the connection of the sexes in all varieties, may be found in nearly every small book and print shop of New York. One on Nassau street, we speak of in particular. We will not give numbers[50] because, by so doing, we may direct those who wish to gloat over such things, and are ignorant of where they may be had, to the shops, and thereby do the venders a service. But, if the officers will call at our office, we will take them to the doors of these bawdy print establishments, with a great deal of pleasure.

Nearly every stand that lumbers up the sidewalks is plentifully furnished with those things, together with libidinous books with most revolting and disgusting contents. We may—if we see no steps taken to confiscate this unlawful property—furnish a list of each stand and shop. How would it operate?

FIGURE 37. "GALLERY OF COMICALITIES.: I HOPE NO PERSON CAN SEE US." ILLUSTRATION FOR A STORY ABOUT THREE SISTERS IN MONMOUTH, NEW JERSEY, WHOSE CLOTHES WERE SNATCHED UP BY SOME YOUNG MEN WHILE THEY WERE BATHING IN A MILL POND. *FLASH*, JULY 31, 1842. COURTESY AMERICAN ANTIQUARIAN SOCIETY.

FIGURE 38. "A STREET VIEW." A GENT PEERS CLOSELY AT A LADY IN A TUMBLE. *WEEKLY RAKE*, JULY 9, 1842. COURTESY AMERICAN ANTIQUARIAN SOCIETY.

The Ex Editor and Ex Manager shall come in for his share of the expose.

ADULTERY

From the *Flash*, October 31, 1841.

The Sunday Flash *editors improbably make common cause here with the New York Female Moral Reform Society, which annually petitioned the New York state legislature to criminalize acts of seduction and adultery. By defending the sanctity of marriage, the flash press can open fire on New York's political and economic elites and charge them with sexual hypocrisy for refusing to pass such a statute. What is really at stake is a paradox in obscenity law: describing adultery in print might be judged obscene, while adultery itself was not illegal.*

ADULTERY AND FORNICATION.

Now that we have a large batch of new fledged legislators about putting on the armour Legislation, we call upon them among the first of their acts, to redeem the common law as it now stands from ridicule and reproach in regard to its treatment of Adultery and Licentiousness. As moral men who have the cause of public virtue at heart, as people who have a regard for the sanctity of the marriage institution, we call upon them to finish what was so well commenced two winters ago, and make the offenses of Adultery and fornication, penal by statute. While the law remains as it is, and every man can be guilty of these crimes at will, without fear of punishment. How weak and wretched to punish the sale and exposure of licentious prints and pictures, on the pretence that they lead to the growth of those very crimes, the commission of which is not punishable by law. Just so that perfection of human folly, the law of libel makes libel a penal offence and punishes it with heavy penalties because "it has a tendency to a breach of the peace," while the breach of the peace itself, is not frequently visited merely by a small fine. O, the blessed laws we live under!

SEXUAL POSSIBILITIES

From the *Whip and Satirist of New-York and Brooklyn*, April 9, 1842.

Some issues of the flash press included illustrated sketches of occupations, trades, and social types that addressed the sexual possibilities of men and women whose work brought them into close contact with each other. Some played to the erotic opportunities of such engagements. In this account, the editors resort to stereotypes implying that the instinctive behavior of maids not only encourages sexual encounters, but such women enjoy the same lustful desires as the men who seek to seduce them. Parts of this essay and its accompanying picture were lifted wholesale from the London Town *of January 20, 1838, shortened, slightly reworded, with American references (such as Harvard, South Carolina) replacing English placenames.*

SKETCHES OF CHARACTERS—NO. 16.

THE CHAMBERMAID.

This buxom wench, of youth and vigour,
A sample, sirs, of legal tact is;
Like pleaders great, she quits the bar
For profitable chamber practice.

The old and young her smiles will seek;
Such is the wantonness of man,
That many stay an extra week
To try the virtue of her pan.

"Sir, I entreat you will not jest;
This gentleman is very amorous,
But I will not submit, indeed,
Though for my favors he is clamorous.

"Give me the young and active fellow,
Who, ripened o'er the flowing can,
Goes to his bed jocose and mellow,
And laughs to scorn the warming pan."

We do not mean to say much of chambermaids in private families; for, should we tell all we know of that interesting class of females, we might let the rising generation into too many secrets; which could not but be subversive of the chastity of youth of both sexes. A few remarks may suffice; chambermaids, we grieve to say it, are but flesh and blood, with the same instinctive desires as their masters, and much of their time is necessarily passed alone, in remote apartments, which usually contain beds. Solitude is the devil, and opportunity only another name for temptation. Beds are as easily spoiled as made, and then how easily they are made up again! A bed of down or feathers is not like a bed of grass, from which the impression of the human form divine can only be effaced by time. A very slight exertion of pretty Sally's physical vigour, restores its symmetry, so that no sagacity,

SKETCHES OF CHARACTERS---NO. 15.

THE PRETTY SERVING MAID.

FIGURE 39. "SKETCHES OF CHARACTERS — NO. 15.: THE PRETTY SERVING MAID." THIS
IS A NEAR-PERFECT COPY OF AN ILLUSTRATION OF A "MAID-SERVANT" IN THE LONDON
TOWN OF FEB. 24, 1838. ALSO SEE FIGURE 26, WHICH ACCOMPANIED THIS ARTICLE.
WHIP AND SATIRIST OF NEW YORK AND BROOKLYN, APRIL 2, 1842. COURTESY
AMERICAN ANTIQUARIAN SOCIETY.

merely human, can discover what has passed between the sheets. There is
a proverb, too, that "stolen waters are sweet, and bread eaten in secret is
pleasant;" and there is no wisdom in exposing any, especially the young,
to temptation. Would not a banker be esteemed mad, who would give
anyone free access to his vaults. We would as soon trust a reputed
thief alone in the Jewel Chamber of the Tower, as two young persons of
different sexes in a chamber where there was a bed. In Christian love, we
caution all married women and mothers of grown up sons against hiring
young and pretty chambermaids. Such a servant will only do for a widow
and her daughters. In all other families the *femme de chambre* should be
ugly and old; forty five, at least; though even this is not always a sufficient

precaution; for there are often stout Irishmen on or about the premises; men of few words and great stomachs, and variety is charming. There never was a wiser prayer than "lead us not into temptation!" Not that chambermaids are naturally more amorous than other women; but they are usually vain and always ignorant, and they are marked by all mankind as lawful prey. A virtuous chambermaid is as hard to find as a pulse in a potato or blood in a turnip.

> 'Tis *in* the bed or *on* the bed,
> Or up against the wall;
> 'Tis on the floor, behind the door,
> Or any where at all.

We now come to the *genus* chambermaid, in inns and boarding-houses, where they never, never escape. Here Sally is, in some measure, identified with Thomas, the waiter, who divides her favours about equally with John, the coachman—the stouter fellow of the two has the preference—without speaking of the way in which, in her loose hours, she smiles upon the guests and boarders, and increases her stock of wearing apparel and millinery. No wonder that she should do so; seeing how ill she is paid. The consequence of her low wages is, that she gets money by the only means in her power, and is not nice about her lovers.

We recollect a girl who made beds at a low inn in Cambridge, Mass. near Harvard University; where of course, she was obliged to bear with the un-hallowed addresses of the students, who were never famous for refinement in manners, language or behaviour. Nevertheless, she had been brought up in the principles of a poor, but pious mother, and heard and bore all, for a while, with a cold indifference, that astonished them; blackguards as they were. At last an adventurous student arrived from Charleston, South Carolina, and put up, for one night, at the inn, where he offered a wager, to any amount, that he would rouse her from her apathy. It was taken, and he retired for the night. Soon after, she was ordered to bring away the candle. When she entered his room for that purpose, she beheld an exhibition that certainly would have startled a fine lady. Not so with Sally—we cannot explain, but she advanced, saying it was a pity the candle should want an extinguisher. She did extinguish it and the wretch lost his bet, and was so burned up that he did not walk at ease for a month.

This anecdote exemplifies the boldness and lack of delicacy which is characteristic of the sisterhood. It is next to impossible to bring the crimson of a blush into their cheeks. They are used to licentious conversation and shamelessness is a second nature to them.

A ludicrous story is told [of] an old tar who had lost a leg in his country's service, and had supplied its place with one of mahogany, splendidly carved. The story goes, that he took up his quarters at a country tavern, where, as, he was somewhat rheumatic, he requested to have his bed warmed, which, however, was not done, and in consequence, he turned in "all standing." The landlady was a careful old soul, and used to visit each of her chambers every night, to see that her guests were comfortably lodged. When she came to Jack's, she observed the specimen of carving before mentioned, sticking out at the foot of the bed; but its owner she did not see; partly because her sight was bad, and partly because he was buried under the clothes.

"Bless me," cried the good woman, "that careless jade Betty has left the warming-pan in the gentleman's bed!" and, with that, she gave a tug at the supposed handle and Jack, of course, awoke.

The worst feature in Sally's lot, if she is placed in a tavern or boarding house, is, that she usually falls to a lower depth of degradation than other female servants. Her more constant intimacy with lewdness, hardens her sooner, and she more readily takes up with chance customers. Hence, it is, that of every two night walkers, one, at least, is a chambermaid, and hence it arises, that there are so many bed houses and places of assignation, where bawds pleasure crowns the labors of the day. It is from this class that brothels are most extensively recruited. We would wager any amount, that if the history of the Hook and the Five Points[51] could be ascertained, that nine tenths of their female poplation would be found to have been chambermaids.

We have heard of lodging houses where the functions of the sisterhood are discharged by chamberlains, or he-chambermaids.

It is an abominable and unmanly practice. Man was not intended by nature to twirl mops and empty jordans,[52] and the occupation of these creatures engenders disgust and abhorrence. Domestic service is the sphere of women. Such men, beasts, we mean, ought to be pelted and hooted wherever they dare to show themselves in the streets. Faugh! they ought not to be suffered to live.

To conclude—it is the true policy of publicans not to hire young and pretty chambermaids. To do so, is not only an offence against humanity; but injuries their own interests. They are all vain and ignorant, and are far more ready to pass their time toying with the men, than in doing their masters' work.

HETEROSEXUAL ENCOUNTERS

From the *Whip*, January 1, 1842.

Some flash press articles offered advice to prospective males in search of a sexual adventure. "Making love in the streets" referred not to a public display of heterosexual intercourse, but rather to the negotiations and foibles associated with men picking up prostitutes. Here both parties engage each other in certain performative roles—the young woman pretends to be chaste, the male suitor hopes she is. The preliminary encounter described here seems to last for several hours, probably an exaggerated description of a transaction that normally took only minutes.

MAKING LOVE IN THE STREETS.

We believe there is a great deal of iniquity committed in this way, partly by a set of females who have given up walking at night and taken to wandering abroad in the morning, not only because it is more healthful, but because, if they are clever at catching flats,[53] they find it more profitable; and partly, on Sunday evenings especially, by numerous classes of damsels who are so badly paid for their meritorious industry during six days of the weeks, that they could scarcely exist without the aid of an occasional "match" on the seventh. In the course of their perambulations, they never stop, but walk steadily along, and, if any gentleman addressed them, will, perhaps at first, start a little on one side, appearing to be somewhat timid and very modest, but this depends entirely on what sort of a man they have to deal with, and whether he is very bold or half bashful. We have often watched one of these modest gents, and have been exceedingly amused by the very scrupulous way in which he makes his approaches. First you will see him taking a view of the damsel's figure behind, and if he approves of that, then he gradually quickens his pace, passes her, and takes a sort of half glance at her features as he goes by; if this does not satisfy him, he walks on still faster, for some distance, turns sharply round, looks her full in the face, and is either pleased with her or not, according to his fancy. If he likes her, he turns back again and still follows her, ruminating, no doubt, on the best mode of addressing her, during which time the lady very condescendingly slackens her pace, till, at last, they are walking side by side together. Now, if in spite of his animal nature, he should happen to exhibit a want of confidence and to continue

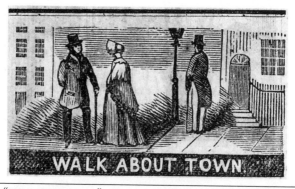

FIGURE 40. "WALK ABOUT TOWN." HEADER ILLUSTRATION FOR A REGULAR COLUMN. *NEW YORK SPORTING WHIP,* MARCH 4, 1843. COURTESY AMERICAN ANTIQUARIAN SOCIETY.

walking on without speaking, the damsel, if she likes his looks, will either turn her eyes upon him by way of encouragement, or should it be on a week day, stop at some shop window where he may speak to her without rendering himself so conspicuous, or perhaps she will suddenly bend her course down some private street, and there, by dropping either her glove or handkerchief at his feet, ascertain whether or not he really does intend to make love to her. We have also seen (aye, and felt too) in the streets and at the theatre, some of these seemingly modest females give sly pinches, even when they have been in company with a gent, who, it might be supposed, had a right to the monopoly of their favo[rs]

[tear in paper that removes five lines]

yield, they feel fully convinced that it has been a victory over chastity, and forthrightly go and boast about it among their male acquaintances. Cunning little Isaacs![54] we have noticed the women laughing at them all the time, not in their sleeve, but in their pocket handkerchief. Making love in the street, to a really modest woman, is an extremely delicate affair, and, in order eventually to prove successful (though one interview will never do it) requires no small share of tact, address, and ingenuity, especially if you have reason to believe that the female is, in every sense of the word, a lady. Perhaps she evinces great alarm; it is your business to make her laugh—but here we must stop. We could throw out many more useful hints, having ourselves a few sins to answer for in this way (though we have long abandoned such naughtiness), but we do not think that it is a subject on which our young readers ought to be enlightened. We will, however, venture upon a few little bits of advice: if you cannot restrain your wantonness, be very careful whom to speak to; always look well in a lady's face before you speak to her, and have nothing whatever to say to her if she persists in keeping down her veil. We know one young gentleman who once walked two or three miles making love to his aunt, who, at last, politely unveiled her features, and told him she could not sufficiently admire all the gallant speeches he had been making to her; another, who being rashly smitten with a lady's shape, when he was walking behind her, went up and gave utterance to some impassioned address that was replied to in the croaking voice of an old woman without a tooth in her head; and so, indeed, the youth found she was. One more little anecdote by way of a warning against all veiled ladies, and we have done. A friend of ours, after much persuasion during a walk of about three hours up and down the Battery, succeeded in inducing the fair one to accompany him to a certain hotel. As soon as they were alone, he assisted his companion to take off her bonnet and veil, when, to his great vexation, he discovered, or thought he discovered, a strong squint in her right eye. Common gallantry, however, compelled him to consummate his bliss, and, though he kept looking at the eye all the while, thinking it a horrible blemish, he gradually proceeded in his advances, and, in another moment would have carried them to the utmost extent, but in the course of a little playful, preliminary struggling, something fell on the floor, he picked it up and discovered that his Dulcinea's[55] squinting optic was a glass eye! He seized his hat, blew out the light, and regardless of all decency, rushed down stairs into the street as fast as the obstructing condition of his dress would allow him. Readers, beware when a woman conceals her face with a veil, and do not take it for granted that she wishes to hide her beauty.

FASHION AND SEX

From the *New York Sporting Whip*, January 28, 1843.

The flash press was full of satire. Here the editors address women readers and complain about bustles, a popular undergarment used to amplify the female fanny. They illustrate their objection by raising a humorous comparison to male genitalia.

FAIR SEX

As we have promised to devote a portion of our sheet to the sole, use, and exclusive benefit of the ladies, and as this first week of our enlargement is well nigh gone at the time we write this, we trust the fairer portion of our friends will be content with the information below:—

FIGURE 41. "SKETCHES OF CHARACTERS,—NO. I.: THE FRENCH CORSET MAKER." A
FASCINATION WITH WOMEN'S UNDERWEAR IS MANIFEST IN MANY ISSUES OF THE FLASH
PAPERS. *WHIP AND SATIRIST OF NEW-YORK AND BROOKLYN,* DEC. 25, 1842.
COURTESY AMERICAN ANTIQUARIAN SOCIETY.

This is the ladies' department of the Whip, and all the Mary Ann's, Jane
Maria's, Sarah Elizabeth's, Eliza's, Catharines and Martha's may blow up[56]
their lovers through it as much and as often as they please.

Fashion is a hard master, (or mistress, we are not certain of the gender,)
and his most faithful followers being the ladies we shall give publicity to his
stern edicts as to dress and materials of dress, as often as he issues them.
We shall not quarrel with the ladies' tastes, only when they overstep the
bounds of reason; they may, as they generally have heretofore, violate the
rules of decency as much as they like; —the bustle for instance. We cannot
see what the male bipeds have to do with such articles. The ladies seek to
enlarge, and render interesting and conspicuous, a plump, fair, and cov-
eted part of their frames, and it is certainly in bad taste for editors to poke
their noses into matters of such a tender and private nature. Take our word

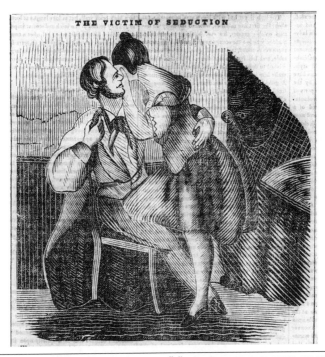

FIGURE 42. "THE VICTIM OF SEDUCTION." "THOU HAST PARTED WITH ALL THAT
IS OF INTRINSIC VALUE TO WOMAN," INTONES THE TEXT, ADVISING THE "FIEND WHO
HAS DESTROYED HER" TO MARRY HER IMMEDIATELY. *RAKE,* SEPT. 3, 1842.
COURTESY AMERICAN ANTIQUARIAN SOCIETY.

for it, gentlemen, you are on a wrong scent, and the girls will tell you so.
Gentlemen, do you suppose, if we, the bewhiskered and breeched members
of the community were in fancy that by sticking a bologna sausage down
into the laps of our unwhisperables we improved our appearance—do you
suppose the girls would trouble themselves, and meddle with such a trivial
affair? No! would you girls?

We will pick out certain professors of the art of dress making, curl making, and all other branches of trade in which females deal, and, if we feel
them worthy, give their names and locations under this head. Dealers in
fancy goods and all sorts of female haberdashery will, if wise, send us their
card, lists of prices &c., immediately. Having figured pretty largely as a
Rake, and being now reformed, we will, in glowing terms, describe the
art of the seducer, and show the innocent daughters of Eve the manner in
which to cheat the intended destroyer of his victim (that would be), and
continue, as she should, a bright light and a virtuous member of society. We

are to use a vulgar conventionalism, "great" at the business, far superior to the religious and misanthropical conductors of the "Advocate of Moral Reform." [57]

FEMALE READERS

From the *Whip and Satirist of New-York and Brooklyn*, March 26, 1842.

The flash press included correspondence from readers. Here a female reader claims that she regularly reads the Whip *and that the weekly is popular among her associates. She also charges that many "respectable" men and women object to the erotic content of the weekly while surreptitiously finding a copy to read themselves. The authenticity of the letter remains unknown; it is possible editors wrote such letters to appeal to the tastes and fantasies of male readers.*

NEW YORK, MARCH, 1842.

To The Editors of the Whip:

It is with pleasure that I inform you that your paper is making great headway among the ladies of my acquaintance, and I am frequently asked if I have seen the "Whip" this week. That false delicacy that has governed the better judgment of the female portion of the community is fast wearing away, and the day is not far distant when the truth can be spoken without the danger of a suit of slander. Some may doubt the respectability of my female acquaintances, but I assure them they are of the highest order; they are not of that class that have such false modesty that they would faint at the mention of a man's leg or body; or who would let a man suffer death before they would enter his death chamber. I have no acquaintances but with whom I can converse freely with on any subject that may be brought on the carpet without thinking of every word before we dare speak it, a fig for the girl that does not read the "Whip." I am acquainted with a family that lives in the central part of the city, who would consider themselves insulted if a young man should mention the name of your valuable paper to them, but who every Monday morning ransack their boarder's rooms to find a "Whip." Their boarders being sensible young men, they generally find one, which they devour with great eagerness, and find out if any of their acquaintances are noticed, and if so, they take the paper and show them—they was highly tickled last week for they found a mare's nest in my last communication and immediately after breakfast one of the family would be seen with the end of a newspaper sticking out of her reticule[58] making towards C_st, where after considerable puffing and blowing she arrived in good order and well conditioned. O Lord, how tired I am! have you seen the "Whip," why dear me, they have got_in it; what is the world coming to the next thing they will have me in it (she spoke the truth for once) they ought to be put down! They are a nuisance to society, &c. &c. Well here you are, my dear madam, in the Whip, and what do you think of yourself. I hope that you will mind your own business—the Lord have mercy on you I say; and the devil take your enemies. My motto is "evil be to them that evil thinks," and I am going to cut all acquaintances with whom I cannot exchange sentiments free and without restraint, that our thoughts on matters and things in general are the same, there is no one that will deny, then why a restraint in exchanging them. Here I am at the end of my sheet.

George you must excuse me for when I hear any thing that relates to your valuable paper, as an old friend I cannot but enjoy the pleasure of congratulating you *vive la Whip* and the girls that patronise it.

Yours in haste,

PHILO.

MARRIAGE IN A BROTHEL

From the *Whip and Satirist of New-York and Brooklyn*, March 19, 1842.

Flash press satire extended to the foibles and predicaments of young men in brothels. Here the fictionalized male Ezekiel Verisopht ("very soft") from rural New England is seduced by the women in Julia Brown's brothel. Smitten by love, Verisopht agrees to a hasty marriage with Ellen Thompson. He learns the next morning that he has been duped, and reacts with destructive anger.

MARRIAGE IN HIGH LIFE.

This is the season when birds begin to couple, and according to nature as well as to old use and wont, a most loving pair of turtles came together and made their nest, (for one night only) at Princess Julia Brown's Palace in Leonard street about a fortnight ago. The cock bird was a young trader from Barnstable, Mass., who had just come into his inheritance, and was in New York to learn something of the world and to purchase goods. His name is Ezekiel Verisopht. The hen was the beautiful and stately Ellen Thompson, with her swan-like neck and breast of snow. The conjunction copulative was brought about as follows:

The fame of the Princess Julia pervades the habitable globe, and has even reached the Fejee Islands. Zeke had heard much of her, and his curiosity was screwed as tight as fiddle strings. Accompanied by several friends, (people flush of money never want friends,) he repaired to her abode and demanded an introduction; but as the Princess happened at the time to be engaged in private business with a gentleman, on the second floor, and as Zeke was very importunate, the fair Ellen represented her. She received Zeke with great dignity and gave him her hand to kiss. Nothing doubting that this was the true Princess, Mr. Verisopht fell in love at first sight, and after a deal of billing and cooing, and the cracking of a basket of champagne at his expense, he proposed marriage, to which the sham Princess graciously acceded, and a day was appointed for the nuptials. The true Princess having by this time dispatched her little affair above stairs, came in, blooming like a rose, and was presented to the amorous Yankee as Ellen's sister. The whole affair was intended as a joke on the part of the ladies—we shall see if they had much reason to laugh at it in the sequel. As for Mr. Zekiel, he was in right down, Yankee earnest.

A sham priest was procured, and preparations were made for a most splendid wedding supper, all of which was to be at Mr. Verisopht's expense. To him the minutes seemed like hours, till the anxiously anticipated moment arrived; and at last, arrive it did, and Zekiel thought himself supremely blessed. The blushing bride appeared in virgin white, emblematic of her spotless purity, supported on one side by Miss Mary Quiffe, and on the other by the Princess herself, who alternately applied their sal volatile[59] to her nostrils. The cager[60] groom was assisted by two of his particular friends, viz., Obadiah Clambake, the skipper of a fishing smack,[61] and Othniel Peabody, a trader in notions. The ceremony was performed; but as soon as the fatal words had been spoken, the Princess swooned away, and was carried to her chamber. It was buzzed about the crowded apartment that she, too, was romantically attached to Mr. Verisopht; and it was confidently predicted that this destruction of her hopes would be the death of her. The company was then regaled with music on the guitar of George Gale, Esq., till the hour arrived when the pair were put to bed with all the accustomed forms and ceremonies. The absence of Mr. George Gage was deeply regretted. He had been summoned, by special express, from Baltimore; but did not arrive in time for the nuptials.

In the morning, surfeited and sick with love, the fair Ellen informed her quasi husband of the deception that had been practiced on him. For a long while, he would not believe her; and when he did—oh Lord!—he swore, he raved, he stamped, he broke things; but was finally soothed by the entrance of the Princess, accompanied by two or three truculent fellows with crabsticks[62] in their hands. Having promised more pacific behavior, these gentlemen were dismissed, and the Princess then presented our friend Zekiel with a bill for a wedding supper, &c., to the tune of $260;[63] at the same time informing him that he must make good the damage he had done, on peril of the law.

"Well," said Ezekiel, buttoning his overcoat and taking up his hat; "I somehow seem to think that I haven't got no wife, and so I can't have had any wedding supper, anyhow you can fix it!"

With these words he bolted, and has not since been heard of. The Princess and the fair Ellen are alike inconsolable—the one for the loss of her lover, and the other, with more reason and greater sincerity, for the loss of her money.

THE SOLITARY VICE

From the *Flash*, July 10, 1842.

The flash press played to the fears of nineteenth-century men. Writers and health reformers like Sylvester Graham warned Americans that masturbation was debilitating and unhealthy. Graham counseled a stern disciplining of sexual urges; the flash editors advised men either to marry or find a mistress. At the same time, the editors rejected the belief of Thomas L. Nichols ("t.l. niggles") that youths as young as fifteen should have regular sexual intercourse, arguing that such sexual activity would result in premature aging. The larger point is that masturbation was condemned by libertines and rakes as well as by health reformers. Both groups feared it led to severe mental and physical debility.

MASTURBATION.

It is roally lamentable to contemplate the misery and deteriviation of the human race brought about by this bestial enjoyment. It is but within a few years that the medical faculty have had their attention properly drawn to it, and when the deleterious influences of such a practice are more properly known, few will indulge in them unless they wish to fill a premature grave.

By mere observation, in walking the streets, one will often see young men with sunken eyes, pallid countenances and emaciated forms, perhaps wrinkles, in their faces, though not over the age of twenty. Such indulge in an unhallowed passion, which, if persisted in, will end in insanity, a broken-down nervous system, or death in its most formidable shape. Many young men thus become victims to their own folly. Some know not that they are killing themselves—while others, with heated temperament, will rush on, regardless of consequences, even if death stood at the door. Having thus wasted the energy and fire of youth, if they become husbands, few ever become fathers—and if so, it is of pale, poor and sickly children.

t. l. niggles,[64] (he that publishes a moral reform paper) proposed not long since that every young man at the age of fifteen should be provided with either a wife or a mistress. This would be making bad worse, with a vengeance. A pretty race would then people the world. For instance, a man of thisty would be looked upon as an old man, and twenty-five would be about the average of man's life. The only proper way to put a check to such indulgences is "to hold as it were the mirror up to nature," and let them have a full insight into the dreadful consequences that must follow, if they persist in a practice so much at variance with nature.

Let this be a warning to all who thus indulge—for of all horrible deaths, we doubt not but this would be the last any of our readers would choose, if they had ever witnessed it. If you are young—not too young—marry a good, virtuous wife. If you cannot afford it, took occasional enjoyment among women, if possible; but above all thihgs, desist from this solitary vice, unless you wish to tenant an insane hospital, drag out a wretched existence, or pay the debt of nature before it is due.

NATIONAL INFLUENCE

From the *Whip*, September 10, 1842.

The influence of the flash press extended well beyond New York. Editors reportedly solicited letters and correspondence detailing sexual intrigue in the American hinterland. This letter adopts the flash press pose of castigating licentiousness and so turns the tables on the Utica Female Moral Reform Society, accusing its leader of spreading sexual vice by explicitly advocating sex education by parents.

UTICA.

CORRESPONDENCE OF THE WHIP

August 28, 1842.

MESSRS. EDITORS,

Our central city, replete with immorality, fun, and frolic, is deemed (as it would seem from your positive and continued silence) unworthy of being served up as a spicy meal, capable of enhancing the gusts of your numerous patrons. The castigations of your esteemed periodical would do much to quell the depravity and licentiousness that pervades all grades of our population. Vice masked under the modest robe of virtue stalks abroad, and under the guise of blessed religion, hoary sinners polute the virtuous minds of the young and beautiful. I will instance an old female wretch, not an unworthy specimen of the ancient Egyptian mummy, (without the preparatory ordeal of embalming and bandaging,) familiarly known as old mother S, this person has for a long time acted as president of the Moral Reform Society, which society (originally designed for good) has done more to contaminate the morals of the public, than all the direct importations of vice from Europe has done for a century past. The venerable Skinner's[65] ideas are now maniac, dwelling ever on the mysterious joys consequent on hymen; her untireing efforts are to decrease the manufacture of babies! and to inculcate in the minds of the young and beautiful of the tender sex, not to lie on feather beds, nor eat meats, nor even set on sofas where married people have sat! for fear that it should make them "fell licentious," and whet their appetite too strongly for animal enjoyment. By her single influence a rule has been adopted in the Society, for mothers of families to acquaint their children as soon as they shall have arrived at the age of ten years, all the minutiae attendant upon marriage, and WHEN CONVE-NIENT (after the theory is duly instilled) allow them to view with their individual optics, practical illustrations. Your chastisement is also necessary for the little boys and girls of all our best families, who acting upon these inflamitory hints, have commenced indiscriminately, and are engaged in "soft delights" nightly, resorting to barns, woodsheds, &c.; and horrible to relate, a pair of these hopeful juveniles were actually caught in the act in broad daylight! O tempora! O mores! We depend upon your chastening influence to withdraw the scourge from among us—do it, and the prayers of a rescued city will rise in grateful incense to Heaven, and shower its blessings on your head. More

"ANON."

COMMERCIAL SEX NATIONWIDE

From the *Flash*, August [7], 1842.

This article, submitted by a Philadelphia reader of the Flash, *exemplifies coverage of the commercial sexual underworld in other U.S. cities. The focus here is on male pimps, and the author adopts negative adjectives—vile, lewd, nefarious, evil—to describe both the men and women involved. Note the coded identifications, which hint at possible blackmail opportunities—or, conversely, bring notoriety and thus pleasure to the young men seemingly exposed.*

PHILADELPHIA PIMPS OF FAME.

Philadelphia, Aug. 3d. [1842]

MR. EDITOR—

I wish to show the public of this place some of the vile beings whom they have living amongst them. There is here at the present time some things in the shape of young men, who mingle with the best society in this city who live by the prostitution of lewd women and appear in the best of clothing, brought, of course, by the harlots whom they mingle with. At times these women go so far as to have cards printed with the names of their paramours on, and their own residence. These cards they distribute freely to every one they have any acquaintance with. Whilst they are carrying on their nefarious business, these pimps can be seen promenading our public thoroughfares with the elite of our city. I happen to know the names of some young men of good birth whose parents discarded them on account of their evil practices. These fellows are now kept by common harlots. There are two or three fellows who are kept by prostitutes living at No. 19 Elizabeth street. One of them is the son of a merchant in Market street, whose name is D E. There is another one by the name of George W . . . . t, who is kept by the notorious bawd Emma Jacobs, of Bryan's Court. The next on the list is J. G. who is kept by Mary S . . . . rs. There is another by the name of Dan V. . . .t, a young man of highly respectable parents, but of a most notorious character himself. In my next I will give you something that will give you something that will astound the pimps of this city.

Yours,   SNIP.

|||||||||||||||||||||||||||||||||||||||||||||||||||||||||||||||||||||||||||||||||||||||||||||||||||||||||||||||

5 GOSSIP, VITUPERATION, AND BLACKMAIL

|||||||||||||||||||||||||||||||||||||||||||||||||||||||||||||||||||||||||||||||||||||||||||||||||||||||||||||||

GOSSIP

From the *Whip and Satirist of New-York and Brooklyn*, April 2, 1842.

The flash press offered mysterious and titillating exposés in certain columns. Here "The Whip Wants to Know" combined local gossip, invective, and possible black-

GALLERY OF COMICALITIES.

A COBBLER CAUGHT WITH HIS "AWL" OUT!

FIGURE 43. "GALLERY OF COMICALITIES.: A COBBLER CAUGHT WITH HIS 'AWL' OUT!"
AN AWL IS A SHARPLY POINTED LEATHERWORKING TOOL. THE ARTICLE TELLS OF
NEIGHBORHOOD MATRONS WHO ARRIVED IN TIME TO PREVENT A SEXUAL ASSAULT
ON A FIFTEEN-YEAR-OLD GIRL (DEPICTED AT RIGHT, IN UNDERCLOTHES).
FLASH, AUG. 14, 1842. COURTESY AMERICAN ANTIQUARIAN SOCIETY.

*mail with sexual wordplay. Readers paid to have their insults or queries published.
Whip editor George Wooldridge used the column to continue his campaign to smear
Adeline Miller, this time through Willis G. Thompson, an associate of her son Nelson
Miller.*

THE WHIP WANTS TO KNOW
New-York.

If Caroline, at Nelly Weaver's, deals in horses. Circus horses?

How many tons freight the Great Western carries in her *hold*.

What has become of Hal Grandy. Has she paid her board at 39
Thomas?

When those three wise men of Brooklyn intend paying a female for
the new dress they spoiled one rainy night about three o'clock in the
morning.

If they will not select better money next time, as shinplasters are out of date.

If the lawyer will not take that X to the broker.

If Johnny will not learn his friends better next time than to knock at peoples doors so early in the morning.

What has become of a lady who is known by the name of M__e who formally lived as a married woman at a respectable boarding house in Spring st., and not far from Hudson.

Why Mr. R__V__ will persist in calling at the Duchess de Berrie's and endeavor to come the sweet over one of her Nymphs where he is fairly detested. Better keep your wife in the city, and bake your own cakes and eat them too.

How often a notorious liar sleeps at the house of Mr. Thompson, and if Mrs. Thompson knows that her husband visits his house in return.

Why the Girls of Mrs. Miller's all use the word soft Mr. Thompson.

Who those seven or eight young men were who left a well known Refrectory late on Friday night last week for a spree.

If it will be any harm to give an account of the houses they visited that night. What say you George and Guss, Eugene, Joe and little Gussy, and others not recollected.

For what purpose Julia Brown keeps onions in her back parlor.

If it is for the purpose of assisting Moll Quiff to shed crocodile tears.

The amount of snuff Jule Barcklen chews per day.

If she would not like to make a contract for a regular supply with a large manufactory in New Jersey.

Why English Mary Elizabeth meddles herself so much with other people's business.

If she would attend to her own she would be much better employed.

Where that beef steak went too that was missed out of the safe at Mrs. Miller's.

If the lady it was taken to knew of its coming from a brothel. Oh! Mrs. Thompson, oh.

If Mr. Thompson knew the company he introduced to his wife when he introduced a notorious liar.

If Mr.__n, son of Mrs. G__n, mentioned two weeks ago, has brought affairs to a close with the pretty Miss M__n milliner, in Division street, not one hundred miles from the office of Dr. Hunter's Red Drop. You are quite safe Hannah though namesake of the great Carthagenian General.

ENEMIES

From the *True Flash*, December 4, 1841.

Invective was just as easily leveled against other and competing editors as well as brothel madams. Here George B. Wooldridge turns his pen against William Joseph Snelling, "Scorpion" in the original flash press team of Scorpion, Startle, and Sly, who founded the Sunday Flash.

SPIRIT-GAS SCORPION.

It is seldom indeed that Proprietor, Editor, Reporter, Printer, nay the veriest penny-a-liner[66] that makes the morsel that shall feed him, by raking the whole universe of thought for an abject and pitiful subject, can find in imagination so degraded a being as some who exist in common life. Never did we sit down to chronicle the life of a more wretched, miserable, God forsaken individual than the one who forms the subject of this sketch. Like Satan of Milton,[67] with far less of his moral courage and redeeming [quali]ties, the thing was gifted by his God with talents of a high and noble order, and as if a Divine Providence designed to show in his person how a human being can degrade his nature, violate every moral obligation, claim a kindred with the most loathsome reptiles that crawl along the face of the earth, and find a damned glee with the abandoned and base, he has been permitted for years to libel his fellow men, scoff at holy things, make himself the pander to lust, and the chronicler of deeds and sayings that might better find a sphere for their action, below the lower deep of the deepest hell, than to stain and spot this fair creation of our God. Our readers already guess whom we mean. For blessed be the ever kind Providence that watches over the destiny of man, and thanks to the unshaken principles of virtue, diffusing itself through civilized society, there is but one such man. This fellow has made himself conspicuous under the cognomen of "Scorpion" in a sheet designed by its projector "Sly" to be a chronicle of life in all its varieties—not the miserable, powerless, unprincipled, contemptible, and reckless organ which this creature made of it! Boasting of his courage, but possessing by nature, education, and habit, every attribute of a coward, when the whip of offended decency was raised to scourge the reptile, he would have fain transferred the blow to the hand that stooped to raise him, that plucked him from the jaws of a death by starvation, by feeding him with the morsel of charity, and, who, when all the would disgusted with his loathsome habits, shunned him as they would the skunk, whose odor polluted the air, in the vain hope of redeeming him from his rags and disgrace, gave him some employment for his faded faculties, and to exert those talents once so brilliant, but now a wreck from dissipation, ingratitude and crime.

In order to commence aright the career of this individual, we will begin with facts.

As to the place of his birth, we spare the unfortunate city or town from the everlasting ignominy and degradation of having spawned forth such a thing from its teeming population. Through a course of years, struggling with the natural vices of his character and the better dictates of his now degraded intellect he obtained a scholarship in the West Point Academy, and from that time we know nothing of him until he was expelled, amid the sneers and contempt with the unmitigated detestation of all who knew him. The causes, we will not mention, we would not stain our sheet with it, for it scarcely has a name. The next we find of him, is when driven by the reckless desperation, and pitiful meanness of his character from all reputable and passable society, charity gave him a berth as Editor of the Boston Galaxy, a paper which he soon ruined. The blight of God seemed to rest on all his labors. He commenced a war on the Gamblers, and the force and sprit of his articles made them flutter again. But he spared the rich rogue, while he scourged the poor one, and fed on the crumbs through as you throw a crust to a yelping cur, to stop his noisy growl.

In this sheet, he attacked one of the Judges of the Municipal court and was committed to the Leverett street prison for seventy days. Here he formed those disgusting habits and fondness for disreputable companionship, which has marked his degraded career. The companion of thieves and libellers, the slanderers of virtue and the victims of intemperance, he defied the law for the society was congenial to his nature. But in the indulgence of pity, honorable to them but uselessly thrown away on its object his friends took him in their charge, believing that some lingering spark might be yet remaining from which they could fan a flame of purer light. But in vain—in vain—he was found a common drunkard, the lowest haunts of the rum suckers, the dirtiest houses where unbridled lust had its sway, aye the gutter at night was his resting place, and the very dog walked along the streets or smelt at his carcase, reeking with the fumes of liquor, and walked on, a greater honor to God's creation that that abject being. An outcast from society, spurned by all, no longer able to keep himself sober enough to write two consecutive lines for his daily bread, or clothes to cover his nakedness, he surrendered himself as an outcast to the authorities, and at his own request was committed to the House of Correction. Here he passed six months of his time, hope fondly dreamed—his heart broken friends had a distant, oh how distant prospect that one thought of a better kind, would flash across his brutalized mind. It was hoped that in solitude his faculties might by a great effort be capable of one reflection, that might bring him back to such a state as would prevent him at least from being a nuisance to society—but no sooner was he released, than "the dog returned to his vomit." He proved himself then what Willis[68] pronounced him abroad, an outcast from society. The scenes of his degraded life were repeated again, until people thought no more of him, than of some public nuisance, which though it could not be endured, could not also be removed.

In the midst of all, like a wanderer with the brand upon his brow, he found his way to this city, and became the protego of the notorious woman Miller. He served her in every capacity, and revelled in his situation as pander to a wanton, nay a common procuress. Obeying the behests of this foul stain on her sex, he attacked the character of Hamblin[69]—the more rum she gave him, the more reckless became his articles. Like a coward, he sneaked behind the apron of his mistress, and trembling for the descending lash, he induced her by his pitiful littleness, and want of courage, to extend the shield of her gold, the wages of sin and damned crime, wrung from broken hearts and diseased bodies. He became connected with a paper called the "Censor," which was made the organ of his foul imaginations, but on the sixth day of its publication, its wretched Editor was found drunk in the street, unable even to string out the abominations so congenial to his nature. The unfortunate printer who had been induced to blast forever his reputation by his connection with him, give up the concern in disgust, and the creature Miller fostered, fed and clothed the tool of her malevolence. She warmed the serpent into life. Oh, how could we here introduce a history of this woman's infamous career, but for the sake of her children,[70] we spare her, till another time, when we will hold her up for the world's loud laugh, to be scorned and despised by the whole creation. In the course of these remarks there should be one word to wound the heart of the child whom she professes to adore and who has already been smiled on by the public, we must be excused. It is that lady's misfortune not her fault. Driven from every employment, and feeding at the board of this woman she endeavored to turn what talents he had left to account. She engaged him to write a play, locked him in a room to prevent him from becoming intoxicated, but he drank the very alcohol placed to feed his lamp and was found in his room in a state of beastly drunkenness.

The hellish disposition which this woman has ever exhibited towards Hamblin is doubtless the cause of the articles which have appeared in the sheet which was under the superintendence of Scorpion Spirit Gas, against that manager. The whole sheet soon became under the influence of this creature. Her house was made the medium through which the recreant tool was to receive the information necessary to the accomplishment of his hellish plans. For a time too a person of independence espoused the cause of the creature Miller, thinking her right in the quarrel, until disgusted with her fiendish spirit, and the hatred and falsehood in which she indulged, he gave up the further defence of her. That defence, generously as it was meant, and under mistaken ideas, has, in all probability been potent to prevent that pest to society from realizing the threatened horrors of lynch law. She may bless the error for it has given her a space to repent of her own. The spiritless vagabond whom she had fostered had before the commencement of his career as Scorpion traveled back to Boston, and there procured the opportunity of abusing New-York and its inhabitants. He poured out the disgusting filth of his polluted mind, in a reckless but impotent attempt to annoy those who had befriended him. Behind the cover of his littleness, he shot what was meant to be the poisoned arrows of sarcasm. Whenever he had received a favor he returned it with ingratitude. Until with a mind perverted from every thing good, and revelling in all that is atrocious, mean, and disgusting,—he again came to New York like a lick-spittle,[71] to fawn himself into favour, where he obtained the power to libel again, the men who endured the insufferable nuisance of his presence. After he obtained a situation on the Flash, he abused the confidence of the proprietors, offended the ear of decency, rolled in filth, and gloried in disgrace, till he was plunged into a prison for his impudent libels on persons of more honorable character than he had grasp of mind enough to conceive of. By the sufferance of charity he was permitted to occupy a room some where in West Broadway, where his habits of filth and indecency compelled the landlady, finding all other means useless, to smoke[72] him from the room. The thing, then, with a view of carrying out that boundless impudence which belongs to a man ignorant alike, as far as experience goes of one decent thought, or one sober reflection, practiced the unparalled imposition of pretending to belong to a temperance society scarcely had the pledge been signed, than the lowest grog shops were sought, and morn broke and evening closed on a wretched forsaken outcast, a confirmed and almost insane inebriate. He then found, with an instinct, which is known to the pig, the place most in accordance with his taste and habits and we find him, though almost incapacitated for its exercise, wallowing in licentiousness in a beastly stew in the five points,[73] with a miserable hag, whom years of disease, and filth, had no further use for her rotten carcase, than to throw herself into the arms of the broken down miscreant, and with a paramour, taint the air with the filthy odor of their persons. The fellow is now indicted for libel, but what a face! He libel? He the fallen, outcast, whom the very reptiles must scorn, whose very praise would be the most damnable libel he could perpetrate on one of God's creatures. The fellow had talent, but he has sunk into a brainless sot. He remembers like a half forgotten dream, his habits of lying and slander, and occasionally, by accident, their flashes power enough on his withered brain to string together a few sentences of his slang, but he is harmless. His best effusions now are the mumblings of a sot, almost in a state of bestial insensibility.

He has gained the name of Scorpion Spirit Gas, and occasionally he may be seen crawling along the public streets. He boasts of his courage, and well he may for he is too unimportant for any one to kick, or for a person of decency to "void his rheum on."[74] He never had a friend he did not ruin, he never had a favor (and he has lived by sufferance all his life) that he did not return with ingratitude. He never had a penny he did not spend in the rum shop, he never went into company he did not dishonor. He never had talents that were not degraded. He never had a patron that he did not insult. There never was a vice he did not practice, there never never was a virtue he did not scorn, there never was an hour when he was decent and his most meritorious productions have been thrown off by accident. Whatever mind he had he was never capable of regulating, he never put his pen to paper but it flowed with filth, he never felt happy but when reveling in bestiality. He never made a promise he did not break, he never spoke a word he did not lie except when he told the Magistrates of Boston that he was unfit for a civilized community. Brutal in his passions, but impodent in their gratification, mean in his spirit, cowardly in his disposition, crushed in his soul, withered in his intelect, despised by the world, looked on as a nuisance, buffeted as a blackguard, punished as a drunkard, receiving the retribution of his filth, the inmate of stews while scorned by their wretched inmates, the companion of the base, the type of ingratitude, the doomed of earth and the * * * * * *, what has he left but to crawl his way through the world, leaving his slime behind him, unless society can find a home where the foot of civilized man never trod and fit only for the irreclaimable outcast and malevolent impotents of creation. So let him go. He never had a prospect in life he did not blast by his own folly, he has no one to thank for his condition but himself, the voice of remonstrance is thrown away on him and pity degraded by its exercise. Let then his impotent malice have its way—let him file sheet after sheet with his ribaldry, blasphemy, indecency, till he sinks into a grave almost polluted by his presence "unwept, unhonored and unknown" except as a disgusting example of human recklessness, folly and impotence. Enough for the present.

The above cut represents "Spirit Gas Scorpion" on the day that he was sent to Blackwell's Island for vagrancy, by Judge Stevens, where he remained several months filling the office of hog reef, ie. feeding the hogs. To this fact John W. Brown, Esq. can testify. Further particulars hereafter.

CRITICAL CORRESPONDENCE
From the *Whip*, September 10, 1842.

Letters to the editor in the flash weeklies offered a range of perspectives, including insinuation and insult. Some letters were hypocritically critical of the growing prominence of commercial sex in New York. "Hickory's" letter below conflicts with the positive presentation of Julia Brown's establishment and male engagement with prostitutes found in other parts of the weekly.

NEW YORK.
City Correspondence of the Whip.

September 1, 1842.

Mr. Editor:

Through the medium of your useful paper I would advise those gentlemen, for they are called such in these degenerate days, the next time they go riding up Broadway in company with such notorious women as Mary and Elvira from Julia Brown's to shut the window's down and keep the curtains drawn, and not expose themselves to the gaze of their friends.

Young men, if you have no respect for yourselves, have a little for those who once thought you incapable of such disgraceful conduct. I warn you that the next time you offend I will expose your names in full. I will make known something more of your shameful conduct. I only hold the Whip ready, and it shall be effectually applied.

Yours,

HICKORY.

BLACKMAIL

From the *New York Sporting Whip*, February 11, 1843.

By 1843, some flash press editors openly admitted they engaged in blackmail. In this excerpt, they imply that Herald editor James Gordon Bennett is guilty of the same, but refuses to admit engaging in such nefarious practices.

MADAME TRUST.

Who does not remember Madame Trust—*danseuse* of some merit, but a *woman* of abominable appearance? Why, do you suppose, do we ask this question? Well, we'll tell you. Scandal enough may always be had for the trouble of procuring it, by any one; but we, more fortunate than our fellows, get it for nothing, and a small *douceur* to boot. Now, the drift of this is that we have on hand a queer, funny, and explicit *exposé* of the doings of a quack who married this *madame*—of her transactions—and of the secret affairs of both. If we can make any blackmail by suppressing it we will. There! we, more daring than Bennett, openly avow that we extort hush money. That's all.

ABORTION

From the *New York Sporting Whip*, February 11, 1843.

Abortion was an increasingly controversial practice in the mid-nineteenth century. Some well-known abortionists like Madames Restell (Ann Lohman) and Costello practiced in several cities. This article attacks abortion while simultaneously advertising the practice.

MADAME COSTELLO, THE "FEMALE PHYSICIAN."

When the means to hide guilt of the most awful nature can be obtained for a few "paltry" dollars, we cannot marvel at the commission—frequent and secret—of those crimes that are denounced in Holy Writ, and rendered a shame, only, by the hypocrisy and queer formation of society.

The existing code of morals, is an exceedingly accomodating one. It is "So that you cloak and hide your enormities from the public eye, there are no enormities at all. Violate your brother or wife—pollute, with unchaste embraces, and through lies and deceit, his daughters—lavish, with a profligate hand, your substance upon harlots—associate with them as often as you please—contract and bear about with you loathsome, cankerous leprosies—perpetuate horrid offences against nature and God—depredate and ruin—and so long as you have cunning and perception enough to keep, locked up within your black and corrupted heart, the knowledge of your weak parts, you are as good as the best, and twice as smart."

Instruments and opportunities for concealment are to be met with on every corner, and the use claimed for the "paltry" (as we said before) sum of five or ten dollars a job.

Madame Costello, the woman who advertises as "Female Physician" is one of those concealing instruments—the tormenting rival of Restell the Abortionist—the one who stands ready to accomplish whatever the opposition may refuse.

Costello exercises, in her damnable vocation, a deal more caution than her rival; and it is not so generally known that she is an abortionist. She does not advertise, openly, "Preventive Powders," but under the comprehensive title of "Female Physician" cloaks her unholy and unnatural business. A young girl; full of life and hope and beauty shows a partiality for a villian, and he, taking advantage of her liking, endeavors, by fair promises and deceptive professions, to rob her of her virtue, and blight her budding hopes, she,—weak, fragile creature—tells him she will yield her honor and peace to his keeping but for the opinion of the world—the fear of detection. "Suppose she gets with child?" she hints. "Madame Costello or Madame Restell will prevent that," answers the villain, and the girl consents to cast herself into irremediable ruin.

Can the authorities remain quiet while these devils' dams are insulting God with their infernal practices?

Will they not make an effort to crush them?

Restell has slipped through the meshes of the law eel-like, three times— try her again—send them all to the State Prison together, and rid us of their pestiferous, blasphemous presence.

Mrs. Bird next week.

6 RACISM AND ANTI-AMALGAMATION

CHARLES DICKENS IN NEW YORK

From the *Whip and Satirist of New-York and Brooklyn*, March 12, 1842.

British novelist Charles Dickens, popularly nicknamed "Boz," visited the United States in 1842. While in New York, he spent an evening walking around Five Points, the nation's most infamous slum, joined by American newspapermen, including one of the flash editors. This article from the Whip *highlights the racial stereotyping and vehement racism of the flash press editors. The dancing scene below was made famous when Dickens described "Juba," a young black man who became a dance sensation, in his book* American Notes.

BOZ AT THE FIVE POINTS

Last Friday evening, Mr. Charles Dickens started from his residence at the Carlton House, in company with one of the city aldermen and police officers Wm. H. Stephens and A. M. C. Smith, on a voyage of discovery into regions hitherto unexplored by men of his dimensions. Frank Mc-Cabe, in Anthony street was honored with their first visit, a white man who keeps a house of public entertainment and prostitution for negroes of both genders. Up stairs they went, and in one of the bedrooms in the attic they found total darkness. With some difficulty, owing to the mephitic state of the atmosphere, they succeeded in igniting a friction match and obtaining a light, when lo! four negresses were discovered without so much as a fig-leaf, far less a rag to cover their nakedness, lying on the bare floor, intermixed with four or five dogs, who were doing their best to keep them warm, and one buck negro. Their alarm was, of course, great, as there was no means of escape and the consequent stench was intolerable. The window was closed, and Boz, keeping between his finger and thumb a pouncet box,[75] which, ever, and anon, he gave his nose, declared himself quite satisfied. Stevens, however would not let him off so, being desirous of shewing him all the beauties of his immediate jurisdiction. Accordingly he was commendably taken into another garret room in which lay four ladies of color and three gentlemen of the same hue in a promiscuous heap, as well as three small children and two big Newfoundland dogs. It was doubtful which of the twelve was least human. The window of this dormitory was also closed and on entering Boz fell back into the arms of one of the officers and could not be persuaded to reenter, till the skylight had been raised and the apartment well ventilated. A great stove was red hot with a fire of the best Peach Orchard, all present were in a beastly state of intoxication, and it is certain that a few minutes more would have ended their earthly existence but for the visit of Boz. The room in which these wretches were lying and this stove was burning was just six feet by six, the size of the police office at the Five Points. "Well, Mr. Stevens," said the male black, as that officer entered, "are you going to take me to prison;" and on being assured he sank back again into an uneasy slumber upon the swinish heap. They entered another bed chamber of nearly the same dimensions, where a stout darkey bawled "Don't come here. We are all sick." "Oh! if you are sick," said Boz, "God forbid that I should disturb you," and with that he turned away. St. Giles, he said had nothing like this.[76]

We do not think Boz is to be commended for saving these wretches from destruction. It would have been better for them to die than live and far better for society. We do suppose that such creatures were created for some wise purpose; but what that purpose was we are utterly unable to imagine.

Boz is not a man of weak nerves, or this would have been sufficient for them. He then went through every house on the north side of Anthony street and expressed his surprise that any sort of order could be kept among such a disorderly crew. We have not room for all his perquisitions[77]—or inclination—it wold be a deplorable exposition of vice and misery. He then went to Almack's in Orange street[78] where only genteel niggers are admitted and there were about a hundred assembled. The place is kept by a fellow named Frazer. The first sound that greeted Mr. Dicken's ear, as he entered, was the voice of a gentleman of color calling to the fiddler for "de Boz Quadrille." Boz laughed a few—not so the company; who were utterly as sound [astounded] at the entrance of the officers and would have made their escape if they could; but that was impossible. They, probably, were each one conscious of deserving the visitation of the law; and the right of officer Stevens was more terrible to them than of their offended maker. Stevens assured them, however, that, for the present, they had nothing to fear, and exhorted them to persevere in cotillions and quadrilles, to the popular airs of "Sitch a gittin up stairs" and "Jim along Josey," which they performed with a zeal and animation excited by the fear of the Penitentiary, greatly to the amusement of Mr. Dickens.

Then he went to Roache's, in Orange street, where there was a promiscuous company half of whom made a simultaneous rush for the door down stairs, trampling upon each other like so many wild elephants and inflicting a great many wounds and bruises. One lady had her leg broken and "the other fractured," and was conveyed to the hospital on a spring cart, and not a few of the gentlemen were not blacker, but rather bluer than they were before. Others made the adodgment[79] up stairs, through the scuttle and down the spout, tearing their clothes awfully in the descent. One big buck of about the size of Ben Caunt, the Champion of England,[80] was seen flying down Cross street with his nether man utterly denuded, as if the avenger of blood was behind him. A few of the fat and forty remained, who were compelled to execute Scotch reels and breakdowns,[81] which they did greatly to the satisfaction of Boz. They executed the figure called the "six"[82] at the Points in very superior style. There were two rooms here front and back. Boz was quite satisfied here and the party adjourned to the Diving Belle at the corner of Orange and Leonard streets, where Peter Williams[83] keeps a ballroom under ground. We have been told that he danced there with Amada Flagrant till the business was well nigh done. Genteel negroes only are tolerated here, and Boz, if he had not been a married man, and, moreover, as well known as he is, might have found a thousand paramours. It was not, however, his taste, and he declined the attentions of Mrs. Julia Simms and Mrs. Amanda Brown, as well as of Clarissa Brown to revel in their embraces. Whereere Boz went, he heard his own waltz called for and as his object was to see life in New-York he put down his foot in tune to the measure. After this he visited the watch house and from thence went home escorted by the faithful police officers, who would not have seen him in trouble. Stephens is the Jonathan Wild[84] of New York, if it be not an insult so to style him, in talent if not in disposition. He has the ability, if he were properly employed and properly remunerated, to do more good than twenty lectures on temperance and twice as many moral reformers. Boz was attended with a crowd in his progress through the Points. Stephens goes single-handed into a congregation of vice and inniquity.

Dickens has learned more by three days residence in New York of the low antipodes of humanity than he could have done by a life spent in any city in Europe. There is more variety in modes and fashions; ay, in morrals too, in ces-Atlantic London than in the old world itself. Boz, however, can never do a nigger. It needs a native to do up a Virginia Negroe or a Western Indian.

AMALGAMATION

From the *Whip*, July 9, 1842.

In this issue, the Whip and Satirist of New-York and Brooklyn *became the* Whip. *The article illustrates the themes of interracial sex, racism, fears of "amalgamation," and the national scope of the flash press based on published correspondence.*

BALTIMORE.

[CORRESPONDENCE OF THE WHIP.]

A Veteran Bawd . . . . A Flower to be saved . . . . Walking Grog Shops . . . . Big Ann Williams and her son.

July 2, 1842.

Dear Whip:

In my rambles through the city the past week I visited many streets and many places. Among the rest Park street, and its thoroughfares, as also Wilk street, better known by the title of 'Crossway.' I went for the express purpose of exposing crime (it is impossible to note the whole.) It would take a year's residence in the midst to become familiarly acquainted with even one half. Park street is in the western part of the city and was once as notorious for its damnable deeds as ever the "Five Points" was in its Palmiest days.[85] This street has improved of late years. The holders of property refused to rent to these women. There is only one house that is fit for a person to enter and that has been recently built. It is kept by one Eliza Randolph, an old veteran Bawd. She has about one dozen girls of all sizes, shapes and ages.

There is one I particularly noted for her extreme youthful appearance and modest deportment; one profane word uttered by any one, would cause a blush to crimson her spotless cheek for very shame. At the first sight of her, I knew the sphere she was then filling was not suited to her nature. Oh! that she could be "plucked as a brand from the burning," she would yet be an honor to her family and society.[86]

She was torn from her home by a wretch, who under the pretence of marriage deceived father and mother, and gained the confidence of the too confiding girl, whom he ruined and then carried her to this "hell on earth." I hope her parents may find where she is and rescue her.

I have often exclaimed inwardly while conversing with ladies: how beautiful is the female character. It is like the placid lake that rolls murmuring onward, as it oe'r flows the bank on either side, beautifies and imparts a healthful vigor to the verdant lawns and gives a refreshing tone to every thing around. But to carry out the analogy, she is when seduced from virtue like a "Freshet as it comes sweeping on in its ruinous course, carrying eternal destruction to the very place it gave life to." In Park street there is some fifteen houses of the very lowest order; these I pass by, and would not put my nose inside to learn the names of the inmates. After leaving this section of the city, I wended my way eastwardly until I reached the "Cross way," as famous a spot as this place can boast of. In these "diggins," girls hardly out of their teens are perfect walking grog shops. The most disgusting sight I know of, is a drunken woman. If the girl leaves the path of rectitude and takes up her abode in this abominable place, she is at once sunk below (in the eyes of every respectable person) the brute creation. There are but few instances where a girl goes to this place to live until she is worn out. If one does, she never can enter a better place. It would be a lasting disgrace on the house to take her in. The most noted one here is big Ann Wilson, an old prostitute of 35 years standing, who keeps a brothel and sailor boarding house; hardened as this old hag is, she brougt her daughters up decently, from home of course, and they married very respectably. But the son was allowed to participate in the business his mother carried on; he became a proficient in the art, he carried it on until the law arrested his progress and placed him in "durance vile." Here you will find houses that surpass the "Five Points" in the richness of filth and putrid matter; enter some and view the Ciracssian[87] and sable race beautifully blended together, and their arms intermingled so as to form a lovely contrast between the alabaster whiteness of the one, and the polished blackness of the other; what a charming sight to thus see two lovly and loving couple entwined in Cupid's Silken Knots. What abolitionist is there but who could admire this? How I admire it, and a Southerner, too. Yes, I love amalgamation as the devil does holy water. I admire it so much, that if I was the mayor, I would with a posse of police officers very politely escort them to the Penitentiary, where they might enjoy the cool, refreshing breeze on the "margin of fair Jones's water," until they were perfectly satisfied with a rural retreat.

Yours, Hornet.

SOUTHERN SLAVERY

From the *Whip and Satirist of New-York and Brooklyn*, April 2, 1842.

Poetry was a common feature in the flash papers. Some poems revealed the racism and pro southern sympathies of certain flash press editors.

CHARITY BEGINS AT HOME.

Look to the South!—behold her golden fields!
Look at the jolly slave—what are his woes?
See him—his toil is over for the day—
Skipping and dancing as he homeward goes?

Look at him, in his go-to-meeting gay,
With Dinah and their charcoal children all;
So blythe and happy as they jog along
To next plantation—"to da nigger ball"

Look to the East; to Britain's cities proud;
Her domes and spires, her palaces and halls;
Her princes, dukes; her noblemen and lords;
Her damp, offensive huts, with mouldering walls.

Oh! How can pen describe or heart conceive
The want, the misery, the vice, the stealth
Of all the million things with human souls
Who die of hunger in this "land of wealth!"

"Lo, the poor slave!" kind hearted Britain cries;
"His wrongs, his woes, his wounds behold, alas!"
At royalty's own door her beggar dies!
He lived, a slave—he dies a putrid mass.

7 HOMOSEXUALITY

GENTEEL FIENDS

From the *Whip and Satirist of New-York and Brooklyn*, January 29, 1842.

The promiscuous heterosexuality promoted by the flash press was magnified by its homophobia. The flash editors initiated some of the earliest known crusades against homosexuals. Here City Hall Park, one of the most publicly accessible spaces in the city, is identified as Gotham's leading meeting place for random homosexual encounters. As with prostitution, the flash press pretended to act as the moral guardian of the city, while simultaneously advertising the very behavior it condemned.

THE SODOMITES.

We hope that in presenting to our readers a sketch of some of the inhuman enormities that a set of fiends bearing the form of men are nightly in the habit of disgusting nature with their monstrous and wicked acts; our excuse must be, that we have undertook to rout from our city these monsters. That it will be a Herculean task, we are well aware, yet we feel assured that in the end we shall be the conquerors.

We know them all by sight, and most of them by name. They are nearly all young men of rather genteel address, and of feminine appearance and manners; among this herd of beasts is one or two old and lecherous villains whom we know well, one of them already, to our knowledge, has murdered, aye that's the word, for by no calmer word can we call the brutal act, that caused a youth of our acquaintance, who was so unfortunate as to fall within the snare of this old sodomite and his beastly crew; he fell into a decline which so emaciated his form that when his body was raised from his bed to be placed within the grave, that the stiffness and coldness of the dead gave place to the shrunken and disjointed corpse.

To what has New York come, if this intolerable nuisance is continued much longer. Our city within the vicinity of the Park will become a second Palais Royale.[88] Their the agents of a horror stricken crime are men or rather miscreants, wearing the appearance of the human form also, their is no difference between the doings of these fiendish agents of the Palais Royale and the brutal sodomites of New York; their diabolical enticements lead to the same end. Fear seizes the mind of the moral man when he is thus accosted and his first impulse is to escape; who would appear at the police

FIGURE 44. "SKETCHES OF CHARACTERS,—NO. II.: FEMALES IN MASQUERADE" SUGGESTS THAT WOMEN AS WELL AS MEN ENGAGED IN HOMOSOCIAL, IF NOT HOMOSEXUAL, ACTIVITIES. *WHIP AND SATIRIST OF NEW-YORK AND BROOKLYN,* MARCH 5, 1842. COURTESY AMERICAN ANTIQUARIAN SOCIETY.

office even to prefer a charge against one of these abominable sinners, why no one in the world; yet we have the names of men who have been acted upon by these fiends, and when we want them, they will be called upon by a tribunal that they dare not refuse to obey—the Law.—

Men of respectability are frequently made the victims of extortion by them, for even death is preferable to the remotest connection with such a charge, we shall pursue this subject again, and endeavor to draw the attention of Justices Matsell and Parker[89] to it, for of a verity we are taught to think these horrible offences foreign to our shores—to our nature they certainly are—yet they are growing a pace in New York—the why and the wherefore in the progress of our strictures we will endeavor to arrive at, as we know where these felons resort for the purpose of meeting and making appointments with their victims, who are generally young men of most prepossessing looks, yes we even know where these abominable and horrd stews are kept, in which these enormities are committed. To show these wretches that we are in earnest in what we say, we will merely ask, Collins Johnson and Adly if they do not believe us.

HOMOPHOBIA

From the *Whip and Satirist of New-York and Brooklyn*, February 5, 1842.

Homophobia and blackmail overlapped. The flash press editors assumed the role of moral guardians by attacking theater impresarios like Ferdinand Palmo for tolerating homosexual performers on stage. Without specifically identifying gay thespians, they urged their removal from the stage.

OUR ARROW HAS

hit the mark! Yes, already do the beastly Sodomites of Gotham quake; they feel their brute souls quiver with fear, and should they not—for, if the bear recital of the deeds of these monsters do not make the honest heart shudder, we are mistaken. One of them nightly performs at one of the Concert Rooms in this city; he shall not do so long, for, even if the task is left to us alone, we will drive his filthy carcase from the place; yet, if he dares insult mankind by appearing among them, when he should herd with beasts, and even they would feel contaminated with his presence. Shame on you; but you have none; now in Pity's name, we warn you of the blow ere we strike, and mark well our words of warning, for we intend to single you out one by one—and you are the first. We warn you not to appear in public again, nor to open your fulsome mouth, that nightly admits, among honest men, a nauseous breath, which it would be certain death to inhale. Palmo, you have one of these monsters among your performers. We tell you of it in plain words, we ask of you, in kindness to your customers, to discharge him. We demand of the performers who are associated with him, to refuse to play, unless he is discharged; and we ask all who visit that place to aid us in driving this monster who wears the human form, and yet carries the soul of a hell-engendered Sodomite from the city.

HOMOSEXUAL MONSTERS

From the *Flash*, August [7], 1842.

Homosexuals were vilified with multiple forms of insult in the flash press: "brutal sodomites," "abominable sinners," "a beastly crew," "old and lecherous villains," "polluted persons," and "monsters." The following two letters not only depict homosexuals as monsters, but even urge their execution.

DOMESTIC COMMUNICATIONS.

A MAN-MONSTER.

New York, July 31st, 1842.

Mr. Editor—

I noticed in the Rake of July 30th, an article headed "Awful Depravity —Sodomy." That paper wanted proof positive, which I can furnish, so that you may show up the hoary headed old villain therein mentioned, and as far as I am concerned, you shall have my oath as well as the oaths (if required) of two other very respectable young men, connected with some of the first families in this city and elsewhere.

To begin—at three different times has this rascal met me in the street and attempted to fool with me as if I were of the sex feminine, till alarmed by his disgusting manner, I intimated to him the propriety of his visiting the Five Points,[90] where possibly he would not be repulsed. He left me as a mob began to collect. This occurred in Broadway near White street, or between White and Franklin streets. Since then, he met me while I was looking into the window of Mr. Howe's bakery, at the corner of Broadway and Howard street. The rascal—my blood boils while I relate it—came up to me, and in a very pleasant humor, apparently, said "Well, sonny, fine cakes, those; very nice for the ladies, hey!" I thought to myself I would see how far he would go. After taking some indecent liberties with me, too indecent to be committed to type, he asked me to walk around the corner in Howard street. It being the way to my residence, I complied. No sooner had we got into Howard street, than the old rascal recommenced his endearments in the same manner; I sung out "watch!" pretty lustily,[91] upon which he struck his large cane upon the side walk angrily, and quickly decamped. Since then, about a year ago, he has not molested me, but I have heard of his abuse of an orphan lad, a relation of mine. To conclude, I would beg of you, Mr. Editor, to wither him with one consuming Flash—that searching flame destined to purify the city of New York, and destroy all vice and wickedness. This wretched name is JFD . . . . , a pretty stout, hale, hoary old rascal. Expose him, then dear sir, and save the bone and sinews of our city—the young men.

If you wish it, I can and will furnish you with the affidavits of half dozen young men of my acquaintance, who have been treated the same way by this unnatural villain.

Yours truly,   F. JUSTICE

A few weeks age we should have rejected the communication above with indignation, for, till quite lately we did not believed in the existence of so abominable a vice, or even in the possibility, history and scripture to the contrary notwithstanding. Nor did it appear to us a thing to be credited that one of these human monsters walked abroad in the form of an American citizen. Certain articles on the subject, that have appeared in sundry of the weekly papers, however, have given us occasion to express our opinion and to make inquiries, and to our infinite regret, we are compelled to believe that the worst and most unnatural of the vices of ancient Athens is extensively practiced in modern Gotham.—There is at least a score of habitual sodomites abiding in this city, who have been pointed out to us, and whom we would expose in the most plenary manner, had we legal proof of their guilt; but there are a thousand notorious truths which do not admit of such proof, and it is dangerous to meddle with them.

One of these miscreants was pointed out to us a few weeks ago in the singing gallery at Palmo's. We were told that he has been detected in the commission of this shocking crime and has mixed very little with society since. His demeanor corroborated the statement—he never once looked up while he was singing and, as soon as his performance was ended, vanished and was seen no more. If that man was not a guilty one, his looks belied him sadly.

Another was shown to us, an elderly man, who keeps a shop in the upper part of Centre St.

Our indignation at the crime is only exceeded by our astonishment that such a morbid appetite should exist. The ancient Israelites and the Pilgrim Fathers punished sodomy with death, and if they ever acted righteously in anything, it was in this.—[EDITOR.]

From the *Flash*, August 14, 1842.

DOMESTIC COMMUNICATIONS.

MONSTERS.

New-York, August 10th, 1842.

Mr. Editor—

I perceived in the last number of the Flash an article headed, "A man monster," and signed Justice. The writer of which deserves the thanks of the greater portion of the community for having come forward to expose the doings of a set of the lowest brutes in creation. It is an astonishing fact, Mr. Editor, that this city has been for a long time flooded with a set of the most bare-faced, impudent, English transported scoundrels that ever breathed the breath of life; I say English, for I venture to affirm, nine out of ten are such, and if there are any other than English, they have been made what they are by these worse than brutes. The amount of evil they are calculated to produce is truly alarming, and calls for the most serious attention. They are continually parading our streets of an evening, watching for their prey, and hundreds of young boys, yes, sir, boys as young as twelve years to eighteen, are victims to their foul and disgusting deeds. I venture to say none of them are married, but hire rooms in various parts of the city for the purpose of bringing their victims to. I shall rid this city of these devils if it is possible, I will spare no pains nor expense to bring them before the world through the columns of your independent and fearless Flash. Show them up in their true colors—give you their names and an account of them as far as in my power lies, will be a pleasure to me, which I shall avail myself of. Before closing, sir, I wish to say a few words in reference to your remarks to 'Justice's' communication. You say one of these miscreants was pointed out to you at Mr. Palmo's singing gallery, and that he never once looked up while he was singing. Now, Mr. Flash, I venture, as a visiter at Palmo's, to say, that no such character was ever engaged there to sing, but there was a notorious one there who presided at the piano, and is styled a music master —Oh that the public knew him!—but his character was not known to Mr. Palmo, and when he discovered who he was, he was discharged, and his place is now supplied by a gentleman in every sense of the word, and one who understands his business, and I think would not be ashamed to look the whole world in the face.

P S—I am certain since the publications in your and other weekly papers, touching these walking nuisances, one half of them, at least, have been compelled to leave the city, and some of them have left off their shameful practices.

I would call on the Old Cap to reform himself immediately, also brutes J, G F, P, H, A, F, W, &c. also a host of young beginners in villainy, pupils of the above reprobates.

Yours, resp'tfully,
EXTERMINATOR.

NAMING NAMES

From the *Rake*, October 1, 1842.

At times, flash press editors identified men charged with sodomy. If blackmail was not the specific goal in such instances, the practice raised the potential threat in other cases.

A SODOMITE NABBED.

A miserable beast in "God's own image" was brought before the Police Court, last Monday, charged with the crime of Sodomy. A friend informs us he was a horrible looking being, as was his accuser. We believe he was let off. He gave his name Grey, or Greigg. For this crime against nature God visited his vengeance upon the heads of the perpetrators, destroying them by thousands. Oh! when will the day arrive that we are to see those guilty of the commission of the terrible enormities now winked at, punished as they should be. Are we to wait until the Ruler of the Universe, outraged and insulted beyond forbearance, blasts us with his destroying wrath, sweeping us from the face of his footstool, into everlasting torture?

‖‖

8 INDICTMENTS

‖‖

PERSONAL ATTACK

From the *Sunday Flash*, October 17, 1841.

One of the principal features of the flash papers was scurrilous attacks on public figures, such as the actor and theater owner Thomas Hamblin. In this case, the article featured a New York businessman Myer Levy, who turned to the district attorney for redress through a prosecution of the editors for criminal libel. The piece was accompanied by a woodcut of "Big Levy" (see fig. 23).

GALLERY OF RASCALITIES AND NOTORIETIES.—NO. 6

BIG LEVY.

After having faintly tried to shadow forth the enormous demerits of Oily Attree[92] and other professing Christians, we began to think that we should be obliged to search the Old Testament for a rascal great enough for our purpose. "The man after God's own Heart" would have served our turn, very well; but his history is already well known, and a moment's reflection has shown us that we have an Israelite nearer home, than whom his whole vile race can shew none viler, from Dathan and Abirain down to little Leah (or Lee, as he falsely spells himself) of the New York Herald.

We spoke of the Jews as they were by their own shewing, until the destruction of the Temple. Since that time, they have been gradually improving, and, at present we have no more valuable citizens. The Quakers are not more moral and exemplary. We believe that no Israelite in New York has ever been convicted before the Police, or chargeable to the public. But there was a Devil in the bright Host of Heaven, and Big Levy belongs, or may belong, to a synagogue in Gotham, if, indeed, he has not already been cast out. It is his birthright.

This walking scarlet sin was born in this city in A.D. 1799, and pity it is that he was not strangled in his birth. The Hebrews are strict in the manner of genealogies, and thus it appears that Levy is a lineal descendant of him who sold his lord for thirty pieces of silver. The younger Judas would sell him for half as many pieces of copper; so true it is that, with that unfortunate race, the sins of the father descend to the children. This is evinced alike by his gambling stock transactions in Wall Street, and by his invariable practice of bilking female sojourners by the way-side, cheating them with counterfeit bills, possessing himself of their trinkets &c. &c. &c. Mrs. Phœbe Doty[93] could give a curious account of his speculations in this line; but what need?—are they not written in the chronicles of every brothel in this city. It is but about three weeks ago that he palmed five counterfeit notes on Catharine—of No. 88 Mott Street; but Kate, who is up to a thing or two, shewed them to the mistress of the house, who looked rather black at the pale color of the impression. This, however, he explained by saying that he had fallen overboard that day, and thereby the color of the ink had been discharged.—Nevertheless, the watchman was sent for; but, as it took three quarters of an hour to arouse that functionary from his slumbers, Levy had time to get on his clothes and make his escape. He did not need to hurry himself.

Melinda Hoag[94] asserts, in his case credibly, that he once gave her an X, and received a V. in exchange. Much did she exult in her unwonted great good luck, till she found that the X. was spurious. The biter was, however, bitten—both bills were alike worthless.

Our hero's father is said to have been as miserly as himself—nevertheless he put his son to school; but took him away again; the young hope of Israel being either so stupid or stiff-necked that no liberality of rod could save the child, or beat anything into him. He, however, shewed an extraordinary aptitude of possessing himself of his schoolfellow's nuts, apples and play-things, and on lending them pocket money on usury. He also drove a brisk trade in peanuts and molasses candy, and so he went on improving, and to improve, till, at last, he reached the summit of his ambition and became a Wall Street broker.

At an early age he assumed the dandy,[95] a character he still retains, and may be seen perambulating Broadway every afternoon, with watch, chain, rings, and dressed in the extreme of the fashion, peering under every woman's bonnet, or following the objects of his especial approval till he compels them to take refuge within the first doors open to them. Many a time has his nose been pulled and his seat of honor been visited therefor. He never resists, though a great, stout hulking fellow; but, like Bennett,[96] seeks a salve for his bruises in a court of law.

He was enabled to begin this career of shew and splendor, by becoming a kind of agent and broker for the famous Mrs. Phœbe Doty, opposite the Old Sugar House, in Church Street, doing the honors of the house and acting as her "fancy man," pouring out the tea, waiting upon the company and doing any little thing for the ladies. So says Phœbe—and she ought to know. She who found most favor in his sight here, was the fair friend of Captain Boardman; Eliza Van Cott by name; with whom he afterwards eloped to Canal Street; where they lived together as man and wife. She bore his name; though most commonly known as Mrs. Boardman.

Eliza was not his only handmaiden, by a good many. His *beau ideal* of manhood was King Solomon—and he tapped as often to the doors of strange women as ever did that salacious sovereign.

> "Black, white or yellow, nothing came amiss;
> 'Give me,' lewd Levy cried, 'a melting kiss.'

And truly, never since the days of Noah,
Had Jew so many concubines before."

Several curious anecdotes are told of his morbid appetites.

One evening he followed a dusky Dulcinea home to the house of Mrs. M__, a very respectable and fashionable lady in Spring Street; where he safely housed her in the kitchen. Somewhat surprised at his unceremonious entrance; the damsel asked him what he wanted. Flushed and eager, he abruptly answered, at the same time giving her a kiss—"a g__," which means something not fit to eat. "A g__!" said she; "is that all? O, yes! Come with me and you shall have it!" She took him by the hand and led him, nothing loth, up a dark staircase. Then, opening a door, she pushed him into an apartment where there was a large party assembled; before he could guess her design or offer her the least resistance. There he stood; petrified—the image of discomfiture and dismay—unable to open his lips. "Mrs. M__, "said the negress, while his knees knocked under him; "this gentleman has come into your kitchen to look for a g__! If you've got such a thing in the house, I'd wish you'd give it to him." It is scarcely necessary to add that he was kicked out of the house in double quick time.

On another occasion, this Levite literally found a soft soap mine. He had been out rather late, to a champaigne supper, and was returning home, somewhat exhilerated, to Sullivan Street, when he was aware of a nymph tripping the pave whose twinkling ankles, gazelle graces and elastic tread raised his ideas to the seventh heaven—*lowered* them, were, perhaps the better word, considering what his ideas of Heaven were. He gave chase instantly, and the strange craft shortened sails and hove in stays as soon. He was at once within hail and she accepted his convey with hesitation. She was leste, sprightly and communicative, and, so much elated was he that he began incontinently to sing,

"____I have pleasure in tow,
And the port where she dwells, I've in view,"

At this juncture, passing a lamp, he perceived that his charmer was black as Erelus,[97] "Never mind," said he—"a black sheep's as sweet mutton as a white one;" and with this philosophical reflection he renewed his endearments. At last they reached a house in Hudson Street. She took him in and led him, in the dark, to a door, which she desired him to enter and wait till she could return with a light. He did so, and she immediately locked the door on him. He did wait, till he was tired, and then set off to explore his whereabout. At the first step, he rolled, heels over head, into the cellar, on the upper stair of which he had been standing.

Seeing, now, that he was caught in a trap, and half frozen, he sought how he might escape. There was a small window, on a level with the street; but he could not reach it—if he could he were saved. Groping about, he found a barrel, half full of something; he knew not what; and open at the end. He rolled it under the window, placed a small piece of board over the top, and mounted. He could now just grasp the sill and made a leap. Confusion!—the board broke—he plumped to his middle into soft soap and rolled, together with his footstool, upon the floor; a most obscene spectacle.

Nothing daunted, however, he turned the barrel the other end up, mounted again and made another and more successful attempt. He was saved and gained the street—some say the watch-house.

We do not quarrel with Mr. Levy's peculiar tastes. He has right to them and to enjoy them. Indeed, they are not peculiar—they are shared by far more than a half of our "brethren of the South." He is far from being the only practical amalgamationist. Only let him and them indulge their preferences decently and lawfully. If they prefer negresses to white women, let them marry them and we shall hear less about amalgamation.—That is the true way to suppress the abolitionists.

We may as well make one story of his mishaps, and have done with them. They may serve as a warning to others—to Tom Hamblin for example. Some years ago, he made a trip to Canada and there he insulted a Miss B__l with his licentious addresses. The lady's brother challenged him. He may be a Jew in other matters; but, when it comes to fighting, he is a Quaker meeker than Moses. On receiving the challenge, he fled the province.

To follow and insult ladies in the street is his constant and daily practice. No longer since than last Monday week he followed a highly respectable lady through Broadway and down Spring to her residence in McDougal Street. There is not a more perfect goat on Snowdbn or Plinnoymmon. Not long ago, he accosted a handsome woman, who is a kept mistress, with very unwelcome addresses; but she could by no means get rid of him. Finally, making the best of a bad bargain, she took him to her house in Sullivan Street and asked him in; no very delicate step; but what could she do? She there requested him to sit down in her parlour and asked him to partake of refreshments. He assented, and she went out, as if to procure them, but, in fact, to call her servant and send her forth to buy a raw hide, which, we are glad for the sake of such fellows as Levy is a very cheap thing and easily procured. The whip was got and placed on a silver salver. The servant was then directed to take it to him. He had the grace to take the hint, and brushed instanter.

Such flesh-flies may not be so wicked or so dangerous as Hamblin, but they are more annoying and as great offenders *contra bonos mores*.[98] They ought to be almost as severely punished.

To return to Mrs. Eliza Boardman. She died about three years ago, regretted by many and missed by more leaving a sister's son in care of our money changer. This little boy now lives with him in Sullivan Street and is taught to bless him with the name of father. His household is under the superintendance of Eliza's sister, who acts as his housekeeper.

Our Pharisee's father once set him up in the dry goods business, in a connection with Mr. E__II__, a very worthy young Englishman. Within three years they failed and Levy now boasts that he has paid every dollar they jointly owed; but he does not say *how*. It was done by compromise— he paid twenty cents on the dollar only—not without compulsion. He next became out door runner to a large house in Wall Street and was afterwards a member of the Board of Brokers. It was not long before he failed to meet his contracts and was turned out of his seat at the Board. To this day, he is largely indebted for differences in stocks.—Nor are all his mishaps on Change. Having called in question the character of Mr. E H, a young gentleman who has been unfortunate in business and was unable to pay him a balance due in stock speculations, the latter publicly horse whipped him in Wall Street, and he had recourse to the law for protection as usual.[99]

We have done with this man's history. He has gone through a life without possessing; certainly without practicing, a single virtue; cringing, avaricious, sordid, ostentatious, lascivious, crapulous, mean. Withot fortune, without morals, principles or religion, he yet enjoys the rights and privileges of the citizens and is not scouted from society. In the South, or the West, he would not be suffered to go at large—no, not to live.—The very wild Indians would not suffer him. "Cut him down!—why cumbereth he the ground?"

COURTS INTERVENE

From the *Flash*, October 30, 1841.

On October 26, 1841, William Joseph Snelling, George Wilkes, and George Wooldridge were arrested on the double charge of libel against Myer Levy and obscene libel for other elements of the October 17 edition of the Sunday Flash. *Here Snelling presents his situation and lashes out against Levy.*

OUR INDICTMENT.

"Now, by St. Paul, the work goes bravely on!" Last Tuesday morning, as Mr. William J. Snelling was sitting quietly smoking his cegar at No. 6, Center Street, thinking no harm, poor man, he was arrested for the Devil knew what, on two indictments found by the congregated wisdom of New York (we mean the Grand Jury) at the complaint of the Devil knows who, which is more than Officer Bowyer did. There are two warrants, one for libel and the other for a misdemeanor, which we since understand to signify publishing the Flash in general and an account of the amorous adventures of a very great rascal designated as Big Levy.—There are several Israelites in this city of that name, and one of them has been kind enough to take to himself the whole contents of that interesting piece of biography, from whic it is fair to infer that he considers any remarks on swindling, cohabitation with negroes, &c. as personal to himself. We trust that he will be able to establish his belief to the satisfaction of the petty jury also. Do it! Levy; nor leave the task to us!

On the same day Messrs. George Wilkes and George Wooldridge were likewise arrested, on precisely the same charges, for no reason that we can imagine but because they happen to be personal friends of Mr. Snelling. The two last immediately gave bail, but the first, in default thereof, was consigned to the Tombs[100] which are not so bad a place after all, and the heart of the circumcised Philistine was mightily exalted and his horn up-lifted. It is written, however, "let not him who putteth on his armour glorify himself like him that taketh it off," and if Mr. Levy does not find that he has caught a Scorpion in gooe earnest, we will be bound to eat him unsalted. He never would have ventured upon such an enterprize, but for the con-currence of several rther upper crust soaplocks[101] and highbinders,[102] who, we understand, joined him in a petition to the Grand Jury. Nor would it have succeeded had there not been several sinners and one fornicator in that sapient and illustrious body, who fear the Flash more than the sum-mons of the last trump to appear before the judgment seat. Before we have done with them, they shall wish they had eaten their bread sweetened with such marmalade as the lord assigned to the Prophet Ezekiel, before they meddled with the Flash and "they shall be consumed with their iniquity." War to the sword hilt and no quarter.

And so Mr. Levy thought he had fastened upon Scorpion, Startle & Sly and utterly quenched the lightning of truth. Never were you more mistaken in your life, friend, not even when you called yourself an honest man. The editors of the Flash walk invisible and intangible; yet they stick to their enemies like tar and are as impalpable to their attacks as feathers. You have sought them without finding them, as an ox goeth to the Slaughter, or the fool to the correction of the stocks.

If Levy had called at No. 6, Center Street, he would have obtained all the information he wanted and have entitled himself to a reward of fifty dollars, for prosecuting, but since he has awakened the wrong passengers, let him make the most of it; for he will get neither information nor money out of us. This we think will go nigh to break his Hebrew heart. As for the Star Chamber to which he applied, we have no patience with it, as will be seen some day soon. Is it not a horrible thing that three innocent men should be accused n d judged in private, on the information of such land sharks as this Levy, arrested without knowing what they are charged with and sent to prison without a copy of the indictment and without a moment allowed to procure bail or engage counsel? Was there anything worse than this in the Inquisition, the Vehmique Tribunal[103] or the mouth of the Lion of St. Marks? Bad as the English common law is, this is the most iniquitous feature. We say, "thou shalt not covet thy neighbors wife, or his servant," and round turns Levy and catches the first man that he sees by the collar with "Do you mean me, Sir?" We say, "thou shall not commit adultery," and we expect that some other inoffencive person will be indicted for it next month by St. Thomas S. Hamblin. When knaves are the complainants and fools the judges, there is no knowing what may happen. Mr. Boggs, Mr. Boggs,[104] you and your fellows have brayed a little too loudly and too early this time. Scorpion, Startle & Sly are not news boys and are not to be silenced so easily.

Reader, did you never see a foolish fowl thrust its head into a haystack, vainly imagining that its body became as invisible as its poll.[105] Just so it is with such turkey buzzards as this Levy. At the first shot he has hidden his head in the Grand Jury room, leaving his tail more exposed than before, and if we do not pepper it for him, it is because there is no powder and shot.—If anybody asks him who the editors of the Sunday Flash are, he had better say that he does not know; for he does not.

THE FLASH PRESS DEFENDED

From the *Whip*, July 23, 1842.

George B. Wooldridge was indicted on charges of obscene libel by the grand jury in New York Court of General Sessions for the July 9, 1842 edition of the Whip. *Here he presents his side, returning to the early conflict with brothel madam Adeline Miller and her son Nelson. The charges against Wooldridge, however, were part of a larger campaign against the flash press, drawing in not only the editor of the* Whip *and the* Libertine *but also those of the* Rake *and the* Flash.

OUR COURSE.

Since the time when the "Whip and Satirist" was indicted by the Grand Jury as an obscene sheet, (the manner in which it was procured we here state,) we have been guarded in the strictest manner as regards the publication of a single article that could in any manner tend to corrupt the morals of the public, or bring a blush on the cheek of the most fastidious; for we not only respect the laws but fear them likewise; and we are not so foolish as to dare the people and the authorities in doing otherwise.

Many who have never read the Whip, labor under the false impression that in its columns is to be found language which would disgrace a bawdy house, or in its illustrative pictures of a kind that would offend all decency. To those thousands who do read our paper, we would refer, and ask if this is so? and we answer for them—no! are we wrong? That there have been, and now are published in this city, papers that should bring the strongest censure of the public upon the authorities did they allow them to go on and publish, in their weekly issues the indecent engravings they do, is without a doubt. Not only should the proprietors be punished, and severely too, but all who have a hand in their publication.

We would not have any one suppose that we speak thus from jealousy, or a desire to injure, for we are now issuing weekly more copies of the Whip than we have ever yet done our circulation at this time being upwards of 12,000! And in one city alone, our agent sells more Whips weekly than the whole circulation of any one of those papers amount to.

How the indictment of the Whip was brought about we will now show, and let the public judge of the purity of the intentions of our prosecutors. We published an article some time since—true in every particular—in which a gentleman, who was in the employ of Nelson H. Miller, a young man well know for his integrity and love of truth, felt himself and his wife injured by our remarks—and, at the persuasion of this man, Miller, and his mother, a suit was commenced against us for libel and damages. He then applied several times to the police magistrates for a criminal warrant, but they would not grant it. His counsel then drew up an indictment for libel and publishing an obscene sheet. The articles selected were the " Diary of a Rake," "The Battery Spy," "Wants to Know," "Nymphs by Daylight," "Split Whiskers," and illustrations of this nature: A chambermaid is lighting an old gentleman to bed, who, do doubt, becomes heated with love and endeavors to kiss her; in the struggle to obtain it, he manages to straddle the handle of a warming pan which she holds in her hand, and in type is made to say, "Take care of the warming pan, sir!"

We do confess that it was rather broad, more so than we would have wished to publish, but it was one of a series that had been published in an English newspaper,[106] and without the slightest intention of doing evil we published it.

These are the articles that those wise men of Gotham selected to obtain an indictment against us by the Grand Jury! how far they succeeded the public already know. Now it will be seen why these gentlemen made themselves so busy: As for Nelson H. Miller, he hated us—and good cause had he, for had we not been instrumental in procuring the indictment of his mother—a woman who has kept a brothel in this city for thirty years, and during that time bid defiance to all law and decency? Yes, she was tried and found guilty, and will soon receive the sentence of the law. We have a witness who will swear that this fellow has boasted that he would have satisfaction for injuries done his mother!

Then, for ridding the city of a corruption, we are to suffer—at least the sapient asses would have it so; but they have fallen short, for the very man intended as their tool has found that the words we had spoken to him in person was truth. Yes, he has found out the characters and intentions of the men who enlisted him against them, and we bid them defiance. For what we have suffered a court of justice will yield us the satisfaction desired; before that court which we were cited to appear we will go, and by good, true, and honest witnesses, show the characters of those who are leagued against us—and the bawd and procuress, whose hate we love, shall be unmasked, her ways and means exposed—and if that court can then punish us, we will abide the issue without a murmur.

||||||||||||||||||||||||||||||||||||||||||||||||||||||||||||||||||||||||||||||||||||||||||||||||||||||||||

9 SPORTS AND THEATER IN THE FLASH WORLD

||||||||||||||||||||||||||||||||||||||||||||||||||||||||||||||||||||||||||||||||||||||||||||||||||||||||||

DEFENDING BARE-KNUCKLE BOXING

From the *Flash*, September 4, 1842.

Prize fighting was illegal in many jurisdictions but increasingly common in antebellum America. Authorities in New York City banned it because it was a violent and bloody sport. Impromptu fights of the 1830s were giving way in the early 1840s to planned matches between trained fighters, often fought outside the city limits in West-chester County, in Brooklyn, in New Jersey, and even on barges in the harbor. Fight-ers often represented rival street gangs or firefighting companies, and settling a quarrel was often the motive. Here the Flash *argues that boxing permits a manly settling of scores in a dispute that might result in worse damage if settled with weapons. Two weeks after this article ran, two young men fought a fight of 108 rounds that resulted in the death of one, casting a momentary pall over the sport.*

FIGURE 45. "THE RING." HEADER ILLUSTRATION FOR A REGULAR PUGILISM COLUMN. *NEW YORK SPORTING WHIP,* MARCH 4, 1843. COURTESY AMERICAN ANTIQUARIAN SOCIETY.

THE RING.

If human passions could be tamed, if all mankind were quakers, there would be no blood-shed, no inadequate punishment for individual wrongs. We should then rejoice to see pugilism abolished. But, as such a state of things cannot be, we think a well regulated prize ring a public benefit. It does look ill, we admit, to see two good men and true stand up and pummel each other to jellies; but which is worst, a punch in the ribs, a tap on the conk, or eighteen inches of a Bowie knife?

Take a dispassionate view of the matter. One Spaniard, Greek or Italian says to another "you lie," and is instantly stretched in his blood. The chastisement far exceeds the offence. One man loses his life outright, and the other, if he has any feeling, is embittered by remorse. An Anglo Saxon who recognizes the rules of the ring and receives the same insult, knocks his slanderer down and is satisfied, for no son of Fancy[107] will strike a man when he is down. The worst that can come of it is a mill, and a drubbing is better than death, even if it falls upon the wrong party.

It has been argued that science enables one man to insult another to trample on another with impunity, for the strong to trample on the weak. It would not be so if the laws of the ring were the laws of the land. No true chick of the game will stand by and see a big 'un oppress a light weight. He will take it up rather, himself and bear the brunt. If the difference must be decided by fistic arbitrement a match is never suffered to take place where there is not, at least, a doubt respecting the ability of the men. All is as regular as clock work and every thing is conducted fairly. Is it so with dueling? What two men were ever equal good swordsmen or shots? For Captain Scott to kill James Watson Webb[108] in a duel would be literal murder, unless he were forced into it, of which there is little danger.—He has the most imperturbable intropodity[109] and could count every button on his coat with a sword or pistol as coolly as he would carve a partridge, whereas Webb's eye would assume the hue of green glass and his hand would shake so that his opponent would run less risk than his seconds. It would be no fair match; yet, physically, Webb appears much superior to Scott. Could they by any possibility quarrel, it would be better for them to settle the matter in a set-to than otherwise;—better for Scott to receive a licking than to make himself a homicide, though we are not quite sure that there is any harm in shooting a calf.

In casual disputes, a powerful man often takes advantage of superior force to inflict every personal indignity upon his feebler neighbor. The aggrieved party goes to the police for redress and is fined five dollars—no redress at all. It is adding injury to insult. In the south and west this leads to dueling and assassination; for who will consent to be horse-whipped or kicked for five dollars. Here the whipper has nothing to do but to grin, bear it and pass for a spiritless dastard or to take the law into his own hands.

FIGURE 46. "PEDESTRIANISM." ANOTHER REGULAR COLUMN HEADER FOR A POPULAR SPORT OF FOOT-RACING, AT WHICH GEORGE W. DIXON EXCELLED. *NEW YORK SPORTING WHIP*, MARCH 4, 1843. COURTESY AMERICAN ANTIQUARIAN SOCIETY.

Hence so many street brawls, outrages, and riots. If every man in the community were imbued with the spirit of the Fancy a hundred hands would be raised at once to resent or chastise every such cowardly outrage, at every corner would start forth a McClusky, a Bell or a Ford to do summary justice on the offender.[110]

It is a common but gross error to suppose that pugilists as a body, are morose, ignorant or vulgar in their manners. Where can be found a kinder or better landlord than McClusky, Ford or George Over? Where are two more gentlemanly men than Jack Sheridan and John Hudson? Many more we could name, but we do not like to make a distinction. The fact is that as large and very powerful men are good natured, so the consciousness of superior power makes most pugilists civil and forbearing. They entertain the feeling of the lordly mastiff, who never attacks a lapdog. There may be exceptions but they are few. Accidents happen, too, in the sports of the ring, so they do in steam boats, rail road cars and other vehicles of public good.

THE RING

From the *Flash*, June 23, 1842.

The flash press satirized street fighters. This account describes a fight motivated both by jealousy over a woman and by firefighter rivalry.

FIGHT BETWEEN TWO COCK-CHICKENS,

ON TUESDAY

This came off in the Fifth Avenue, between 10th and 11th streets, and a pair of game bantams the combatants are. The thing has been on hand, we believe, for more months than one, and right manfully did the disputants come to the scratch. The parties are two firemen, and, if we have been correctly informed, jealousy, the green-eyed monster, has caused their quarrel.

The report runs, too, that there was some engine department dispute. These heroes are Dick Blauvelt, of No. 27, and John Reed, of No. 36. Dick "The Blower," as he is called, is much the largest of the two.

The men peeled in the street, and a pretty pair of potatoes they seemed as ever had their coats taken off. For five rounds they fought in fair style, no shying, no dropping. When either fell it was because he was fairly knocked down, and there was no calling to time. Up to this moment Dick stood no chance—his science and perhaps his practice was quite inferior to that of his game little antagonist. But in the sixth round Dick rushed in—a clench took place, and both came down, Dick uppermost. Very hard to say which had the worse of it. We have seldom seen four bunches of fives used more industriously or expeditiously. In fact, it was impossible for our eyes to keep count of the knocks. Both lost their temper, and the seconds were obliged to drag them apart, both foaming at the moth. The seconds kept them apart about three minutes, and to it they went again, Dick with his eyes in by no means a new sort of mourning, and his proboscis in no order for sneezing. Though rather groggy, he stood well upon his pins, till Johnny caught him with his left, and then it was up with him.

Seventh Round—No chance for Dick; but still the gallant fellow made play and planted one excellent, but feeble hit on John's bread-basket. He took nothing by his motion but a right-handed counter, when he closed again, and John went down, very like a spread eagle.

For three more minutes John had the game to himself—hitting pretty much as he pleased. Dick, nevertheless, refused to give in, till the close of 10th round, when he could not come to time, and his seconds withdrew him, very unwillingly. The fight lasted but twenty minutes; but there were as many hard blows given and taken in that time, as in the hard contested fight between Tom Hyer and Country McClusky.[111] We have never seen anything like the severity of the punishment.

DOG FIGHTS

From the *Whip*, November 12, 1842.

Animal fights were popular with gamblers. Such accounts rarely mention female spectators. Wallabout was a section of Brooklyn adjacent to Wallabout Bay, the location of a naval shipyard in the East River.

CANINE FANCY.

We are requested to lay before our readers a true account of the late "turn-up" between the celebrated dogs Wallabout Snap, and Madison street Bill, for twenty dollars a side. The fight took place at a spacious barn at the Wallabout, on the 18th of October last. The Wallabout dog was on the spot long before the appointed time, and looked all fight, being in first rate condition. At about ten minutes before the appointed time, the New

York boys made their appearance with their dog; but what a contrast their dog presented; he was at least ten pounds lighter than the Wallabout dog, and, as I have been told by his hander, on three legs at that.

After the judges were appointed, the two dogs went at it, and fought for 33 minutes without a turn; and up to the 26th minute, bets were freely exchanged on both sides, when Snap straightened his dog out, and the handler of Snap claimed a turn, but was not quick enough to take it; so both dogs went at it again; and while fighting, the handler of Snap put both hands on his dog, and the New Yorkers claimed the money.

REMARKS. The Wallabout dog was at least ten pounds the heaviest dog. The New York dog is said to have received but three days training, when he received his lameness, and was in no condition to fight; but the fight was claimed on account of bad handling on the part of Snap. The foregoing remarks can be proved by a disinterested person.

The owner of the dog Hangman are now open to fight him against any sixty pound dog, give or take two pounds, for no less than $50, or as much more as they feel inclined to make it. If the challenge is accepted, the party accepting will name the time and place where the money can be put up, through the columns of the Whip.

AQUATIC SPORTS

From the *Whip*, November 12, 1842.

Boat racing attracted spectators of both sexes. This contest took place on the Hudson River in front of crowds at Elysian Fields, a popular Hoboken, New Jersey, riverside park easily reached by ferryboat from New York City. Vendors of food and drink worked the crowd, as did card-trick gamblers.

DAY AT HOBOKEN.—THE REGATTA.

This regatta, which took place on Wednesday, July 27, was well attended. Many of the sporting men of the city were present—as were most of those noble souls, the "Battery boatmen." The day was beautiful, but the sun was rather warm; which, had there been no other inducement, would have been sufficient to bring thousands to that delightful spot, the Elysian Fields. A large number of the "frail sisterhood" were also present; among whom we noticed the fearnaught, Mary Turner, who tripped o'er the green fields as gay as a lark; she was accompanied by her friend, the fair Rose Berri. Having arrived a short time before the race took off, we strolled over this second paradise, and having become rather dry from the exposure to the

FIGURE 47. "SKETCHES OF CHARACTERS—NO. 38.: GRAND PIC-NIC IN HOBOKEN"
REFLECTS THE HETEROSEXUAL POSSIBILITIES AT A POPULAR PICNIC GROUNDS ALONG
THE HUDSON RIVER IN NEW JERSEY. *WHIP,* SEPT. 10, 1842. COURTESY
AMERICAN ANTIQUARIAN SOCIETY.

sun which we were subjected in the crossing over, we called upon our old
friend McCarty, whom we found busy attending to the wants of his numerous customers; after partaking of one of his "cobblers," we found ourselves
extremely refreshed. . . .

Among the many bucks present, we noticed several busily engaged with
"swells;" but to our astonishment not a solitary "five, ten or fifteen can't
tell where the little joker lays" player was present—although we *did* notice one with the knee-prop in his hand. Perhaps they were afraid of being
thrown overboard. . . .

At half past three o'clock the first race came off . . . [the last race] lay
between the Jefferson and the Duane. On starting the Duane took the lead,
which was kept for a few rods, when the Jefferson passed her, and on the turn
was full five lengths ahead, which was maintained during the remainder of
the race. The astonishment at this result was great, and much dissatisfaction
was evinced by friends of the Duane—they asserting it was foul, and offered
to prove it on oath a "throw off" race. We hope, for the satisfaction of both
parties, that this race may again be tested. Will not that be the case?

... We then took up our homeward march, and walking leisurely along, fell in with a lot of young "sparks" who had been enjoying themselves during the afternoon, by testing the different qualities of Mac's Liquors, and were in high glee; two of them had "picked up" two of the identical females we had met during the afternoon, and were inclined to be jealous of the man with the "prop," he having our beauty in tow. . . .

THEATER REVIEWS

From the *Weekly Rake*, October 1, 1842.

Four or five major theaters provided drama in New York City. Numerous daily papers posted playbills and curtain hours along with reviews by drama critics. The sporting weeklies also covered the theater, but sometimes with an extra spark of attention to the flash underworld. This example from the Rake *reviews not only the actors on stage but also the prostitutes in the famous third tier in each house. Note that in every case the* Rake *condemns the prostitutes and threatens exposure of clients.*

PLAYS, PLAYHOUSES AND THEIR PLAYERS;

OR, A PEEP AT THEIR PERFORMANCES:

We have been unable to attend the Theatres regularly this week. However what we have gathered will be found below.

PARK.—The houses have been *rayther* slim, and not very flattering to the tragedian, Mr. VANDENHOFF, JR.,[112] who is in every way a "chip off the old block."—We have not enough space to devote to a criticism of his merits. We do not think he will "set the North River on fire," though we have heard a great deal of "praise preliminary." He has been, to tell the truth, miserably supported, and this may have added to our disappointment; for we were sadly deceived! Messrs. Simpson and Barry will have to try another tack.[113] The harlots in the third tier were very unruly and filthy both in speech and person. Gentlemen, will you exclude them from the house, or are you determined to compel us to publish the names of the frequenters of your assignation house? Correspondents are sending names fast, and we will not "hold over" much longer.

OLYMPIC.—The little band plays sweetly, the women are strong in numbers and all beautifully fascinating, aye! enchanting, especially Miss Taylor. Little Singleton used to be the belle of *them* boards;[114] but Miss Taylor takes the shine off.

The "Lady in Black" made her appearance by proxy, last Monday evening; for the first time Mrs. Timm becoming her substitute; though why she is called the Lady in Black, is to us a mystery, as they are all ladies in opaque garments. The piece resembles Saratoga Springs in two particulars. Mitchell[115] plays Mr. Brown, and is taken for another Mr. Brown, and in consequence, suffers considerable, getting into all sorts of dilemmas from which he is in the end extricated, of course! Then, it is exceedingly smutty, and the *double entendres* saved it. We call that catering to the depraved taste of the millions, when, to please a few "gallant" bloods, are uproarious and insulting towards the gentlemen in the boxes, the few females in the house are obliged to hide their blushes from their male companions. All we have to say, is, that such a course, though profitable for a short time is ruinous in the end. In short, "The Lady in Black" is a "stale, flat, and unprofitable" affair. . . . The Third Tier here is small, but—oh!—The women who make their sales here are low and miserable in appearance, though pretty civil. We have seven names furnished us by a correspondent, who is a responsible man. Reform, or—. . . CHATHAM.—Mr. Sinclair, the father-in-law of Mr. Forrest, has been here during the week.[116] Mad. Lecompte and the *ballet corps* have exceedingly fine legs, and know how to show them to advantage. She does not kick lower than formerly; but, of course, dreads no more "prosecuted pictures!"[117] Mr. Sinclair sings sweetly for so old a man, but he is too old and had better retire. We cannot imagine how he can sing at all with such accompaniment—the band is composed of men who have anything but "music in their souls," and send forth sounds as melodious as the strains of a barrel organ and Pan pipes. The houses have been middling, only. The women who fill the Third Tier are beastly, disgusting sots, and are removed but one degree from those on the Hook and on the Five Points.[118] They emit an effluvia similar to the perfume of a skunk. . . .

BOWERY.—The people mustered strong on Monday and every other night to welcome back Celeste. We consider her improved since her departure. Marie du Cange is a very good drama, and admirably adapted to Madame's powers of pantomime. In some parts she is pathetic and affecting in the extreme, and we were as well pleased as any body. This house is noted for looseness, both before and behind the curtain, and we are sorry that Madame engaged with the manager. Prize fighting (after a fashion) was exhibited here; and many beastly exhibitions presented upon the boards. . . . The slaves who sell themselves here are culled from the commonest trulls in and about the neighborhood—in fact, most of them are miserable Walker-street cruisers—and are very insulting and repulsive in their deportment. They would turn the stomach of a boz.—We have five names of gents who visit here; and if Tom S. Hamblin[119] or Mr. S. do not make a clean sweep upstairs, we shall be compelled to "go our death."

THE THIRD TIER

From the *Whip and Satirist of New-York and Brooklyn*, January 29, 1842.

The infamous third tier of theaters (actually the second balcony) was reserved for prostitutes and their customers. The Whip *here instructs its readers on the boundaries of proper sexual behavior.*

The third tier of the Olympic was crowded on Monday evening last with the pretty nymphs of Gotham. We noticed two gentlemen (we call them so now) making themselves familiarly acquainted with the ankle and foot of one of Mrs. Franklin's LADIES. We would request these gentlemen for the sake of decency, to wait for a proper time, and then there will be no danger of disgusting many who visit that part of the house, and we would inform them that the saloon is furnished for the purpose of accommodating ladies and gentlemen with eatables and drinkables, nothing else, so we acquaint Mr. Raffle-ring and Mr. $1100 that if they are caught in the same ungentlemanly conduct again they will either receive a kick from Mr. Napoleon, or a severe WHIPping from us.

10 THE ILLUSTRATIONS OF JOHN H. MANNING

John H. Manning was the only named illustrator for the flash press. Born around 1820 in Massachusetts, he began his career in 1841 as an engraver and designer of comic almanacs. He worked in New York from 1842 to 1844 in the shop of Robert H. Elton, a master printer who supplied humorous illustrations to newspapers, including the flash papers. Manning's work in the *Whip* and in the other sporting weeklies appeared in summer and fall of 1842. In 1850, perhaps after a time in California during the Gold Rush,

Manning resurfaced in Boston, where he primarily did more refined drawings. His artistic career ended in 1859.

Manning was the delineator for the masthead of the *Whip and Satirist of New-York* (fig. 3), the "Pewter Mug on a Saturday Night" (fig. 6) and "A Cobbler Caught with His 'Awl' Out!" (fig. 43), as well as the four illustrations pictured here. He returned to his comic New York style in his later Boston years when he designed the masthead for *Life in Boston and New England Police Gazette* (fig. 29).

FIGURE 48. MANNING, "GRAND TRIAL DANCE BETWEEN NANCE HOLMES AND SUSE BRYANT," *WHIP AND SATIRIST OF NEW-YORK AND BROOKLYN,* JUNE 25, 1842 (ALSO *LIBERTINE,* JUNE 15, 1843), IS A ZESTFUL AND COMIC LOOK AT THE PURPORTED DANCE COMPETITION OF TWO BOSTON PROSTITUTES. COURTESY AMERICAN ANTIQUARIAN SOCIETY.

FIGURE 49. MANNING, "RIPTON AND AMERICUS," *WHIP*, OCT. 1, 1842, IS A
STRAIGHTFORWARD PRESENTATION OF A SPORTING EVENT, ENLIVENED BY MANY MALE
CHARACTER TYPES. COURTESY AMERICAN ANTIQUARIAN SOCIETY.

FIGURE 50. MANNING, "THE DANDY AND THE SOAP-FAT MAN," *WEEKLY RAKE*,
OCT. 1, 1842, SHOWS A FOPPISH "PUPPY" OR DANDY BEING DUNKED IN A PAIL OF FAT BY
AN INSULTED IRISH WORKMAN WHO RECYCLES COOKING FATS FOR SOAPMAKING. NOTE
THE NEWSBOY CLUTCHING COPIES OF THE *RAKE*. COURTESY AMERICAN ANTIQUARIAN
SOCIETY.

LOOK ON THIS PICTURE

The AMERICAN "Merchant Princes" of the city of New-York responding to the toast in honor of the President of the United States.

AND ON THIS!!

The AMERICAN "Merchant Princes" of New York responding to the toast of the "Queen of England," at the same time proclaiming her "Queen of the Seas!!"

"Can such things be."—SHAKSPEARE.

THE ENGLISH RING.

FIGURE 51. MANNING, "SKETCHES OF CHARACTERS—NO. 39.: LORD ASHBURTON DINNER—ILLUSTRATED," *WHIP,* SEPT. 24, 1842. AFTER CONCLUDING A HIGHLY SATISFACTORY U.S.-CANADA BORDER TREATY, BRITISH NEGOTIATOR LORD ASHBURTON WAS HONORED IN SEVERAL U.S. CITIES. BUT A DINNER HOSTED BY WEALTHY NEW YORK MERCHANTS SCANDALIZED MANY WHEN A FEEBLE TOAST TO PRESIDENT TYLER WAS MET WITH STONY SILENCE WHILE A TOAST TO QUEEN VICTORIA GAINED STANDING ACCLAIM. MANNING'S CARTOON REFLECTS FLASH CRITIQUES OF THE MERCHANT ELITE, SEEN AS SOUR AND UNPATRIOTIC. COURTESY AMERICAN ANTIQUARIAN SOCIETY.

ACKNOWLEDGMENTS

Although the flash press weeklies remained in business for less than two years, we have lived with them for nearly two decades. The three of us began working together in 1998. Horowitz was researching the sporting press for a chapter in *Rereading Sex* and consulted Cohen and Gilfoyle, already working with the flash weeklies. All three realized the richness of the subject of the sporting press and wanted to probe it further. The three coauthors first collaborated on a panel at the American Studies Association annual meeting in 1999. Although some of the material in this new work was significantly influenced by Horowitz's earlier study, important new research and thinking has emerged from the collaboration.

In the course of our research and writing, we incurred considerable debts to librarians, archivists, and collectors, whose labors preserved and made accessible these obscure but important publications. Most important has been the American Antiquarian Society in Worcester, Massachusetts. This institution carefully preserved the largest known collection of flash press weeklies, made them available to us on numerous occasions, and microfilmed the entire collection when we reached the end of our research. Georgia B. Barnhill, Joanne D. Chaison, Ellen S. Dunlap, Vincent L. Golden, John B. Hench, Thomas G. Knoles, Dennis R. Laurie, and Joyce Ann Tracy offered invaluable assistance over many years at different stages of this project. The Society also supported Cohen and Horowitz with fellowship grants that allowed them to read and examine the flash papers in greater depth. Finally, we are particularly indebted to Leo Hershkowitz for saving and sharing these and other documents with us on numerous occasions.

We also thank Kenneth Cobb, Leonora Gidlund, and Evelyn Gonzalez at the New York City Municipal Archives and Reference Center; Marguerite Lavin at the Museum of the City of New York; Meg Rich and Charles Greene at the Princeton University Library; the Chicago History Museum; the Newberry Library; the New-York Historical Society; and the New York Public Library for making parts of their collections available to us. Terry Delaney, the granddaughter of George Underwood, shared her knowledge of her family and grandfather at a key point in determining the provenance of the flash weeklies.

Others offered valuable suggestions, provocative interpretations and sometimes their own research, including: Gail Bederman, Donna I. Dennis, Elliott J. Gorn, James R. Grossman, Leon Jackson, David Rabban, Jonathan D. Sarna, Renée M. Sentilles, Timothy Spears, Richard Stott, and Alfred Young. We also thank the providers of recent online databases of nineteenth-century U.S. serials—19th Century U.S. Newspapers (Thompson/Gale Group), Early American Newspapers (Readex), the Civil War Era (ProQuest), and the American Periodical Series (ProQuest)—whose vast digitized collections enabled us to recover many elements of the public careers of our largely forgotten flash editors. We are grateful to the University of Connecticut, the University of Nebraska and the Great Plains Humanities Center, and the Pennsylvania State University for inviting us to discuss portions of our work, and to the American Studies Association and the American Antiquarian Society for allowing us to present our findings at their annual meetings in 1999 and 2004, respectively. Sharon Davenport, Crystal Fryer, and Sarah Miller provided research assistance during the course of the project.

Our respective institutions—Loyola University Chicago, Smith College, and the University of California, Santa Barbara—have supported us in multiple ways during our careers. Our colleagues in the History and American Studies Departments have provided intellectually stimulating environments.

At the University of Chicago Press, we owe considerable thanks to the positive and detailed criticism we received from the anonymous peer readers. Their suggestions enabled us to write a much better book. We appreciate the time, support, and, most importantly, patience our editor Robert Devens gave us. Emilie Sandoz and Katherine M. Frentzel saved us much time and anguish in moving the manuscript through production.

Our spouses and families have lived with the flash weeklies almost as long as we have. They deserve special mention and have our unbounded affection: Mary Rose Alexander, Benjamin J. Cohen, Danielle Gilfoyle, Maria Gilfoyle, and Daniel Horowitz.

APPENDIX

Below follow variant titles of the flash papers, their full runs as imputed from their issue numbers, and their known editors (in parentheses).

The *Sunday Flash*: August 8, 1841, to October 24, 1841 (Snelling, Wilkes, Wooldridge)

The *Flash*: Oct 31, 1841, to January 29, 1842 (Snelling)

The *Flash*: June 10, 1842, to January 14, 1843 (Snelling, Scott, Vandewater)

The *True Flash*: December 4 and 5, 1841 (slightly variant editions) (Wooldridge)

The *Whip and Satirist of New-York and Brooklyn*: December 25, 1841, to July 23, 1842 (Wooldridge, Colburn, Renshaw)

The *Whip*: July 9, 1842, to January 21, 1843 (Wooldridge, Colburn, Renshaw)

The *New York Sporting Whip*: January 28, 1843, to March 4, 1843 (Wooldridge, Meighan)

The *Libertine* (twice a month): July 1, 1842, to September 1, 1842 (Wooldridge)

The *Weekly Rake*: June 18, 1842, to November 26, 1842 (Meighan, P. Henry). (One issue in this set is titled the *Rake*, September 3, 1842.)

NOTES

INTRODUCTION

1. The main successful exemplars of the so-called penny press were the *Sun*, the *Transcript*, the *Herald*, and the *Tribune;* less well known were 1840s papers like the *Daily Express*, the *Atlas*, the *Aurora*, the *Tattler*, and the *Planet*. On the early chronology and development of New York's penny press, see Isaac Clark Pray, "A Journalist," in *Memoirs of James Gordon Bennett and His Times* (New York: Stringer and Townsend, 1855); James Parton, *The Life of Horace Greeley* (New York: J. R. Osgood & Co., 1872), 103–10, 157–65; Horace Greeley, *Recollections of a Busy Life* (New York: J. B. Ford & Co., 1868), 91–97, 136–43; William L. Stone, "Newspapers and Magazines," in *Memorial History of the City of New-York*, vol. 4, ed. James Grant Wilson (New York: New York History Co., 1893), 155–59; Frank Luther Mott, *American Journalism: A History of Newspapers in the United States through 260 Years* (New York: Macmillan, 1949), 215–20 (statistics), 222–28, 243; Gunther Barth, *City People: The Rise of Modern City Culture in Nineteenth-Century America* (New York: Oxford University Press, 1980), 58–92; John D. Stevens, *Sensationalism and the New York Press* (New York: Columbia University Press, 1990); Michael Schudson, *Discovering the News: A Social History of American Newspapers* (New York: Basic Books, 1978); Dan Schiller, *Objectivity and the News: The Public and the Rise of Commercial Journalism* (Philadelphia: University of Pennsylvania Press, 1981); James L. Crouthamel, *Bennett's New York Herald and the Rise of the Popular Press* (Syracuse, N.Y.: Syracuse University Press, 1989); Andie Tucker, *Froth & Scum: Truth, Beauty, Goodness, and the Ax Murder in America's First Mass Medium* (Chapel Hill: University of North Carolina Press, 1994); Alexander Saxton, "Problems of Class and Rank in the Origins of the Mass Circulation Press," *American Quarterly* 36 (1984): 211–34; idem, *The Rise and Fall of the White Republic: Class Politics and Mass Culture in Nineteenth-Century America* (London: Verso, 1990), 77–108; Peter Buckley, "Culture, Class, and Place in Antebellum New York," in *Power, Culture, and Place: Essays on New York City*, ed. John H. Mollenkopf (New York: Russell Sage Foundation, 1988), 36–38. None of these works discuss the flash press.

2. The *Working Men's Advocate* and the *Subterranean* addressed the laboring classes; the *Spirit of the Times* devoted itself to the theater and the turf, among other sports; and papers like the *Aurora*, the *Atlas*, the *Censor*, the *Uncle Sam*, the *Arena*, and the *Two-Penny Trumpet* were among dozens of enterprises that aimed to entertain readers with gossip and local news. On reading and New Yorkers, see Isabelle Lehuu, *Carnival on the Page: Popular Print Media in Antebellum America* (Chapel Hill: University of North Carolina Press, 2000); David Henkin, *City Reading* (New York: Columbia University Press, 1999); and Ronald J. Zboray and Mary Saracino Zboray, *Literary Dollars and Social Sense* (New York: Routledge, 2005).

3. The *Oxford English Dictionary* gives examples of the slang adjectival meaning of *flash* in three senses: gaudy, showy, and smart; counterfeit, sham; and knowing,

in-the-know. It ascribes its use to the realms of thieves and prostitutes in the eighteenth century and then to sporting men, especially those associated with boxing, in the mid-nineteenth century. *OED Online*, 2nd. ed. (Oxford: Oxford University Press, 1989), http://www.oed.com (third adjective entry for "flash"). The glossary: Ned Buntline (E. Z. C. Judson), *The Mysteries and Miseries of New York: A Story of Real Life* (New York: Bedford, 1847), 113–16; George W. Matsell, *Vocabulum; or, The Rogue's Lexicon* (New York: George W. Matsell & Co., 1859), 82. For British usage: *The Slang Dictionary, Etymological, Historical, and Anecdotal*, 2nd ed. (London: Chatto and Windus, 1874), 163–64. For its early coinage: Charles Hitchin, *The Regulator; or, A Discovery of the Thieves, Thief Takers, and Locks, alias Receivers of Stolen Goods in and about the City of London: with the thief takers proclamation, also an account of all the flash words now in vogue amongst the thieves, with an explanation of each word* (London, 1718). A later reference work continues the usage: Humphry Tristram Potter, *Dictionary of all the Cant and Flash Languages, both Ancient and Modern, Used by Gypsies, Beggars, Swindlers, and Shoplifters* (London, 1790). See Helen Berry, "Rethinking Politeness in Eighteenth-Century England: Moll King's Coffee House and the Significance of 'Flash Talk,'" in *Transactions of the Royal Historical Society*, 6th ser. (Cambridge, Eng.: Cambridge University Press, 2001), XI: 65–81. For nineteenth-century flash culture in London, see Gregory Dart, "'Flash Style': Pierce Egan and Literary London, 1820–28," *History Workshop Journal* 51 (2001): 181–205. For "flash men" in Australia in the 1840s, see http://www.investigator.records.nsw.gov.au/ebook/book.asp?3406/a001 (accessed Aug. 16, 2007), which reproduces a manuscript kept by William Augustus Miles, superintendent of the Sydney Police from 1840–48, documenting the flash underworld imported there by English convicts.

4. Louis Hewitt Fox, *New York City Newspapers, 1820–1850, A Bibliography* (Chicago: University of Chicago Press, 1928). Fox's source for the flash titles was Frederic Hudson, *Journalism in the United States from 1690 to 1872* (New York: Harper and Brothers, 1872), 525, which presents a comprehensive list of New York papers as of November 1842. Fox does note four extant issues of the *New York Packet* (1845) edited by George Washington Dixon, filled with what he called "lurid sex stories." While there is indignant sexual humor and the satire on moralism characteristic of the flash press, we class this paper as a near-flash, but still rather more tame than the titles of 1841–43. For Dixon's involvement with the birth of the flash papers, see chapter 1, this volume. Fox listed scattered issues of other humor papers that we also judge not to be in quite in the same league as the flash papers: the *Arena* (1842), *Life in New York* (1842), the *New York Trumpet* (1841), the *Uncle Sam* (1841), the *Evening Tattler* (1839–42), plus at least one satirical gossip paper from a decade earlier: *Ely's Hawk and Buzzard* (1826–34). Scattered issues of all but one of these titles are owned by the American Antiquarian Society, which also now has five issues of the *Owl* (1830), from the Hershkowitz gift. The *Owl* and the *Hawk and Buzzard* consisted of short complaining or tattling letters to the editor, many of which broached indelicate topics (i.e., complaints about "golden showers" from upstairs neighbors, or admonitions to clerks visiting young girls at 3 a.m.; *Owl*, July 10, 1830, p. 1).

5. Thomas O. Mabbott's research note, "Brief Notes on Four Obscure New York Scandal Sheets," *American Notes and Queries* (Nov. 1944): 115–16, discussed the *Weekly Rake* and the *Libertine*, each a single issue, and two others with no extant copies, the *Flash* (mentioned in the *Rake*) and another called the *Figaro* (1833), referenced as a gossip sheet in the *New York Mirror*. Letters between Mabbott and Clarence Brigham, President of the American Antiquarian Society, establish that before 1946 the AAS owned the *Libertine* and issues of the *Broadway Belle* and *Venus's Miscellany*, two erotic weeklies of the late 1850s. We thank Vincent Golden, curator of newspapers and periodicals at the

AAS, for unearthing this correspondence of five letters, three by Mabbott to Brigham (Sept. 14, 1935; Jan. 30, 1945; Sept. 25, 1946) and two by Brigham to Mabbott (Jan. 29, 1945; Sept. 27, 1946).

6. Cohen's first use was in "Unregulated Youth: Masculinity and Murder in the 1830s City," *Radical History Review* 52 (Winter 1992): 33–52. Articles by Dale Cockrell are "Callithumpians, Mummers, Maskers, and Minstrels: Blackface in the Streets of Jacksonian America," *Theatre Annual* 49 (1996): 15–34; and "Jim Crow, Demon of Disorder," *American Music* 14 (1996): 161–84.

7. Horowitz learned about Prof. Hershkowitz from Gail Bederman of Notre Dame University, who had tracked original court records about the New York City abortionist Madame Restell to his Queens basement, where he invited her to look at his 1840s through 1850s newspaper collection. (The Restell records are now at the Schlesinger Library in Cambridge, Massachusetts.) On Leo Hershkowitz and his aptitude for finding castoff documents, see Murray Schumach, "Papers Reflect Bias of Bygone Era," *New York Times,* Aug. 6, 1976; and Douglas Martin, "A 'Bum' Gleans the Discarded to Find History," *New York Times,* July 28, 1990. The donation to the American Antiquarian Society consisted of twenty-seven issues, most of which bore the marks of the district attorney's pen as he considered possible prosecutions. The seventeen not from the flash set were relevant to other libel cases; several were papers with a racy or sporting character, but not qualifying as fully flash. See http://www.americanantiquarian.org/Thebook/July2004.pdf.

8. We thank Thomas G. Knoles, the Marcus A. McCorison Librarian of the American Antiquarian Society, for his persistence in locating acquisition records including letters exchanged between George B. Underwood Jr. of Portsmouth, N.H., and Joyce Ann Tracy, then curator of newspapers for the Society (Nov. 8, 16, 20, and 27, 1984). See also Lucien Marcus Underwood, *The Underwood Families of America* (Lancaster, Pa.: New Era Printing Co., 1913), 143; "Former Sports Editor, Sports Star, Dies," *Portsmouth (N.H.) Herald,* Aug. 30, 1943; and http://www.zoominfo.com/people/Underwood_George_48369238.aspx (accessed May 4, 2007). We thank Underwood's granddaughter, Terry Delaney, for sharing her knowledge of her grandfather. The flash editors who continued with sports journalism careers were George Wilkes, editor of *Wilkes' Spirit of the Times* from 1857 to the early 1880s; and George B. Wooldridge, who wrote a column "Old Sports of New York" for the *New York Leader* in the 1860s. A final intriguing fact is that George Underwood's grandmother's maiden name was Colburn, according to the 1913 family genealogy; George Colburn was an editor of the *Flash* in 1842. We were unable to establish any relationship between the editor in New York and Mary Colburn Herrick in Massachusetts, who was probably born no later than 1835.

9. Elliott J. Gorn, *The Manly Art: Bare-Knuckle Prize Fighting in America* (Ithaca, N.Y.: Cornell University Press, 1986); Elliott J. Gorn and Warren Jay Goldstein, *A Brief History of American Sports* (Urbana, Ill.: University of Illinois Press, 2004); Howard P. Chudacoff, *The Age of the Bachelor: Creating an American Subculture* (Princeton: Princeton University Press, 1999); Allan Stanley Horlick, *Country Boys and Merchant Princes: The Social Control of Young Men in New York* (Lewisburg, Pa.: Bucknell University Press, 1975); Patricia Cline Cohen, *The Murder of Helen Jewett: The Life and Death of a Prostitute in Nineteenth-Century New York* (New York: Knopf, 1998); Richard B. Stott, *Workers in the Metropolis: Class, Ethnicity, and Youth in Antebellum New York City* (Ithaca, N.Y.: Cornell University Press, 1990); Thomas Augst, *The Clerk's Tale: Young Men and Moral Life in Nineteenth-Century America* (Chicago: University of Chicago Press, 2003).

10. Timothy J. Gilfoyle, *City of Eros: New York City, Prostitution, and the Commer-*

cialization of Sex, 1790–1920 (New York: W. W. Norton, 1992), 58–59. Gilfoyle estimates that between 5 and 10 percent of young females may have engaged in prostitution. The city population given here does not include nearly 80,000 more in the towns immediately surrounding Manhattan. The "Fair Sex" column appeared in the *New York Sporting Whip* when it enlarged to an eight-page format in January 1843.

11. The raw data from 1801–5 and successive five-year intervals: 444, 548, 586, 678, 1240, 1670, 2089, 2651, 3179, 2352, 1293, 1154, 702.

12. Clare A. Lyons, *Sex Among the Rabble: An Intimate History of Gender and Power in the Age of Revolution, Philadelphia, 1730–1830* (Chapel Hill: University of North Carolina Press, 2006).

13. But we should note that for most of the papers listed, there remain just scattered issues by which to judge their character. Perhaps if we had a longer run of each, they would look more flash. For one paper we do have a long run: the *Polyanthos*, edited by George Washington Dixon in New York City. For Dixon's gradual slide into publishing a flash paper by 1841, see chapter 1.

14. Other scholars who have used these papers in publications: Dale Cockrell, *Demons of Disorder: Early Blackface Minstrels and Their World* (New York: Cambridge University Press, 1997); Jonathan Ned Katz, *Love Stories: Sex between Men before Homosexuality* (Chicago: University of Chicago, 2003); George Thompson, *"Venus in Boston" and Other Tales of Nineteenth-Century City Life*, ed. David Reynolds and Kimberly Gladman (University of Massachusetts Press, 2002); Jill Fields, "Erotic Modesty: (Ad)dressing Female Sexuality and Propriety in Open and Closed Drawers, USA, 1800–1930," in *Material Strategies: Dress and Gender in Historical Perspective*, ed. Barbara Burman and Carole Turbin (London: Blackwell, 2003), 122–45; Jill Fields, *An Intimate Affair: Women, Lingerie, and Sexuality* (Berkeley: University of California Press, 2007); James W. Cook, "Dancing Across the Color Line: A Story of Markets and Mixtures from New York's Five Points," *Common-place* 4, no. 1 (October 2003), http://www.common-place.org/vol-04/no-01/; Peter Baldwin, "Mapping Time: Day and Night in the Nineteenth-Century City," *Common-place* 6, no. 1 (October 2005), http://www.common-place.org/vol-06/no-01/; Mark Caldwell, *New York Night* (New York: Scribner, 2005); E. Haven Hawley, "American Publishers of Indecent Books, 1840–1890" (Ph.D. diss., Georgia Institute of Technology, 2005); Donna I. Dennis, *Obscenity Regulation and the Rise of Erotic Publishing in Nineteenth-Century New York* (Princeton: Princeton University Press, forthcoming). Dissertation projects currently in process include Katherine Hijar, "Sexuality, Print, and Popular Visual Culture in the United States, 1830–1870" (Johns Hopkins University); Kenneth Cohen, "'To Give Good Sport': The Making and Meaning of Sporting Leisure in Early America, 1750–1840" (University of Delaware); and Maura D'Amore, "Country Life within City Reach: Masculine Domesticity in Suburban America, 1819–1871" (University of North Carolina at Chapel Hill). Finally, Gail Bederman of Notre Dame University has research in progress on New York City abortionist Madame Restell.

CHAPTER ONE

1. *New World*, ed. Parke Benjamin and Rufus Griswold, July 16, 1842, p. 47.

2. *Philadelphia Journal*, quoted in "Libidinous Publications," *Gazette Extraordinary* (New York), Aug. 27, 1842, p. 3

3. *Gazette Extraordinary*, Aug. 27, 1842. District Attorney James R. Whiting saved this paper too, as potential evidence in obscenity indictments.

4. The only two mentions of the flash papers in the *Advocate* occurred in quotations of male writers from other periodicals; *Advocate of Moral Reform*, Aug. 1, 1842, p. 119; and Dec. 1, 1842, pp. 177-78.

5. In 1839 Whiting prosecuted George Cragin, the agent of the *Advocate of Moral Reform*, on a libel, and Cragin complained that Whiting was "thoroughly prejudiced against the Moral Reform movement." G. Cragin, "Story of a Life," *Circular*, Dec. 18, 1865, p. 316.

6. A blood was "a fast or high-mettled man," a flash word popularized in England in the time of King George the Fourth (the 1820s) but "nearly obsolete" a half century later. See *The Slang Dictionary, Etymological, Historical, and Anecdotal*, 2nd ed. (London: Chatto and Windus, 1874), 87. (*High-mettled* describes race horses of a fiery disposition.)

7. Mr. and Mrs. R. A. Lyon advertised for their young ladies' day and boarding school at 60 Livingston St., Brooklyn, amidst other ads for corsets, dressmakers, pianos, patent medicines, and insurance, in the *Weekly Rake*, Oct. 1, 1842, p. 4.

8. The article features on "The Sodomite" ran in the *Whip*, Jan. 29; Feb. 5, 12, 26; and March 5. The *Weekly Rake* ran occasional items; "Awful Depravity! Sodomy!" was a letter complaining of "vile wretch" of initials J. F. D., July 30, 1842; and "A Sodomite Nabbed" complained that this "crime against nature" was winked at far too routinely at the police office, Oct. 1, 1842. Jonathan Ned Katz discusses the *Whip* series in *Love Stories: Sex between Men before Homosexuality* (Chicago: University of Chicago, 2003), 45-59.

9. *Weekly Rake*, Aug. 13, 1842 (no. 9); issue is missing first and second page; date implied.

10. George B. Wooldridge, the *Whip* editor, leveled this charge against William J. Snelling of the *Flash*, claiming he told the compositor "Why, we write all our letters. . . . To be sure, why that's the way to make any paper take, although you must never mention it because we manufacture all our Ancient Pistols and Notorieties in the same way. No, no, we have had enough trouble about the truth, we go humbug now." *Whip and Satirist*, Jan. 29, 1842, p. 3. But Wooldridge was wrong: the *Flash*'s "Ancient Pistols and Notorieties" columns generally adhered to a recognizable and checkable biography of each profiled person, with the one exception being their unflattering portrait of Myer Levy, who sued them.

11. *Whip*, Sept. 10, 1842, p. 4.

12. *Flash*, July 3, 1842 (which also reprinted the "wants" item from a June 16 issue no longer extant); *Middletown Courier*, June 23, 1842. We thank Bryan V. Knapp for locating the *Courier* article. Other articles in the *Courier* did not use overheated language; the paper was a normal village weekly. No Newcome/Newcomb family appears in the 1840 census in Orange County; but in 1850, Thomas Newcomb and family resided in Wallkill, New York, today contiguous with Middletown, a mile to the northeast. The oldest Newcomb daughter listed is twenty-three; she would have been fifteen in 1842.

13. "Obscene Papers," *Albany Microscope*, Dec. 10, 1842. Grand juries seemed to show some reluctance: In Boston, a warrant was issued charging a man named Lewis Wheeler for selling the *Flash* of Sept. 22, "filled with matter of an indescribable description" ("A Move Against the New York Flash Papers," *Boston Post*, reprinted in the *New-York Spectator*, Sept. 24, 1842), but the grand jury refused to pursue an indictment (*Boston Post*, reprinted in the *New-York Spectator*, Oct. 12, 1842).

14. Larry Howard Whiteacker, "Moral Reform and Prostitution in New York City,

1830-1860" (Ph.D. diss., Princeton University, 1977), 179-95; Patricia Cline Cohen, *The Murder of Helen Jewett: The Life and Death of a Prostitute in Nineteenth-Century New York* (New York: Knopf, 1998), 275. On McDowall's suspension, see the *New York Journal of Commerce*, reprinted in the *New Bedford Mercury* (Mass.) of April 29, 1836, p. 2. McDowall died suddenly in 1836, a broken man.

15. On the female moral reformers: Whiteacker, "Moral Reform and Prostitution"; Carroll Smith-Rosenberg, "Beauty, The Beast, and the Militant Woman: A Case Study of Sex Roles and Social Stress in Jacksonian America," *American Quarterly* 23 (Winter 1971): 562-74; Cohen, *Murder of Helen Jewett*, 275-76; Lori D. Ginzberg, *Women and the Work of Benevolence: Morality, Politics, and Class in the Nineteenth-Century United States* (New Haven: Yale University Press, 1990); Mary P. Ryan, "The Power of Women's Networks: A Case Study of Female Moral Reform in Antebellum America," *Feminist Studies* 5 (Spring 1979): 66-85. The single issue of Whitmarsh's New York paper has gone unnoticed in this historical literature: *The Light; or, Two-Edged Sword* vol. 1, no. 13, n.d., but internal evidence indicates July 1835. The New York district attorney presented the *Light* as a "nuisance" to the grand jury; *New Bedford Mercury*, July 24, 1835, p. 2. In Boston, Whitmarsh, then twenty-five years old, published the *Illuminator*, Sept. 1835 to Dec. 1836. The American Antiquarian Society owns the one issue of the *Light* and a complete run of the *Illuminator*. A libel trial arising out of the *Illuminator* sent Whitmarsh to jail in Boston in 1838; the Boston female moral reformers folded his subscription list into their periodical, the *Friend of Virtue*, Jan. 1838, p. 16.

16. *Whip and Satirist of New-York and Brooklyn*, April 23, 1842, p. 2.

17. *London Town*, Sept. 29, 1838, p. 556; and March 21, 1840, p. 1171. A long run is available at the Library of Congress and at the Lilly Library at Indiana University. See Donald J. Gray, "Early Victorian Scandalous Journalism," in *The Victorian Periodical Press: Samplings and Soundings*, ed. Joanne Shattock and Michael Wolff (Toronto: Leicester University Press and University of Toronto Press, 1982), 317-42; Philip Howell, "Sex and the City of Bachelors: Sporting Guidebooks and Urban Knowledge in Nineteenth-Century Britain and America," *Ecumeme* 8 (2000): 20-50. Definition of *swell* from *The Slang Dictionary*, 316.

18. The five main editors are: William J. Snelling (1804-48), born in Boston; George Washington Dixon (1804-61), born probably in Virginia; George Wilkes (1817-84), born in New York City; George B. Wooldridge (1818-c. 1870), born in New York City; and Thaddeus Warsaw Meighan (1822-74), born in Westchester County, New York. Thomas L. Nichols, who was in constant dialogue with the flash editors throughout 1842, lived from 1815 to 1901, and was born in New Hampshire. Other names more resistant to tracking are: Charles G. Scott, John Vandewater, George Colburn alias Searl, and Henry Renshaw alias McVey. The following names also appeared in issues, but they may be aliases; none appear in city directories or the U.S. census: A. D. Munson, P. Henry, and Garrit Lansing.

19. *Weekly Rake*, Aug. 20, 1842 (no. 10); issue missing first and second front page, date implied.

20. C.B.F., "Boston Correspondence," in a lengthy obituary of Snelling, *Literary World*, Feb. 10, 1849, p 125. On Josiah Snelling's career, see the entry from *Appleton's Cyclopedia of American Biography* (New York: 1887-89), online edition Virtualogy.com, at http://www.famousamericans.net/josiahsnelling/ (accessed Feb. 9, 2006); and Barbara K. Luecke and John C. Luecke, *Snelling: Minnesota's First First Family* (Eagan, Minn.: Grenadier Publications, 1993). Luther Stearns' classical boys' school opened in 1814 with ten students, half of whom boarded with the Stearns family, Snelling included. See

biographies of Luther Stearns' well-known abolitionist son: Frank Preston Stearns, *The Life and Public Services of George Luther Stearns* (Philadelphia: J. B. Lippincott, 1907), 17-19; Charles E. Heller, *Portrait of an Abolitionist: A Biography of George Luther Stearns, 1809-1867* (Westport, Conn.: Greenwood Press, 1996), 7.

21. Leaving West Point before graduation was a common experience at the military academy; the combination of rigorous mathematics and military discipline posed a major discouragement. A good quarter of each class was held back to repeat a year, Snelling included for both of the years he appears in the Register of the Officers and Cadets of the U.S. Military Academy, June 1819 and June 1820, available online at http://www.library. usma.edu/archives/archives.asp (accessed May 12, 2005). Snelling started in a class of 116; a year later, only 86 remained, and then 54 the next year. Only 42 graduated at the end of four years. (He is listed as Joseph Snelling in the West Point and Minnesota records.) Data in a congressional report of 1823 showed that 44 percent of all cadets from 1802 to 1823 dropped out or were discharged; "Condition of the Military Academy at West Point," American State Papers, House of Representatives, 18th cong., 1st sess., *Military Affairs* 2:632-33. For the West Point curriculum, see ibid., 649-50.

22. An obituary of Snelling by "C.B.F." of Boston reported the difficulty with a West Point teacher; "Boston Correspondence," *Literary World* (New York), Feb. 10, 1849, p. 125. A variant story was offered by a young woman who worked as a servant for the Snelling family in Minnesota; she later recalled that young William Joseph "led a rather ungoverned life for several years" and had "committed some breach of discipline" at West Point and was sent home; Mrs. Ann Adams, "Early Days at Red River Settlement and Fort Snelling: Reminiscences of Mrs. Ann Adams, 1821-1829," *Collections of the Minnesota Historical Society* 4 (1894): 96.

23. "He mixed constantly with the Dakotas . . . acquiring a very perfect knowledge of their habits, religion and legends," recounted the editor of the *Collections of the Minnesota Historical Society* in 1872 when it reprinted Snelling's 1830 essay "Running the Gauntlet," vol. 1:439. On his winter sojourn: Edward H. Keating, *Narrative of an Expedition to the Source of St. Peter's River, Lake Winnepeek, Lake of the Woods, &c, Performed in the year 1823*, vol. 1:314; available online at the Library of Congress, American Memory site, "Pioneering the Upper Midwest," http://memory.loc.gov/ammem/umhtml/umhome.html. On Indian women and traders, see "The Auto-Biography of Maj. Lawrence Taliaferro," *Collections of the Minnesota Historical Society*, vol. 6 (1894): 249, where a list of twenty-six licensed traders, including Snelling, is followed by the comment that "most of these traders, and many of their hands, had the use of Indian women as long as it suited their convenience, and children were born to them." Snelling worked in 1822 as a bonded and licensed trader employed by the Columbia Fur Company of St. Louis; the *Lawrence Taliaferro Papers, 1813-1886*, Minnesota Historical Society, reel 1, "List of licenses granted at the Indian Agency at St. Peter's Office."

24. James R. Newhall, *The Legacy of an Octogenarian* (Lynn, Mass.: The Nichols Press, 1897), 75-76. Newhall was a Boston typesetter who read the proofs of Snelling's first book, *Tales of the Northwest*, in 1829. Newhall recalled that Snelling was "a striking character; vigorous, fearless and industrious"—but also "caustic." On the 1823 expedition: Leucke, *Snelling: Minnesota's First First Family*, 121, 195. Adams, "Early Days at Red River Settlement and Fort Snelling," 98-99. On William J. in a duel: *Old Fort Snelling, 1819-1858* (online at http://www.ancestry.com), 102, describes how young Snelling accepted a duel with an officer who had challenged his father; William was wounded, and the officer was court-martialed. An 1849 obituary says the duel originated in William's objections to an unfair court-martial, and that just before shooting com-

menced, Snelling shouted to halt fire because he thought his opponent's ball had rolled out of his gun. The duel then recommenced, and Snelling was hit. C.B.F., "Boston Correspondence," *Literary World,* Feb. 10, 1849, p. 125. See also Josiah Snelling to Lawrence Taliaferro, Aug. 26, 1826, Taliaferro Papers, reel 1. On the "loss of a portion of one of his hands," see Newhall, *Octogenarian,* 76. A good summary of these events is Edward D. Neill, "Fort Snelling, Minnesota, while in Command of Colonel Josiah Snelling," *Magazine of Western History* 8 (Aug. 1888): 373-81.

25. The marriage is recorded in a letter from J. Marsh to Lawrence Taliaferro, Sept. 16, 1826: "The only news at this place is that J. Snelling was married last night to a Swiss girl who lately passed St. Peters," Taliaferro Papers, reel 1. Ann Adams later recalled that "Jo. Snelling married, while quite young, a French girl from Prairie du Chien, very handsome, but uneducated. They lived in a sort of hovel for awhile, and, owing to cold and privation during the ensuing winter, the poor girl took sick and died." Adams, "Early Days at Red River Settlement and Fort Snelling," 96. The wife was Dionice Fournier; Dyonise Fournier appears on documents posted on http://www.ancestry.com as an immigrant from Switzerland to the Red River in Canada in 1821; the story of this Swiss migration of eighteen families is told in General A. L. Chetlain, "The Red River Colony," *Harper's New Monthly Magazine* 58 (Dec. 1878): 47-55. On knowing French: in 1843 and 1844, Snelling translated and published two books by the French popular writer Eugene Sue into English. See George Harvey Genzmer, "Snelling, William J." in *Dictionary of American Biography,* vol. 9 (New York: Charles Scribners, 1936).

26. Leucke, *Snelling: Minnesota's First First Family,* 194, 198; Helen M. White, "A Soldier Disguised," in *The Tale of a Comet and Other Stories* (St. Paul, Minn.: Minnesota Historical Society Press, 1984), 1-22.

27. [William J. Snelling], *Tales of the Northwest,* reviewed in the *North American Review* 68 (July 1830): 200-213. The book was reprinted in 1936 (ed. John T. Flanagan) and again in 1971, 1975, 1976, 1983, and 1985. Snelling continued his advocacy of Native Americans in New England when, in the mid 1830s, he assisted William Apess, a Pequot minister, in drafting his writings; Barry O'Connell, ed., *On Our Own Ground: The Complete Writings of William Apess, A Pequot* (Amherst: University of Massachusetts Press, 1992).

28. Newhall, *Octogenarian,* 77. The anti-Jackson portrayal was probably a piece of work-for-hire, campaign propaganda, written "By a Free Man" and cynically titled *A Brief and Impartial History of the Life and Actions of Andrew Jackson, President of the United States* (Boston: Stimpson and Clapp, 1831). A long review of "Truth" allowed that bad poetry might deserve sarcasm, but rebuked Snelling for "condescend[ing] to petty scurrility and personal abuse." See *American Monthly Review* (May 1832): 408-13, quotes on 409 and 412. A more favorable review allowed that possibly Snelling's coarse and critical language was warranted; "Literary Notices," *New-England Magazine* (March 1832): 266-68. The duel is noted in "Error," *Boston Pearl, A Gazette of Polite Literature,* July 6, 1836, p. 4. The error was that an earlier report named George Washington Dixon the go-between in the duel, and Dixon and Snelling wished to set the record straight. The typesetter Newhall later heard that Willis wanted "to whip Snelling on sight" but in view of Snelling's easy athleticism, Willis would have lost; Newhall, *Octogenarian,* 77-78.

29. The *Providence Patriot, Columbian Phenix* of Rhode Island reprinted his lively *Galaxy* essays along with the claims of "extraordinary demand" for reprintings and the rapid circulation boost; "Snelling's 'First Impressions,'" May 4, 1833. Snelling was

clearly adept at self-promotion. For the "sensation," see Frederic Hudson, *Journalism in the United States, from 1690 to 1872* (New York: Harper & Brothers, 1873), 384-85. Fears for honor: C.B.F., "Boston Correspondence," *The Literary World*, Feb. 10, 1849, p. 125. Snelling kept a short diary of his 1833 incarceration and published it: W.J.S., "Reflections of a Jail Bird," *New England Monthly* (Nov. 1834), 366-71. The trial report was also published: *Trial of William J. Snelling, for a Libel on the Honorable Benjamin Whitman, Senior Judge of the Police Court* (Boston, 1834). The case contributed a signal precedent about rules of discovery in Massachusetts law: Alan Rogers, "Murder in Massachusetts: The Criminal Discovery Rule from Snelling to Rule 14," *American Journal of Legal History* 40, no. 4 (Oct. 1996): 438-54. A contemporary account of the trial appeared in the *Spirit of the Age and Journal of Humanity*, July 18, 1833, pp. 4-6. The abolitionist David Child was Snelling's defense attorney; for more, see note 72. In 1836 Snelling issued a prospectus for a weekly called the *Balance*, which never got off the ground. The *Boston Courier* publicized it and noted that "Mr. Snelling has had a stormy life" but "he is entitled to sympathy" (Sept. 22, 1836). He also published short stories and poems in a variety of other journals and gift books.

30. Snelling's self-committal was noticed in the *Boston Atlas*: The "talented man" of constant intemperance wanted to "hide from public observation"; item reprinted in the *New Bedford Mercury*, Feb. 17, 1837. The *New York Daily Express* titled an editorial "The Infirmities of Genius," in which the brilliant Snelling was described as "a keen, powerful, but vindictive satyrist" who had lost all his friends and succumbed to drink; reprinted in the *Pensacola Gazette*, April 1, 1837. Many years later, the highly popular *Frank Leslie's Illustrated Newspaper* of New York ran a comic dialogue between Snelling and the magistrate who sentenced him, showing the prisoner's pithy wit: "A Drunken Philosopher," Nov. 1, 1862. [William J. Snelling], *The Rap-Trap; or, Cogitations of a Convict in the House of Correction* (Boston, 1837), 75-76; "Old Boston Criticism," *The Literary World: A Monthly Review of Current Literature* (Boston), Aug. 1, 1876, 41-42; and "Literary News," ibid., Sept. 1, 1876, 58-59. The acquaintance who contributed the memory of Snelling's alcoholic odor to this article was not identified. On Snelling's dissipation, see Joseph A. Willard, *Half a Century with Judges and Lawyers* (Boston: Houghton Mifflin, 1896), 33. Another linked Snelling's early death at age forty-four with his "convivial nature" which made him "his own worst enemy"; Neill, "Fort Snelling, Minnesota," 381. The obituary in the *Literary World* by C.B.F. proclaimed in its opening lines that "Had he not been a victim of an appetite which has clouded many noble minds, he would have been one of the highest ornaments to the literature of America." James Newhall wrote that his "brilliant and promising early life" ended intemperately in "misery and degradation"; *Octogenarian*, 78. The *Boston Courier*'s deaths column of Sept. 27, 1837, noted that Mary Adelaide, wife of William J. Snelling, died at age thirty.

31. On Native Americans, see Todd G. Willy, "Literary Realism as Anti-Racism: The Case of William Joseph Snelling," *The Old Northwest* 15 (Fall 1990): 143-61; Maureen Konkle, "Indian Literacy, U.S. Colonialism, and Literary Criticism," *American Literature* 69, no. 3 (Sept. 1997): 457-84. See also Laura L. Mielke, "'Native to the Question': William Apess, Black Hawk, and the Sentimental Context of Early Native American Autobiography," *American Indian Quarterly* 26 (2002): 246-70. On antislavery, see Roman J. Zorn, "The New England Anti-Slavery Society: Pioneer Abolition Organization," *Journal of Negro History* 42 (July 1957): 160. Poems and songs by Snelling appeared in the *Liberator*, Aug. 6, 1831, p. 128, April 14, 1832, p. 60, July 5, 1839, p. 107, and Nov. 1859, p. 176. The latter was a song as sung by "slaves in insurrection," kept by Gar-

rison and published as the Civil War approached. Possibly the seedbed for Snelling's antislavery views was laid early; his Medford academy training was under the tutelage of Rev. Luther Stearns, whose son George Luther Stearns, close in age to Snelling, became a major abolitionist figure in the 1850s, known as one of the six main backers of John Brown's raid at Harper's Ferry in 1861; David S. Reynolds, *John Brown, Abolitionist* (New York: Knopf, 2005), 3-6. On his lecture: "New England Anti Slavery Society," *Liberator*, Sept. 1, 1832, p. 139. The lecture was reprinted in the *Abolitionist* in three installments in 1833: March (pp. 35-37), April (pp. 53-56), and May (pp. 70-73). Snelling claimed to have witnessed the whipping of a slave woman, but the rest of the speech does not rely on first-person testimony. He tackled racism and fears of racial amalgamation squarely, arguing that slavery had already led to rapid racial mixture (April 1833, p. 56), and he gloried in being called a "fanatic" on the question of slavery (p. 53).

32. The U.S. Federal Census of 1850 for Chelsea, Massachusetts, shows Lucy Jordan Snelling, 36, with her daughters Josephine, 12, Mary F., 2, and Anna, 1. The 1900 census in Charlestown, Massachusetts, lists Josephine Gerrish, widowed and living with an adult son; her birth is noted as June 1839. The link from Snelling to Gerrish is established by the 1880 census, where Lucy Snelling shared quarters with Josephine and her son-in-law G. W. Gerrish in Boston. Lucy's father was Simon Jordan; in 1809 and later he was listed as a baker in the *Boston City Directory*, ed. Edward Cotton (Boston, 1809). See also Tristram Frost Jordan, *Jordan Memorial: Family Records of the Rev. Robert Jordan and his Descendants in America* (Boston, 1882), 226.

33. The *Censor* is held by the New-York Historical Society. On Willis: Thomas Nelson Baker, *Sentiment and Celebrity: Nathaniel Parker Willis and the Trials of Literary Fame* (Oxford: Oxford University Press, 1999).

34. Missouri Miller appears (without the Louisa) in three issues of the *Catalogue of the Members of the Troy Female Seminary*, for 1832-33, 1833-34, and 1834-35. The cost of attending was $200 a year, with $75 extra for classes in music, the arts, dancing, and languages. Minister's daughters could attend at reduced rates, and other girls without sufficient means were offered a student loan program, paying tuition out of future earnings as schoolteachers; Mary Kelley, *Learning to Stand and Speak: Women, Education, and Public Life in America's Republic* (Chapel Hill: University of North Carolina Press, 2006). We thank Barbara Weiz, archivist at what is now the Emma Willard School in Troy, for sending us copies of the Troy Academy's catalogues.

35. The 1840 census lists Adaline Miller (*sic*) in the third ward of New York City in a household of 19 people: 13 females aged 20-30, 1 aged 50-60, 5 free blacks, 3 of them females aged 10-36. The 1850 census lists Adeline Miller as household head in the fifth ward, age 70, with 5 white women ranging in age from 18 to 26, and 3 young black women described as servants. See also Timothy J. Gilfoyle, *City of Eros: New York City, Prostitution, and the Commercialization of Sex, 1790-1920* (New York: W. W. Norton, 1992), 67, 70-71, 73, 79, 81, 83, 84, 86, 104, 169, 324, 327; Helen Lefkowitz Horowitz, *Rereading Sex: Battles over Sexual Knowledge and Suppression in Nineteenth-Century America* (New York: Knopf, 2002), 166-68, 171, 174-75, 185, 186, 222. Emma Willard to Thomas Allen, editor of the *Madisonian* (Washington, D.C.) and reprinted in the *Spirit of the Times* in New York, Aug. 25, 1838, p. 217.

36. Vincent's mother was reputed to be Mary Gallagher, a prominent madam during two decades of New York's prostitution scene. See Cohen, *Murder of Helen Jewett*, 12, 259, 264, 301, 317. For a hostile account of Hamblin's liaisons with Vincent, Clifton, and Louise Medina, see Mrs. Mary Clarke, *A Concise History of the Life and Amours*

of Thomas S. Hamblin as Told by Elizabeth Blanchard Hamblin (Philadelphia and New York: n.p., n.d., but circa 1838). This rare pamphlet is available online from the library of Stanford University, https://dlib.stanford.edu:6521/text1/dd-ill/hamblin.pdf (accessed Dec. 22, 2005).

37. Faye E. Dudden, *Women in the American Theatre: Actresses and Audiences, 1790–1870* (New Haven: Yale University Press, 1997), 64–70; Miriam Lopez Rodriguez, "Louisa Medina, Uncrowned Queen of Melodrama," in *Women's Contribution to Nineteenth-Century American Theatre*, ed. Maria Lopez Rodriguez and Maria Delores Narbona Carrion (Valencia, Spain: Universitat de Valencia, 2004), 29–42. Medina, an orphan born to Spanish parents, came to the United States in 1831 and moved in with Hamblin in 1833. Before her death in 1838, she wrote ten very successful melodramas produced at the Bowery Theatre. In theater histories her birth year is usually given as 1813; the manifest of her ship of arrival in Philadelphia (the *Thames*, June 20, 1831) gives her age as nineteen (Louisa Honor de Medina, in Philadelphia passenger lists, 1800–1945, online database at http://www.ancestry.com, accessed Nov. 7, 2006). On Attree, see Cohen, *Murder of Helen Jewett*, 41, 52, 61, 78, 85, 56, 91, 110, 215, 250, 357.

38. Snelling also had close connections to another young actress making her debut on the New York stage that summer, Charlotte Cushman. In 1835 in Boston Snelling had lodged in a boarding house run by the Cushman family, and had thus come to know Charlotte, destined to be one of the most famous actresses of the nineteenth-century stage. "We speak warmly, because we know her well, having long lived under the same roof and sat at the same table," *Censor*, April 12, 1838. Missouri Miller premiered in Hamblin's play in 1837 in Boston; so possibly via Cushman, Snelling had met Missouri then. Clarke, *Concise History*, 37. For the sexual insinuation, see "Spirit-Gas Scorpion," *True Flash*, Dec. 5, 1841, ed. by "Sly," George B. Wooldridge, Snelling's ex-partner. The two men were locked in a legal battle by this date.

39. *Polyanthos, and New-York Visiter*, June 9, 1838. Also see Horowitz, *Rereading Sex*, 167.

40. The quote appeared as a reprint in the *Lynn Record* in Massachusetts, June 30, 1838. A New Hampshire paper announced that an "abusive article" in a penny paper was "calculated to destroy all her prospects of success"; *New Hampshire Sentinel* (Keene, N.H.), June 28, 1838. Distant newspapers took their material from the *New York Herald* of June 20, 1838, which had featured one seemingly authoritative report, "The Singular Death of Miss Missouri," reprinted in Clarke, *Concise History*, 38–40; Clarke says the article's author was Louise Medina, Hamblin's playwright paramour, whose motive was to clear Hamblin of innuendoes of seduction and homicide. Medina laid all blame on "the wretched woman" [Mrs. Miller] and her associates whose *Polyanthos* article was so venomous that Missouri fell down dead upon reading only half of it. *Herald* reporter William H. Attree first set in motion the chain of events removing Missouri from Mrs. Miller's house. The *Herald*'s coverage included the full autopsy report on Missouri's body. A somewhat more judicious assessment appeared in a weekly edited by a young Horace Greeley, who noted that New York papers charged the *Polyanthos* with shocking her to death, but then left it to readers to judge the merits of that charge; *New Yorker*, June 23, 1838. One other New York paper condemned Hamblin: William Porter's *Spirit of the Times*, a sports and theater weekly, claimed the "vivacious, confiding" girl suffered inflammation of the brain due to the greedy struggle to control her brilliant stage career; June 23, 1838. Extant issues of the early *Polyanthos* were recovered from the deaccessioned papers from the New York City Municipal Archives and Records Center (here-

after NYCMA), gathered along with a dozen of the 1840s flash papers. A full run of the weekly paper from Jan. to June 1841 is held by the New York Public Library.

41. On Medina's death and Hamblin's flagging fortunes, see Dudden, *Women in the American Theater*, 70-74. The two-part *Sunday Flash* profile of Attree appeared Sept. 12 and 19, and the two on Hamblin on Oct. 24 and 31, both in 1841. Another comic paper of New York, edited by Thomas L. Nichols, defended Attree from Snelling's verbal assault: "Attree has faults enough . . . but we are bound to say that the article in question is grossly and malignantly false in many particulars." See *Uncle Sam*, Sept. 18, 1841.

42. The most extensive discussion of Dixon is by Dale Cockrell, who devotes a chapter to his career in *Demons of Disorder: Early Blackface Minstrels and Their World* (New York: Cambridge University Press, 1997), 92-102. On hints on his African ancestry: "Melodious Squabble," *New York Herald*, Aug. 4, 1837, p. 1. Louise Medina had called him "a half-negro" in her "Singular Account"; Clarke, *Concise History*, 40. The black swan retort was reprinted in the *Spirit of the Times* (New York), July 22, 1837, p. 187, a paper that had earlier suggested that Dixon's pedigree included "the kings of Kongo"; July 2, 1836, p. 156. In 1849 that same paper ran a humor essay in white dialect that mentioned Dixon as a man with a "mixtur of chockylet about his komplexion"; N. O. Delta, "The War Opinions of Billy White," *Spirit of the Times*, Aug. 15, 1846, p. 293. Snelling, at one time friends with Dixon, declared the singer was "as white as so dusky a man can be"; "The Passages in the Life of G. W. Dixon, the American Coco La Cour, Negro Dancer and Buffalo Singer," a generally disparaging profile in the *Sunday Flash*, Dec. 11, 1841. Dixon tried to squelch rumors he had African ancestry in a short article, "Our Private History," in the *Polyanthos*, March 6, 1841, p. 68. He claimed his opponents said it because "we performed our parts [in blackface music] as naturally as the *genuine nigger*. Even it if had been our misfortune to be a descendant from one of Africa's sable sons, there is one thing which must be admitted: that whether we had been red, black, yellow or green, we can make any harebrained sinner look *blue* in the eyes of every true moralist."

43. For Dixon's outdoor performances: "The Great Dixon Monody—Take Care and Don't Be Among the Missing" describes his speech on the Hudson River shore at Weehawken to memorialize the murder of Mary Rogers, in early October 1841. The monody, or funeral oration, provided a public ritual on the site of the murder for New Yorkers agitated over the recent unsolved mystery (one that Edgar Allan Poe transformed into the "Mystery of Marie Rogêt" a few years later). The same news item claimed that "The Dixon" had recently given a two-hour ex tempore speech out a window on Chambers Street to a crowd of two thousand, after the highly publicized murder of Samuel Adams by John Colt; *Sunday Times*, Oct. 3, 1841. From the slightly irreverent title of the Rogers oration, the hyperbole of the article, and the jokester personality of "the Dixon," it is entirely possible that neither of these performances actually occurred, at least not as serious rituals of public mourning. Cockell quotes at length from colorful newspaper accounts of Dixon's court fiascos; *Demons*, 104-11. "Lack of discretion": *Boston Daily Advocate*, June 14, 1836.

44. Snelling later ran a two-part profile of Dixon in the *Sunday Flash*, Dec. 11 and 18, 1841, at a time when their friendship was irrevocably broken. *Polyanthos Extra*, Jan. 15, 1839, gives Dixon's point of view on the case of Rev. Francis L. Hawks and of the suicide of Minturn. The *Advocate of Moral Reform* noted a marriage in trouble, and Dixon lifted that text but slyly inserted the names of the parties, causing one party, the auctioneer Rowland S. Minturn, unbearable shame sufficient to provoke suicide. "Auctioneer

in wrong Roome" was the Dixon headline, Mrs. Roome being the illicit lover, and "Mint" and "turn" were used repeatedly. See testimony by George Cragin, agent for the *Advocate of Moral Reform*, in the *New York Sun*, April 16, 1839.

45. On Miller's bail: Minutes of the Sessions, New York Court of General Sessions of the Peace, reel 17, docket book for July 1838-March 1839; Jan. 7, 1839, p. 486; Feb. 6, 1839, p. 572. Cockrell's book offers abundant documentation on these colorful trials; *Demons*, 116-27.

46. For the campaign against Restell, see Feb. 16, 1841, and later *Polyanthos* issues usually with the headline, "Keep it Before the People"; the issue of Feb. 16 also contains the list of fourteen seducing men with a description of each; Nov. 7, 1841 listed houses of prostitution. These same issues, however, carried admiring profiles of prostitutes ("Sketches of Character" featuring Ellen Thompson) and seduction news stories that both castigated male wretches and gave readers the sensational details of their rake-like ways. On sublime mission: Sept. 18, 1841. On fearless determination: March 20, 1841. On Julia's ball: Nov. 7, 1841. By this time, the *Sunday Flash* was underway and Dixon no longer had Snelling's help on his paper. Minutes of the Sessions, New York Court of General Sessions of the Peace, docket book for May-Dec. 1841, p. 356; Nov. 20, 1841; and docket book for Jan.-Aug. 1842, pp. 57, 281, NYCMA. None of these minor legal events gained coverage in the major New York newspapers.

47. For Snelling's association with the *Sunday Times*, see Louis Hewitt Fox, *New York City Newspapers, 1820-1850, A Bibliography* (Chicago: University of Chicago Press, 1928); William J. Snelling to Rufus Griswold, Sept. 24, 1841, Griswold Mss., no. 968, Boston Public Library, on his need for excitement.

48. *Longworth's Directory* of New York shows George Wooldridge (senior) in 1837-38 running a bath and refectory at 41 Chambers Street, and in 1838-39 running the Clarendon house at 301 Broadway. George Wooldridge (junior), according to the 1839-40 directory, sold oysters at 240 Broadway; two years later, in 1840-41, he sold oysters at 289 Broadway while his home was at 69 Duane Street. In the 1841-42 directory he is simply listed as living at 69 Duane. In 1842-43, George B. identified himself as an editor at 21 Ann Street with home at 21 Centre Street; Lydia Wooldridge, widow of George, shared that address and ran a refectory there. Ads for the "Court Lunch" at 21 Centre Street near Chambers ran in Wooldridge's *Whip*; July 9, 1842. A year later, George now took the work identity of "late editor" in the city directory, still living with his mother, now on Elizabeth Street. Wooldridge Sr. appears in the 1820 and 1830 censuses, in the Sixth Ward, and in the 1840 census as Geo. Wooldredge. Young men of the right age to be George and his younger brother Napoleon, soon to be a policeman, are in the father's 1840 household. At least once the Wooldridge family came in serious contact with the law: In August 1835, an Irish servant girl died from eating a pie laced with arsenic at the Wooldridge home. Apparently no one had warned her of the poisoned treat left out to fool rats; the coroner's inquest ruled negligence. *New York Transcript*, Police Office Column, Aug. 18, 1835. Ad for the Elssler saloon: *Sunday Flash*, Sept. 26, 1841. On the Elssler saloon as a site for illicit sex and publishable gossip, see the *Sunday Flash*, Dec. 11, 1841.

49. Wooldridge v. Smith, July 20, 1836, Police Court Papers, NYCMA. The July 4 marriage was performed at the Methodist Green Street Church. According to the police court papers, one of the witnesses to the happy event was Charles Scott, who might well be the same Charles G. Scott who became the editor of the *Flash* in mid-1842. Testimony in the trial of Wilkes and Snelling in the libel on Myer Levy brought forth further details of Wooldridge's marital history, when Snelling testified that Wooldridge

was "a sorrow" to his father for marrying a prostitute and then remarrying without obtaining a divorce; thus George had a new partner in 1841. Methodist records from another church show only one further union by George: he married Mary Louisa McCabe on Aug. 6, 1848. The 1850 census shows Wooldridge with the twenty-year-old Mary L. and five children ranging in age from eight to one; the four oldest probably derived from George's union of the early 1840s. William Scott Fisher, comp., *New York City Methodist Marriages, 1785-1893*, vol. 2, *Index of Grooms* (Camden, Maine: Picton Press, 1994); 1850 U.S. Census, 8th Ward, New York City. For the trial coverage, see *Sunday Flash*, Jan. 22, 1842. Wooldridge appears in the 1860 U.S. census with wife Mary and seven children; Bethel, Sullivan County, New York.

50. The only partial biography of Wilkes is Alexander Saxton's essay "George Wilkes," in *The Rise and Fall of the White Republic: Class Politics and Mass Culture in Nineteenth-Century America* (New York: Verso, 1990), 205-226. See also Genzmer, "Wilkes, George" in *Dictionary of American Biography*, and Cohen, *Murder of Helen Jewett*, 191-92. George Wilkes, 33, appears (unindexed) in the 1850 census in the Sixth Ward living with a woman named Sarah, 36, born in England, and two servants; New York City Sixth Ward census, p. 264. In 1860 he lived with women surnamed Wilkes, again Sarah G., born in England, his mother Ellen Wilkes, 67, born in Germany, and a third woman, Matilda E., 36; New York City Fifteenth Ward census. In 1870 Helen Wilkes (spelled Wilks in the listing) was household head, with age reported as 70, born in New York, living with Catherine, 46, George ("editor, Spirit of the Times"), 41, and Helen, 24; Sixteenth Ward, Fourteenth Election District census, p. 55.

Wilkes declared in court in Nov. 1842 that he was "the principal writer" and "had the control of the paper"; Court of Common Pleas, *New York Herald*, Nov. 12, 1842. Adeline Miller's financial help is detailed in that same article, the trial of *Wm. Applegate vs. Adeline Miller*. For an earlier clue of Miller's backing, see *True Flash*, Dec. 4, 1841, ed. Wooldridge: "Query-Can Mrs. Miller of 133 Reade Street deny that she placed in the hands of her son Nelson H. Miller, the bonds of two houses for the purpose of enabling her to justify himself as bail for the notorious Scorpion Snelling and Startle Wilkes, and has she advanced any money to purchase a Power Press." On Wilkes' city knowledge, see Hudson, *Journalism*, 338.

51. On the Mike Walsh group, see Robert Ernst, "The One and Only Mike Walsh," *New-York Historical Society Quarterly* 36 (January 1952): 43-65; Peter Adams, *The Bowery Boys: Street Corner Radicals and the Politics of Rebellion* (Westport, Conn.: Praeger Publishers, 2005). For Wilkes's 1836 arrest, Gilfoyle, *City of Eros*, 326.

52. "Two Trials for Libel," *Subterranean*, Sept. 20, 1845, p. 2.

53. "Caution," *Subterranean*, July 7, 1845. Walsh seems never to have written for any flash paper. He edited the *New York Aurora* for about a month in 1842, and then started the *Sunday Knickerbocker* with Enoch E. Camp in 1843, which died after "one pot of ale"; Hudson, *Journalism*, 338. Next he started the *Subterranean*, which ran from 1843 to 1845, ending when Walsh was jailed for libel. If there were a prize for compulsive aggressive insult in print for the 1840s, Walsh would win it. On his love for Snelling: "Wm. J. Snelling," *Subterranean*, Aug. 16, 1845.

54. On the *Police Gazette*: Elliott J. Gorn, "The Wicked World: The *National Police Gazette* and Gilded-Age America," *Media Studies Journal* 6 (1992): 6-10; Dan Schiller, *Objectivity and the News: The Public and the Rise of Commercial Journalism* (Philadelphia: University of Pennsylvania Press, 1981), 57-65. A diary of a police officer exhibits periodic use of the *Police Gazette* to track the whereabouts of professional criminals; see the Diary of William H. Bell, 1850-51, New-York Historical Society, March 15, 1851,

p. 74. Enoch E. Camp attended Columbia College and was admitted to the New York bar, but he mainly was a Democratic politician and a Washington correspondent for the *New York Herald*. He admired Wilkes enough to name a son born in 1846 George Wilkes Camp; U.S. Census, 1850, New York City. Camp died suddenly in 1853; the *New York Atlas* profiled his career on Jan. 20, 1853. On Wilkes's alleged connection with the prostitute Kate Ridgely, see New York Supreme Court, *The Answer of John F. Chamberlin to the Complaints of George Wilkes, in an Action to Recover Damages for Defamation of Character* (New York, Wm J. Reed, Law and Job Printer, 1873), 2, 10-12. Wilkes's serialized novel about the prostitute Helen Jewett appeared in the *National Police Gazette* over many months in 1848-49.

55. Three long obituaries each noted Wilkes' physical qualities: the *New York Herald*, Sept. 25, 1885; the *New York Times*, Sept. 25, 1885; and the *New York Clipper*, Oct. 3, 1885. The latter paper published a fairly hostile obituary. We thank Richard Stott for providing us with the *Herald* and *Clipper* notices. Snelling's rascalities articles in the *Flash* often reference events in his life, making his authorship apparent. See the profile of James Watson Webb, editor of the *Courier and Enquirer*, Nov. 20, 1841, where Snelling mentions first meeting Webb in Detroit in 1823.

56. The two issues of the *True Flash* were Dec., 4, 1841 and another, now lost, probably a week later. For the feature on Dixon, see the *Sunday Flash*, Dec. 11 and 18, 1841. The swindling stories of Boston are confirmed in reprintings from the *Boston Post* appearing in the *Spirit of the Times* (New York), June 18, 1836. The "negro swindler" epithet appears in the *Flash*, Jan. 22, 1842, p. 3, in an item set in upside-down type.

57. *Sunday Flash*, Sept. 26, 1841, p. 3.

58. A poem by Snelling appears in the *Whip*, March 12, 1842, p. 1. Snelling still worked there in mid-April, when a libel suit against Wooldridge also named Snelling in the action. *Whip*, May 21, 1842, p. 2. Possibly Wilkes worked on the *Whip* at times as well: one of his obituaries noted that he had once written for the *Flash* and the *Whip*. *New York Herald*, Sept. 25, 1885.

59. A George Colburn appears in the 1870 and 1880 censuses for New York as a printer and compositor; based on the ages reported then, the Colburn was twenty in 1842. A search on his alias in the police docket books, George Searl or Serle, turns up only one candidate, a man born in New York in 1816 who became a farmer in Wisconsin and Minnesota in the 1850-80 censuses. Renshaw aka Henry McVey is a complete mystery.

60. *Libertine*, June 15, 1842. Ads for its contents in the *Whip* show that it only lasted two months.

61. Charles G. Scott married Jane Clements, Sept. 21, 1844, in Fisher, *New York City Methodist Marriages*, vol. 2, 566. Wooldridge was married at the Green Street church; Scott at the Roosevelt Street church. For attacks on Nichols: "The Arena," *Flash*, June 23, 1842, p. 2. The *Whip* of July 2, p. 2, attributed this *Flash* attack to Snelling, and its nasty tone is unmistakably his. Thomas L. Nichols started the daily *New York Arena* in March 1842; it ran at least until August. Eight extant issues show a progression of increasingly overt attention to the sexual underworld of New York. Nichols himself was constantly caricatured in the *Flash*, the *Whip*, and the *Rake* for his brothel connections.

62. On Meighan, see a website maintained by a descendant, Matthew Meighan, based on obituaries held by the family: http://home.earthlink.net/~mdmeighan/thaddeus .html (accessed May 2005). For Meighan's work on the *Star*, see Hudson, *Journalism*, 339. For attacks on Meighan, see *Whip*, Feb. 16, p. 3; Letter from J.M.L., Feb. 26, 1842, p. 2. For Meighan's truce: *Weekly Rake*, no. 8, date page missing, implied Aug. 7, 1842; loathing libertinism: Sept. 3, 1842; Restell, no. 10, implied Aug. 21, 1842.

63. In Sept. 1841, Snelling lived at 60 West Broadway, a street formerly named Chapel in the 1830s; Snelling to Griswold, Sept. 24, 1841, Boston Public Library. Nearby houses at 64, 70, 72, and 74 Chapel were all well-known brothels around 1840; Gilfoyle, *City of Eros*, 318, 325. *Applegate vs. Miller*, Court of Common Pleas, *New York Herald*, Nov. 12, 1842. The debt was also at issue in a judgment contested in court the prior July; Court of Common Pleas, *New York Herald*, July 18, 1842. For a typical advertisement for Applegate's services: *New York Herald*, Sept. 8, 1840.

64. Adeline Miller's taxable net worth was $16,500 in 1857; William H. Boyd, *Boyd's New York City Tax-Book* (New York, 1857), 137. On the printing press trial, see the *New York Herald*, Nov. 14, 1842.

65. Applegate and the *Whip*: "General Sessions," *New York Herald*, Dec. 22, 1843. For contemporary estimates of the costs of a weekly paper see the *Merchant's Ledger and Statistical Messenger*, May 28, 1848, p. 4; and the *New York Times and Evening Star*, July 22, 1841. On cub reporters, see "Our Indictment," *Flash*, Nov. 6, 1841. p. 2; *Whip*, Jan. 29, 1842, p. 2.

66. In a pitch to advertisers, the *Sunday Flash* claimed it was selling 5,000 copies a week by its eighth issue: Sept. 26, 1841, p. 1. "Our Course," *Whip*, July 23 1842. "Our Experiment," July 2, 1842, p. 2, and Nov. 12, 1842. For mainstream press circulation, see Hudson, *Journalism*, 357, whose figures derive from a data source relating to the new Bankruptcy Act of 1842.

67. On income from "wants": the *Weekly Rake* announced it charged twenty-five cents per item; Sept. 3, 1842. On puff from Brown: *Weekly Rake*, Oct. 22, 1842.

68. *Whip*, January 21 and 29, 1843 ("if you wish to hide"). Of course, this could be a joke: the *Whip* was alleging that it intercepted this blackmail note by a *Flash* editor to a private citizen and was righteously exposing a shakedown. The testifying editor was the turncoat Wooldridge, ratting on Snelling and Wilkes; "Court of Sessions," *New-York Spectator*, Jan. 19, 1842. Wooldridge later blatantly bragged of extortion; see "Madame Trust," *New York Sporting Whip*, Feb. 11, 1843; "To Mr. J.R.L.," *Whip*, Dec. 24, 1842, p. 2. For more on Livingston, see Cohen, *Murder of Helen Jewett*, 102-9, and Gilfoyle, *City of Eros*, 20, 42-46.

69. Thomas L. Nichols, ed., *Uncle Sam*, Sept. 18, 1841, p. 1.

70. "The *Whip* Triumphant," *Whip*, April 16, 1842, p. 2.

71. Different newspapers reported different defendants; it appears that all seven men faced indictments. Scott and Vandewater pled guilty, while Wooldridge tried unsuccessfully to argue that the *Libertine* was not obscene. Scott, Wooldridge, Colburn, and Renshaw drew sixty-day sentences on Blackwell's Island, while Vandewater got ten days in the city prison. "Court of Sessions," *New-York Spectator*, Sept. 17 and 28, 1842; "Court of Sessions," *New York Sun*, Sept. 10 and 15, 1842; *New York Herald*, Sept. 29, 1842. Thaddeus W. Meighan's arrest did not make the papers but he appears in the General Sessions docket book for Jan.-Aug. 1842, pp. 501, 535. Three out of town papers carried news of the Snelling case, which focused on the issue of Oct. 31, 1841, and specifically on the profile of Thomas Hamblin. Wooldridge testified that Snelling was the author; Snelling conducted his own defense, based on the claim that the articles were not obscene. The jury convicted him. *Boston Courier*, Sept. 12, 1842; *Pennsylvania Inquirer and National Gazette*, Sept. 12, 1842; and *Boston Recorder*, Sept. 16, 1842.

72. Lydia Maria Child republished her series in book form: Letter XXIX, dated Oct. 6, 1842, in *Letters From New York* (New York: C. S. Francis & Co., 1844), 189. Presumably Mrs. Child did not read the flash papers, but she did know William Snelling. Child grew

up in Medford, Massachusetts, where Snelling attended academy. Her husband David
Child, also from Medford, worked with Snelling in the early antislavery movement in Boston. He represented Snelling in his legal dispute with the Boston judge in 1833 and then
employed Snelling in his publication's office in 1835; D. L. Child to W. J. Snelling, May 20,
1835, *Massachusetts Journal* Papers, 1829-35, Massachusetts Historical Society. After
his September conviction on obscenity, Snelling won delayed sentencing on account
of "the representations of his physician of his indisposition," probably his usual health
problems, so he was not among the incarcerated editors Child saw that day (*New York
Express*, Sept. 29, 1842). It seems likely that Child's acquaintance with Snelling enabled
her to think more charitably about the flash editors.

73. Meighan pled guilty to the indictment. Daniel Austin fought a misdemeanor
charge of obscenity and was found not guilty by the jury, because he was only the compositor for the paper; "General Sessions," *New York Herald*, March 11 and 16, 1843.

CHAPTER TWO

1. For examples of using gossip to embarrass rivals, see the depiction of Moses
Beach of the *Sun* in *Weekly Rake*, July 9, 1842, and Sept. 3, 1842; *Flash*, Sept. 4, 1842,
and Aug. 14, 1842. On gossip, also see Helen Lefkowitz Horowitz, *Rereading Sex: Battles
over Sexual Knowledge and Suppression in Nineteenth-Century America* (New York: Knopf,
2002), 172-73. George Wilkes can be identified a "brothel bully" based on his involvement and later indictment in the assault on Mary Gambel in her brothel at 28 Crosby
Street on Nov. 20, 1836. See People v. Garret Dikeman, James Morton, George Wilkes,
Thomas Thorne, William Story, Benjamin Story, Lewis Blanch, Alexander Bates, Dec.
14, 1836, Court of General Sessions, District Attorney Indictment Papers, New York
City Municipal Archives and Records Center (hereafter DAP); Timothy J. Gilfoyle, *City
of Eros: New York City, Prostitution, and the Commercialization of Sex, 1790-1920* (New
York: W. W. Norton, 1992), 76, 326. The term "bawdy-house bully" appears in *Sunday Flash*, Sept. 26, 1841. For more on Wilkes, see George Harvey Genzmer, "Wilkes,
George" in *Dictionary of American Biography*, vol. 20 (New York: Charles Scribners,
1936), 218; Patricia Cline Cohen, *The Murder of Helen Jewett: The Life and Death of a
Prostitute in Nineteenth-Century New York* (New York: Knopf, 1998), 191; Alexander Sax-
ton, "George Wilkes: The Transformation of a Radical Ideology," *American Quarterly*
33 (1981): 437-40; idem, *The Rise and Fall of the White Republic: Class Politics and Mass
Culture in Nineteenth-Century America* (London: Routledge, 1990), 205-26; Horowitz,
Rereading Sex, 190-91. Thomas Nichols was a water-cure vegetarian and a supporter
of hydropathy, mesmerism, vegetarianism, spiritualism, and women's rights after 1847.
See Horowitz, *Rereading Sex*, 286-96. William Joseph Snelling was a Whig and an abolitionist in the 1830s. See chapter 1; and Horowitz, *Rereading Sex*, 166. Thomas Dixon
was affiliated with the Whig Party and among the first to introduce blackface minstrelsy
to the stage, and he developed a national following singing "Old Zip Coon" in theaters
during the 1830s. See Dale Cockrell, *Demons of Disorder: Early Blackface Minstrels and
Their World* (New York: Cambridge University Press, 1997), 96-98, 108-9. Wooldridge,
Wilkes, and Nichols were at various times Democrats.

2. The literature on the importance of social conditions shaping political and per-
sonal ideology is vast. For examples, see Barbara Jeanne Fields, "Slavery, Race and
Ideology in the United States of America," *New Left Review* 181 (1990): 111-12; and
Winthrop Jordan, *Tumult and Silence at Second Creek: An Inquiry into a Civil War Slave
Conspiracy* (Baton Rouge: Louisiana State University Press, 1993), 181-211, esp. 200.

3. The "religion of libertinism" held that sexual organs and acts of sexual intercourse were symbols of a great life-giving force and worthy of human worship as Christian sacraments. See Randolph Trumbach, "Erotic Fantasy and Male Libertinism in Enlightenment England," in *The Invention of Pornography: Obscenity and the Origins of Modernity*, ed. Lynn Hunt (New York: Zone Books, 1993), 254.

4. For the "monster," see "The Libertine," *Boston Weekly Magazine*, June 26, 1841. For examples of corruption equated with licentiousness, vice, and libertinism, see "The Progress of Corruption," *Rutger's Literary Miscellany: A Monthly Periodical*, Aug. 1842; "Clerical Libertines," *Evangelical Magazine and Gospel Advocate*, July 30, 1841; "The Libertine," *Evangelical Magazine and Gospel Advocate*, Dec. 24, 1841; "Clerical Libertines," *Liberator*, Sept. 17, 1841; "Unpunished Crime," *Liberator*, July 14, 1843. On the definition of libertinism, see Catherine Cusset, "Editor's Preface: The Lesson of Libertinage," *Yale French Studies* 94 (1998): 1–2; Michel Fehr, "Libertinisms," in *The Libertine Reader: Eroticism and Enlightenment in Eighteenth-Century France*, ed. Michel Fehr (New York: Zone Books, 1997), 11–12, 14. On republicanism, see J.G.A. Pocock, *The Machiavellian Moment: Florentine Political Thought and the Atlantic Republican Tradition* (Princeton: Princeton University Press, 1975); Gordon Wood, *The Creation of the American Republic, 1776–1787* (Chapel Hill: University of North Carolina Press, 1969); idem, *The Radicalism of the American Revolution* (New York: Knopf, 1992). A good, brief summary appears in Gordon Wood, "Republicanism," in *The Readers' Companion to American History*, ed. Eric Foner and John Garraty (Boston: Houghton Mifflin, 1991), 930–31. On libertine behavior and "vice" to be in conflict with republican values, also see Clare A. Lyons, *Sex among the Rabble: An Intimate History of Gender & Power in the Age of Revolution, Philadelphia, 1730–1830* (Chapel Hill: University of North Carolina Press, 2006), 227–28. The term *republicanism* is admittedly problematic in wake of recent critiques of the ubiquitous employment of the term by historians. See Daniel T. Rodgers, "Republicanism: The Career of a Concept," *Journal of American History* 79 (1992): 11–38. Yet flash press editors borrowed certain republican themes while simultaneously glorifying others that were the antithesis of what earlier republicans considered "virtue." Furthermore, little, if any, of the literature on reinterpretations of republicanism in the nineteenth century discuss libertine themes.

5. Libertinism first emerged in sixteenth-century Europe and peaked in the eighteenth century. See Trumbach, "Erotic Fantasy and Male Libertinism," 253–82; Fehr, "Libertinisms," 10–16; Iain McCalman, *Radical Underworld: Prophets, Revolutionaries and Pornographers in London, 1795–1840* (Cambridge: Cambridge University Press, 1988), 208–11; David Foxon, *Libertine Literature in England, 1660–1795* (London: The Book Collector, 1964).

6. On the "profligate press" and "licentious press," see *Herald*, Sept. 15, 1842; Greeley, *Tribune*, Jan. 16, 1843. The *Herald* referred to the flash weeklies as "The Ann Street Licentious Press." See Horowitz, *Rereading Sex*, 244. Mike Walsh described George Wilkes as a "brothel chronicler." See *Subterranean*, Sept. 20, 1845. Greeley never discussed the sporting or flash press in his autobiography, *Recollections of a Busy Life* (New York: J. B. Ford, 1868), nor did Isaac Clark Pray, "A Journalist," in *Memoirs of James Gordon Bennett and His Times* (New York: Stringer and Townsend, 1855). Mike Walsh charged George Matsell with keeping an "infidel bookstore" on Chatham Street which sold both erotic and radical literature. See *Subterranean*, Dec. 2, 1843. In 1845, Walsh charged that Matsell was "an atheist book seller." See *Subterranean*, June 21, 1845. Matsell's brother

Augustus J. Matsell assumed control of Frances Wright and Robert Dale Owen's Hall of Science bookstore in 1832. George Matsell later joined his brother in operating the enterprise. See Horowitz, *Rereading Sex*, 74–75, 209.

7. Eric Foner, *The Story of Freedom* (New York: W. W. Norton, 1999); David Hackett Fischer, *Liberty and Freedom* (New York: Oxford University Press, 2005). Richard Godbeer, *Sexual Revolution in Early America* (Baltimore: The Johns Hopkins University Press, 2002), 285–88, briefly discusses eighteenth-century American perceptions of libertine behavior, but primarily in the relation to courtship etiquette. Most discussions of libertine behavior focus on male predatory sexuality and the negative associations with such behaviors. For example, see Rodney Hessinger, "'Insidious Murderers of Female Innocence': Representation of Masculinity in the Seduction Tales of the Late Eighteenth Century," in *Sex and Sexuality in Early America*, ed. Merril D. Smith (New York: New York University Press, 1998), 262–82. On the eighteenth-century "pleasure culture" and its decline in Philadelphia, see Lyons, *Sex among the Rabble*.

8. Norma Basch, "Marriage, Morals, and Politics in the Election of 1828," *Journal of American History* 80 (1993): 890–918, esp. 895–96; E. Anthony Rotundo, *American Manhood: Transformations in Masculinity from the Revolution to the Modern Era* (New York: Basic, 1993); Carol Smith-Rosenberg, "Davy Crockett as Trickster: Pornography, Liminality, and Symbolic Inversion in Victorian America," in *Disorderly Conduct: Visions of Gender in Victorian America* (New York: Knopf, 1985), 90–108; James A. Shackford, *David Crockett: The Man and the Legend* (Chapel Hill: University of North Carolina Press, 1956); Gail Bederman, *Manliness and Civilization: A Cultural History of Gender and Race in the United States, 1880–1917* (Chicago: University of Chicago Press, 1995), esp. chap. 5.

9. The literature on Paine and his republicanism is extensive. Good overviews include Harvey J. Kaye, *Thomas Paine and the Promise of America* (New York: Hill and Wang, 2005); Eric Foner, *Tom Paine and Revolutionary America* (New York: Oxford University Press, 1976); and David Freeman Hawke, *Paine* (New York: Harper and Row, 1974). The literature on the Marquis de Sade is also large. See Marquis de Sade, *Philosophy in the Bedroom* (1795), trans. Richard Seaver and Austryn Wainhouse (digitized and typeset by Supervert32, Inc., 2002); Marquis de Sade, *120 Days of Sodom* (1789), trans. Richard Seaver and Austryn Wainhouse (digitized and typeset by Supervert32, Inc., 2002); both available at http://supervert.com (both accessed Feb. 8, 2005). Good summaries of Sade are in Francine du Plessix Gray, *At Home with the Marquis de Sade: A Life* (New York: Simon and Schuster, 1998), esp. 363–65; Fehr, "Libertinisms," 31–35; Marcel Henaff, "Oedipus, Baroque Portrait with a Woman's Face," in Fehr, *Libertine Reader*, 1256–75; Camile Paglia, *Sexual Personae* (New Haven: Yale University Press, 1990), 2, 235–47; Octavio Paz, *An Erotic Beyond: Sade*, trans. Eliot Weinberger (New York: Harcourt Brace & Co., 1993); Lucienne Frappier-Mazier, *Writing the Orgy: Power and Parody in Sade* (Philadelphia: University of Pennsylvania Press, 1996); Roger Shattuck, *Forbidden Knowledge: From Prometheus to Pornography* (New York: St. Martin's Press, 1996), 289–99; Laurence L. Bongie, *Sade: A Biographical Essay* (Chicago: University of Chicago Press, 1998); Geoffrey Gorer, *The Revolutionary Ideas of Marquis de Sade* (London: Wishart, 1934); Iwan Bloch, *Marquis de Sade: His Life and Works* (New York: Brittany, 1931); Walter Drummond, *Philosopher of Evil* (Evanston, Ill.: Regency Books, 1962); Caroline Warman, *Sade: From Materialism to Pornography* (Oxford, Eng.: Voltaire Foundation, 2002); Catherine Cusset, ed., "Special Issue on Libertinage and Modernity," *Yale French Studies* 94 (1998).

10. On Paine's republicanism, see Foner, *Paine*, esp. 89–90 (possessive individualism), 106 (cosmopolitanism), 181–82 (market). On the freethinking and sexual theories of Owen, Kneeland, and Knowlton, see Horowitz, *Rereading Sex*, 45–85.

11. On polite libertinism, see *Flash*, Sept. 11, 1842. On Owen and Knowlton's dislike of libertinism and prostitution, see Horowitz, *Rereading Sex*, 59, 60, 79. On these elements in Sade's philosophy, see Paz, *Erotic Beyond*, 49, 69; and Fehr, "Libertinisms," 33. The flash press never endorsed the sexual violence, rape, castration, mutilation, flagellation, cannibalism, tribadism, incest, and other cruel tortures, i.e., the sadism, found in Sade's writings.

12. *Whip*, Sept. 17, 1842 (moral paper), and July 9, 1842 (Dr. B., pimps); *Flash*, Jan. 29, 1842 (Jones), and Sept. 11, 1842 (fashion); *Whip and Satirist of New-York and Brooklyn*, April 16, 1842 (chroniclers), May 14, 1842 (chroniclers), and April 30, 1842 (prostitutes); *Weekly Rake*, July 30, 1842 (prostitutes). For a similar idea ("We are no libertine ourselves, though occasionally the chroniclers of their malpractices"), see *Rake*, Sept. 3, 1842. Also see the one issue of the *Libertine*, June 15, 1842, with the motto: "Vice is a monster of such hideous mien,—That to be hated needs but to be seen."

13. *Libertine*, June 15, 1842 (epicures); *Life in New York* (epicures); *New York Sporting Whip*, Jan. 28, 1843 (Man is endowed); *Rake*, Sept. 3, 1842 (pregnant); *New York Arena*, May 27, 1842 (intercourse); *Whip and Satirist of New-York and Brooklyn*, April 9, 1842 (time is no more). Also see "Licensed Stews" in issue of March 5, 1842.

14. For example, " . . . beautiful WOMAN! is the centre of all our joys. . . . With her, a man naturally exclaims—One little hour of joy to me is worth a dull eternity!" See Old Man of Twenty-five, *Guide to the Harems, or Turkish Palaces of the Empire City . . . and all Other Large Cities in the United States and British Provinces* (New York, 1855 and 1856), in the personal collection of Leo Hershkowitz, Queens College, City University of New York. We are indebted to Professor Hershkowitz for sharing this and other documents with us on numerous occasions.

15. *Weekly Rake*, July 30, 1842. On Jewett, see Cohen, *Murder of Helen Jewett*. On the poverty associated with prostitution in Five Points and Corlears Hook, see Gilfoyle, *City of Eros*, 36–46, 51–53. A brothel guide similarly asserted that "all mortals" sought "pleasure." "The old and the young; the blooming boy, and the buxom girl; the man in his prime, and the voluptuous woman; the chaste and virtuous, as well as those who have 'fallen from their high estate'—are all votaries of PLEASURE." See Old Man, *Guide to the Harems*, 3.

16. *Weekly Rake*, July 30, 1842; *Whip and Satirist of New-York and Brooklyn*, June 25, 1842 (Sappho); *Rake*, Sept. 3, 1842 (immortal lust, quote). For a story on Sappho, see *Libertine*, June 15, 1843. A similar reference to ancient Greece and Rome in support of regulating prostitution appears the *Sportsman*, July 22, 1843. Brothel guides made similar references to the classical world of antiquity. See Old Man, *Guide to the Harems*, 3–4. The *Herald*'s James Gordon Bennett referred to the murdered prostitute Helen Jewett as "a regular Aspasia." See Cohen, *Murder of Helen Jewett*, 47.

17. *Flash*, Sept. 18, 1842 (Hero and Leander), and Sept. 4, 1842 (Arethusa); *Whip*, Jan. 14, 1843 (Venus de Medicis). On Artemis as an erotic image, see Paz, *Erotic Beyond*, 13–14. The *Venus de Medici* was a popular ancient Greek statue acquired by the Medici family in the late sixteenth or early seventeenth century and now on display in the Uffizi Gallery in Florence, Italy. Nineteenth-century writers often confused the classical Greek sculpture *Venus de Milo* as the *Venus de Medici*. For another example, see Lisa Sigel, *Gov-*

erning Pleasures: Pornography and Social Change in England, 1815-1914 (New Brunswick, N.J.: Rutgers University Press, 2002), 4.

18. The Alcibiades Club House on Mercer Street is mentioned in *Flash*, Aug. 14, 1842; *Weekly Rake*, July 30, 1842, and Nov. 12, 1842; *Whip and Satirist of New-York and Brooklyn*, May 21, 1842; *Whip*, Aug. 27, 1842. Alcibiades (c.450-404 B.C.) was an Athenian statesman and general, a ward of Pericles and an attendant of Socrates. During the Peloponnesian War, he was the leader in agitating against Sparta. When the Athenian forces were defeated, Alcibiades fled to Sparta and gave advice against Athens. He later escaped to Persia. He was recalled to Athens at the request of Thrasybulus, and Athens had a short era of greatness after Alcibiades directed the Athenian fleet to victory over the Peloponnesian fleet and recovered Byzantium. When Lysander, a new Spartan commander, defeated the Athenian fleet at Notium in ca. 406 B.C., Alcibiades was exiled. In 404 B.C., at the behest of Lysander, Alcibiades was murdered. Sappho's presumed lesbianism is based upon her residence on the isle of Lesbos and her poetry in which females were the target of her affections. See http://www.sappho.com/poetry/sappho.html (accessed April 5, 2005). On perceptions that Erinna was a Lesbian poetess like Sappho, see Luis Guichard, "Review of *Erinna*," *Bryn Mawr Classical Review* (2004.07.24), available at http://ccat.sas.upenn.edu/bmcr/2004/2004-07-24.html (accessed April 5, 2005).

19. Lawrence Levine, *Highbrow/Lowbrow: The Emergence of Cultural Hierarchy in America* (Cambridge, Mass.: Harvard University Press, 1988); Nigel Cliff, *The Shakespeare Riots: Revenge, Drama, and Death in Nineteenth-Century America* (New York: Random House, 2007); Terri Marsh, "Epilogue: The (Other) Maiden's Tale," in *Pornography and Representation in Greece and Rome*, ed. Amy Richlin (New York: Oxford University Press, 1992), 274. On *Ariadne*, see Cohen, *Murder of Helen Jewett*, 108-9, 269, 272. On tableaux vivants, see Gilfoyle, *City of Eros*, 127. Lais was a courtesan from Corinth who lived with the philosopher Aristippus according to Dioenes Laertius. Pythonice was the mistress of Harpalus in Plutarch's *Phocion*. On the accessibility of classical writings to the working classes, see Jonathan Rose, *The Intellectual Life of the British Working Class* (New Haven, Conn.: Yale University Press, 2001), esp. chap. 1. Elsewhere, an article on the editor James Watson Webb began: "Troy had her Hector, Rome her Caesar and France her Napoleon. New York has her James Watson Webb." See *Flash*, Nov. 20, 1841.

20. *Whip and Satirist of New-York and Brooklyn*, Jan. 29, 1842 (Palais Royale, beastly, lecherous), and Feb. 12, 1842 (monster); *Whip*, Feb. 9, 1842 (polluted); Jonathan Ned Katz, *Love Stories: Sex between Men before Homosexuality* (Chicago: University of Chicago Press, 2001), 45-59. On the Palais Royale as a center for prostitutes, pimps, sodomites, and criminals, see Katz, *Love Stories*, 54, 357 note 54.

21. *Weekly Rake*, July 30, 1842 (vile wretch), and Oct. 1, 1842 (enormities); *Flash*, Aug. [7], 1842 (unnatural of vices, habitual sodomites).

22. *Whip and Satirist of New-York and Brooklyn*, Feb. 5, 1842 (Palmo's); Feb. 12, 1842 (beasts); Feb. 26, 1842 (feminine parts); and March 5, 1842 (unnatural intercourse). Palmo's was attacked by a mob of approximately 100 a decade later. See various indictments, Jan. 1852, DAP; *New York Times*, May 13, 1852. Palmo's Opera House (later Burton's Theater and the Federal Court House) was located at 39-41 Chambers Street. Palmo was a wealthy Italian immigrant who used his fortune to introduce opera to New York. Palmo's opened on Feb. 3, 1844, but the venture proved unprofitable. In 1845, William Dinneford turned it into a Grecian theater. From 1848 to 1857, William Evans Burton leased the facility until he opened the Metropolitan Theater on Broadway. From

1857 to 1876, it was leased to the federal government until its demolition. See *Frank Leslie's Illustrated Newspaper*, May 13, 1876. For a more detailed account of the anti-immigrant elements of the *Whip*'s homophobia, see Katz, *Love Stories*, 46–55.

23. *Weekly Rake*, July 9, 1842 (necessary as bread), and July 30, 1842 (essential); *Whip and Satirist of New-York and Brooklyn*, Jan. 15, 1842. Also see similar language in Old Man, *Guide to the Harems*, 4–6 (endowed with passions). Augustine allegedly wrote: "Abolish the prostitutes and the passions will overthrow the world; give them the rank of honest women and infamy and dishonor will blacken the universe." Quoted in Alain Corbin, *Women for Hire: Prostitution and Sexuality in France after 1850*, trans. Alan Sheridan (Cambridge, Mass., 1990), vii.

24. *Whip and Satirist of New-York and Brooklyn*, March 5, 1842, June 11, 1842 (France), April 9, 1842 (bullies, less streetwalking), and April 30, 1842; *Whip*, July 9, 1842 (oppressed), in People v. George B. Wooldridge, July 14, 1842, DAP; *Weekly Rake*, July 30, 1842 (male libertine). On brothel bullies, see Gilfoyle, *City of Eros*, 76–91.

25. *Whip and Satirist of New-York and Brooklyn*, March 26, 1842 (false notion); *New York Sporting Whip*, Feb. 25, 1843 (fashionable ladies). On the lack of portrayals of illicit sex as "anything other than sinful and dangerous," see Cohen, *The Murder of Helen Jewett*, 61. On stories in the *Transcript* and *Herald*, see ibid., 40–43.

26. *Weekly Rake*, July 3, 1842, July 23, 1842, and July 30, 1842; *Flash*, Dec. 11, 1841, Dec. 18, 1841, and Jan. 22, 1842; *Whip and Satirist of New-York and Brooklyn*, April 2, 1842, and April 9, 1842. The *Rake* also included a feature entitled "Houses of Bad Character."

27. *True Flash*, Dec. 4 and 5, 1841. The *Whip and Satirist of New-York and Brooklyn* published equally effusive descriptions of prostitutes. For an example, see the description of "the Divine Fanny Winslow" in the column "Nymphs By Daylight" in the issue dated April 2, 1842. The reference to "young Buonaparte" [*sic*] is unclear, as several Bonapartes resided in and visited the United States. Napoleon's youngest brother, Jerome (1784–1860) visited the United States and married Elizabeth Patterson in 1803. Napoleon refused to recognize the marriage, arranged a new marriage with Catherine of Württemberg, and later installed Jerome as king of Westphalia (1807–13). Elizabeth Patterson, however, produced a son Jerome Napoleon Bonaparte (1805–70). Charles Lucien Jules Laurent Bonaparte (1803–57), a nephew of Emperor Napoleon, lived in the United States from 1824 to 1833. Another possibility was Napoleon's older brother Joseph who abdicated the Spanish throne Napoleon gave him in 1813. From 1815 to 1841 he lived in Bordentown, New Jersey. See http://www.answers.com/topic/bonaparte (accessed May 1, 2005).

28. *Whip*, Oct. 29, 1842 (head of profession); *Whip and Satirist of New-York and Brooklyn*, Jan. 14, 1843 (ball). Brown was referred to as "Princess Julia" in the following: *Whip and Satirist of New-York and Brooklyn*, Feb. 26, 1842, March 19, 1842, and May 14, 1842; *Whip*, Aug. 6, 1842, Oct. 22, 1842, Oct. 29, 1842, Dec. 3, 1842, Dec. 24, 1842, Dec. 31, 1842, Jan. 28, 1843, and Feb. 11, 1843; *New York Polyanthos*, June 6, 1841; *Polyanthos*, July 1841; *Dixon's Polyanthos*, Nov. 7, 1841; *New York Sporting Whip*, Feb. 11, 1843; *Flash*, Sept. 11, 1842. Brown was mentioned or discussed in the *Whip and Satirist of New-York and Brooklyn*, April 2, 1842, June 4, 1842, and June 25, 1842; *Whip*, Sept. 3, 1842, and Sept. 10, 1842; *Sunday Flash*, Oct. 3, 1841; *Flash*, Dec. 18, 1841, Sept. 25, 1842, and Jan. 14, 1843; *Weekly Rake*, Oct. 29, 1842, and Nov. 12, 1842. Negative coverage of Brown appeared in the *Weekly Rake*, Nov. 26, 1842.

29. *New York Arena*, May 27, 1842 (bewildering); *Weekly Rake*, Nov. 12, 1842 (Dickens);

Flash, Sept. 11, 1842 (charm man). For similarly effusive praise, see *New York Sporting Whip,* Jan. 28, 1843. Also see *Dixon's Polyanthos,* Nov. 7, 1841, for coverage of Brown's ball. Brown was even the subject of poetry:

> Oh, dearest Julia Brown
> Is it possible you're in town,
> And that you were at the ball
> With the ladies from City Hall—
> We cannot believe it teue, [*sic*]
> Though we suppose that you
> Were invited—but if not
> 'Twas the fault of Mrs. Mott.

See *True Flash,* Dec. 4 and 5, 1841.

30. *New York Sporting Whip,* Jan. 28, 1843, March 4, 1843 ("suppression"), and Feb. 4, 18, and 25, 1843. Brothel guidebooks also followed this pattern of condemning sexual profligacy while attracting ever more attention to it. One guide complained: "Vice stalks abroad in the community—the young and the thoughtless are its victims, and how awful are its effects! There is no check on the libertine and the seducer—no bar to the debaucheries of the rake and the public and private votaries of prostitution." See Butt Ender, *Prostitution Exposed; or, A Moral Reform Directory, Laying Bare the Lives, Histories, Residences, Seductions, etc. of the Most Celebrated Courtezans and Ladies of Pleasure of the City of New York* (New York, 1839), 3, in the personal collection of Leo Hershkowitz.

31. *Rake,* Sept. 3, 1842 (show vice); *Whip,* Dec. 25, 1841 (Mary Robinson), and Jan. 1, 1842 (Mary Robinson). Also see the description of Mary Gallagher in the *Whip,* July 23, 1842.

32. *Weekly Rake,* Sept. 24, 1842, and Oct. 1, 1842. Also see *Whip,* Jan. 1 and 8, 1842 (fancy women, favorite prostitutes), and March 9, 1842 (brothel fixtures). For examples of issues identifying specific names and addresses of prostitutes, see *Whip,* Oct. 15, 1842.

33. *Whip,* July 16, 1842 (hugely fat); Oct. 15, 1842 (old); Oct. 22, 1842 (in Almshouse); *Whip and Satirist of New-York and Brooklyn,* Feb. 26, 1842 (over the hill); March 12, 1842 (notorious).

34. *Sunday Flash,* Oct. 17, 1841 (Levy); *Flash,* Dec. 18, 1841 (Dixon); *Whip,* Oct. 29, 1842 (Nichols); *Whip and Satirist of New-York and Brooklyn,* Feb. 26, 1842 (Beach, Bennett). On Doty, see Gilfoyle, *City of Eros,* 71–73, 82, 86, 324, 325. Doty appeared in Federal Census Population Schedules, City of New York, 1820 (Sixth Ward), 1830 (Fifth Ward), and 1840 (Fifth Ward). In 1842, she was between forty-two and forty-seven years of age. On Levy as a merchant, see *Longworth's American Almanac, New-York Register, and City Directory* (New York, 1831 and 1832); as a broker, see ibid. (New York, 1839). An "M. Levy" or "Myer Levy" is identified as a physician in later directories. See *Doggett's New York City Directory* (New York, 1849, 1850, 1853); *Goulding's New York City Directory* (New York, 1870 and 1875).

35. *Whip and Satirist of New-York and Brooklyn,* June 25, 1842 (degraded being); *Whip,* July 9, 1842 (dirty, slovenly), and July 30, 1842 (she-male, cow-hide); *Sunday Flash,* Oct. 17, 1841 (fight; Gingerballs); Horowitz, *Rereading Sex,* 170, 187. During another brothel fight, Grandy reportedly showed "some signs of uneasiness; but, as the challenge only extended to men, she was restrained by her fancy man Ginger Blue." See

Flash, Dec. 25, 1841. Grandy was also discussed in *Flash,* Jan. 29, 1842, and Sept. 18, 1842; *Whip and Satirist of New-York and Brooklyn,* Jan. 8, 1842, Feb. 5 and 12, 1842, and June 25, 1842; *Whip,* Oct. 1, 1842, and Oct. 22, 1842. On the numerous brothels on Church Street, see Gilfoyle, *City of Eros,* 46–49.

36. *Whip,* Nov. 19, 1842 (professing Christian); *Whip and Satirist of New-York and Brooklyn,* July 9, 1842 (the vicious); *Flash,* Aug.14, 1842 (Alcibiades Club); *Weekly Rake,* Nov. 12, 1842 (recherche).

37. *Whip,* Jan. 1 and 8, 1842 (dandies, fancy men, fancy women); *True Flash,* Dec. 4 and 5, 1841 (frail sisterhood); *Flash,* July 31, 1842 (harlots). A dandy was a young gentleman "classed as one of the 'Puppy' order, a financial conceited fop, whose ideas are not a whit above a good suit of clothes." See *Weekly Rake,* Oct. 1, 1842. References to fancy men as pimps or associates of prostitutes appear in *New York Sporting Whip,* March 4, 1843; *Flash,* Dec. 25, 1841, June 23, 1842, and Sept. 18, 1842; *Weekly Rake,* Oct. 22, 1842; *Whip and Satirist of New-York and Brooklyn,* June 4, 1842. Other criticism of pimps appear in: *Sunday Flash,* Sept. 26, 1841 (Alick Hoag), Oct. 3, 1841, and Oct. 24, 1841 (Pimp Richards); *Flash,* Nov. 20, 1841 (Wooldridge called a pimp), Dec. 11, 1841 (Wooldridge), Dec. 18, 1841 (Wooldridge), and Dec. 25, 1841 (Wooldridge); *Flash,* June 23, 1842 (Nichols); *Weekly Rake,* Sept. 24, 1842 (Bennett); *Whip,* July 9, 1842, July 23, 1842, July 30, 1842, Oct. 29, 1842, and Dec. 24, 1842. Also see the description of "Sucker Joe" in *Flash,* Oct. 17, 1841.

38. *Whip,* Jan. 8, 1842. When the *Sunday Flash* instigated its campaign against the merchant and broker Myer Levy, he was described as the "fancy man" for Phoebe Doty and Eliza Boardman. See *Sunday Flash,* Oct. 17, 1841. The *Whip* claimed that brothel bullies had "gone out of fashion. Robberies, and even murders, at brothels were not infrequent.—Now they are seldom heard of." For more on brothel bullies, see Gilfoyle, *City of Eros,* 76–91. Brothel guides directly associated New York's gentry and merchant elites with Gotham's brothel subculture. See Old Man, *Guide to the Harems,* 15–18. Some guides, however, occasionally poked fun at plebeian groups. In one, a prostitute adopted the name "Red Rover," probably a pun on the Red Rover Engine Company No. 34, a rowdy volunteer fire company whose members also included Mike Walsh. "Red Rover" is listed as the madam at 105 Mercer Street in Butt Ender, *Prostitution Exposed.* Similarly, the "Butt Enders" were also the name of another volunteer fire company. See Cohen, *Murder of Helen Jewett,* 371 note 28. On the Red Rover fire company, see Robert Ernst, "The One and Only Mike Walsh," *New-York Historical Society Quarterly* 36 (1952): 46. For a more detailed discussion of the historiography of pimps, see Timothy J. Gilfoyle, "Prostitutes in History: From Parables of Pornography to Metaphors of Modernity," *American Historical Review* 104 (1999): 131–33.

39. *Flash,* Oct. 31, 1841 (judgement seat), Nov. 12, 1841 (SALONS), and Nov. 20, 1841 (Snelling is poor). Snelling and Bennett were both under indictment at this time. On the legal system, see George Wilkes, *The Mysteries of the Tombs: A Journal of Thirty Days Imprisonment in the New York City Prison for Libel* (New York: The Author, 1844).

40. *Whip and Satirist of New-York and Brooklyn,* Feb. 26, 1842.

41. *Whip and Satirist of New-York and Brooklyn,* April 16, 1842 (vagabonds); *Flash,* Nov. 12, 1842 (niggers, darkies), and July 10, 1843 (niggers); *Whip,* Jan. 14, 1843 (nigger, darkey), and Jan. 21, 1843 (niggers, darkeys); *Sunday Flash,* Oct. 17, 1841 (practical amalgamationist), and Sept. 26, 1841 (Tappan); Horowitz, *Rereading Sex,* 179–83. On Quinn as the "father" of the panel game, see *Whip and Satirist of New-York and Brooklyn,*

March 12, 1842. For another reference to Tappan's abolitionism, see the description of John Scaley in *Flash*, Dec. 25, 1841. This incident illustrates the confusing views of flash press editors. Although Wooldridge, Wilkes, and Snelling were editors of the *Sunday Flash* at this time and all were later accused of libel, later issues claimed that the attack was written by Wooldridge. See *Flash*, Dec. 18, 1841, and Jan. 22, 1842. Wooldridge's anti-abolitionist views appeared in *Whip and Satirist of New-York and Brooklyn*, May 7, 1842. On Snelling as a founding member of the New England Antislavery Society, see chapter 1.

42. *Whip and Satirist of New-York and Brooklyn*, March 12, 1842 (morbid appetite); *Sunday Flash*, Sept. 12, 1841, (Nigger Ball); *New York Sporting Whip*, Jan. 28, 1843 (Dinahs); *Weekly Rake*, Nov. 26, 1842 (kiss negroes, beastly desires). Also see "Horrible Effects of Depravity," *Flash*, Sept. 18, 1842.

43. *Whip and Satirist of New-York and Brooklyn*, July 9, 1842.

44. *Whip and Satirist of New-York and Brooklyn*, March 12, 1842. Also see criticism of Fanny Perry and her "consorting with negroes" in *Flash*, Dec. 11, 1841; Katz, *Love Stories*, 56–57. The racism in the *Whip* mirrored that of proslavery members of the Democratic Party. For example, see the poem entitled "Charity Begins at Home" in *Whip and Satirist of New-York and Brooklyn*, April 2, 1842.

45. David Reynolds, *Beneath the American Renaissance: The Subversive Imagination in the Age of Emerson and Melville* (New York: Knopf, 1988), 64–65; Ray Allen Billington, *The Protestant Crusade, 1800–1860: A Study of the Origins of American Nativism* (New York: Macmillan, 1938), 98–108; Peter Wagner, "Anticatholic Erotica in Eighteenth Century England," in *Erotica in the Enlightenment*, ed. Peter Wagner (New York: Lang, 1991), 166–209. American brothel guides borrowed this salacious convent imagery. See Butt Ender, *Prostitution Exposed*, 8 (Raydon and Benson), 15 (Phillips), and 20 (Lewis).

46. *Sunday Flash*, Sept. 12, 1841. Other issues with excerpts from *Decameron* include *Sunday Flash*, Sept. 19, 1841, Oct. 17, 1841, and Oct. 24, 1841; *Rake*, Sept. 3, 1842; *Weekly Rake*, Sept. 24, 1842, and Oct. 1, 1842.

47. *New York Sporting Whip*, Feb. 11, 1843 (unholy act); *Flash*, Dec. 11, 1841 (dunghill). The dunghill quote refers to William G. Boggs, publisher of William Cullen Bryant's *Evening Post* and a member of the grand jury which indicted Snelling. See chapter 3. For complaints about the popularity of Paul DeKock novels in New York, see *Herald*, Jan. 16, 1843. On millennial evangelicism, see Whitney Cross, *The Burned-Over District: The Social and Intellectual History of Enthusiastic Religion in Western New York, 1800–1850* (New York: Harper and Row, 1950); Paul E. Johnson, *Shopkeeper's Millennium: Society and Revivals in Rochester, New York, 1815–1837* (New York: Hill and Wang, 1975).

48. *Flash*, Oct. 17, 1841.

49. *Whip and Satirist of New-York and Brooklyn*, July 9, 1842 (innocent nature); *Sunday Flash*, Sept. 26, 1841. For examples of boxing match coverage, see *True Flash*, Dec. 4 and 5, 1841. On nineteenth-century male sporting life, see Elliott J. Gorn, *The Manly Art: Bare-Knuckle Prize Fighting in America* (Ithaca: Cornell Univ. Press, 1986); idem, "'Good-Bye Boys, I Die a True American': Homicide, Nativism, and Working-Class Culture in Antebellum New York City," *Journal of American History* 74 (1987): 388–410; idem, "'Gouge and Bite, Pull Hair and Scratch': The Social Significance of Fighting in the Southern Backcountry," *American Historical Review* 90 (1985): 18–43.

50. *Sunday Flash*, Oct. 31, 1841 (circumcised Israelite), and Nov. 6, 1841 (Jew, noxious vermin). Also see *Sunday Flash*, Oct. 17, 1841. Mallan's dentistry was also associated

with debauchery. See "Samuel DuBoif and His Wig" in *Weekly Rake*, Sept. 24, 1842. For other examples of anti-Semitism, see criticisms of the "Chatham Street Auctioneers" in *Sunday Flash*, Sept. 19, 1841; "The Jew in Paradise" in *Sunday Flash*, Sept. 26, 1841.

51. *Whip and Satirist of New-York and Brooklyn*, March 5, 1842; Katz, *Love Stories*, 51. For other examples of anti-Semitism, see *Whip*, Dec. 3, 1842; "two Jew looking dogs" in *Whip*, Dec. 31, 1842; the criticisms of the "Chatham Street Auctioneers" in *Sunday Flash*, Sept. 19, 1841; complaints in "The Jewish Sabbath" in *Sunday Flash*, Oct. 17, 1841; Hamblin called an "English Israelite" in *Flash*, Oct. 31, 1841; a reference to "defiance alike to Jews and negroes," and an anti-Semitic attack on Goslin in *Flash*, Nov. 6, 1841; a complaint about the "ugly-looking Jew with a long nose," in *Flash*, June 23, 1842.

52. On Sade's interpretation of commercialized sexuality as liberating and the supreme form of sexual relations, see Frappier-Mazier, *Writing the Orgy*, 23.

53. Randolph Trumbach, "Erotic Fantasy and Male Libertinism," 259–62. One of the earliest reinterpretations of pornography was Steven Marcus, *The Other Victorians* (New York: Basic Books, 1964), esp. 45 (definition of "pornotopia").

54. H. Montgomery Hyde, *A History of Pornography* (New York: Farrar, Straus and Giroux, 1964), 1; Walter Kendrick, *The Secret Museum: Pornography in Modern Culture* (New York: Viking, 1987), 1–3; Sigel, *Governing Pleasures*, 4, 24–25. The earliest use of the term was Nicholas Edme Restif de la Bretonne's tract on public prostitution, *Le Pornographe*, in 1769. See Kendrick, *Secret Museum*, 18–21; Hunt, "Introduction: Obscenity and the Origins of Modernity, 1500–1800," in *Invention of Pornography*, 12–16.

55. Kendrick, *Secret Museum*, 1–69; Amy Richlin, "Introduction," in *Pornography and Representation in Greece and Rome*, ed. Amy Richlin (New York: Oxford University Press, 1992), xx ("whore-writing"); Reynolds, *Beneath the American Renaissance*, esp. 170–99, 214, 223; Karen Halttunen, "Humanitarianism and the Pornography of Pain in Anglo-American Culture," *American Historical Review* 100 (1995): 317–18 (quote), 324–25; Peter Wagner, *Eros Revived: Erotica of the Enlightenment in England and America* (London: Secker & Warburg, 1988), 7; Sigel, *Governing Pleasures*, 4; Robert Darnton, "Sex for Thought," in *New York Review of Books*, Dec. 22, 1994 (*Le Pornographe*); Ian Hunter, David Saunders, Dugald Williamson, *On Pornography: Literature, Sexuality, and Obscenity Law* (New York: St. Martin's Press, 1993). Julie Peakman, *Mighty Lewd Books: The Development of Pornography in Eighteenth-Century England* (New York: Palgrave Macmillan, 2003), 5–10, distinguishes pornography as a form of erotica. Helen Horowitz expressly avoids the term "pornography" because it usually stigmatizes that which a commentator finds unacceptable. See Horowitz, *Rereading Sex*, 447 note 22. On the evolution of obscenity law in New York and elsewhere, see Helen Lefkowitz Horowitz, "Victoria Woodhull, Anthony Comstock, and Conflict over Sex in the United States in the 1870s," *Journal of American History* 87 (2000): 403–34.

56. Recent European historians have uncovered important political meanings in the popular pornographic publications, substantially revising Steven Marcus's findings. See Sigel, *Governing Pleasures;* Hunt, *Invention of Pornography;* Wagner, *Erotica in the Enlightenment;* Robert Darnton, *The Literary Underground of the Old Regime* (Cambridge, Mass.: Harvard University Press, 1982). For a brief account of pornography in antebellum New York City, see Gilfoyle, *City of Eros*, 130–35. On Marcus, see Brian Harrison, "Underneath the Victorians," in *Victorian Studies* 10 (1966–67): 239–67. Darnton argues that the world of the printed word in eighteenth-century France was too complex to be sorted into categories like "enlightened" and "revolutionary." Today, some identify the *Social*

Contract as political theory and *Histoire de Dom B****** as pornography, something too crude to be treated as literature. But eighteenth-century bookmen lumped them together as "philosophical books." Looking at the material their way, the distinction between pornography and philosophy breaks down. One can perceive a philosophical element in the prurient and an erotic element in the philosophical. See Robert Darnton, "Philosophy Under the Cloak" in *Revolution in Print: The Press in France, 1775–1800*, ed. Robert Darnton and Daniel Roche (Berkeley: University of California Press, 1989), 49; ibid., *Literary Underground*, esp. 199–208. For an insightful examination of the employment of sexual imagery in a national election, see Basch, "Marriage, Morals, and Politics in the Election of 1828," 890–918.

57. *Weekly Rake*, Aug. 20, 1842 (no. 10), issue missing first and second page, after Aug. 18, 1842 (smutty papers); *The Diary of Philip Hone, 1828–1851*, ed. Allan Nevins (New York: Dodd, Mead and Company, 1927), 240–41 (Feb. 4, 1837), 275 (Sept. 23, 1837), 289 (scurrilous), 518 (ribaldry), 632 (licentiousness). For similar critiques, see *Diary of Hone*, 195, 275, 335, 464, 549, 585, 667–68, 908.

58. Frank Luther Mott, *American Journalism* (New York: Macmillan, 1949), 231–40 (quotes 237). The flash press sometimes vilified Bennett. See *Sportsman*, July 22, 1843. On the *Herald* as "humbug," see *Whip and Satirist of New-York and Brooklyn*, Dec. 25, 1841. Wooldridge published Dixon's attack on Bennett for publishing a Sunday *Herald*. See *True Flash*, Dec. 4 and 5, 1841. Walt Whitman described Bennett as "a reptile marking his path with slime wherever he goes." See Reynolds, *Beneath the American Renaissance*, 174.

59. People v. Thaddeus Meighan, July 14, 1842, DAP. For more on the language contained within libel indictments, see chapter 3.

60. On British pornography, see Sigel, *Governing Pleasures*, 33–49. For continental pornography, see the notes above. For more in-depth coverage of the "Duchess de Berri," see Cohen, *Murder of Helen Jewett*, 86–88, 112–15. References to the New York madam residing at 128 Duane Street as the "Duchess de Berri" appear in *Sunday Flash*, Sept. 19, 1841; *Flash*, Dec. 18, 1841, June 23, 1842, July 3, 1842, and Sept. 18, 1842; *Whip and Satirist of New-York and Brooklyn*, March 12, 1842, April 2, 1842, April 9, 1842, April 30, 1842, May 21, 1842, May 28, 1842, and July 2, 1842; *Whip*, Aug. 6, 1842, Oct. 15, 1842, Oct. 22, 1842, Oct. 29, 1842, and Nov. 12, 1842. The "Countess de Roberts of Mott Street" appears in *Flash*, Dec. 3, 1842. On "Queen Sweet," see *Whip*, Dec. 31, 1842. For "queen-like Fanny Winslow," see *Whip and Satirist of New-York and Brooklyn*, April 30, 1842. Excerpts from *Decameron* appeared in *Sunday Flash*, Sept. 12, 1841, Sept. 19, 1841, Oct. 17, 1841, and Oct. 24, 1841; *Rake*, Sept. 3, 1842; *Weekly Rake*, Sept. 24, 1842, and Oct. 1, 1842.

61. *Flash*, Oct. 31, 1841. Also see *Flash*, Dec. 11, 1841; *Sunday Flash*, Oct. 24, 1841: "there is scarcely a married man who is not an adulterer, and the city authorities justly regard the Flash as a vehicle dangerous to their interests."

62. *Sunday Flash*, Oct. 17, 1841 (Costello); *New York Sporting Whip*, Feb. 4, 1843 (bawdy house), and Feb. 11, 1843 (bawdy house); *Whip and Satirist of New-York and Brooklyn*, June 25, 1842 (Princess Julia). Nichols's favorable description of Brown appeared in *New York Arena*, May 27, 1842. On references to Brown as "Princess Julia," see note 28.

63. *Sunday Flash*, Oct. 17, 1841. For similar statements, see *Sunday Flash*, Oct. 24, 1841. For an example of moral reform rhetoric, see *Advocate of Moral Reform*, Nov. 15, 1838.

64. *Sunday Flash*, Oct. 24, 1841. For similar examples, see Wooldridge's attack on

panderers and pimps in *True Flash,* Dec. 5, 1841, p. 2; the criticism of "obscene pictures" sold in New York print and book shops in *New York Sporting Whip,* Feb. 11, 1843; complaints regarding "latter-day sinners" in *Flash,* Dec. 11, 1841.

65. *Sunday Flash,* Sept. 26, 1841.

66. *Whip and Satirist of New-York and Brooklyn,* May 28, 1842 (create evil). References and comparisons to the *Advocate of Moral Reform* appear in *Whip and Satirist of New-York and Brooklyn,* March 19, 1842, April 16, 1842, April 23, 1842, and May 7, 1842; *Whip,* July 30, 1842.

67. Cohen, *Murder of Helen Jewett,* 269-72, 402; Horowitz, *Rereading Sex,* 217. The best introduction to Robinson is Peter C. Welsh, "Henry R. Robinson: Printmaker to the Whig Party," in *New York History* 53 (1972): 25-53; Harry T. Peters, *America on Stone* (New York, 1931), 337-42. For listings of other Robinson prints, see Frank Weitenkampf, "The Eno Collection of New York City Views: Its Significance in the Library's Print Room," in *Bulletin of the New York Public Library* 29 (1925): 340, 349; Allan Nevins and Frank Weitenkampf, *A Century of Political Cartoons* (New York, 1944), 36-37, 40-41, 48-49, 54-55, 60-63 66-67.

68. People v. Henry R. Robinson, Sept. 20, 1842 (forfeited Dec. 14, 1842), and Sept. 28, 1842, DAP (both indictments were received from the district attorney on June 7, 1844); *Herald,* Aug. 18, 1842; *Tribune,* Aug. 18, 1842; Horowitz, *Rereading Sex,* 116, 212-19, 222-25; Gilfoyle, *City of Eros,* 133, 145-47. Robinson owned a Wall Street bookstand in addition to a warehouse at 56 or 58 Cortlandt Street. The arresting officers were recently elected Sixth Ward Alderman Clarkson Crolius Jr. and Justice (and future *National Police Gazette* editor) George Matsell. Robinson was quickly released and still selling the articles in December 1842. See James Craft's testimony, March 17, 1843, in indictment for Sept. 28, 1842. The indictment of Sept. 20, 1842, included the following titles: *Memoirs of a Woman of Pleasure; Memoirs of the Life and Voluptuous Adventures of the Celebrated Courtesan Mademoiselle Celestine of Paris; The Cabinet of Venus Unlocked in a Series of Dialogues between Louisa Lovstone and Mariana Greedy; Two Cyprians of the Most Accomplished Talent in the Science of Practical Love; The Lustful Turk: An Interesting History Founded on Facts; The Curtain Drawn Up; or, The Education of Laura, translated from the French; The Confessions of a Voluptuous Young Lady of High Rank; The Amourous Songster; or, Jovial Companion, Being an Entire New and Choice Collection of Modern Songs of Distinguished Taste, Humor, Mirth and Merriment* (also called *Flash Songs); The Amourous History and Adventures of Raymond DeB——and Father Andouillard, Detailing Some Curious Histories and Disclosing the Pastimes of a Convent, with Some Remarks in the Use and Advantages of Flagellation;* and *The Autobiography of a Footman.* The indictment of Sept. 28, 1842, included prints entitled: *A Standing Member of the Abolition Society, Giving an Example of Practical Amalgamation—a man in the dress of a member of the Society of Friends in an obscene, impudent, and indecent position with a negro woman; Victoria Studying Her Comfort;* and *Queen Victoria and Her Page in Attendance.* Robinson appears to have never been tried; both indictments indicate that the case was received from the district attorney on June 7, 1844, with no indication of a verdict or sentence. He continued to be identified as a caricaturist and lithographer in city directories. McCalman, *Radical Underworld,* 204-37, describes the progression from politicized libel and libertinism to more money-grubbing efforts to produce pornography for the market in early nineteenth-century England.

69. Sade recommended mixing the moral with descriptions of orgies: "And through-

out the whole, introduce a quantity of moral dissertation and diatribe, above all at the suppers." See De Sade, *120 Days of Sodom,* 390; Paz, *An Erotic Beyond,* 69.

CHAPTER THREE

1. "Our Indictment," *Flash,* vol. 1, no. 1 (Oct. 30, 1841), p. 2.

2. One such was Robert H. Elton. An ad placed by Elton in the *Arena,* a two-penny sheet, stated that Elton was a "Publisher, bookseller and stationer[,] engraver on wood, and colorist." In his shop at 98 Nassau Street, between Ann and Fulton, can be found "a general assortment of Toy and Song Books, Prints, Almanacs, &c.," as well as wood engravings. He has on hand "upwards of 3000 engravings on wood, new and second hand, adapted to newspaper and other publishers," ranging in price from ten cents to $2 each. See *Arena,* April 16, 1842 (vol. 1, no. 29), p. 1; Helen Lefkowitz Horowitz, "Another 'American Cruikshank' Found: John H. Manning and the New York Sporting Weeklies," *American Antiquarian Society Proceedings* 112, part 1 (2002): 93-126. The term "fancy man" has no exact twenty-first-century equivalent; here it means the lover or kept man of a prostitute or madam. While a "fancy man" might do services or run errands, he was not a procurer or pimp in the modern sense, as prostitution was largely organized in female-run brothels. "Gallery of Rascalities and Notorieties, No. 6," *Sunday Flash,* Oct. 17, 1841 (vol.1, no. 11), p. 1.

3. *Longworth's American Almanac, New-York Register, and City Directory* (New York, 1841).

4. David de Sola Pool, *Portraits Etched in Stone: Early Jewish Settlers, 1682-1831* (New York: Columbia University Press, 1952), 334; David and Tamar de Sola Pool, *An Old Faith in the New World: Portrait of Shearith Israel, 1654-1954* (New York: Columbia University Press, 1955), 179, 180-81; Hyman B. Grinstein, *The Rise of the Jewish Community of New York* (Philadelphia: The Jewish Publication Society of American, 1945), 149, 553; Malcolm H. Stern, comp., *First American Jewish Families: 600 Genealogies, 1654-1977* (Cincinnati, Ohio: American Jewish Archives, 1978), 169. On Levy as a merchant, see *Longworth's American Almanac, New-York Register, and City Directory* (New York, 1831 and 1821; as a broker, see ibid. (New York, 1839). Beginning in 1849, the directories list him for several years "segar maker." Levy ultimately became or styled himself a physician: see *Doggett's New York City Directory* (New York, 1849, 1850, 1853); *Goulding's New York City Directory* (New York, 1870 and 1875). This is confirmed in the census of 1850 and 1870, in which Myer Levy, occupation "physician" appears, born in the West Indies, 1798. Myer Levy died Jan. 2, 1877.

5. Hart was identified as providing Woodridge with notes on Levy in "Court of Sessions-Friday January 14," *New-York Spectator,* Jan. 19, 1842. Myer Levy's sister was the wife of Moses B. Seixas, Emanuel Hart's uncle. Hart was about a decade younger than Levy. His association with gamblers and prostitutes came to light in a confidential letter from Robert R. Hunter to John C. Calhoun (Democratic senator from South Carolina), Feb. 24, 1845, in the *Papers of John C. Calhoun,* ed. Clyde N. Wilson (Columbia: University of South Carolina Press, 1993), 21:353-54. Despite this reputation, Hart became an important Tammany figure. He served as member of the House of Representatives in 1851-53, surveyor of the port of New York in 1857-61, alderman and commissioner of immigration, 1870-73. Both Hart and Wooldridge were close associates of Dan Sickles, a sporting man who rose from the streets of New York to become a member of Congress. In 1859 Sickles murdered his wife's paramour, Philip Barton Key, in plain sight,

0

and was acquitted. Wooldridge was his private secretary. Hart escorted Sickles's mother to Washington to visit her son in jail. See Pool, *Portraits Etched in Stone*, 338-39; Stern, *First American Jewish Families*, 97, 169, 265, 266; Ned Brant, *The Congressman Who Got Away with Murder* (Syracuse: Syracuse University Press, 1991), 149; Thomas Keneally, *American Scoundrel: The Life of the Notorious Civil War General Dan Sickles* (New York: Doubleday, 2002), 50, 71.

6. "Our Indictment," *Flash*, Oct. 30, 1841 (vol.1, no.1), p. 2.

7. "Trial of The Sunday Flash," *New York Herald*, Jan. 16, 1842, p. 2; "General Sessions" *New York Herald*, April 20, 1842, 2. Nelson H. Miller put up security for Snelling. No length of Snelling's sentence appeared, but a month's time was typical.

8. For vendetta, see *Whip*, April 2, 1842 (vol. 1, no. 15), p. 2.; for charges, see "Our Late Course and Future Intentions," *Whip*, April 23, 1842 (vol. 1, no. 18), 2.

9. The People vs. George B. Wooldridge, July 14, 1842, District Attorney Indictment Papers, Court of General Sessions, New York City Municipal Archives and Records Center, New York, N.Y. (hereafter DAP).

10. Legal scholars have typically relied on the printed and bound state compilations in law libraries, which contain cases that went to appeal at the state level (hence knowledge of Sharpless and Holmes). To take a case to appeal required resources: the flash press editors charged with obscenity in the 1840s were for the most part persons who lacked money and influence. To learn about their cases required research of a different nature.

11. Morton J. Horwitz, *The Transformation of American Law, 1780-1860* (Cambridge, Mass.: Harvard University Press, 1977), 4-9; quote from John Randolph, Attorney General of Virginia (1768), 7. Recent scholarship, focusing on common law, include Hendrik Hartog, *Public Property and Private Power: The Corporation of the City of New York in American Law, 1730-1870* (Chapel Hill: University of North Carolina Press, 1983); Charles Grier Sellers, *The Market Revolution: Jacksonian America, 1815-1846* (New York: Oxford University Press, 1991).

12. David Yassky, "Eras of the First Amendment," *Columbia Law Review* 91 (1991): 1699-1755.

13. *Dominus Rex v. Curl*, 2 Stra. 788, reproduced in Edward De Grazia, *Censorship Landmarks* (New York: R. R. Bowker Company, 1969), 3-5.

14. William Blackstone, *Of Public Wrongs, Commentaries on the Laws of England*, vol. 4, Facsimile of the First Edition of 1765-69 (Chicago: The University of Chicago Press, 1979), 41-42, 64. To this reader, these words seem to establish a right of privacy built into the structure of the Anglo-American legal system.

15. Blackstone, *Of Public Wrongs*, 150-51 (italics added); David M. Rabban, *Free Speech in Its Forgotten Years* (Cambridge, Eng.: Cambridge University Press, 1997), documents "bad tendency" extensively; see especially discussion, 132-46, 255 (we are grateful to David Rabban for pointing this out to Helen Horowitz in a communication, Jan. 26, 2000).

16. Blackstone, *Of Public Wrongs*, 151-53 (italics added).

17. Francis Ludlow Holt, *The Law of libel; in which is contained a general history of this law in the ancient codes, and of its introduction, and successive alterations, in the law of England* (London: J. Butterworth and son, 1816), esp. chap. 3; quotes from 72, 283-84. Blackstone's discussion of the relation of criminal libel law to freedom of the press contained an important footnote on the history of printing licensing (Blackstone, *Of Public*

Wrongs, 152 note a) that Holt expanded into the text into a history that freed the law of libel from the onus of the Star Chamber.

18. The case went to appeal, leaving a printed record easily available for legal research: *Commonwealth of Pennsylvania v. Sharpless,* 2 Serg. & R. 91 (1815), reproduced in De Grazia, *Censorship Landmarks,* 35-40.

19. *Report of the Arguments of the Attorney of the Commonwealth at the Trials of Abner Kneeland for Blasphemy* (Boston: Beals, Homer & Co., 1834), 13-14, reprinted in Leonard Levy, ed., *Blasphemy in Massachusetts: Freedom of Conscience and the Abner Kneeland Case: A Documentary Record* (New York: DaCapo Press, 1973), 189-90.

20. Starkie, *Treatise on the Law of Slander and Libel,* vol. 2 (1830), 155, 16, 248, 255, 158-59. Many state constitutions, in contrast to English common law, established that truth could be used as justification.

21. Starkie, *Treatise on the Law of Slander and Libel,* vol. 2 (1830), 240. Italics in quote added.

22. Starkie, *Treatise on the Law of Slander and Libel,* vol. 2 (1830), 241; quote from 258.

23. Starkie, *Treatise on the Law of Slander and Libel,* vol. 2 (1830), 331, 333. David Rabban pointed out to Helen Horowitz the modifications of American law in a communication, Jan. 26, 2000.

24. Thomas Starkie, *A Treatise on the Law of Slander, Libel, Scandalum Magnatum, and False Rumours . . . ,* first American ed., with notes and references to American and the late English Cases (New York: George Lamson, 1826). A lengthy footnote (569) establishes the state protections. The earliest edition in the collection of the Harvard University Law School of Starkie, *A Treatise on the Law of Slander,* is 1813.

25. Starkie, *Treatise on the Law of Slander and Libel,* vol. 2 (1830), 420 (appendix 24).

26. The 1826 American edition, Thomas Starkie, *A Treatise on the Law of Slander, Libel, Scandalum Magnatum, and False Rumours . . . ,* does not contain the critical appendix 24 that provided the text for obscene libel indictments, including that of Wooldridge.

27. Full discussion of popular physiology can be found in Helen Lefkowitz Horowitz, *Rereading Sex: Battles over Sexual Knowledge and Suppression in Nineteenth-Century America* (New York: Knopf, 2002), chaps. 2-5.

28. Robert Cover, "Violence and the Word," in *Narrative, Violence, and the Law: The Essays of Robert Cover,* ed. Martha Minow, Michael Ryan, and Austin Sarat (Ann Arbor: University of Michigan Press, 1992), 203.

29. Lawrence M. Friedman, *Crime and Punishment in American History* (New York: Basic Books, 1993), 125. Rabban, *Free Speech in Its Forgotten Years,* argues that court judgments in matters of obscenity do not mirror public opinion but lag long behind it, responding only very slowly to changing standards.

30. Iain McCalman, *Radical Underworld: Prophets, Revolutionaries, and Pornographers in London, 1725-1840* (Cambridge: Cambridge University Press, 1988); "Duties on Imports," section 28, *Public Statutes at Large of the United States,* vol. 5, ed. Richard Peters (Boston: Little, Brown and Company, 1856), 566-67; James C. N. Paul and Murray L. Schwartz, *Federal Censorship: Obscenity in the Mail* (New York: The Free Press of Glencoe, 1961), 248-49, details the authors' efforts to track down the statute's origins. Attached to nine snuffboxes imported from Germany in three boxes of toys were paintings of "an indecent scene or figure of so very obscene a character that they were unfit to be produced in court." One of them, with the offending scene covered by ink, was

exhibited to show that way the paintings were attached to the boxes under a false bottom. Without leaving the courtroom, the jury agreed that the entire shipment be confiscated by the government, despite the fact that the importers did not know of the hidden paintings. See Jane Clapp, *Art Censorship: A Chronology of Proscribed and Prescribed Art* (Metuchen, N.J.: The Scarecrow Press, Inc., 1972), 130.

31. Horowitz, *Rereading Sex,* treats the arrest of Restell, 200-201; arrests of purveyors of pornographic prints and texts, 211-22.

32. Philip Howell, "Sex and the City of Bachelors: Sporting Guidebooks and Urban Knowledge in Nineteenth-Century Britain and America," *Ecumene: A Journal of Environment, Culture, Meaning* 8 (Jan. 2001): 41, explores the uses of brothel guidebooks by men navigating the city.

33. David McAdam et al., *History of the Bench and Bar of New York,* vol. 1 (New York: New York History Company, 1897), 495; *Trial of Hon. Frederick A. Tallmadge* (New York: Baker & Godwin, 1858), 64; obituary, *New York Times,* Sept. 19, 1868, p. 4; Nigel Cliff, *The Shakespeare Riots: Revenge, Drama, and Death in Nineteenth-Century America* (New York: Random House, 2007), 209, 224, 239.

34. On Noah's life and full career, see Jonathan D. Sarna, *Jacksonian Jew: The Two Worlds of Mordecai Noah* (New York: Holmes & Meier Publishers, Inc., 1981); for a fresh understanding of Noah, especially in relation to African American theater in New York City, see Shane White, *Stories of Freedom in Black New York* (Cambridge: Harvard University Press, 2002).

35. "District Attorney," "Court of General Sessions," *New York Herald,* June 5, 1838, p. 2, discusses the odd choice of Whiting.

36. "General Sessions," *New York Herald,* Oct. 5, 1841, p. 2; "City Intelligence: Court of Sessions," *New York Tribune,* Oct. 5, 1841, p. 3; *Longworth's American Almanac, New-York Register, and City Directory* (New York: Thomas Longworth, 1840); ibid., (New York, 1841); *The New York Business Directory, for 1841 and 1842,* 2nd ed. (New York: J. Doggett, Jr., 1841); "General Sessions," *New York Herald,* Sept. 7, 1841, p. 1. For Tallmadge quote, see ibid., Oct. 5, 1841, p. 2.

37. "City Intelligence, Court of Sessions," *New York Tribune,* Oct. 20, 1841, p. 3; quote from "General Sessions," *New York Herald,* Oct. 20, 1841, p. 2.

38. "Our Indictment," *Flash,* Oct. 30, 1841 (vol.1, no.1), p. 2. (This issue is dated both Oct. 31 and Oct. 30.)

39. "Curious Proceedings in the Court of Sessions," *New York Herald,* Jan. 4, 1842, p. 2.

40. "Trial of the Editors of the Sunday Flash," *New York Herald,* Jan. 15, 1842.

41. "Court of Sessions-Friday January 14," *New-York Spectator,* Jan. 19, 1842. Hart was closely associated with Levy both as a broker and the son of Rebecca Seixas Hart (Levy's brother-in-law was Moses Seixas). On Hart, see note 5 above.

42. "Trial of the Editors of the Sunday Flash," *New York Herald,* Jan. 15, 1842, p. 1; "State's evidence," *Flash,* Jan. 22, 1842 (vol. 1, no.18), p. 2.

43. "Trial of The Sunday Flash," *New York Herald,* Jan. 16, 1842, p. 2.

44. "General Sessions," report on proceedings of Nov. 21, 1843, *New York Herald,* Nov. 22, 1843.

45. "General Sessions" *New York Herald,* April 20, 1842, p. 2. The normal prison term was a month.

46. *True Flash,* Dec. 4, 1841, p. 1, American Antiquarian Society.

47. *Whip and Satirist,* April 2, 1842 (vol. 1, no. 5). Willis G. Thompson, a business

associate of Nelson H. Miller, regarded himself as libeled by George B. Wooldridge; Wooldridge was indicted on the two counts of libel and obscenity. The weeklies that became a part of the court record were rescued by the U.S. historian Leo Hershkowitz, and since 2000 have been in the collection of the American Antiquarian Society.

48. Wooldridge faced indictment for the *Whip* and the *Libertine*, a weekly along the same lines as the *Whip*, and at the same address, 31 Ann Street. Snelling was included in the April indictments of the *Whip*, something that a writer for the paper regarded as wrong—"Has not he been persecuted enough?"; *Whip*, April 23, 1842 (vo.1, no.18), p. 2.

49. *Whip*, July 23, 1842 (vol. 2, no.3), pp. 1-2. The engraving appeared in the *Whip*, April 9, 1842 (vol. 1, no. 16), p 1.

50. *Whip*, July 9, 1842 (vol. 2, no.1).

51. The People vs. George B. Wooldridge, July 14, 1842, DAP.

52. "General Sessions: Trial for publishing an obscene paper," *New York Herald*, Sept. 15, 1842.

53. James M. Smith Jr. first appeared in the city directory in 1841, as an attorney with an office at 3 Wall Street. He may have been the son of an established attorney of the same name. For discussion of the trial, see "General Sessions: Another of the same kidney," *New York Herald*, Sept. 15, 1842; "General Sessions: Pleaded Guilty," *New York Herald*, Sept. 16 and 29, 1842.

54. "General Sessions: Another of the same kidney," *New York Herald*, Sept. 15, 1842; "General Sessions: Pleaded Guilty," *New York Herald*, Sept. 16 and 29, 1842. Vandewater received a lighter sentence. Although informative on the whole, these newspaper reports contain some inaccuracies.

55. See Horowitz, *Rereading Sex*, chap. 10.

56. *Whip*, Feb. 11, 1843 (vol. 3, no. 3), p. 7; "General Sessions," *New York Herald*, March 16, 1843. Interestingly enough, the jury acquitted a compositor for the paper. For a later Meighan publication, see Thaddeus W. Meighan, *Jenny Lind Mania in Boston; or, A Sequel to Barnum's Parnassus, by Asmodeus* (Boston: [s.n.], 1850).

57. "General Sessions: April 20, 'The Whip,'" *New York Herald*, April 21, 1843.

58. "General Sessions," report on proceedings of Nov. 10, 1843, *New York Herald*, Nov. 11, 1843.

59. "General Sessions," report on proceedings of Nov. 21, 1843, *New York Herald*, Nov. 22, 1843.

60. "The Tweedle-dum and Tweedle-dee in Morals—The Ann Street Licentious Press, and the Wall Street Licentious Press," *New York Herald*, Sept. 15, 1842.

61. "To Our Readers," *Whip*, July 10, 1842 (vol. 2, no. 1); for Snelling quote, see "Our Indictment," *Flash*, Nov. 6, 1841 (vol. 1, no. 14), p. 2.

62. "Our Indictments," *Flash*, Dec. 11, 1841 (vol. 1, no. 16).

63. *Whip*, Oct. 1, 1842 (vol. 2, no. 13), p. 2, and Oct. 15, 1842 (vol. 2, no. 15), p. 2.

64. George Wilkes, *The Mysteries of the Tombs; A Journal of Thirty Days Imprisonment in the New York City Prison; for Libel* (New York: sold at all the booksellers, 1844), 2, 63.

65. These arguments played in the defense of Victoria Woodhull, Ezra Heywood, and D. M. Bennett. See Horowitz, *Rereading Sex*, chaps. 18 and 19.

CHAPTER FOUR

1. Wilkes obituary, *New York Times*, Sept. 25, 1885.

2. For Snelling's partnership with Whitman, see the obituary of Mordecai Manuel

Noah, *Sunday Times and Noah's Weekly Messenger*, March 30, 1851, which describes the agreement among the three men to merge their two New York papers in 1843. For choice samples of Snelling's rants in the *Boston Herald*, see "A Subscriber" and "Elizur Wright," May 27, 1848; "A Soldiering We'll All Go!" July 29, 1848; "Sketch of the Life and Services of Gen. Lewis Cass-no. 3," June 8, 1848; "Mr. Signal, A Reminiscence of the of Days that are Gone By," Dec. 12, 1848; and "Lard Oilpot," June 15, 1848. On Snelling's death in the *Herald*: "Death of William J. Snelling, Esq.," Dec. 25, 1848; "The End of All," Dec. 27, 1848; "The Snelling Benefit," Feb. 8, 1849; see also "The Snelling Benefit," *Boston Daily Atlas*, Jan. 31, 1849. For the *Herald's* early history, see Edwin A. Perry, *The Boston Herald and Its History* (Boston: 1878), 17-30.

3. In addition to city directories and censuses consulted, see Alexander Saxton, "George Wilkes: The Transformation of a Radical Ideology," *American Quarterly* 33 (1981): 437-58; Clarence B. Bagley, "George Wilkes," *The Washington Historical Quarterly* 5 (1914): 3-11; Dan Schiller, *Objectivity and the News: The Public and the Rise of Commercial Journalism* (Philadelphia: University of Pennsylvania Press, 1981); Patricia Cline Cohen, *The Murder of Helen Jewett: The Life and Death of a Prostitute in Nineteenth-Century New York* (New York: Knopf, 1998), 191-92; Obituaries in *New York Clipper*, Oct. 3, 1885; *New York Times*, Sept. 25, 1885; *New York Tribune*, Sept. 27, 1885; *Spirit of the Times*, Sept. 26, 1885; George Harvey Genzmer, "Wilkes, George" in *Dictionary of American Biography*, vol. 20 (New York: Charles Scribners, 1936), 218. On Wilkes's family: "George Wilkes Adopts Two Children," *St. Louis Globe-Democrat*, reprinted from the *New York Herald*, July 1, 1884. Mrs. McKay had just died, and Wilkes adopted George, 19, and Alicia, 4; the mother was abandoned by her husband "long ago." Within a year, Wilkes disinherited George and left everything to Alicia. His will was contested by his sister, Catherine Ten Eyck, said to be his only living relative; *New York Times*, Oct. 10 and 21, 1885.

4. Dale Cockrell, *Demons of Disorder: Early Blackface Minstrels and Their World* (New York: Cambridge University Press, 1997), 154-55; Hans Nathan, *Dan Emmett and the Rise of Early Negro Minstrelsy* (Norman: University of Oklahoma Press, 1962), 116-18, 138; Charles White, "Negro Minstrelsy: Its Starting Place Traced Back Over Sixty Years, Arranged and Compiled from the Best Authorities," *New York Clipper*, April 28, 1860, available online at http://www.banjofactory.com/negro_minstrelsy.htm (accessed Jan. 29, 2007). On political activity: "The Empire Club-a Chapter in Democracy," New York *Express*, Aug. 18, 1844. In an issue a week later, Mike Walsh, editor of the *Subterrean*, wrote the *Express* to deny that he was the source for their story on the Empire Club. Even so, Walsh could not resist bashing Wooldridge (but without using his name); his acceptance by the Empire Club marked it as a degenerate group. Wooldridge was, he wrote, "a hang-dog, white livered, States' evidence wretch, who was loathed and despised even by his fellow convicts, and whose acquaintance would be spurned by the most depraved villain on the five points"; *New York Express*, Aug. 26, 1844. For a more positive account, see "A Sketch of the Famous Empire Club, of the City of New York, By a Lover of the Spoils of Office," where the club members were described admiringly as "half horse, half alligator, with a touch of the wildcat"; *New York Herald*, Feb. 6, 1845. The character played by Daniel Day Lewis (Bill the "Butcher") in Martin Scorsese's film *The Gangs of New York* (2002) was a combination of Isaiah Rynders and Bill Poole. Through the 1860s, Rynders was a leader of a Five Points gang.

5. "Died," *New York Herald*, Feb. 18, 1848, for the death of Margaret Ann Wooldridge, wife of George B. and daughter of Andrew J. Von Orden. Von Orden was a hotel keeper in Brooklyn in 1850. The new Mrs. Wooldridge shown in the 1850 census was named

Mary, and she (or someone of the same name) appears in the 1860 enumeration, living with George B. Wooldridge in Bethel, New York.

6. "Serious Accident on the Hudson River Railroad," Special Dispatch to the *New York Tribune*, reprinted in the *Milwaukee Daily Sentinel*, March 25, 1856. Two passenger cars derailed and overturned near Albany, and Wooldridge broke both legs along with other injuries. He was "maimed for life," said the *New York Herald*, Nov. 26, 1857, "though not to an extent to interfere with his capacities" for the doorkeeper job in the House of Representatives. Sickles has attracted considerable attention, beginning with the transcript of his trial, *Trial of the Hon. Daniel E. Sickles for Shooting Philip Barton Key* (New York: R. M. DeWitt, 1859); *Frank Leslie's Illustrated Newspaper*, March 12 and 19, 1859. See Sickles's obituary in the *New York Times*, May 4, 1914. Recent scholarship includes W. A. Swanberg, *Sickles the Incredible* (New York, 1956); Robert M. Ireland, "The Libertine Must Die: Sexual Dishonor and the Unwritten Law in the Nineteenth-Century United States," *Journal of Social History* 23 (Fall 1989): 27-44; Ned Brandt, *The Congressman Who Got Away with Murder* (Syracuse: Syracuse University Press, 1991); Hendrik Hartog, "Lawyering, Husbands' Rights, and 'the Unwritten Law' in Nineteenth-Century America," *Journal of American History* 84 (June 1997): 67-96; Allen D. Spiegel and Peter B. Suskind, "Uncontrollable Frenzy and a Unique Temporary Insanity Plea," *Journal of Community Health* 25 (April 2000): 157-79; Thomas Keneally, *American Scoundrel: The Life of the Notorious Civil War General Dan Sickles* (New York: Doubleday, 2002). Few copies of the *New York Leader* are extant; the several remaining Tom Quick columns say nothing of the flash press. On the hotel in Bethel, see James Eldridge Quinlan, *History of Sullivan County* (Liberty, N.Y.: G. M. Beebe and W. T. Morgans, 1873), 136-37.

7. *Philadelphia North American and Daily Advertiser*, Feb. 11, 1842; "Match Walking," *Cleveland Daily Herald*, Feb. 14, 1842; *New York Herald*, Feb. 16, 1842; "Snatches of Editorial," *New England Weekly Review* (Hartford, Conn.), April 30, 1842; *Pennsylvania Inquirer and National Gazette*, Sept. 30, 1842; "Philadelphia," *New York Herald*, Aug. 30, 1842; *Weekly New York Herald*, Oct. 26, 1844; *New York Herald*, Jan. 14, 1845.

8. *New York Packet*, Aug. 31 and Nov. 9, 1845. About a half dozen issues in toto, all that exist, are held by the American Antiquarian Society (AAS) in Worcester, Mass., and the New-York Historical Society. The *Advocate of Moral Reform* of Nov. 15, 1845, rejected Dixon's claim in no uncertain terms, p. 170.

9. The rally: "Editor's Correspondence," *Raleigh Register and North-Carolina Gazette*, May 29, 1846. The libel suit: "General Sessions," *National Police Gazette*, June 6, 1846, p. 336. Notices in papers: *Weekly Nashville Union*, June 17, 1846; the *Liberator*, June 19, 1846, copying from the *Norfolk County Whig American* (puzzling about the strange bedfellows, Rynders and Dixon); the *Boston Daily Atlas*, Aug. 6, 1846, quoting the *Maysville (Ky.) Eagle* of July 28 and the *Wheeling Times* of West Virginia. *Boston Daily Atlas*, Aug. 22, 1846, reprinting articles from the *New Orleans Picayune* of Aug. 12, 1846; the *Cleveland Herald*, Aug. 26, 1846; the *Milwaukee Daily Sentinel and Gazette*, Aug. 27, 1846; the *Raleigh Register and North Carolina Gazette*, Aug. 28, 1846. George Wilkes revived claims of Dixon's racial ambiguity with reports that Dixon was jailed for frequenting New Orleans coffeehouses late at night without a permit from a white person; "George Washington Dixon in Limbo Again," New York *National Police Gazette*, July 24, 1847, p. 364.

10. For tidbits of wacky coverage, see the following. *Arkansas Democrat*, Oct. 23, 1846 (on his tendency for heated speech); *Boston Daily Atlas*, Oct. 26, 1846 ("blockhead," "quack"); *Boston Liberator*, March 12, 1847, and July 30, 1847 (on jail sentences);

Boston Daily Atlas, Apr. 21, 1848 (proclamation calling Yucatecos to fight for independence); *Dover (N.H.) Gazette and Strafford Advertiser,* May 13, 1848 (reporting Dixon had sailed to the Yucatan with twenty men); *Boston Daily Atlas,* Aug. 31, 1849 (on the *Southwestern Police Gazette*); *Cleveland Herald,* Oct. 4, 1850 ("dunce," "knave"); *Boston Emancipator and Republican,* Oct. 24, 1850 (on jail again for stealing tools); *Boston Daily Atlas,* Aug. 26, 1851 (on plans to run for Congress); *Boston Daily Advertiser,* Jan. 12, 1835 ("Prince of Humbugs"); *New York Herald,* Nov. 16, 1859 ("Duke of Yucatan," "Earl of Poydras Market").

11. Both men became members of the Society of California Pioneers, which recorded arrival dates. An early membership list contains John Vandewater, Frank Soule, John H. Ghion, and James Nisbet, *The Annals Of San Francisco* (San Francisco: D. Appleton & Co., 1855), 822-24, available at http://www.rootsweb.com/~casanfr2/annalssf.txt (accessed Jan. 28, 2007). Scott became an officer of the group in 1853-54; see *Constitution, By-Laws and List of Members of The Society of California Pioneers, Since its Organization* (San Francisco: The Society of California Pioneers, 1874), online at http://www.sfgenealogy.com/caldatanook/scp74/officera.htm#53 (accessed Jan. 28, 2007).

For the vigilance committee list, see http://www.books-about-california.com/Pages/Academy_Pacific_Coast_History/Papers_Committee_text.html (accessed Jan. 28, 2007). Scott's wife Jane and daughter appear in the 1850 census in the New York City household of James Godfrey, Jane's brother-in-law. Relatives named Clements also live there, confirming the link to the Jane Clements who married Charles G. Scott, noted in chapter 1 note 61. News of the Aug. 20 marriage of John Vandewater to Justice Jackson was printed in "Notices of Marriages in California," *New York Herald,* Sept. 28, 1856. A forgery case where a John Vandewater was a victim appears in *The Alta California* (San Francisco) Jan. 3, 1857. San Francisco's *Daily Evening Bulletin* carried several notices of the shooting and wounding of John Vandewater by an assailant; see Aug. 10, 13, 14, Sept. 16, and Oct. 14, 1857. The link that establishes John Vandewater and Charles G. Scott in San Francisco appears in a column titled "New Suits" that appeared in the *Daily Evening Bulletin,* Aug. 14, 1860, in which Mrs. Charles G. Scott, now a widow, sued the administrator of her late husband's estate for wrongly distributing to heirs a piece of San Francisco real estate that she claimed was given to her alone as a gift by John Vandewater in August of 1852.

Charles G. Scott, 33, wife Jane, daughter Indiana, 6, and baby Charles, 2 months, appear in the 1852 special census of San Francisco. Widow Jane Scott ran a boarding house in 1860 and 1870, reporting her property value as $17,000 — a quite substantial sum — in the second entry. By 1880, daughter Indiana had married William Willis, a boarder with Scott in the 1870 list, who was one of San Francisco's richest men, serving on the board of directors for some twenty mining companies with stakes all over the West. A newspaper noted the newlywed couple's purchase of a mansion for $53,000; six servants staffed it in the 1880 census entry. Charles G. Scott's heirs achieved rapid upward mobility, compared to their standing in the 1850 census, when Jane Clements Scott lived in New York's Seventh Ward in a house with twelve inhabitants headed by a gunsmith. In addition to the U.S. census entries, see: "Important Real Estate Changes," *Daily Evening Bulletin* (San Francisco, Calif.), Feb. 4, 1879; "Passed Away: Death of Three Well-Known Citizens of San Francisco," *Daily Evening Bulletin* (San Francisco, Calif.), Feb. 12, 1887.

12. The aliases are noted in the New York Court of General Sessions Docket Book,

Jan.-Aug. 1842, p. 291, held at the New York City Municipal Archives and Records Center (hereafter NYCMA). For Renshaw/McVey's non-appearance, see "General Sessions," *New York Herald*, Sept. 30, 1842; *New York Sportsman*, July 22, 1843, held at the AAS.

13. Http://home.earthlink.net/~mdmeighan/thaddeus.html (accessed Sept. 22, 2006).

14. *Subterranean*, May 24, 1845 ("hush" and "lusts"), and July 25, 1846 (rape).

15. *Subterranean*, Jan. 3, 1846 (pimps), Sept. 20, 1845 (Wilkes), March 13, 1847 (Furman), June 21, 1845, July 25, 1846, Aug. 29, 1846, and Dec. 26, 1846 (all for Matsell). An Irish immigrant and lithographer, Walsh was identified as a "soft-shell" Democrat and noted for his radical, democratic, and pro-Southern sympathies. The *Subterranean* began publication in 1843 and integrated obscene rhetoric with "highbrow" culture, publishing the fiction of Herman Melville, Washington Irving, and George Lippard, and poetry by Henry Wadsworth Longfellow. See *Subterranean*, May 23, 1846 (Melville), Oct. 31, 1846 (Irving), Aug. 22, 1846 (Longfellow), and March or April 1846 (Lippard). Walsh also admired the poet Lord Byron, linking him with the combined elements of libertinism: liberalism, anticlericalism, and eroticism. See *Subterranean*, June 7, 21, and 28, 1845, and July 26, 1845. Walsh was later elected to the state assembly in 1846 and again in 1848. He served in the U.S. House of Representatives from 1853 to 1855. He died in New York City on St. Patrick's Day, March 17, 1859, and was interred in Greenwood Cemetery, Brooklyn, N.Y. See Robert Ernst, "The One and Only Mike Walsh," *New-York Historical Society Quarterly* 36 (1952): 44; Matthew P. Breen, *Thirty Years of New York Politics Up-to-Date* (New York: The Author, 1899), 303; Sean Wilentz, *Chants Democratic: New York City and the Rise of the American Working Class, 1788-1850* (New York: Oxford University Press, 1984), 326-35. Matsell was convicted of obtaining money under false pretenses on March 8, 1878, and sentenced to three years in prison. His term was later commuted to two years in New York County Penitentiary. See entry for Nov. 6, 1879, New York State Assembly, *Documents: Annual Report of Pardons, Commutations and Reprieves*, Assembly Doc. 13 (Albany, 1880), 13.

16. Elliott J. Gorn, "The Wicked World: The *National Police Gazette* and Gilded-Age America," *Media Studies Journal* 6 (1992): 6-10. For Wilkes's claim to virtue and moral reform, see "A Woman's First and Last Step in Crime," *National Police Gazette*, Oct. 17, 1847, pp. 25-26. For later complaints about the "police papers" claiming "in their editorial columns that their mission on earth is a pure and good one," while filling their papers with "scantily dressed women and black-moustached villains," see *Minneapolis Tribune*, Dec. 14, 1880.

17. The New-York Historical Society has one *Arena*, April 12, 1842, that could be a family newspaper. The AAS owns three others that chart the progressive change: April 8, April 16, and May 27, the latter from the New York District Attorney's collection, held as evidence in a potential charge against Nichols for obscenity. The *Arena* is mentioned many times in the flash papers over the summer of 1842, noted for its descent into indecency.

18. Jay Monaghan, *The Great Rascal: The Life and Adventures of Ned Buntline* (Boston: Little, Brown and Company, 1951), esp. 157-67, 328. *Ned Buntline's Own* was inconsistently published from 1848 to 1854. Few copies survive. We examined the copy in the Chicago History Museum dated April 21, 1849. According to WorldCat, single copies of other issues are held in the libraries of the University of Pittsburgh, Cornell University, Rutgers University, and the University of Texas.

19. The *Spy and Philadelphia Paul Pry*, Oct. 5, 1842; copy owned by the University of Southern California library; *Viper's Sting and Paul Pry*, Aug. 18, 1849 (vol. 1, no. 32), p. 4. The AAS copy carries the stamp of collector Thomas O. Mabbatt.

20. There are no known copies of the *Manchester Owl;* it is described in Howard A. Chamberlen, "The First Ten Years of Printing and Publishing in Manchester, New Hampshire, 1839-1849: A Preliminary Survey" (Manchester Historic Association, 1948), 9. The *Gleaner* was edited by one John Caldwell who had earlier published the *Manchester Representative*. Caldwell specialized in heated language with a heavy class antagonism expressed in 1840s slang: "blowfistical nincompoops" is one elegant example of his invective. The AAS recently acquired a good run of the *Gleaner* (1842-44).

21. The *Boston Satirist & Punch* of Aug. 30, 1845, turned up in an uncatalogued box of miscellaneous Massachusetts newspapers in UC Santa Barbara's Special Collections. Patricia Cohen then inquired at the AAS for this title and learned of fourteen more issues, not catalogued as of 2004. Likely there are more such ephemeral papers, uncatalogued and awaiting discovery in libraries around the country.

22. *Broadway Omnibus*, Nov. 1, 1858; *Life in Boston and New England Police Gazette*, April 27, 1850. These publications, as well as issues of the *Monthly Cosmopolite*, the *Broadway Dandy*, and the *Broadway Omnibus* are located in the collections of the AAS. For more on Thompson, see Helen Lefkowitz Horowitz, *Rereading Sex: Battles over Sexual Knowledge and Suppression in Nineteenth-Century America* (New York: Knopf, 2002), 229-39.

23. *Broadway Omnibus*, Nov. 1, 1858; *Monthly Cosmopolite*, May 1, 1850; *Life in Boston and New England Police Gazette*, Aug. 10, 1850. For similar critiques and warnings regarding prostitution, see *Life in Boston and New England Police Gazette*, April 27, 1850, May 18, 1850, and Jan. 4, 1851; *Weekly Whip*, Feb. 12, 1855.

24. *Venus' Miscellany*, May 9, 1857, Department of Rare Books and Special Collections, Princeton University Libraries. The May 9, 1857 issue was identified as number twenty-six of volume one, and claimed a readership of 49,000. On readership numbering approximately 7,000, see Horowitz, *Rereading Sex*, 242. *Venus' Miscellany* probably began in 1856, but no issues survive. The earliest known extant issue dates from Jan. 31, 1857 (vol. 1, no. 12). See Horowitz, *Rereading Sex*, 471 note 43. Some flash newspapers reportedly reappeared in the 1850s. A *Herald* editorial in 1858 complained about "flash newspapers" and the new obscenity. See *Herald*, Aug. 5, 1858. It is unclear if this is a reference to *Venus' Miscellany*. For later complaints about "flash literature," see *Minneapolis Tribune*, Dec. 14, 1880. For more on authors of city mysteries and their serialized publications, see Paul Erickson, "New Books, New Men: City-Mysteries Fiction, Authorship, and the Literary Market," *Early American Studies* 1:1 (2003).

25. Ackerman operated under the pseudonyms of James Ramerio and "Jean Rosseau," worked in both New York and Boston, published several George Thompson novels, and sold abortifacients under the name of Dr. Ashwell. On Ramerio, "Jean Rosseau," and Ackerman being the same person, and his early career as a pornographer, see Horowitz, *Rereading Sex*, 239-42; Donna I. Dennis, "Obscenity Law and the Conditions of Freedom in the Nineteenth-Century United States," *Law & Social Inquiry* 27 (2002): 390-94. According to Anthony Comstock, Ramerio published Thompson's *Venus in Boston: A Romance of City Life* (1849) and *Anna Mowbray; or, Tales of the Harem* (n.d.), as well as Sparks's *Flora Montgomerie, The Factory Girl: Tale of the Lowell Factories* (1856). See Society for the Suppression of Vice Papers, vol. 2, 1872, Library of Congress, Washington, D.C. "Clarke" was also listed as an editor on the masthead of *Venus' Miscellany*. As

Donna Dennis points out, Ackerman's name was also spelled "Akarman." See *Tribune,*
Sept. 17, 1857 (Ackerman), and Sept. 22, 1857 (Akarman); *Times,* Sept. 15, 1857 (Ackerman), and Sept. 21, 1857 (Akarman). City directories identify George Akarman, publisher, 82 Nassau in 1853. George W. Ackerman is identified with the following occupations, workplace addresses, and homes: music printer at 40 Vestry in 1837; 527 Pearl in
1838 and 1839; 228 Church in 1840; 146 Mulberry in 1841; printer at 169 Fulton and
home at 450 Broome in 1847; printer at 25 Howard and a home at 5 W. Broadway in
1849-50; music printer, at 25 Howard and a home at 217 Mulberry in 1853; printer at
377 Broadway and home at 210 Mulberry in 1855; printer or engraver at 53 Mercer and
residing at 210 Mulberry from 1856-61; home at 78 Spring in 1862; engraver with home
at 157 W. 38th in 1863; painter, 117 Fulton, home at 7 W. 20th in 1865. See *Longworth's
American Almanac, New-York Register, and City Directory* (New York, 1837-42); *Doggett's
New York City Directory* (New York, 1842-50); *Wilson's and Trow's Directory of New York
City* (1852-53); *Rode's Directory of New York City* (New York, 1853); *Wilson's and Trow's
Directory of New York City* (1855-59); *Trow's New York City Directory* (New York, 1860-
65). Also see Harry T. Peters, *America on Stone* (Garden City, N.Y.: Doubleday, Doran,
and Company, 1931), 72.

26. *Venus' Miscellany,* May 9, 1857 (rich, rare, racy), May 16, 1857 (Priapus), May 23,
1857, May 30, 1857, June 6, 1857, July 4, 1857, and July 11, 1857. The image in the May 9,
1857 issue was the most erotic image in the collection. The plain and colored illustrated
plates were entitled *The Wedding Night; or, Advice to Timid Bridegrooms* and *Secret Passion.*
Other publication titles for twenty-five to fifty cents included: *Flora Montgomery; The
Bridal Chamber and its Mysteries; Anna Mowbray; or, Tales of the Harem; The Amours of a
Quaker; or, the Voluptuary; The Loves of Byron, his various Intrigues with Celebrated Women;
Chevalier De Faublas; or, Debauchery of the Old Nobility of France; Merry Wives of London;
being a Picture of Licentiousness of the Court; The Chevalier; a Thrilling Tale of Love and Pas-
sion; The Gay Deceiver; or, Man's Perfidy and Woman' Frailty, Dissipation; or, Crime and
its Consequences; Julia King; or, The Follies of a Beautiful Courtezan; The Irish Widow; or,
The Last of the Ghosts; Harriet Wilson; or, Memoirs of a Woman of Pleasure; Madeline, the
Avenger; or, Seduction and its Consequences; Paul the Profligate; or, Paris as it is; Adventures
of a Country Girl; or, Gay Scenes in my Life; Simon the Radical; or, The Adventures of a Bonnet Rouge; Amelia Moreton; or, Life at a Fashionable Watering Place; The Countess; or, My
Intrigues with the Bloods; Venus in Boston, An Exciting Tale of City Life; City Crimes; or, Life
in New York and Boston; Jack Rann, alias Sixteen String Jack the Highwayman; The Adventures of a Libertine; Evil Genius; or, The Spy of the Police; Sharps and Flats; or, The Perils of
City Life; The Lame Devil; or, Asmodeus in Boston; Dashes at Life, by Our Ned; The Mysteries and Iniquities of a Private Madhouse; The Brigands; or, The Murrill Conspirators of the
West; Kate Montrose; or, The Maniac's Daughter; Demon of Gold; or, The Miser's Daughter;
Aristotle Illustrated; the Complete Masterpiece.* While some of these works undoubtedly included political content, no such commentary appeared in *Venus' Miscellany.*

27. On George Thompson's use of eroticism and portrayal of sex unconnected with
love, governed by violence, entrapment, and manipulation, see David Reynolds, *Beneath
the American Renaissance: The Subversive Imagination in the Age of Emerson and Melville*
(New York: Knopf, 1988), 224; Horowitz, *Rereading Sex,* 229-39. Also see Herbert
Spencer Ashbee (Pisanus Fraxi), *Catena Librorum Tacendorum: Bio-Biblio-Icono-graphi-
cal and Critical Notes on Curious, Uncommon and Erotic Books* (London: privately printed,
1885), reprinted as *Bibliography of Prohibited Books,* vol. 3 (New York, 1962): 201-21.
For similar developments in late eighteenth-century France, see Antoine de Baecque,

"Pamphlets: Libel and Political Mythology" in *Revolution in Print: The Press in France, 1775-1800*, ed. Robert Darnton and Daniel Roche (Berkeley: University of California Press, 1989), 165-70.

28. Excerpts of Thompson's *Adventures of a Pickpocket; or, Life at a Fashionable Watering Place* and *Venus in Boston; A Romance of City Life* appeared in the same issue of *Life in Boston*. See *Life in Boston: Sporting Chronicle, and Lights and Shadows of New England Morals*, Sept. 1, 1849. *The Mysteries of Bond Street; or, The Seraglios of Upper Tendom* (New York, 1857), chap. 13, appears to have been serialized in *Venus' Miscellany*, May 9, 1857, p. 4, but under authorship of "Appollonius of Gotham." *The Amourous Adventures of Lola Montez; Otherwise Known as the Madame the Countess of Lansfeldt* was serialized in *Venus' Miscellany*, June 6, 1857 (chap. 1), June 20, 1857 (chaps. 3 and 4), June 27, 1857 (chaps. 4 and 5), July 4, 1857 (chap. 6), and July 11, 1857 (chap. 7), all under the authorship of Eugene de Orsay. This appears to be a serialized version of George Thompson's *The Amorous Adventures of Lola Montes* (1857). One issue included an image of Lola Montez entitled "Lola Discovered in the Act by her Husband," depicting Lola in a lifeboat with a man fondling her breast as her voyeuristic husband observes from the deck. See *Venus' Miscellany*, June 27, 1857.

29. *Weekly Whip*, Feb. 12, 1855, and March 5, 1855, both at the AAS. The *Weekly Whip* described itself as "a weekly journal devoted to fun, frolic and fashion—the drama, the fine arts, and the gossip about town—to ladies of the 'upper ten' and ladies of the 'lower twenty,'—to Broadway by day-light, by moon-light, by gas-light, and in total darkness—and all other matters and things pertaining to the busy spirit of the age we live in." Much of the publication, however, appears to have been a vehicle to promote the sale of Thompson's works. Among the Thompson novels prominently advertised were: *Adventures of a Pickpocket; City Crimes; The Gay Deceiver; The House Breaker; Jack Harold; Julia King; The Ladies' Garter; The Outlaw; Radcliff; The Road to Ruin;* and *Venus in Boston*. The *Weekly Whip* was published by Gillen and Co., which was prosecuted for obscenity in 1856. See Edward Rice v. Thomas Gillen, March 22, 1856, box 7955, Police Court Papers, NYCMA.

30. Fuller treatment of this case appears in Horowitz, *Rereading Sex*, chap. 19.

31. For discussion of crucial 1960s U.S. Supreme Court obscenity rulings, see Edward de Grazia, *Girls Lean Back Everywhere: The Law of Obscenity and the Assault on Genius* (New York: Random House, 1992), chap. 22.

FLASH PRESS EXCERPTS

1. An exotic term for brothels. *Seraglio* referred to the secluded apartments confining the harem of a Turkish nobleman.

2. References to the Greek god Jove, who threw lightning bolts from the top of Mt. Olympus.

3. Common abbreviation for "criminal conversation," a legal term for adultery.

4. *Brother Jonathan* was a weekly literary periodical published in New York City in 1842, founded by Rufus Griswold and Parke Benjamin, who also published the *New World* (cited in chapter 1 note 1). On Aug. 31, 1842, *Brother Jonathan* issued an entire novel as a supplement issue, "The Tempter and the Tempted," by Baroness de Calabrella.

5. The *New York Sunday Times*, published from 1841 to 1843, was edited by William J. Snelling. It had no relationship to the weekly *New York Times*, published in the 1830s and 1840s, nor to the daily newspaper of the same name started in 1851 by Henry Raymond and still in existence.

6. Imprimis, Latin: in the first place.

7. Jeremiad: a lament or a prophecy of doom.

8. Ochone, O wira sthrue: Gaelic for alas, a pity; known from Irish folks songs of the period.

9. Hunter's Red Drop: a popular nostrum for treating venereal disease, including syphilis, one of whose visible symptoms was an eating away of the nose.

10. From the Greek Elysium, where the blessed go after death in Greek mythology; hence, a state of perfect happiness.

11. A reference to Benjamin Rathbun of Buffalo, New York, a spectacular and well-known entrepreneur who gained millions in a mere decade and then lost it all in 1836 when his credit transactions contracted.

12. A reference to the celebrated Viennese dancer Fanny Elssler, who toured the U.S. in 1840-41 to sell-out crowds. She showed her gratitude by contributing a large sum to an American Revolution memorial on Bunker Hill near Boston.

13. Dixon makes a sly jab at Rev. Francis L. Hawkes, doctor of divinity, whom he libeled in 1839 over a sexual charge; see chapter 1. Dixon confessed and went to jail, but here he takes a little revenge.

14. This is another joke, building on Dixon's claim in 1839 in the Minturn case that he was only reprinting an adultery charge from the Moral Reformers' newspaper. Here the report of the moral reform committee that visits unfortunate girls becomes a sexual aid on the bedside table of a prostitute.

15. Samuel Swartwout was collector of the Port of New York for a decade when a massive corruption scandal exposed his embezzlement of millions of dollars in 1838. Swartwout fled to Europe to evade arrest.

16. Fanny Elssler and Maria Taglioni were famous European dancers; Taglioni was a leading ballerina of the Paris Opera. Reichstad and Waterford were likely celebrity noblemen from Europe. Charles Kemble of the famed Kemble family was a British stage actor. Arbaces was an Assyrian general of the eighth century B.C., perhaps known as a character from a popular play.

17. A slang word for face, from physiognomy, a popular science claiming an ability to read a person's character from facial features.

18. A pun on breach of the peace, a traditional term for disorderly behavior; "breeches" refers to pants and "piece" was a common slang word for penis.

19. A synonym for a penitent prostitute, from Mary Magdalen of the New Testament. Institutions founded to "save" prostitutes were frequently called "Magdalen Homes."

20. "Swellish" was characteristic of a "swell," a person who dresses in high style. Pavé from the French was widely adopted in English to mean the street and a woman of the pavé was a prostitute; here used to connote a high style man of the street.

21. Patent: open, accessible to the public.

22. Mantue-maker, actually mantua-maker: an archaic term for women's dressmakers.

23. An ancient Persian collection of stories, popularly read in antebellum America.

24. Two British brothers, James William and Henry John Wallack, ran the National Theater around the corner from Julia Brown's brothel in the late 1830s. The theater was destroyed in a fire in 1841.

25. Quadrille: a French dance involving four couples in a square formation.

26. From the New Testament: a fallen angel now a demonic figure, literally "destroyer" in Greek, who presides over a bottomless pit in a scene of hell in the Book of Revelations.

27. Five Italian operas.

28. Praxiteles, a fourth century B.C. Greek sculptor; Antonio Canova (1757-1822), a Venetian sculptor famed for his marble nudes.

29. Venus de'Medici, a first century B.C. nude statue representing the goddess of love acquired by the Medici family in the late sixteenth or early seventeenth century and displayed in the Uffizi Gallery in Florence.

30. Sarah Siddons (1775-1831), a famous British stage actress.

31. Spencer: a tightly fitted jacket or bodice for women.

32. From Greek mythology, a female creature with a head of snakes instead of hair; hence, a monstrously ugly woman.

33. Thomas L. Nichols, journalist and editor of the *Arena* in 1842, a paper veering towards flash. The flash papers linked him romantically with Sal Wright of Thomas Street repeatedly.

34. Recherché: sought after, choice.

35. See note 22.

36. Negus: a hot, sweet wine drink, flavored with lemon, sugar, and spices.

37. *Flagrante delicto*, Latin: "while the crime is blazing"; i.e., being caught in the act.

38. *Vi et armis*, a Latin legal term: violently and forcibly.

39. At least three Bonapartes of the French ruling family spent time in the United States in the 1830s. See chapter 2 note 27.

40. Crack as an adjective commonly meant excellent in the nineteenth century; as in a crack shot, an excellent shooter.

41. A popular café on Broadway near Duane Street in New York City, owned by Ferdinand Palmo. Palmo opened a music hall in 1844.

42. Sloped: American slang for slinking away, departing (OED 1839 usage).

43. Mary Berry, aka Mary Cisco, a madam for two decades at a brothel on Duane Street in New York. Like "Princess" Julia Brown, she adopted an aristocratic title and was well known as the Duchess de Berri. The pseudonym was probably borrowed from *The Authentic Memoirs of the Countess de Barre*, first printed in English in 1771.

44. Houris: beautiful maidens of the Muslim paradise.

45. Cove: British flash slang for a fellow or chap.

46. Harridan: a scolding, shrewish woman.

47. Lampblack is a fine carbon soot released as a by-product in oil lamps and used to make black pigments. Blackface minstrels of the era sometimes were called "lampblacked Negroes"; burned cork offered a safer form of stage makeup. The action recommended here, putting lampblack and flour on Grandy, suggests a version of tarring and feathering, a method in favor during the American Revolution to humiliate and deter men thought to be disloyal to the Patriot cause.

48. Sharps was an admiring slang term for clever cheats and swindlers, often paired with flats, the easy dupes of sharps. Drummers were young men in the employ of mercantile firms who escorted out-of-town merchants to brothels and gambling dens, treating them to the pleasures of the town as a way of drumming up business for their employers. Suckers and pimps have the same meanings today; diners out were men who habitually had dinner outside of the home or boarding house and thus were known as bon vivantes, or high livers. Libertines and roués were words for men who indulged in sexual pleasure and sensuality.

49. Carbuncles: large red pimples.

50. Numbers meaning street addresses.

51. The Hook refers to Corlears Hook, an impoverished neighborhood in lower Manhattan along the East River and a hangout of sailors. Five Points was an immigrant

and working-class neighborhood just north of City Hall in the blocks surrounding an intersection of five streets.

52. Jordan: a chamber pot.

53. Flats: flash slang for the easy dupe of a swindle; opposite of sharps.

54. Cunning little Isaacs: plural version of a phrase popularized in a 1780 British comedy, *The Belle's Stratagem*, where a character attends a masquerade ball dressed as a Jewish figure (Isaac Mendoza) from a 1775 play, *The Duenna*. Its use here signifies deceptive masquerade practiced by women of ill-repute.

55. Dulcinea, the sweet, beautiful, and completely unattainable female character sought by the hero in the seventeenth-century novel *Don Quixote* by Miguel de Cervantes.

56. Blow up: flash slang meaning to expose, betray.

57. The *Advocate of Moral Reform* began in 1834 as the bimonthly journal of the New York Female Moral Reform Society, edited by evangelical Christian women. Its aim was to illuminate the evils of licentiousness and reform male sexual misconduct. The *Advocate* took almost no notice of the flash papers.

58. Reticule: a women's pocketbook.

59. Sal volatile: smelling salts, to revive someone in a faint.

60. Cager: meaning unknown.

61. Smack: a fishing vessel.

62. Crabstick: a cudgel or large stick originally made of wood from a crab tree.

63. The bill of $260 in 1842 would equal over $6,000 in 2008 dollars, using a formula based on the Consumer Price Index. A journeyman printer of 1842 typically might earn $12 a week, so this sum would take twenty-two weeks to earn.

64. Thomas L. Nichols was then publishing a daily newspaper, the *Arena*, only six issues of which are now extant. It shared some features with the flash papers, with correspondents writing in about sexual escapades and editorials justifying prostitution, but it was not explicitly about the sexual underworld.

65. Fanny Skinner was indeed the longtime and quite aged president of Utica's Female Moral Reform Society. In 1837-38, a group of male clerks strongly protested the tactics of Skinner and her group.

66. Penny-a-liner: a newspaper writer who gets paid by the printed line; not on salary as a reporter.

67. John Milton's *Paradise Lost* (1667) presented the story of Adam and Eve in epic poetry, with Satan a main character.

68. Nathaniel P. Willis, literary writer and celebrity editor first in Boston and then New York.

69. Thomas S. Hamblin was an actor and the manager of the Bowery Theater from 1830 to 1853.

70. Adeline Miller's children were Nelson Miller, a New York lawyer, Josephine Clifton, a stage actress, and the late Louisa Missouri Miller.

71. Lickspittal: a toady, a flatterer.

72. Smoke was commonly used to de-bug rooms infested with insects or vermin.

73. Five Points: see note 51, this chapter.

74. "Void his rheum on" means spitting saliva on; it is a phrase used in Shakespeare's *Henry V* and *Merchant of Venice*.

75. Pouncet box: A small, perforated box holding perfumed material, used as a personal deodorizer.

76. St. Giles: one of the worst slum neighborhoods in nineteenth-century London.

77. Perquisition: a careful inquiry or diligent search.

78. Almack's: a Five Points dance hall located at 67 Orange Street and sometimes called "Pete Williams's Place" after its African American proprietor. Almack's was named after a swank private club in London of the 1820s.

79. Adodgment: probably a made-up word for a hasty departure or escape.

80. Ben Caunt, a bare-knuckle prizefighter of England of the 1830s and 1840s. He stood 6' 2" and weighed 210 lbs.

81. Reel: a lively couple dance of British origins. Breakdown: an energetic dance associated with African Americans.

82. The "six": a dance unknown to the authors.

83. Pete Williams, impresario of popular dance in Five Points and owner of a dance hall.

84. Jonathan Wild (1683-1725) was a renowned policeman in London until he was unmasked as a major criminal and leader of a gang of thieves. His unusual dual career became the stuff of legend and satire.

85. Five Points: see note 51, this chapter.

86. "Plucked as a brand from the burning" was a common biblical quotation referring to the removal of a coal (a near sinner) from a fire of damnation; from Amos 4:1 in a passage about Sodom and Gommorah.

87. Circassian: pertaining to the northern region of the Caucasus, used to denote Caucasian people in contrast to the "sable race."

88. The Palais Royale was an area of Paris known for illicit heterosexual and homosexual liaisons.

89. George Matsell was a police court justice at this time, and later a police superintendent; in the late 1850s he became the editor of the *National Police Gazette*. Milne Parker was a police court justice.

90. Five Points: see note 51, this chapter.

91. "Watch!": a call for the local watchman; they were stationed every couple of blocks to be on the lookout for crime or fires.

92. William H. Attree was a reporter for the *New York Herald*; he was thoroughly roasted in the previous week's Rascalities column.

93. Phoebe Doty ran a brothel over several decades in New York; by 1841 she was close to fifty in age. Also see chapter 2 note 39.

94. Melinda Hoag, locally well-known wife of Ike Hoag, both swindlers and con artists.

95. Dandy: a fashionable man of the 1820s and 1840s, often seen by others as putting on airs.

96. James Gordon Bennett, editor of the *New York Herald*.

97. Erelus, or Herulus, in Greek mythology, the god of the darkness of Hades.

98. *Contra bonos mores*, Latin: against good morals.

99. Mr. E. H.: a likely reference to Emanuel Hart, who later was named in court as the source for this story. The initials earlier in the paragraph appear to read E.-II——, though this could be a faint *H*. Probably these initials do not stand for Hart, who was not an Englishman nor known to be a business partner of Levy.

100. New York's Halls of Justice (1838) contained the city jail, court rooms, and offices, and was built to resemble Egyptian tombs, hence its nickname.

101. Soaplocks: young men of New York's Bowery area, known for sideburns grown into long curled locks of hair, held in curl by soap or heavy grease.

102. Highbinders: a New York City term for ruffians.

103. Vehmique Tribunal: a secret tribunal, or court of the Holy Vehme, from the time of Charlemagne.

104. William G. Boggs, the publisher of William Cullen Bryant's *Evening Post* and a member of the grand jury which indicted the flash press editors in 1841.

105. Poll: the head.

106. Wooldridge borrowed much material from the *London Town*.

107. The Fancy refers to people deeply interested in sports; later shortened to "fan."

108. James Watson Webb was the publisher and editor of the *New York Courier and Enquirer* (1829-61) and a leading figure in the Whig and Republican parties. He was involved in several canings and beatings during his editorial career.

109. Intropodity: probably a humorous mangling of "intrepidity," meaning fearlessness.

110. A reference to well-known bare-knuckle prize fighters. Country McClusky was an Irish immigrant allied with the Democratic Party and Tammany Hall in New York. His real name was John McCleester. Bill Ford was also associated with Tammany Hall.

111. Tom Hyer was an American-born prizefighter allied to various nativist and anti-immigrant groups. In 1849 he was acclaimed to be the first "American Champion" after defeating "Yankee" Sullivan.

112. George Vandenhoff, an actor, was later author of *Leaves from an Actor's Note-Book* (1860).

113. Edmund Simpson and Thomas Barry were the stage managers of the Park Theater.

114. The boards: the stage flooring.

115. William Mitchell was manager of the first Olympic Theater at 422 Broadway from 1839 to 1850.

116. John Sinclair was a popular English singer whose daughter, Catherine Norton Sinclair, was the wife of Edwin Forrest. Forrest was the leading American tragedian and Shakespearean actor of the antebellum period.

117. This is a reference to a famous bare-breasted image by E. W. Clay, "Madame Lecompte, Principal Danseuse . . . in the Character of the Abbess," published in 1837 by Henry R. Robinson, who added, below the copyright line, these printed words: "The Prosecuted Picture."

118. See note 51, this chapter.

119. See note 69.

INDEX